# ALAN BROOKE: CHURCHILL'S RIGHT-HAND CRITIC

A Reappraisal of Lord Alanbrooke

ANDREW SANGSTER

**CASEMATE**

*Oxford & Philadelphia*

Published in Great Britain and the United States of America in 2021 by
CASEMATE PUBLISHERS
The Old Music Hall, 106–108 Cowley Road, Oxford OX4 1JE, UK
and
1950 Lawrence Road, Havertown, PA 19083, US

Hardback Edition: ISBN 978-1-61200-968-1
Digital Edition: ISBN 978-1-61200-969-8

A CIP record for this book is available from the British Library

Printed and bound in the United Kingdom by TJ Books

Typeset by Versatile PreMedia Services (P) Ltd.

For a complete list of Casemate titles, please contact:

CASEMATE PUBLISHERS (UK)
Telephone (01865) 241249
Email: casemate-uk@casematepublishers.co.uk
www.casematepublishers.co.uk

CASEMATE PUBLISHERS (US)
Telephone (610) 853-9131
Fax (610) 853-9146
Email: casemate@casematepublishers.com
www.casematepublishers.com

# Contents

# Preface

Field Marshal Lord Alanbrooke is a familiar name to many historians, most of whom ignore his impact or gloss over his contribution during the war years, and he is almost unknown to the public. A quick check of the internet will show there are schools, barracks, industrial estates, avenues and roads named after him, but few know why they are so named, and who he was, or what he did. A quick survey of non-historical acquaintances confirmed this with only one in ten having any inkling of the name.

Based on his book *Destiny in the Desert*, Jonathan Dimbleby produced a television programme in 2013 called *Churchill's Desert War: The Road to El Alamein*.[1] The programme, which has enormous appeal when compared to reading history books, helped underline why Brooke can be described as the unknown field marshal. The programme was a clever and well-researched survey of the events which culminated in the battle of El Alamein, and underlined the massive political machinations, especially in the Anglo-American camp. The television production conveyed, with a sense of accuracy, insights into such men as Wavell, Auchinleck and Montgomery, which tended to place the emphasis on the genius of Churchill's personality, and was astute in occasionally questioning his approach and sometimes his strategy. However, as this book will demonstrate, the Chiefs of Staff, commonly known as the COS, and Brooke in particular, were at constant loggerheads with Churchill, toning down his ideas and blocking his more risky and madcap projects. This was a prolific task with major political ramifications and they, through Churchill, managed to conduct the war to a safe conclusion, but Brooke's name is not mentioned once in the programme. In this television presentation he is mentioned in passing, but only by his title, not his name.

In a survey of British generals it was written that 'had Brooke not had his ghost-written diaries published [*The Turn of the Tide* and *Triumph in the West*] in the late 1950s, it is unlikely that he would be remembered as anything other than a rather colourless back-room figure of the war years, a man whose experience in the field was slight and whose staff work was dutifully anonymous'.[2] This viewpoint reflects an overall impression of Brooke even amongst many historians, but it is a sweeping statement, and as this biography will demonstrate the statement is fundamentally flawed. Brooke was a powerhouse of energy, the driving force behind much of the Allied strategy, and the only man generally believed to be able to curb some of Churchill's more impetuous if not 'madcap' ideas. His strategic ideas have often been questioned both during and after World War II, but he was the man who originated many of them, who argued the Americans into agreement, and who helped organise the field commanders to implement them into action.

There is no doubt that Churchill deserved the praise heaped on him since 1945, but the Chiefs of Staff, and especially Brooke, not only kept him in line but were the powerhouse of his success. In 1945 Brooke was not well known and little has changed since, but the title 'Churchill's right-hand critic' arises from his stormy relationship with the prime minister of the day.

It was during the critical period of 1939–45 that four men dictated the lives and deaths of people in the Western world: Winston Churchill and Franklin

Brooke's portrait (National Archives)

D. Roosevelt, backed by their most senior military advisers, Brooke in Britain, and General George Marshall in the USA. The former two political leaders are both well known and Marshall has been much studied in America, but Brooke, apart from a biography written nearly 40 years ago, is the least known of the four. Names such as Montgomery, Alexander, Mountbatten, Slim, Eisenhower, Patton, MacArthur and Bradley are better known, and more referenced in histories of World War II than Marshall and especially Brooke.

In this reappraisal of Field Marshal Lord Alanbrooke, he will always be addressed as 'Brooke' because it is the man, his background, his personality, his profession as a soldier and his major contribution which will be studied, rather than his rank. His diaries, his first biography, personal papers and archives are used as sources, but the war years of 1939–1945 are central not only because of the critical nature of these years, but because Brooke was a major figure in the conduct of the war, although he remains largely unknown. His life, his decisions, the controversies in which he was involved will be explored. Near the end of the study, time will be given to a brief analysis of how his contemporaries regarded the man Brooke, and how popular histories have portrayed him, if at all.

His contentious relationship with Churchill is frequently commented on whenever he is mentioned in general histories. When his first diaries became public in the

1950s he was often denigrated for his blunt rudeness about Churchill, the hero of the times; this study will indicate how and why these scenarios arose, and why they were important to the survival of Britain. Churchill has long been adored as the saving hero of the day by the British, who in 2002 voted him as the greatest British figure of all times. He was and still is regarded by many as a genius, but there is no question he was impulsive and prone to madcap ideas, and it needed a man of Brooke's strength of personality to sometimes tone him down, while at other times to have the courage to tell him he was wrong, something few people were prepared to risk with Churchill.

Brooke's clash with the Americans, especially Marshall and Eisenhower, will be explored to understand the climate of the day. There are no easy conclusions about who was right and wrong in the Anglo-American struggle over military strategy, and the question as to whether the American enthusiasm for an early offensive action, rather than the perceived British defensive attitudes, was correct. Both sides in their differing views had a 'curate's egg – good in parts'. The initial problems were more to do with the timing of the cross-Channel invasions into France, but they later developed into more geopolitical tensions. The timing of Operation *Overlord* was one issue, and whether Brooke and Churchill were right to cling on to the Mediterranean campaign in order to take the war to the northern Italian borders another, and these issues became even more sensitive over national prestige in the final months of invading Germany. It could be argued that the Americans provided a counterpoint to Brooke's policy of nibbling away in the Mediterranean theatre, and Churchill's policy of administering a 'punch on the nose' of the enemy, but historical truth defies easy explanations, and this study examines the problems through a re-appraisal of Brooke the man, and does not attempt to supply answers to these issues, which often dominate the history of these fraught times.

A biography of a major figure of historical significance will constantly be open to some form of contention, and the human side of Brooke has not always been easy to unravel. His love of family and his enjoyment of ornithology become self-evident, but always tangled with critical and often damming statements about his close friends. At times his human side is revealed in his depression over the death of close acquaintances, family members and colleagues, and a degree of amusement as bewildered Russian guards watched him wandering around the Kremlin gardens looking at great tits, and then in a nearby Moscow wood looking for a rare species called the black woodpecker. It is always tempting to rush to the defence of the subject under study, but a major effort has been made in this work to remain objective.

# Introduction

## The Subject Brooke

Brooke has been described as pig-headed, stubborn, obdurate, and kind, loving and affectionate. He had mannerisms which were not always appreciated, a blunt staccato way of expressing opinions, and at times he could appear abrasive. This often meant Brooke did not always get along with some Americans; his downright speed, take-it-or-leave-it attitude, and rapid bluntness inclined the Americans to prefer the military-diplomat John Dill to Brooke, just as they preferred Lord Alexander to Field Marshal Montgomery who tended to be even more abrasive than Brooke. The Americans never appreciated Brooke's attitude and could not accept that there might be another point of view; the feeling was mutual. The Americans were equally aware that in 1939–41 Britain had stood alone, using civilian brains and scientific genius, and survived, which was mainly due to Churchill's political strength and Brooke's military experience and ability. For this reason, they held both men in some esteem, but with growing suspicion. The images and impressions of Brooke are as kaleidoscopic as those of Churchill.

There are many photographs of Brooke alongside Churchill, Roosevelt and Stalin, but perhaps one of the best pictures was painted in words by Anthony Powell (who served in Military Intelligence Liaison in the war) in his series of novels called *Dance to the Music of Time*. The narrator was standing on the pavement when the CIGS (Chief of the Imperial General Staff), namely Brooke, suddenly appeared: 'the hurricane-like imminence of a thickset general, obviously of high rank, wearing enormous horn-rimmed spectacles burst from a flagged staff car almost before it had drawn up by the kerb…he tore up the steps of the building at the charge…an extraordinary current of physical energy suddenly pervaded the place.'[1] The incident gave the 'outward appearance of exceptional magnetic impact', and the 'CIGS glanced for a split second, as if summarising all the facts of one's life'.[2] In his obituary in *The Times* in 1963 Brooke was described as 'universally recognised as one of the greatest – intellectually and in military knowledge probably the greatest – soldiers of his generation'.[3]

To those who knew him well he was not the stern forbidding character seen by many of his professional colleagues and opponents, but this remains the broad picture of a man frequently termed the 'CIGS' who was often regarded by historians as the architect, alongside Churchill, of Britain having survived and eventually succeeded in the war against Nazi Germany. It has been stated that Roosevelt and Churchill

Brooke in his War Office (IWM TR 151)

'both knew talent, hiring (and retaining) soldiers like George Marshall and Alan Brooke, who were the central figures making their respective planning staffs function'.[4] According to many historians and observers Brooke, like any human being, was not infallible in all his decisions, policies and estimates of others, but for many more he was the astute and tireless worker behind the scenes of power, historically well read and intellectually gifted.

In his autobiography the American General Omar Bradley wrote that in America, Brooke had hardly been heard of by the general public, whereas Brooke's field commanders such as Montgomery and Alexander were well known. On Victory Day in London Lady Grigg (wife of the secretary of state during most of the war years) observed that when the public watched Brooke climbing into the processional car, they had no idea who he was and what he had achieved. Brooke avoided the limelight, unlike Montgomery and Churchill, and unlike Churchill, Brooke was the reluctant warrior, and he never suffered from too much military ardour. His preferences were life at his home in Ferney Close, or standing up to his waist fishing or photographing waterfowl.

Mainly because some parts of his private diaries were published by Sir Arthur Bryant in the 1950s, he was known as the 'moaner' or 'groaner' with his frequent and vitriolic attacks on other commanders, politicians, national leaders, and especially Churchill and Churchill's friends and cronies such as Beaverbrook, Mountbatten and countless others. When read, these attacks feel personal, but they were nearly always based on his estimation of the subject's lack of strategic ability. Brooke had been appointed to high command because of his professional ability in military and strategic matters, which caused him to be recognised as the best available expert, and he developed a deep loathing of amateur views, especially those of interfering politicians which, in his opinion, could deflect the national goal of survival and hopefully victory.

Brooke once wrote that having a hobby was essential in a busy professional life, and this was more important for a person like Brooke, who apart from his family and a few close friends almost lived the life of a monk. His love of nature, especially birds, saved him time and time again from the pressures of his work, and he was well known for this pursuit and often regarded as a pioneer in bird photography. It was said of his birder friend Eric Hosking that he was one of 'the very few people who have told Field Marshal Alan Brooke to keep quiet', which was close to the truth, and only because in the field of ornithology Brooke recognised his friend as the senior commander.[5]

He may have appeared in world-famous photographs of World War II leaders at international conferences, but he deliberately left no memoirs, no autobiography, only his personal letters and diaries which have often been used to besmirch his character. The only time that Brooke became clearly visible to the public eye was when he appeared, albeit briefly, on British television in the 1950s following the publication of *The Turn of the Tide* when there was a BBC television broadcast, in which Lieutenant-General Brian Horrocks with historian Hugh Trevor-Roper interviewed Brooke. Horrocks in his introduction admitted that even then Brooke was virtually unknown, despite the fact that he had been Churchill's right-hand man, and quoting Montgomery, whom Horrocks said never handed out praise lightly, who had stated that he believed Brooke was the 'greatest soldier ever'. Horrocks emphasised that when he had been in France in 1939–40, he had personally known Brooke who had closed the gap against the Germans which allowed Dunkirk to succeed.\* Horrocks stated that Brooke had been Churchill's right-hand man and questioned him about Churchill. Brooke explained he always called Churchill 'Sir' and unlike the Great War, politicians and military men worked closer together in World War II; that they would argue 'hammer and tongs', but Churchill never overruled the COS. The 30-minute programme was full of compliments for Churchill with some amusing anecdotes by Brooke. It is, with the benefit of hindsight, easy to suspect

---

\*  This BBC broadcast is somewhat old and badly presented by today's standards, but it is worth watching for a personal insight and is available online.

this was an effort to heal the wounds of the conflict between these two leaders, one well known, the other hardly heard about outside military circles.

When Brooke was asked about strategy it was possible for the viewer of this programme to have an openly presented view of the character of Brooke. He spoke rapidly as the Americans had often noted, in a staccato fashion, and answered the questions with total self-assurance, waving a stick at the map too rapidly for the cameras. He did not wait for the question to finish because he immediately understood what was being asked, and he answered without the slightest hesitation and with a total self-confidence that he was correct. He never smiled in the entire programme, and it was possible to detect a degree of nervousness in Hugh Trevor-Roper as he posed his questions. Any reader of Brooke's life would find this 30-minute television clip revealing, mainly because it is possible to sense the respect and awe that the Americans had first felt, the deference for a determined and well-informed man, while seeking some inroad into questioning his strategy which was, even in the 1950s, well argued. Brooke was dressed like an everyday civil servant in a dark suit, and not once did he try to sing his own praises; he just answered the questions, while exhibiting no signs of pleasure when he was complimented or praised. When one later historian described Brooke as a 'self-conscious, not to say self-advertising person', and later as a 'self-satisfied, self-pitying, ungenerous, and disloyal man', it was far from the truth.[6] It is generally accepted that Brooke avoided the limelight, and none of these acerbic criticisms ring true, even when this BBC television interview is watched.

This interview had taken place in the 1950s when Bryant's publications had caused something of a scandal, mainly because of Brooke's often pungent and even brutal words about Churchill, which not only offended those who understandably adored Churchill, but set loose historians questioning the editing of the diaries by Bryant. The new edition by Danchev and Todman of the diaries, published in 2001, included the later comments added by Brooke, which have attracted their own criticism, but at least the new edition tended to show that the strains and stresses of war were the main cause of the frictions which Brooke reflected; these tensions were shared by both Churchill and Brooke, because they had both been regarded as 'old war-horses', and it is not surprising there was some conflict. Churchill had taken part in the last British cavalry charge at Omdurman, experienced the Boer War and even life in the trenches in the Great War. Brooke in that war was awarded the DSO with Bar and was mentioned in dispatches six times, and his length of army service started in 1902, lasting uninterrupted until 1946; they were similar in some experiences, both dedicated to the defeat of Nazi Germany, and with the inherent dangers of 1939–45 it would have been surprising had they not clashed.

Nevertheless, because he was a private man who loved ornithology and nature, he was hardly known by those outside his professional military league and a few close friends. This reappraisal of the largely unknown field marshal is an attempt not only to unravel his contributions during the war years, but to try and understand the nature of a highly significant man of whom few people are aware, and the sort of an he was, and what he achieved, especially with Churchill.

## Diaries

In studying Brooke's contribution during the critical years of 1939–45, his personal war diary is a central piece of evidence about the nature of the man and what he accomplished, and it provides an insight into events behind the scenes during the war years. This raises the initial and reflective question as to why people keep diaries in the first place.

This question can have no definitive answer, and at the best it can only amount to a series of speculations. Samuel Pepys' diary was one which recorded important and interesting events but was interspersed with his amorous love life in detail, and he is probably one of the most acknowledged British diarists of all times. It has been claimed that keeping a diary is a matter of self-discipline and even a productive way to conclude a day. Anne Frank's famous diary helped her cope with her fear and sense of loneliness; it was almost a matter of having a hidden friend to whom one could confide the deepest innermost thoughts. Others might keep a diary because they then have a constant reference to their side of the story or the events of the day. Chips Channon once wrote that when he asked himself why he kept a diary, he was unsure whether it was to relieve his feelings, or act as a consolation in his old age, or to dazzle his descendants. Some may be meant to be entirely personal, but the possibility that others will read it at a future date can never be cast aside by the diarist. The personal side is important, and for some people it is a means of coping, a matter of debriefing.

Many ordinary people do this, but their literary efforts are only of interest or value to their family, and usually when they have died. If they were important people of social or political standing, or were witness to great events, they then become of interest to historians. A person who writes out of self-discipline or as a way of being productive may find it fulfilling and useful, but that is a matter of personal judgement. It has been projected that this type of diary writing can almost amount to a healing process when the days and weeks are mulled over and put into perspective. Again, this is of importance only to the individual and his or her closest family, but it throws some light on Brooke's motivations.

Sometimes diary writing might be a matter of reinforcing self-confidence when the actions of the day are given some form of perspective. It may be assumed such a person tends to be a motivated type of character, seeking perspective in life and especially at a personal level. It could be that the diarist uses the process as a means of keeping the brain uncluttered, giving a sense of order to incidents, and simply recording events or feelings in order to remind the writer if similar occasions or experiences occur in the future. One thing is clear: the person keeping the diary is a motivated type of character. There are multitudinous reasons for diary writing, and ambition, self-propaganda, or even using it as a means of contact with loved ones or a future generation of the family, may be among the many motivations.

The diary gives a new dimension to the past. When David Margesson reported on Chamberlain's serious illness he and John Colville spoke of how the ex-prime minister had been greatly maligned, and Colville wrote, 'but I believe historians, if they try to throw themselves back into the conditions in which decisions were taken, and refrain from judging solely by what happened afterwards, will mix their censure with much praise for his honest efforts'.[7] Historians have occasionally been somewhat guilty of passing a judgement based first on the benefit of hindsight and on what eventually happened. The reading of an original diary helps in throwing historians 'back in time' to understand the feelings and circumstances of the day in question. When any person writes a diary, which is honest to themselves, it inevitably tells the reader more about the nature of that person than even an autobiography, which often benefits from later and perhaps more mature or even self-serving reflections. Unexpurgated diaries, on the other hand, with careful reading can reveal something of the nature of the writer, and the circumstances which reveal the feelings and atmosphere of the day.

Much of the above reflects Brooke's motivations. He had always been a prolific diarist and letter writer from his youth, especially throughout the Great War. He consistently wrote to his mother until the day she died. During World War II his military, political and personal diary was ostensibly addressed to his wife. However, it was also his way of 'letting off steam' and revealing his own anxieties and pressures of responsibility, which he experienced but could not disclose publicly. His diaries were written as his means of communicating with his wife. He was fond of his wife and trusted her, and the impression was that this was a home diary to share his life with her. This is another reason for diary writing for those people who out of necessity must live away from family; many prisoners used and still use this method, and Brooke was a prisoner to his high rank and the importance of his work. In Brooke's case he expected his wife to read about his hopes and fears because it was his means of talking to her. It was an expression of his love and loneliness in his isolated position of responsibility.

Officially British people who were in State service were not supposed to keep diaries for the sake of security. Many did, including John Colville (Churchill's secretary), Sir Alan Lascelles (the king's secretary), Lord Mountbatten, Lieutenant-General Pownall, Anthony Eden and many others. Perhaps the thought had crossed their minds that they were making or witnessing a momentous time in history, although this did not seem to be part of Brooke's motivation. Many were more than happy to write memoirs and autobiographies, but Brooke told Major-General John E. Hull 'that he would never write a book, since he could not bring himself to speak frankly about some people'.[8] In terms of public image it may have paid him to write a book rather than publish the sheer honesty of his forthright diary entries.

However, after the war Brooke was obliged to go through his diary because it contained elements which needed to be censored, and sometimes his downright criticisms of others could almost be libellous. Despite this editing the reader is often astonished by his frank disclosure of his thoughts about Churchill, other generals in the British army, and especially the American and French commanders. It was not a diary seeking public applause, but Brooke had an incisive mind and his revelations are both interesting and useful for historians. As will be noted from time to time these diaries were deeply personal and intended for his second wife Benita. Brooke had always been a 'stickler' for security, yet he often mailed his diaries home to Benita, using the offices of the Royal Mail, not that they would have changed the course of the war had they fallen into the wrong hands.

In 1957 and later in 1959 Sir Arthur Bryant published sections of Brooke's diaries in the books *The Turn of the Tide* and *Triumph in the West*. The first publication in 1957 'created a considerable stir…because it portrayed the irritations as well as the glories that fell to those who worked under Sir Winston Churchill in the direction of the war', and Bryant had somewhat liberally edited the chosen passages and caused a degree of controversy at the time.[9] The diary appeared to readers to demonstrate a bad-tempered moaner and groaner, but who happened to be the master strategist. It was not helped when the *Sunday Times* in 1957 produced a lurid serialisation which was somewhat embarrassing, and which, along with Bryant's input, drew a muted response from Churchill, who stated he was against keeping diaries which were written under the stress and events of the day.[10] It also transpired that Bryant's texts were not always reliable and in places were misleading, which sent serious scholars scurrying to the Liddell Hart archives where Brooke's personal papers are kept.* The diaries were heavily censored both on the grounds of national security 'and for fear of antagonising powerful figures such as the then American President Dwight Eisenhower, and the past and present serving Prime Ministers Winston Churchill, Anthony Eden and Harold Macmillan'.[11]

These first efforts by Bryant 'set the cat among the pigeons' as the press revelled in extracting and publishing the more personal comments, and the thesis that Bryant proposed – that 'the greatest soldier in the world' had been neglected, resulting in 'the legend of how the war in the West had been directed' – was not that accurate, and this stirred some controversy. Churchill's six-volume war history had just been published, leading Bryant to write that his version of Brooke's contribution 'might somewhat modify the prevailing conception of the PM's omniscient part in directing and dictating the entire course of the war – one which, if left uncorrected, will almost certainly be followed by a violent damaging reaction after his death.'[12] This

---

* The Liddell Hart Centre for Military Archives at King's College London was founded in 1964.

somewhat melodramatic and over-cooked sentence by Bryant nevertheless carried a degree of justification in so far that it raised many questions, especially for historians.

On reading Churchill's history, it was soon apparent that Brooke was often regarded as a background figure in a remote department, Brooke more often than not being referred to as 'the CIGS', and the work of the COS is given little priority. Churchill wrote six volumes, but the first was before the time when Brooke became an important participant in major events. The remaining five volumes make up some 3,622 pages. Brooke is mentioned mainly as the CIGS (most of the references occur when Brooke, mainly expressed through his title of CIGS, appears in the appendix of formal memos) only 162 times, and only 13 of these refer to him personally, compared to Alexander who is referred to some 306 times.[*] The personal references to Brooke amounted to only some 0.35 per cent (see footnote below).

Even though it is widely acknowledged, with considerable justification, that Churchill is a national hero of British history, his account of the war in its six volumes concentrates more on his role than others. In Brooke's diaries, if only half of what he wrote were true (and his integrity has never been doubted), Churchill was heavily reliant upon the COS, and especially Brooke. Churchill once referred to the fact that he had argued with Brooke who generally followed his line of thinking in strategy, which was highly misleading. Churchill had, for example, often longed to send troops into the Istrian Peninsula, and Brooke had argued that it would be potentially dangerous to withdraw forces from Alexander's command, but Churchill later wrote that 'the CIGS agreed with me that there should be no question of withdrawing any of Alexander's troops until Kesselring had been driven across the Piave'.[13] If in Churchill's work Brooke were set in the background of events, so was the COS which, like Brooke, was more often mentioned *en passant*, and it was not until the penultimate page of the final volume, in an appendix publishing his victory broadcast (13 May 1945), that the COS was properly mentioned. He wrote that 'in Field Marshal Brooke, in Admiral Pound, succeeded after his death by Admiral Andrew Cunningham, and in Marshal of the Royal Air Force Portal, a team was formed, who deserve the highest honour in the direction of the whole British war strategy and in its relations with that of the Allies.'[14]

The general lack of reference in Churchill's history books to Brooke and the part he played probably helped account for Brooke's image as the unknown field marshal. Churchill's history was regarded as the first authoritative history of the war. The hundreds of formal memos mainly listed in the appendix sections simply contain the state of affairs as suggested by Brooke and the COS, and finally approved by Churchill (usually after much wrangling and heat) but in their formal appearance

---

[*] In percentage terms for each time a name or a title appears in the last five volumes of Churchill's history, Montgomery appears 4.3 per cent, Brooke 4.4 per cent and Alexander 8.4 per cent. Given their relative importance in the war effort this is a curious statistic.

there are always three impressions given by Churchill: the first that all are in agreement, secondly that Brooke and COS generally agreed with Churchill and not *vice versa*, and finally that Churchill was a master of military logistics.

Brooke and Bryant consulted various trusted friends about the proposed publication of the diaries, and Sir Norman Brook (secretary to the Cabinet 1947–62) and Montgomery both warned that Churchill would not appreciate the diaries. They were correct. Despite Brooke's mollifying foreword to the book, and his genuine admiration if not love for Churchill, it was met first by silence, then a letter which saddened Brooke. As an historian the integrity of the diaries with their personal asides makes the work invaluable, but as an initial publication during the immediate postwar time, this writer suspects that if the personal emotions had been moderated, and Benita's advice of making Brooke more human and showing his real character had been taken seriously, they may not have been met with such discord, and provided such tasty meat for journalists. That Brooke was a man of feelings and emotions is known today from these diaries, but unsuspected by many during the war years, although Churchill's personal secretary identified this insight when she wrote: 'The CIGS always appeared to me something of an enigma; he seemed so calm and well controlled, and yet the expression on his face sometimes betokened that he had strong feelings beneath the surface.'[15] However, the diary's integrity comes first and foremost, and demonstrates Brooke's strength of personality. Because these initial published works proved to be highly controversial, they sold well.

The trustees of Brooke's papers later allowed Alex Danchev and Daniel Todman full access, producing the text that this biography has extensively plundered. The work of these two editors helped recover the damage done by Bryant and went a long way in restoring Brooke's reputation by publishing the raw works without Bryant's comments. In the *Telegraph* newspaper when the whole diaries were published, the writer who referred to Brooke as the 'Ulster-born brass hat' claimed that Brooke's influence on global strategies 'cannot be overestimated', claiming his strategies were better than those of Churchill, Roosevelt and Stalin; but whether they were that brilliant will always be a point of contention, especially in America.[16] If Churchill had been angry over Bryant's work, which seemed to undermine his wartime reputation, as the *Telegraph* newspaper of the day noted in 2001, 'he would have been apoplectic if he read what Alanbrooke and Bryant had excised from the diaries and which we publish today'.[17] It would take more than Brooke's diaries to blemish Churchill's reputation, and it should be recalled that part of Churchill's 'greatness lay in the fact that he appointed Brooke, and, albeit often grudgingly, always accepted his advice'.[18]

The first thought that crosses the reader's mind on examining Brooke's diary was that he had deep emotions, which after a difficult day welled up and were released in his notes to his wife Benita, written down almost religiously nearly every day when he was not taking a break or a holiday. It also becomes clear he was something of an 'isolate' and not a natural member of society with which he was obliged to mix.

It is easy to compile a long list of people of whom Brooke was heavily critical, and often his criticisms focused on a person's leadership abilities or their understanding of strategy, though 'at times...he admits that his initial judgement, as in the case of General [Henry Maitland] "Jumbo" Wilson was wrong'.[19] Brooke is always glaringly honest with his views which naturally upset Churchill and probably many others when they became public, especially in America. He was critical of many of his British colleagues and French and American commanders, but his relationship with Churchill was never easy and demands its own subsection in this study.

His diary frequently reflects the necessity of releasing pent-up steam, and while his 'almost nightly entries provided a psychological safety valve (and further allowed him to regain self-mastery), he had numerous other means – fishing, hunting, ornithology, spending portions of almost every weekend at home for relieving the often overwhelming tensions under which he worked'.[20] The wholeness of the diaries further 'help[s] us realize that besides having mettle and a quick mind, he also had a fine sense of humour and was an engaging conversationalist', but he was a man alone, often isolated even at dinner parties, and more at home watching a marsh warbler sitting on its nest.[21] The photographs of Brooke and multitudinous descriptions of a stern-looking horn-rimmed bespectacled man belie the fact that he enjoyed and offered humorous moments, Major-General Sir John Kennedy noting that 'Brooke had a great sense of humour and his descriptions of meetings with Winston are very good fun'.[22]

Another example of the riches of the diaries, expressed by many at their publication, was that despite Brooke's marvellous grasp of strategy, the diaries show that he probably held on to the Mediterranean strategy far too long and failed to appreciate Eisenhower's so-called broad front strategy, to be explored later. 'One further wished,' an American writer noted, that it would have been better 'had he got on with his American counterpart, General Marshall, particularly since they shared so many qualities and were both individuals of the highest character. Nevertheless, the diaries give us a wonderful portrait of a complex, highly intelligent person, who had faults, but who also played a stellar role in helping lead the British nation during one of its most trying times.'[23] Most especially his clash with Marshall and Eisenhower raised a few eyebrows, but he liked the men; it was the strategy, his professional theology, which caused such serious dissent.

The diary also revealed his deeper nature as a man who loved his wife and depended on friendships which were not always apparent during these fraught years. When his friend Dill died, he was upset and angry that Dill had never been given a peerage, about which Brooke wrote, 'I never forgave Churchill for not doing this.' When his son Tom was taken seriously ill he often visited him even during the heat of battle in France, and when his aide de camp Barney Charlesworth was killed in an aircraft accident he was almost beside himself with sheer grief; it cast a deep shadow over him for weeks. He felt sorrow for men like General Władysław Sikorski and Admiral

Ramsay when they died in similar circumstances, and for Lady Halifax on the loss of her son. His public image was of a stern puritanical man, feared, admired and liked by many, but remote and isolated. When these occasional entries are read, they disclose his compassion at the loss of friends or for people who had suffered bereavement, and the true nature of the man becomes revealed. He may have had the nickname of 'Colonel Shrapnel' in the War Office, but the diary paints a picture of a man who cared for his friends and neighbours.*

When Major-General Sir John Kennedy permitted Bernard Fergusson to publish his notes and memoirs in 1957, his only instruction was that 'nothing was to be included that hurts people's feelings', and yet there is something more valuable in those diaries which remain undiluted by after-thoughts. Fergusson had noted the outcry against Bryant and Brooke's book *The Turn of the Tide*, expressing the view that 'we should not be debarred from reading history', and with specific reference to the impact of the years 1939–45, writing: 'We should never have escaped the full penalty of our unpreparedness for war if we had not had a national leader whose imagination and zest were matched by his aggressiveness, and Chiefs of Staff who were not afraid to stand up to him. It was our good fortune that their opposite numbers in Germany lacked that essential characteristic.'[24]

## The Churchill Relationship

As characters, Brooke and Churchill were socially and in many other ways virtually diametric opposites. Churchill loved his cigars, his alcohol, late nights, erratic hours and boisterous dinner parties. At the Russian banquets Brooke always squirmed in disgust at the amounts of food, carefully watching his own intake of wine and vodka, whereas Stalin found a serious contender in Churchill for his drinking prowess. Churchill loved the limelight and Brooke avoided it at all costs. Most people would have enjoyed meals at Chequers and felt honoured to be invited, but Brooke detested these evenings and especially the late hours. If Churchill were the Cavalier, Brooke epitomised the Puritan with a self-mastery over himself. Churchill's secretary later recounted the story of Churchill speaking to Brooke over the telephone when he was in bed. The cat suddenly bit Churchill's toe; he exclaimed down the phone, 'Get off you fool,' ejected the cat, then saw the cat whimpering in the corner and said, 'Poor little thing.' Brooke, on the other end of the telephone, had been told 'to get off, and called a fool' and then found himself addressed as 'poor little thing'. He put the phone down at once, and called Churchill's private secretary wondering what was going on. Churchill was eccentric, lovable, but not always easy to work alongside.[25] In military matters, for which he was employed, Brooke was Churchill's aggravating tutor. Brooke may have been Montgomery's mentor and guardian, but he

---

* *Shrapnel* was his code name initially. Marshall's name was *Tom Mix*, an actor who played cowboys.

was Montgomery's commander; with Churchill the relationship was reversed, often causing bad-tempered moments in their constant disagreements with or without cats.

There were times when Brooke simply boiled over in his diary, wishing the prime minister would die before he tarnished his reputation, other times believing he had an 'unbalanced mind', but as General Hastings 'Pug' Ismay noted in his memoirs, Brooke wrote his diary last thing at night when he was simply exhausted. Churchill and Brooke were both blunt and angry with one another on many occasions, Brooke wondering at one time whether he would be dismissed, but Churchill had deliberately chosen a strong man who could challenge him. Brooke would often tone down Churchill's telegrams, wires and memos with the backing of the COS which was often necessary for diplomatic and military reasons; more to the point Churchill generally accepted the changes.[5] However, Churchill was always unhappy when at conflict with his military advisers or with the Americans, 'but when he had to make a choice between them, he came down firmly on Brooke's side'.[26]

The historian Michael Burleigh wrote that 'first there was the problem of dealing with Churchill, who behaved like a petulant *prima donna*, no matter how much Brooke otherwise respected him'.[27] When another historian wrote that Brooke 'could have exercised far more control over Churchill than he did' this was a patent underestimation of the force of Churchill's personality.[28] Brooke stood out for his ability to challenge a man few others would dare, including his predecessor Dill, who had held the post of CIGS.

Brooke told many amusing stories about Churchill, how he could be like a spoilt child and trying to take away 'from him a dangerous toy, it could take days or weeks!'[29] His battles with Churchill occurred many times, but the relationship was not always highly contentious; there were funny moments, amusing days, and laughter. Brooke often quoted some of Churchill's lines because of their amusement or literary succinctness, and even in heated discussion others found their exchanges amusing. When Churchill was complaining about all the accessories and men the army required, he compared the service to a peacock with an unnecessarily large tail, to which Brooke immediately retorted that without its large tail the peacock would lose its balance. Despite the general impression it was not always friction, there were good times, fun times, and as Kennedy noted 'the war would certainly have been much duller without him [Churchill]'.[30]

Brooke has been referred to as the 'dour, humourless Roundhead' and Churchill as 'the impulsive, expansive Cavalier' and their relationship has long been 'discussed to the point of exhaustion'.[31] Naturally, there are a variety of viewpoints, but the clashes between these two men, although providing a degree of historical bemusement, are essential in trying to understand the critical events of those days, and they provide an insight not only into Churchill, but chiefly for this biography of Brooke himself.

In the postwar years when Churchill had completed his *History of The Second World War*, which some considered to be an egocentric enterprise about how he won the war, his references to Brooke, as noted above, were minimal. This was somewhat surprising because there was not a campaign or strategy or military policy in which Brooke had not been involved, and yet he is often found only in the footnotes, and as a minimal character lurking in the background of the great events. As these books emerged onto the public shelves, Brooke was somewhat baffled by Churchill's neglect of the role that he had played in decision making. People who had been involved in minor ways in major events were given many more sentences and references. Churchill was equally if not more annoyed at Brooke's diaries and the tension of the war years continued into the postwar era. In Churchill's visitors' book kept at Chartwell there is a list of signed visitors with many being regular: Montgomery appears some 46 times, frequently Alexander, but there is not a single entry for Brooke.[32] Colville later noted that 'Brooke was the only man on whom I ever saw him [Churchill] deliberately and ostentatiously turn his back.'[33] This postwar time was much sadder than all the internal conflict of the war years.

## The American Conflict

His obituary in *The Times* stated that Brooke 'established the best possible relations with the Americans and exercised a strong influence upon the future course of Allied strategy, especially before the military expansion of the United States had reached its greatest heights and the American commanders had acquired experience'.[34] By the year 1943 and well before 1944 this had changed as the Americans were less inclined to listen to any foreigner, however able and experienced they were, but they always held Brooke in high esteem and tried to handle him with care. The initial conflicts had been over the British insistence on the North African and Mediterranean campaigns, the timing of invading the north-west coast of France, whether to invade the south of France, the pressure of the British trying to keep Hitler rather than Japan as the priority, and Eisenhower's and Montgomery's differing strategies for invading Germany. In broader terms the Americans had been seriously attacked by the Japanese, they understood that a Nazi-dominated Europe posed a serious risk for their future, and yet the British were demanding that they committed themselves to a desert battle in remote North Africa. This is a broad and somewhat sweeping analysis, and none of this strategic confusion was helped by the occasional outbursts of antagonism. Brooke could hardly hide his contempt for Marshall's and Eisenhower's strategy, and Montgomery, known as Brooke's protégé, did little to help. The response was not helped by a degree of Anglophobia – Generals Patton, Bradley, Stilwell and Clark were known for this as well as General Wedemeyer, who became bitterly Anglophobic after reading Brooke's diary entries when they were first published. Prior to this publication Wedemeyer had said of Brooke that he 'was articulate sensitive and one who would nibble away to gain his own ends'.[35]

As will be noted later in this exploration the question of strategy had a hidden and almost subconscious dilemma. The British, as with other nations, had a form of 'cultural strategy' of defence based on the Royal Navy and the defence of the colonies and essential economics, and an inbuilt policy of gnawing away at the problem, whereas the Americans had already developed a sense of 'go, get and win' as soon as possible, a version of the Roman *veni vidi vici*, 'I came, I saw, I conquered'.

As such, the timing of D-Day in Normandy was an ongoing issue ranging from 1942 which the Americans wanted, to 1943 upon which they tried to insist, and then 1944 which they demanded. 'Viewed from fifteen years later, the British conception still seems sounder in the light of our then knowledge; but the Americans would have none of it. It was just as well: for had the landings in Normandy been abandoned or postponed, the rocket-launching sites in the Pas de Calais would not have been overrun in time to prevent incalculable damage to London and southern England.'[36] A French historian wrote that 'Alanbrooke considered that the Americans' reasoning was rigid and over simplified, and they did not appreciate the magnitude of the problem.'[37] As noted above, both sides held views which had some plausibility.

Over the last 70 years considerable attention has been given to the relationships between the three Allied leaders, Churchill, Roosevelt and Stalin, along with the military advisers Marshall and Brooke. There have been comparative studies made between Hitler and Stalin but not with the Japanese or Italian leadership. The Germans never had conferences like the Allies, and when small internal summits were convened 'Hitler hogged the meetings'.[38] Roosevelt's closest adviser was Harry Hopkins who moved into the White House, and Roosevelt always deferred to Marshall, and Churchill always prepared himself to listen to Brooke. Churchill enjoyed and used his frequent Chequers meetings to relax but also to discuss the war and possible strategies; Hitler enjoyed his coteries where even he must have seen them trying to stay awake during his long and tedious monologues.

There was a vast difference between the war machine of Nazi Germany and the Anglo-American camps. In Germany there were no Cabinet meetings because in 1938 Hitler had abolished the War Ministry after Field Marshal Blomberg's dismissal, and had made himself the supreme commander to whom all military personnel had to swear an oath of allegiance. Keitel and Jodl are often regarded as the key figures in the OKW (*Oberkommando der Wehrmacht*, German high command) but they never dared contradict the wisdom of the Führer. Roosevelt actively sought the advice of Marshall, and 'Brooke could generally save Churchill from the mistakes he was making' but there was nothing like this in the German system.[39] If Churchill were the resounding gong, Brooke was the hand that tempered his mallet, and this was especially true when Brooke toned down Churchill's angry telegrams to Roosevelt as Churchill found to his chagrin that he was becoming the junior partner, none of which helped in the essential and critical Anglo-American alliance.

In short, in the issues outlined above there were few meetings with the Americans which were not contentious, and Brooke was often the perceived focus of the problem with his staunch and differing views of strategy. From the timing of D-Day and whether North Africa was the right fixture, they increased in heat over the public relations concerning the Battle of the Bulge, to the bitter confrontation over Eisenhower's plans for entering Germany. They often reflected the cultural strategic differences mentioned above, but despite the in-house skirmishes Brooke managed to keep his friendship with the individuals, and he was always held in high respect. After the war Marshall invited Brooke over the Canadian border to stay and dine with him. The conflicts at the conferences and meetings may have sounded personal, may have been regarded as personal, Brooke's diary often sounded personal, but in real life it was a technical debate about strategy.

## Author's note

'Speech marks' are used to indicate a quotation which is then end-noted. There are also many times when these marks are used to indicate that they have been extracted from a letter, diary or conversation when an endnote is not required because the reference is self-evident. If, for example, Brooke's arguments or Churchill's words are being outlined the use of a speech mark indicates that this word or expression was used on the occasion, and at other times to indicate an emphasis.

## CHAPTER I

# Early Background

As with many officers born in the later 19th century Brooke was born into a well-known and traditional family, based in Ireland with a history of loyalty to the British crown, stretching back to the middle 17th century. The Brooke family had been rewarded with lands and the Castle Donegal because they had defended the crown in the 1641 uprising. They were minor aristocrats and belonged very much to the upper echelons of society. They were sometimes known as 'the fighting Brookes' and came from that strong Northern Ireland Protestant element often known as the Ulstermen. They were one of the largest landowning families and 26 Brookes served in the Great War, 27 in World War II (12 were killed), confirming their fighting reputation.[1] The family were well known and later Brooke was to discover that Churchill had known and served with two of his brothers, and even President Roosevelt had met elements of his family.*

His father was Sir Victor Brooke (born 1843 and named Victor after his godmother Queen Victoria) who had married Alice Bellingham at an incredibly young age for those days. Victor Brooke was not a politician, but he was known for speaking out against Irish Home Rule thereby continuing the views of his ancestors. He was a

---

\* Churchill wrote: 'His brother Victor was a subaltern in the 9th Lancers when I joined the 4th Hussars, and I formed a warm relationship with him in 1895 and 1896. His horse reared up and fell over backwards, breaking his pelvis, and he was sorely stricken for the rest of his life. However, he continued to be able to serve and ride, and perished gloriously from sheer exhaustion whilst acting as liaison officer with the French Cavalry Corps in the retreat from Mons in 1914. He had another brother, Ronnie, he was older than Victor and several years older than me. In the years 1895–98 he was thought to be the rising star in the British Army. Not only did he serve with distinction in all the campaigns which occurred, but he shone at the Staff College among his contemporaries. In the Boer War he was adjutant of the South African Light Horse, and I was for some months during the relief of Ladysmith his Assistant Adjutant, the regiment having six squadrons. Together we went through the fighting at Spion Kop, Vaal Krantz, and the Tugela…he was stricken down by arthritis at an early age, and he could only command a reserve brigade at home during the First World War. Our friendship continued till his premature death in 1925.' See Churchill, Winston, *The Second World War, Vol II* (London: Cassell and Company, 1949) pp.223–4.

magistrate, a deputy lieutenant and sheriff of Fermanagh, but he was more interested in sport and nature, not least hunting, fishing and exploring. For these activities he became well known and somewhat famous and he passed his enthusiasms on to his sons.

Typically for that era, Victor and Alice had eight children, and then as the late comer Alan Francis Brooke was born on 23 July 1883. His birth came as something of a surprise. He was not born in Ireland, or anywhere in the United Kingdom or British Empire, but at his family's favourite long-term holiday house in France, at Bagnères-de-Bigorre in the French Pyrenees not far from Pau. It was a beautiful setting with mountains and a better climate than Ireland enjoyed. The family, because they were wealthy enough, spent most winters and other months at this climatic haven; it was a fashionable area and the family purchased a villa in Pau and saw less and less of Ireland.

As a young child Brooke occupied himself and was 'totally absorbed in what he was doing, in his own private life', which given that he was the youngest in the family, was not surprising.[2] Being the youngest his interests probably differed to a degree from his older siblings. It is curious that one of Britain's major military leaders in World War II was born in France and spoke French as his first language, although his early education was in English. This did have the consequence that there were times in later life when his written English tended to have grammatical flaws. Being bilingual was a major asset which undoubtedly helped him, and he became a sound linguist in many languages, including German.

His father died from pneumonia in November 1891 aged 48 when the youngest Brooke was only eight years of age, and his eldest son Douglas assumed the baronetcy and the estate. Douglas had a son called Basil born five years after Brooke, and he became more like a traditional brother to Brooke as the eldest son took on the paternal role. If Brooke were closest to any of his brothers, it was Victor who was his immediate brother in age. Curiously, they were educated in a school in Pau which was run by a German teacher for English families. Brooke at an early age was alreay receiving an international background, which would serve him well in later years. During his summers in Ireland and other times in France, Brooke developed a love of nature, shooting and fishing, which as he grew older never diminished, apart from the fact that he later preferred to photograph rather than kill wildlife. His father was widely known for his sporting ability, his hunting and adventurous exploits, and Brooke and his brothers followed the same paternal lines in their various ways. He learnt to ride, as most of his social class did, and enjoyed hunting from a horse, especially in Pau. The Pau area was famous for its hunting and was sometimes known as the Leicestershire of France for this reason, and it would always hold happy memories for Brooke. His French education and background were later to be useful, endearing him to many French people, and later in life he would be honoured in his place of birth and in Pau during the postwar years.

Despite this vigorous type of lifestyle, the youngest Brooke was believed to suffer from frail health, so under his mother's influence he avoided the English prep-school and boarding system, which for some was enjoyable but for others something of a nightmare. He thought for a time he wanted to join the medical profession, but by the age of 16 he was looking towards the army. Even at this age he was deeply interested in hunting sports and nature; undoubtedly something he had gathered from his father who was reputed 'to have a great efficiency with both gun and rifle', and passed this DNA onto his children.[3]

Naturally, a man from his social background was expected to become an officer and not join the ranks, so he went to a cramming school in Roehampton for the entrance exam to try and enter the Royal Military Academy at Woolwich. This well-known establishment of the day (often called The Shop) trained young gentlemen, known as cadets, for commissions in the Royal Artillery (RA) and the Royal Engineers (RE). The result depended on a person's entry mark, and the Field Artillery was considered the best of places; further down the ladder was what was called Garrison Artillery.[4] He came 65th out of the 72 entry candidates but presented well during his time at this establishment.

The training camp was at Perham Down (in Wiltshire on the edge of Salisbury Plain) where he enjoyed the physical and field exercises. He was considered by many to be excellent in horsemanship and was good at shooting, but rarely participated in team games, probably because unlike most of his companions he had never experienced the boarding-school background. Being born in France, educated in English by a German teacher, it was no great surprise that he excelled in languages, and was awarded a prize for his linguistic abilities by the French ambassador. He was further commended because he applied himself to all the tasks and exercises which were demanded from him. When he left this training organisation, he was a highly regarded cadet who could mix with others; he had worked his way up to 15th position and hoped for a place in the RE. It has been suggested that perhaps he worked too hard in the summer of 1902 because he often complained of headaches, and he dropped two places. At the end of his training there were only 15 RE commissions given, but this left him in second place for the RA, and on 24 December 1902 the Secretary for War (St John Brodwick, 1856–1942) signed a commission of King Edward VII appointing him to the Royal Regiment of Artillery.

## Fun in the Army

Brooke spent the first three years of his military life in Ireland, and the next eight in India. The catastrophic Boer war had caused many in the army to rethink traditional British strategy and tactics, and the war had sent a warning to the more astute that perhaps British military power should no longer be taken for granted. As he started his military career, he could not have foreseen that he was facing the prospect of two major world wars, but during this Edwardian time life was peaceful and for most of Brooke's social class the world was simply full of fun. He was sent to join a battery at Fethard in Tipperary where he occupied his time pursuing his growing love of fishing, horses with steeplechases and point to point, and he purchased a motorcycle which he utilised to dash to his mother's home at Colebrooke. As with most motorcyclists he probably enjoyed the sense of speed and driving too fast, which was later to create a serious tragedy in his life.

Brooke was a man deeply rooted in the wish for family love, and this was to become one of his enduring characteristics. He wrote letters to his mother and started a lifelong habit of keeping a personal diary, in which he expressed his innermost thinking, which was later to be an invaluable gift to historians. Later, with the immense strain of leadership during World War II the diary was a means by which he could relieve the inner tensions. His letters to his mother when she was away in France clearly indicated that he was having a pleasant and fun-filled life. This sense of enjoying life as a young army officer was also reflected by Churchill's early autobiography *My Early Life*.[5] However, Churchill had experienced the Boer War, and as mentioned above, there were some salutary lessons which the British military had to take on board, and Brooke's attention to army duties increased despite the background of fun and sport. From these earliest of days as a young officer Brooke developed a feeling for the call of duty, and like most young men a sense of ambition. He even submitted a design for a timed percussion fuse, but it was not deemed to be good enough for testing trials. It was, however, a prescient thought, and such devices would soon be developed not only for shells but for aircraft bombs. He pursued with some relish the study of military history (later even finding time to pursue this in France during the Phoney War), and in 1904 he became a qualified interpreter in French and German.

In those days India was regarded by many young officers to be the place for fun and work, and it offered many opportunities for potential excitement. During this period, it was generally regarded that the Royal Navy guarded Britain with its empire and British interests, and the only anxiety was Tsarist Russia which was possibly considering further expansion in India's direction. This was not deemed to be too serious, but more of a precautionary view, and life for a young military officer in India was regarded as a learning process about overseas, and an opportunity for hunting, sport, excitement and fun. As such, in 1906 Brooke volunteered to go to India, and in the same year he took over a draft of the East Lancashire Regiment and guided them from the Curragh (a flat open plain of common land in Newbridge, County Kildare), outside Dublin, to Bombay. They embarked at Southampton on Boxing Day, from where he eventually travelled to Bombay, and he joined the 30th Royal Field Artillery Battery at Meerut in the Punjab.

This period in India, he later reflected, was the happiest of his life. This is not a surprising revelation because most of the rest of his life would be lived in the vexed turmoil of two world wars. While in India Brookecontinued his love of nature, but being a young man in the company of others he enjoyed hunting and pig-sticking; he also found photography interesting which would one day become part of his love for hunting but without the killing. It was probably during this time in India he started to question himself about killing; he enjoyed the stalking and the pursuit but not seeing the dead animal. In later life he would exchange the gunsight for camera lens and the trigger for the shutter release. He was able to indulge in horse sports including polo, all games associated with the well-off and the upper classes, not that this social distinction, taken for granted by many, would have occurred to a young officer in those days.

Forever the linguist, he qualified in Urdu in 1908 and in Persian in 1910, but at this stage he turned his thoughts to the Indian Staff College because a driving ambition, as in many young officers, was considered the only way forward. His brother Victor was the military secretary to the Viceroy and the future seemed assured. However, on a visit to London an ear specialist said his left ear suffered from a deafness which meant he should no longer be near loud guns, which was his specific task as an officer of the Royal Artillery. He decided the specialists were wrong (which they were) but in the meantime to err on the safe side he considered joining the Staff, which he believed to be the best way forward for making progress. Before he could apply, he had to pass the examinations for the rank of captain which he duly passed in 1909, but he would have to wait for war for the promotion to happen. He was then ordered to join a battery of the Royal Horse Artillery known as Eagle Troop at Ambala (in the state of Haryana, near the Punjab border).

His application for Staff College failed when he scored badly on the Law papers, which was a common problem with this entrance requirement. Later, in 1919, he would be nominated to attend the Staff College at Camberley, thus by-passing the need to sit examinations in law.

In the meantime, he stayed with Eagle Troop and thoroughly enjoyed the experience, developing good friends and a sharp wit in the banter of their club; his ability at the quick verbal response was one day to be regarded as one of his characteristics. It was in this social camaraderie that he developed a keen sense of humour, which emerged even in the darkest days. He lived in a class-ridden society, with the officer class, and at a time when the British were superior and India was regarded as a mere possession. There were times when he appeared to find certain aspects of the social life distasteful, but nevertheless, he gained a school-boyish sense of fun by using a catapult to fire at the natives' backsides. His first biographer wrote that 'in his general attitudes he was a young man of his time'.[6] He would have been in his twenties, and there is little doubt that as he matured, he would have found this memory embarrassing, like most young men when they looked back at their more juvenile days.

In 1908 he was granted the traditional six months' leave, and on returning home he became engaged to his first wife Jane Richardson. Her father was a Colonel John Richardson and there was not only a similarity in the two men's chosen way of life, but they came from the same social class. He was concerned that on a subaltern's pay he could not support a wife and the engagement lasted for six long years. As it transpired it was not until 1914 that he was at last given permission to marry, which he duly did on 28 July from Jane's home in Ballinamallard in Fermanagh. He was engaged for six years, and after the sixth day of his honeymoon he received orders to embark for India.

Brooke was in a complex situation. He had just married and was at the start of his honeymoon, and well aware that war in Europe was a likely scenario, and now, with all his equipment in India he was being ordered back when he would have preferred to remain in Europe. He attempted unsuccessfully to stay, but he obeyed orders as much as he expected commands he issued to be followed. He had no choice but to leave his wife Jane and set sail with many others caught in the same situation through the Mediterranean to Port Said, a major crossroad in those days. As he waited for the next step he moved into Cairo and attached himself to a battery of the Royal Horse Artillery in Abassia (a neighbourhood of Cairo). Brooke with his gift for languages, started to learn Arabic in case the war spread to his area. In the meantime, he was, like many others, reading about the developing conflict in Western Europe, and the growing casualty lists; amongst the first names Brooke read was that of his favourite brother Victor, a devastating blow and the first of many more to come.

## World War I

Brooke was fortunate that on 18 September 1914 he discovered his Eagle Troop had been in transit and were passing through Egypt. He only had a few minutes to spare to join their convoy which was heading towards Marseilles; he was pleased to find a fellow officer had thoughtfully packed his equipment and brought it along with all the troop's baggage. From there they travelled north where Brooke, with his language ability, interviewed some German prisoners. For his entire life he never regarded the enemy as 'despised or hated' but saw them in a purely objective light as the enemy of the day. He also developed a high regard for German military professionalism, which was to later serve him well, and cause him concern in the Phoney War when others felt too relaxed. He would also be criticised by some for his regard for the German military, but he was well justified in his opinion. In the next world war, the German General Rommel would claim the policy of *krieg ohne hass* (war without hate), which reflected Brooke's thinking, as he regarded good soldiers as those who were committed and doing their duty.

By the time Brooke had reached the front and reunited the Ammunition Column with the Artillery Brigade, the first Battle of Ypres was nearly over. It was immediately apparent that this was not the war soldiers had anticipated, and the populace had envisaged. The war had almost immediately settled into the well-known trench warfare of attrition: there were no merging Napoleonic armies, no Light Cavalry charge as in the Crimea, but men dug into the trenches stretching from Switzerland to the sea. The advent of the machine gun which defended the trenches made a frontal attack virtually impossible, though it was tried time and time again and the casualty rates were simply unbelievable. Brooke would have found the soldier's life vastly different from India and even his recent stay in Egypt, because in Europe it was wet, cold, dreary and dangerous. Most of his time was spent on a horse travelling between batteries and the various headquarters. In November he was at last promoted to captain which had taken 11 years and a war to happen.

He had last seen Jane on their interrupted honeymoon five months previously, but at the beginning of 1915 he was given some leave so he could at last catch up with his wife. They would snatch whatever time they could, Jane frequently travelling from Ireland to London so they could spend maximum time together. He often referred to her as Janey and they were evidently a loving couple. The contingencies of war meant Brooke was elevated further; in peace time his senior officers may have noted he was good on horses and hunting, but war drew their attention to his efficiency and sound common sense, and as soon as he returned to the front he was promoted to staff captain and was the adjutant to the commander of the Royal Artillery. This was a Colonel Askwith, who according to Brooke was not a man given to work. This may have worked in Brooke's favour because he had to be more than an official lackey and news conveyor, and he had to assist in the planning. When his Artillery Brigade were moved in support of others in an attack on Neuve Chapelle (March 1915) Brooke had his work cut out. He was responsible for the supervision of some 54 guns, and he worked desperately hard because his colonel preferred to play cards.

Naturally, given his training and background as an artillery man he stayed with this work throughout the war, concerned about supplies, their arrival, their condition, and at times he felt frustrated as the senior commanders did not appear to recognise the critical part guns could play. This sense of frustration at others not understanding a situation was to become a lifelong habit; during the Phoney War of 1939–40 he would become more and more critical of Field Marshal Lord Gort for failing to see the 'bigger picture'. This was not because Brooke was by nature a moaner and groaner, which he would be accused of many times by a variety of people, but he was already developing a highly professional military perceptiveness about what was required. There were many commanders he admired, but he was more than capable, perhaps too adept, at spotting those who were deficient.

During 1915 it was evident that the armies had settled down to a long period of attrition, and the only tactic was to pound the enemy with indirect fire; all sides increased their artillery campaigns and Brooke was occupied with this throughout the war. Artillery, when accurate, was lethal to the enemy: these guns were highly destructive, and their shells moved faster than men and vehicles. The process of recognising the power of artillery was slow, and it was not until 1917 that high-explosive shells with instantaneous percussion fuses, which caused the projectile to detonate on impact but above the ground, were devised and used.[7] During World War II the British army was often criticised but their artillery was always praised.

In order to be efficient, the artillery needed direction, target analysis and good timing. There were at this stage no easy radio or even telephone links. On the other side of the divide was the future Field Marshal Albert Kesselring, who like Brooke was also watching the technological developments. As Kesselring was regarded as something of an 'expert with an understanding of the interplay between tactics and technology', Brooke was always looking for improvements especially in locating targets for the artillery.[8] Both Kesselring and Brooke practised artillery accuracy, and became interested in balloon-observation for directing artillery fire and for observing enemy movement, but with the arrival of aircraft and improved optics, balloons soon became redundant. For most of the early part of 1915 the basic work for Brooke was one of visiting, selecting, and organising observation posts.

He spent much of the 1915 summer in reserve and he managed to visit his mother, and on return found orders posting him as brigade major, Royal Artillery to the 18th Infantry Division. This was commanded by the efficient Major-General Ivor Maxse, who had once been attached to and impressed by the Prussian Guard before the war, and he was one of the commanders Brooke much admired.* He may have been critical of some commanders, but he was also capable of noting the better ones (see footnote on Maxse).

The year of 1916 will always be associated with the Battle of the Somme, and 1917 with Flanders, known as the Third Ypres, marked by battles which have scarred British memory with the massive slaughter and loss of lives. Brooke, now a brigade major, played a vital part in the Battle of the Somme. As would become his lifelong habit he prepared extensively for the coming onslaught, making use of diorama models showing not only the terrain but the essential targets. The overall concept of attack tactics appeared to the generals of the day to be sound, namely a heavy bombardment for days of the other side, then hoping that the British troops only had to walk towards what were anticipated to be empty German trenches. The Germans had planned their gunnery and enfilade concentrations well, but in Brooke's sector of the front, with XIII Corps and the 18th Division sector there was a swift British success.[9] Brooke had observed and copied the French system of the creeping

---

* Ivor Maxse was described by the military historian Correlli Barnet as 'one of the ablest officers of his generation, a man…driven and a formidable personality.' See online edition of *Oxford Dictionary of National Biography* (Oxford: OUP, 2008). He took up fruit growing on retirement and died in 1958. See *The Concise Dictionary of National Biography*, Volume II, (Oxford: OUP, 1995) pp.1993-4.

barrage; 'the barrage to "creep" by lifts, at ninety-second intervals, of fifty yards'.[10] It must have been a terrifying attack for the Germans, but there is no question that their trenches were better, deeper, and often reinforced with concrete. The 18th Division was there for months, often supporting other formations. Looking back with the benefit of hindsight it appeared a hopeless and useless waste of lives, but the generals and senior officers like Brooke had become immured in the consequences, and it never seemed to occur to any of them that it was a mindless method, and as soldiers of that tradition the call for sacrifice had always been a feature of their training and expectations. The breakthrough never happened in 1916 despite Field Marshal Douglas Haig's forecast, but Brooke was awarded the Distinguished Service Order for the part he had played in his sector.

The following year in February 1917 Brooke received new orders to leave the 18th Division, and he was posted as a staff officer to the RA of the Canadian Corps, making him chief of staff to the commander of the Corps artillery. Brooke gained the immediate impression that his new commander was a good man but seemed to know little about the tactical handling of artillery; Brooke wrote out all the orders and his superior never questioned them. This was once again an example where the demands of a war situation provided men who were good professionals with an opportunity to shine more than in peacetime. During the Battle for Vimy Ridge (April 1917), where the fire power was intense, it was greatly helped by Brooke's developing barrage system. He started to use plane flights for observation, and he walked incessantly on the front line inspecting the situation; this sense of dedication and purpose was noted by others, and it was a constant feature of his military life.

He was not a fanatical automaton, and he still enjoyed his golf and horse riding whenever he could take a break from the front lines. In October 1917, the Corps moved north to take part in the closing stages of what was called the Third Ypres, which, as is well known, was another tragedy for the infantry. However, between 26 October and 13 November the Canadian Corps took their final objectives, namely the ridge and village of Passchendaele; Brooke was appalled by the slaughter and sheer destruction, a memory, along with the other disasters he witnessed, which never left him. It was unquestionably these memories which would later concern him with the American strategy of engaging the Germans in France as early as 1942 and 1943.

After Christmas of 1917 Brooke returned to Britain for a short staff course where he was joined by his wife. This must have been like stepping into heaven, but it was only a brief time, because on 21 March, as the last German assault started with Operation *Michael*, all personnel including Brooke were recalled to frontline duties. Brooke was not directly involved, and in June he was appointed temporary general staff officer 1 (lieutenant-colonel) RA at the HQ of the First Army. Brooke had been 31 when war had been declared, and up to that moment he had led a carefree life, but war brought to light his leadership gifts, accelerated his promotion, and changed him as it did many others with the loss of friends and family. He wrote: 'If stones could talk and could repeat what they have witnessed, and the thoughts they had read on dying men's faces I wonder if there would ever be any wars.'[11] This thought would dog him for the rest of his life, but most especially in the opening months of the next global conflict, which in 1939 he barely believed was happening yet again.

In the immediate aftermath, during the first weeks of peace, he heard the Germans in occupied territory had stolen items at a national and personal level, which would have run counter to his own strict morals and almost puritanical feelings. He did, however, notice that the Germans had treated dead soldiers well in the carefully maintained cemeteries, and for this he gave them some respect. He was never to forget, however, their proficiency in military matters; it was a timely warning for him in 1939. On the personal level on 3 November 1918 he returned to England on leave; his eldest daughter Rosemary had just been born, and he witnessed the London scene when the Armistice was announced. The war had given him rapid promotion and marked him out as a highly efficient military officer, a man of duty, and capable of independent thought.

## CHAPTER 2

# Interbellum Years

After the Great War, the two decades of the 1920s and 1930s were scarred by the memory of the massive fatalities and serious life-changing injuries caused by the conflict. The carnage and destruction had been so enormous that most people believed it could never happen again. The economic side of life in Britain was at its lowest ebb, and returning soldiers found unemployment and poverty awaiting them, not the new world they had anticipated. The government introduced the Ten-Year Rule which was an economic device to ensure that not too much money was spent on the military, as it was thought a major war was unlikely within that allotted period. The army was reduced in size and was thinly spread around the globe policing the empire and various colonies, and the intelligence agency (known as the SIS) had its budget cut to a mere annual £125,000 on which it was expected to run a global network. The home intelligence service, MI5, was treated like the SIS. Politicians were no longer worried about impoverished disrupted Germany, but more about the possible success of Bolshevism and the fear that its international programme, known as Comintern, was infiltrating Britain with a view to a revolution. It was almost as obsessive as the panic started by William Le Queux's novels before the Great War, suggesting there was a German spy in every port; this time it was communist spies. The General Strike was believed to be a communist inspired revolution (which the Soviets may have hoped for), but it was not, and the Wall Street Crash heralded the global financial crisis.

Brooke returned to a country with financial problems, in decline, suffering from extreme poverty and unemployment, obsessed with communism, and believing that the Versailles Treaty had made Germany harmless. In Italy, a theorist called Guilio Douhet was proving more influential than any other single Italian military expert, and this was mainly due to the translation and publication in the United States of his book *Il dominion dell'aria* (*Mastering the Airspace*). This publication was widely read abroad, and its theory of demonstrating large-scale bombing of civilian areas clearly indicated that this policy did not originate in the United States or in Great Britain as many have believed.[1] In 1927, in response to a potential air threat against Britain, Joseph M. Kenworthy theorised on this controversial subject in his book *Peace or War?*. Air forces, he argued, would replace armies and navies. Much of this went unheeded for a time in Britain where the economic situation and the communist threat remained the centre of political attention. In the 1920s Germany was no longer considered a danger, and the fact that the German General von Seeckt was working with the other pariah state of the Soviet Union in preparing a reformed military with new tactics (part of which would one day be dubbed the Blitzkrieg) was probably known, but not raising concerns. It would not be until the mid-1930s that attention would be drawn to the lurking dangers of fascist Germany, and then only by the more astute; most were concerned about Bolshevism.

## Staff College and Army Duties

'Brooke emerged from the war with the reputation as being a most capable and promising staff officer', but he was hoping, like so many others, for a peaceful life and simply looked to his career as a professional soldier, the war having raised his rank so he could be regarded as permanent.[2] At a personal level he left the war able to unnerve people with his speed of analysis, speech and action: this would become one of his enduring characteristics. The war had changed him to a degree by making him sharper and discerning, with an increasing dislike for what he might have called 'the company of fools'. He had seen too many inept officers making ill-judged decisions during the Great War, and he always had a strong puritanical streak and disliked 'moral as well as physical flabbiness'; he was strong man in every aspect of the word.[3]

In 1919 he was selected for the first postwar course at Staff College, Camberley, something which had eluded him before the Great War, and indicating that he was perceived as an up-and-coming officer destined for high places. The instructors and his fellow officers had all experienced this bitter war, and his fellow students were men with whom he would soon have some close acquaintance over the next three decades. They included Gort, Freyberg, Foss, and he especially liked the instructor Dill whom one day he would succeed as the CIGS. Dill was an Ulsterman like Brooke which would have assisted in their lifelong friendship. Brooke was already gathering a reputation for his military knowledge, his mental dexterity, and most people appeared to enjoy his company. On the personal side he led a normal family life and his son Thomas, known as Tom, was born in 1921. Brooke was always a family man, and it came as a great shock when his mother died in 1920. Despite his chosen profession, when it came to family Brooke was a deeply sensitive man, and this family loss profoundly struck him.

Following his time at Staff College Brooke spent three years on the General Staff of the 50th Northumbrian Division, a Territorial division with its HQ in Newcastle. He found a house in Warkworth, Northumberland, which was some 30 miles north of Newcastle, and on the peaceful side of life which he always sought, he developed his passionate hobby of birdwatching and photography which almost verged on the compulsive. Gone were the days of pig-sticking; now he hunted his prey with a camera, consumed with his love of ornithology.

His professional military life was somewhat darkened by the industrial strife and fear of a Bolshevik revolution. It infected much of central Europe in the aftermath of the Great War, but more concerning in Brooke's life was the suggested evidence that there was a strong communist branch in Newcastle, part of his area as a military commander. He was informed, probably by Special Branch, that the communists had planned a May Day demonstration, and Brooke was instructed that his troops were to be prepared. When the day came the local public turned out for the event but went home for tea. Quite how the troops, many of them from the same working-class background, would have reacted was fortunately never to be tested. The politicians and many others during this period were totally convinced that a communist revolution would happen at any moment. As mentioned, this fear rapidly re-emerged with the General Strike of 1926, which Soviet Russia had hoped would turn into a revolution, but it was a democratic outburst at the sheer poverty and unemployment endured by the working population. As these worries simmered not far below the surface the 50th Division moved to Catterick, and Brooke moved into a house owned by his wife's sister.

## Camberley and Tragedy

Brooke was not there long: in January 1923 he returned to the Staff College at Camberley as an instructor, meeting amongst others Gort and General Sir Bernard Paget a future commander-in-chief, and also Montgomery and John Fuller. This was the time when immense intellectual debate and military theory came under intense scrutiny in command circles. In the outside world most people paid little attention to these arguments, as there was a general belief that the horrors of the Great War necessitated the end of all wars, but in military circles at the higher level, this war had raised many issues. The nature of the new industrial war had opened new dimensions and ramifications, and the advances in technology and science were having a major impact. The desire not to repeat trench attrition war was pivotal in all the military debates. This explained the sudden interest in aircraft power mentioned above. For his part, and not surprisingly, Brooke was recognised as the authority in artillery; he gave a series of lectures on the subject, and they were published in the *Journal of the Royal Artillery*. Brooke regarded artillery as the real firepower and having watched the helpless loss of life in the infantry attacks, he saw the artillery as the only remedy against this form of devastating attrition.

This was not a view shared by everyone. Many politicians still held to the Royal Navy, the Senior Service, to offer defence, a form of cultural strategy which will be explored later in this study.* Others looked more to aircraft as the problem or

---

* See Chapter Five on the post of CIGS.

answer to another war. Douhet, mentioned above, and others believed that aircraft bombing would destroy weapon production and the workers in the factories, and that it would rapidly bring a country to its knees, thus avoiding another war of attrition; though it sounded more like a Hobson's choice as it switched the killing from the battlefields to the civilians. In Brooke's army circles the future conduct of a war revolved around army issues of artillery, tanks, gas, machine guns and so forth. The debates gave a sense that all was in a state of ferment as different would-be senior commanders tried to predict or warn of future practices, at least in theory. The dispute over the use of tanks became the major debating area, and Colonel Fuller wrote extensively on the subject, especially his work called *The Tactics of Penetration.*[*] This emphasised that tanks offered surprise, a serious power when they were concentrated as a force, sudden deep penetration, and the possible envelopment of enemy infantry forces. Brooke, like many others, believed that guns could match tanks, which was eventually regarded as misleading.

Fuller was convinced that tanks were the answer. He saw war as 'a science and an art' with settled principles. He concluded in one of his published works that the tank would revolutionise war and offered three aspects: '(i) It increases mobility by replacing muscular force by mechanical power. (ii) It increases security by rendering innocuous the effect of bullets through the feasibility of carrying armour plate. (iii) It increases offensive power by relieving the man from carrying his weapons or the horse from dragging them, and by facilitating ammunition supply it increases the destructive power of the weapons it carries.'[4] He ended this early book by concluding that 'if ever war is forced upon us' the tanks 'will compel victory at the smallest possible course'.[5] It was not just in Brooke's circle, or England, that the power of the tank was being considered. In Germany the soon-to-be-famous Panzer leader Heinz Guderian wrote under the heading *Feuer und Bewegung* that the engine and the tank claiming it 'is as much a weapon as its gun'.[6] In France, Charles de Gaulle as a military man would also be looking closely at tanks and publishing his views. Within 20 years German tanks would crush the Polish, the French and the British Expeditionary Force (BEF), not least because Guderian had paid full attention to Fuller's ideas and those of Basil Liddell Hart. They used the tank in full, and with surprise, especially supported by infantry and aircraft, and it became a German strength when first used, only halted at the largest tank battle ever recorded, when the Soviets stopped the Germans at Kursk (July–August 1943). Brooke took the tank argument on board, but he still believed in the priority of the artillery which he regarded as critical, with the tank simply replacing the foot soldier, and moving forward using the artillery to support the mobile tanks. Guderian had realised that

---

* John Fuller (1878–1966) had been in the Tank Corps, and wrote many articles and books projecting a new model army based on tanks; see *The Concise Dictionary of National Biography*, Volume I, (Oxford: OUP, 1995) p.1086.

the infantrymen were not replaced but followed closely behind. Brooke had been trained as an artillery officer and it was imbued in him; British artillery was later praised, but the role of the tank remained prominent.

As Brooke and his military colleagues debated the various ways of conducting a possible war, Germany and Russia were already rebuilding their forces. To the consternation of the Allies, Germany and Russia signed the Treaty of Rappallo in 1922, to normalise relationships between the two countries: this was not just an economic arrangement, but meant to circumnavigate many of the Versailles restrictions. Rappallo underlined the weakness of the Allied victory in that 'it revealed that Moscow and Berlin in concert could defy the West with impunity. Often unspoken, it underlay all of Europe's peacetime deliberations until the nightmare finally turned to reality.'[7] In the treaty there was a secret clause stating Russia would supply heavy weapons to Germany and provide pilot-training facilities. The Germans even carried out tank exercises by using cars, and under von Seeckt they were developing the principle of surprise and using air attack to support ground forces. This was to prove effective, but no concern over this development was expressed in Britain at the time because German production of tanks had been forbidden by the Versailles Treaty. In Brooke's circle, Fuller's views would become more advanced and interesting in the years ahead, and always contentious, and Brooke ensured he listened with attention.

As these academic military discussions were underway Brooke, after 18 peaceful and interesting months at Camberley with all the debates about tanks and artillery, was suddenly shaken by an emotional explosion when he was hit by a deep, almost soul-destroying tragedy. He owned a Bentley, was reputed to be a fast driver but not always skilful, and when a cyclist (April 1925) suddenly swerved in his direction he hit the brakes and the car turned over. The Bentley had the sporting soft roof, and he broke a leg and some ribs, but his wife Jane never recovered and died from her injuries which had damaged her spine, and then she had suffered from pneumonia after medical operations. It would be a shock to anyone, especially when through possible dangerous driving a much-loved wife is killed. Not only the loss of someone deeply loved, but Brooke, probably with some justification, realised he was the cause of her death, and the children had lost their mother. Brooke reeled from this shock more than anything he had experienced in the war. He turned in on himself, losing that sense of extrovert conviviality he had developed in the officers' mess, and was struck down by guilt and grief. This was a totally understandable reaction. Even facing his children became deeply painful; he felt a sense of guilt that they were now without a mother, and their very presence reminded him of her. He almost appeared incapable of smiling and developed a stoop as if he were in 'a dark night of loneliness'.[8] It would take him a long time to recover from this mind-changing tragedy.*

---

\* It was one of those ironic twists of fate that his second wife also died in a car crash in 1965, a couple of years after Brooke's death.

## Imperial Defence College, Army, and Benita

From early 1927, having spent four years at Camberley, Brooke left and went to the newly formed Imperial Defence College as one of the first students. It was situated at number 9, Buckingham Palace Road, and was intended to be the centre for the study of conducting war. Its original intention was stated in its founding principles: 'To prepare senior officers and officials of the United Kingdom and other countries and future leaders from the private and public sectors for high responsibilities in their respective organisations, developing their analytical powers, knowledge of defence and international security, and strategic vision.' The main project was to offer preparations for a defence policy among selected officers of the three fighting forces, along with the civil service and the dominions. It was intended to broaden horizons and demanded that traditional thinking in these matters should be challenged and questioned. Following this academic interlude, Brooke returned to regimental duty. He was a brevet lieutenant-colonel (temporary rank) but still a major in the list of the Royal Regiment. Unlike the war years, and all too typical of peacetime, promotion was less rapid, and following the loss of his wife, he was still somewhat depressed and lonely. He had considered the possibility, before his selection to the Imperial Defence College and for a brief time only, of leaving the army and going to New Zealand, and he had pondered an appointment in India again. It was clear he was trying to re-discover himself and restore happier times.

Other possibilities arose and in February 1929 he was offered the post as commandant of the School of Artillery in Larkhill where he became a brigadier. He worked diligently at Larkhill with his usual dedication to duty to bring this establishment up to his standards. He improved the living quarters for the civilian and military staff, but the tactical and technical side of guns were his main interest. His knowledge and experience had always centred on artillery and guns in general, and everyone who met him understood he was good at his subject. He had experienced these weapons first-hand, read and studied their application almost with a sense of dedicated fervour. He was regarded by his superiors as a highly educated professional officer, more so than many others of his rank.

New Zealand and India were put aside because at Larkhill he once more discovered a sense of well-being, and a degree of happiness was at last returning to his life. This was enhanced in 1929 at the age of 46 years when he first met Benita Lees, the eldest daughter of Sir Harold Pelly, Baronet of Gillingham in Dorset. She was 37 and the widow of Sir Thomas Lees, who had died from wounds at Gallipoli.

Brooke was a man of diaries and letters, an outstanding communicator not only in his professional work but at the personal level, and his early letters to Benita clearly indicated a deep attraction and growing affection between the two of them. Their marriage was organised for 7 December 1929, and thereafter he placed her on a highly elevated emotional dais almost with a sense of personal worship. His later war diaries were always addressed to her, and even in the toughest moments of the war he found time to address his adoration of her and expressed their mutual love. Benita had praised him for his manner and efforts in dealing with his children following the tragic loss of his first wife, which probably helped restore some of his personal self-esteem. He also found in Benita a companion in his religious beliefs. He had never been a person to pay much attention to the formalities of religion, he was not denominationally inclined although from a strong Irish Protestant background, but he had a fundamental if not a core belief in the existence of an all-knowing God who loved and cared for mankind. He and Benita often read the same Biblical text on a daily rota arranged before he had left home. Time and time again in his war diaries he alluded to God's existence, especially when reflecting on man's propensity for self-destruction. Meeting Benita had given him a sense of well-being again, and a better emotional balance, and this was undoubtedly helped by the fact that his two children also loved Benita. This time he was not called away to war at the start of his honeymoon, and a sense of domestic peace settled into his new family. They had two children, Kathleen born in 1931 and Victor in 1932, the situation was one of happiness, and his personal future looked brighter for him in the ensuing years.* How to fight another war was all part of his professional life – tanks, artillery, strategy and tactics – but no one at this stage felt it was likely to be used again on a global scale.

## Imperial College Again

In 1932 Brooke returned to the Imperial Defence College, this time as an instructor, where the emphasis had reverted to issues about planning defences for the empire. This was more of a concern than a possible European war, though the experience of the Great War still dominated the thinking processes of senior commanders, especially in matters of strategy and tactics. It was during this time that Brooke, who was always thoughtful and interested in these matters, took in the wider ramifications of national defence and the need for a unified strategy. This included the wider tensions between the Royal Navy and the army who all too frequently held different opinions, a debate which had probably been simmering from Napoleonic times, if not before.

Brooke had always paid attention to the overall national scenario, which would become one of his important attributes in the years to come. His main criticism of Lord Gort during the Phoney War was this commander's inability to grasp the 'broader picture'. Brooke's aptitude for looking at the wider circumferences and estimating long-term goals would be one of the major factors which enhanced him in the views of others, especially when this attribute was recognised by Churchill.

---

* Kathleen Benita was born on 23 January 1931, and Alan Victor Harold on 24 November 1932.

Brooke was one of those military men who knew that within the British democratic system he had to listen to the politicians of the civilian world. This was especially true of the opinions expressed by Sir Maurice Hankey.* Hankey was in many ways a Victorian type of imperialist who demanded that British domination on a worldwide basis was critical, and it was therefore necessary to steer clear from European conflict. This often led to the criticism that Hankey, although he was deeply patriotic, failed to grasp the enormity of the fascist threat emerging in Europe. Another significant figure had been that of Richard Haldane, a Liberal Imperialist who had been secretary of state before the Great War. He had carried out the 'Haldane Reforms' of the British army during this time, and had set up the Imperial General Staff rather than just a Defence Committee of the Cabinet. Haldane had died in 1928, but Brooke had always been interested in his views. It was also Haldane who helped create the invaluable Territorial Force, the Officer Training Corps, and the Special Force. It was Haldane who had recommended a Secret Service Bureau (later known as SIS and MI5) and his interest in Britain's military for Brooke made him an interesting person. Throughout the 1920s Brooke had paid serious attention to the views of many political leaders and men of military influence.

It could be argued that there was a potential fissure which needed resolving within the national democratic structure over the direction of a war: a matter of coordination, direction, and whether it should be in the hands of a military command, or merely politicians, or a clever combination. Over this major issue of coordination and ultimate command it was generally agreed that it should be resolved by a body known as the COS, Chiefs of Staff, which was regarded as a sort of supreme military council, and Fuller looked to an Imperial Council which by its title included inter-dominion thinking.† However, Britain by this stage was a liberal democracy and it was clear that the elected prime minister in his position was always to be regarded as paramount. Parliamentary committees had studied the possibility of a Ministry of Defence, although it was considered somewhat contentious, and there was the question of a separate air ministry and a separate air force, which naturally the Royal Navy by its traditional values tended to oppose as the Senior Service. Brooke held the considered opinion that each service needed its own dedicated control administration, not least because of their specific technological

---

\*   Maurice Hankey (1877–1963) started life in the Royal Marine Artillery, was later in Naval Intelligence, became Chief of War Cabinet Secretariat, and held many other critical positions from circa 1910 onwards. He wrote many publications, was part of Chamberlain's War Cabinet and later Churchill's administration, and held strong views.

†   COS was a body not widely known by the general public, and it was used for the first time during World War II; it was basically the 'trinity' of the three service chiefs supported by planning and intelligence officials, and was essentially the critical War Headquarters. It had come into being, it has been argued, because the British were often aware that they lacked the professionalism of the German/Prussian military war direction methods.

demands, in a world where advances appeared to be rapidly developing. He wrote that 'the ultimate military control of the next war must be political as it has been since the days of Pitt'.[9] This statement clearly indicated that Brooke recognised the basis of a democratic society and that he was well balanced in political principles. Later he would frequently disagree with politicians, especially when Churchill interfered directly in military matters. He would become angry with their limited military thinking; nevertheless, he always understood the priority of the politician within the democratic structure.

## Army Duties

Brooke left the Imperial College in 1934 and for 18 months he held the command of the 8th Infantry Brigade, which was unusual for an RA officer. The fact that he was given this infantry command was a clear sign that he was seen to be ready for a more important role; such a shift of command from artillery to infantry was rare. The 8th Brigade consisted of several battalions and was based in Plymouth, which at least provided a change of scene. Brooke was a man of purpose, and he set about organising training in the fashion which he perceived should be realistic, arranging battlefield tours and lectures on the conduct of a battle scenario. His experience had made him a good trainer, and he was soon expressing a high degree of concern about the state of the army training, especially amongst the subalterns. He wrote that 'I could see the most usual method to teach them was to put them direct into a platoon to learn for themselves under the very doubtful tutelage of a platoon Sergeant,' which Brooke found somewhat disconcerting.[10] (This writer's first priest was a Father Harold Budgen who as a subaltern in the Great War claimed he survived only because he listened to his sergeant's advice.) Many of the soldiers had some experience, but many of the subalterns came from public schools, and by this time had not experienced the trenches and the reality of conflict; Brooke was undoubtedly correct in his observations. No doubt due to the financial crisis of the day Brooke found it difficult to gather interest in his suggestions, so he immediately established his own Brigade School for young officers; his dedication to their improvement would not go unnoticed, and in 1935 he was promoted to major-general. His purpose was based on the straightforward claim that he did not want the lives of soldiers in the hands of untrained leaders. He demanded that officers leaving military college should have specialised courses in command, a proposal he put to the CIGS, General Deverell, who rejected it on the grounds it had not worked in the past. As forceful as his argument was, he made no headway, but he was tenacious and waited until he was appointed the CIGS. He had the support of the other infantry brigadiers, but top command rejected what today would seem like sound military common sense. This reflected the military historical viewpoint that during the interbellum years there was a degree of stagnation within the top army ranks.[11]

He also projected the thought that better training was needed for night fighting; many opposed this policy, but Brooke fought on with this issue. Many remembered the chaos of fighting at night in the Great War, but they had done so without the appropriate training. At a conference he talked about the problems of attack, and he expressed some doubts about armoured fighting vehicles because of their limited numbers. This was interpreted by many as a lukewarm approach to the issue of the role of the tank, a debate which arose almost yearly in one form or another.

Having been promoted to major-general he left the Brigade to become inspector of artillery in November 1935. He personally felt that in this role he had no authority, because he was subordinate to the director of military training. This situation did not last long and in August 1936 he was appointed director of military training; an appointment in which the *Evening Standard* described him as a 'benevolent eagle', which was probably close to the truth in its picturesque style, or even possibly an aside at his love for birds.[12]

During this period, even in the mid-1930s, there was still a degree of economic shortcomings and the army fared less well than the other services. During the 1920s the Ten-Year Rule had operated as an economic measure and was not removed until 23 March 1932. Even at this stage it felt highly unlikely that there would be another European and global conflict, and the focus of attention tended to be on the traditional and culturally imbued defence of the shores and the dominions. From this perspective the Royal Navy was regarded as essential, with the air defence also gathering some momentum. The army appeared to be only necessary for anti-aircraft guns and search lights. By 1934 only a few astute politicians and senior military officers were becoming aware that Hitler's Nazi hold in Germany might just mean a war; this was mainly based at this stage on the sudden growth of the Luftwaffe.

The debates surrounding the tank-weapon continued to dominate Brooke's circle and many others. Britain had led in the design and use of the tank and only continued to do so in the theoretical debates, which could often be contentious. It is sometimes claimed that it was J. F. C. Fuller who invented the Blitzkrieg with his plan dating back to 1919. He had proposed that tanks should move rapidly through the enemy and thereby destroy their rear and supply bases and lines of communications. This, he suggested, was far better than the war of attrition by destroying the enemy's command and control systems.[13] It was the German General Guderian who understood this policy, and the British, including Brooke, remained somewhat conservative, with others highly sceptical about such plans. It was one thing investigating machine guns and gas, which were recent technologies, but converting to numerous tanks was not only expensive and demanding specialist manpower, but the question still reverberated as to whether tanks were overrated. It was commonly believed that well-sighted artillery could stop them in their tracks. Finance and the efficacy of the tank continued to play a major role in the ongoing debates. There were basically two schools of thought: to ignore them as a major weapon or to give them freedom to develop as fast as possible.

In 1927 an experimental mechanised force had been established on Salisbury Plain, from which eventually emerged the tank brigade, and from 1937 the Royal Tank Corps was brigaded annually on Salisbury Plain. Even at this juncture the question of tactics was under continuous scrutiny, and whether tanks were to be an independent force or part of all arms. The pro-tank lobby was dominated by Fuller, as noted above, and his books are still published to this day, and strongly supported by Basil Liddell Hart who had published on operational themes. Unlike Fuller, Liddell Hart believed they needed to work alongside the infantry and others. Liddell Hart at this time was working for *The Times* having been invalided out of military service in 1924. He was widely respected by many, but he had his critics, and this is still true to this day.

A critical moment came in 1937 when Leslie Hore-Belisha was appointed secretary of state for war. He was interested in army reform and mechanisation, which was music to Fuller and Liddell Hart. As a politician he was very much out of favour with the senior officers, including Brooke, who found him offensive. He in turn thought the senior officers to be somewhat inane, and they thought him vulgar. The situation was not helped when he made Liddell Hart a personal consultant on army matters, as he too was not thought well of by those in command, and they were both unpopular.

How far the criticisms of these men were valid remains a point of contention, as it was at the time. Brooke was not happy with either of them, but at least Hore-Belisha sacked Deverell as CIGS, the man who had clashed with Brooke over training officers; however, he then appointed Lord Gort who was to have his critics in time, including Brooke. Hore-Belisha had made serious efforts to bring in much-needed innovations, not least the post-Great War stagnation of senior officers seeing their time out. 'The promotion system was partly blocked in the early 1930s by ageing senior officers playing "musical chairs." Weed-killer was needed, and it was applied with some gusto by Hore-Belisha.'[14] However, Brooke was conservatively minded and Hore-Belisha was a politician; they were two opposites in personality and views.

Near the end of 1937 a mobile division was formed and was to be the forerunner of the future armoured divisions. It was established in Southern Command and Brooke was given command. Liddell Hart made it clear he preferred General Hobart because he was a tank specialist, yet another name which was contentious in the machinations of these military-political circles, somewhat unfairly in Hobart's case. The question raised was whether Brooke was too conservative for such a command, because when commanding the infantry division, it was known that he had expressed doubts about the tank. But he brought a sense of tactical reality and was always practical and pragmatic. He also recognised, after the debates, that the tank needed other armed support, and he was proved right by subsequent experience. The next war would expose the errors of tank deployment, but as always mere rehearsals were not enough, and it took the reality of conflict to understand the consequences of theory. It was a hard lesson. Brooke was fortunate to have as his superior commander General Wavell, whom he considered a sound and understanding officer of wide experience. The staff to man the tanks had to be found and Brooke, a keen lover of horses, realised that the cavalry had to learn the new arts of this type of warfare, fighting not from the saddle in time-honoured tradition, but from a pedestal mounted on the inside of a mobile armoured box.

Brooke appeared to be moved rapidly from one situation to the next and in July 1938, he was selected for promotion to Lieutenant-General and given command of a new Anti-Aircraft Corps, which had long suffered from starvation of resources like so much else. He made the sensible effort to liaise with Air Chief Marshal Sir Hugh Dowding and fortunately the two men appreciated one another's views. It was essential they worked together when it came to searchlights and anti-aircraft guns. In June 1936, the committee responsible (Reorientation Committee) had demanded the requirement of 76 AA (anti-aircraft) batteries and 2,500 searchlights, but only 60 guns and 120 lights were available. Brooke's initial task was therefore a paper one demanding the necessary resources. The TA (Territorial Army), which manned these responsibilities, was a volunteer force working for a modest remuneration, but now it faced a major and necessary expansion. The TA had been financially deprived and often treated badly and given below-standard accommodation. Brooke also had to try and make sure the men were properly treated and cared for, knowing it was all too easy to take the TA for granted.

Once again Liddell Hart, who had argued for a director-general anti-aircraft with a seat on the Army Council, which would have been a new department, voiced his opinions which made Brooke somewhat unhappy. Liddell Hart soon disapproved of Brooke's appointment to his command at Stanmore, but at the same time Hore-Belisha and Liddell Hart parted company. As it was, Brooke's tenure of command at Stanmore only lasted 13 months and in May 1939 he was appointed colonel commandant RA. He handed over his TA post to General Pile who held AA Command throughout the war. For his part Brooke was pleased to be designated to succeed Wavell as commander-in-chief Southern Command with HQ in Salisbury, in August 1939, the last month of peace.

## CHAPTER 3

# War

The last months of 1939 and the first months of 1940 were for the army a period of tedium in waiting for something to happen. In Britain it was known as the Phoney War, in France the *drôle de guerre*, joke of war; in Germany it was *Sitzkrieg*, in Polish it was *Dziwna Wojna*, Strange War, Churchill called it the Twilight War, and some the Bore War. The Phoney War did little generally to prepare men or officers for the outbreak of battle when it eventually happened. Often the French soldiers were returned to their industrial jobs, many more helped in the harvest, and as the months passed and 1940 spring approached, many started to ask why they were there in the first place, and why they were expected to fight. The Germans with polished propaganda played on this sense of self-questioning and boredom.

The deployed French and British soldiers from September had been waiting in nervous anticipation for an attack with frequent false alarms, and they endured one of the coldest winters on record. February, often regarded by many as the dullest month of the year, was for many the height of boredom, and there seemed as if nothing but the threat of war was in the air. The first man wounded by a British bullet in France was a stone-deaf French farmer who did not hear the British sentry's challenge to stop.[1]

There had always been an inbuilt deep distrust between the British and the French. During the Phoney War 'officials spent considerable time discussing schemes to make the British and French populations view each other more favourably. These ideas ranged from the sublime to the ridiculous.'[2] Edward Spears made the comment to Churchill that 'many French people…believe…that they have perhaps been duped and are fighting for England'.[3] French and British temperaments were sometimes very different, and much was later made of senior French staff bursting into tears, such as General Billotte when informed that his powers had been increased at a critical time.[4] The British considered the French to be temperamental, while the British were seen through the myth of their stiff upper lip; no room for emotion or sentiment. Stories and accounts abound of unpleasant tensions, disagreements, personality conflicts and divergent styles of leadership. Many of the French generals were frequently criticised, especially by Brooke. In 1939 'the French military leadership lacked the confidence that they had had in their own and the British armies before 1914. To some extent this must be attributed to the British failure to create and sustain a harmonious military entente in the late 1930s.'[5] There was also, understandably, the personal element of the individual commanders, which was to be a dominating issue in many countries throughout the war.

It was not just the French generals who came under the scrutiny of historical hindsight. Historians have disagreed over the British Command figure of General Gort; Julian Jackson cast him in a rather poor light, and Alistair Horne painted a vastly different picture.[6] Brooke held both views; he admired Gort's courage and liked him as a person, but felt he was more concerned about trivia than the broader picture. The French generals were often accused of bickering, but among the British there was a lack of communication, especially between Ironside and Gort, and the traditional friction between military commanders whatever their nationality appeared to be a common feature of military command throughout this war. Finding the right choice of military commander was always going to be a problem for the Allies, and one which would constantly vex Brooke in the years ahead.

Once the war had been declared the French mobilization had started with some efficiency. The French employed a man called Raoul Dautry, known as the 'Napoleon of Railways', making the French railway system outstanding for the transportation of troops, but nearly 100,000 soldiers had to be returned to other work during this period.[7] As a matter of passing observation, 'French military spending in 1938 was in real terms 2.6 times greater than it had been in 1913', but ironically France was less ready for war in 1914 than in 1939.[8]

The Phoney War had not helped in preparing the men for battle. It was not only, as mentioned, the coldest winter for half a century, but the sheer boredom had eaten deep into the souls of the waiting men. This had ramifications, and the fact was that 'France was deceived by the passivity of the Phoney War and lulled into complacency about her military strength and moral resilience'.[9] The Allied propaganda was poor, and no amount of entertainment provided by the army and the French eradicated the gathering gloom of uncertainty.

The Germans with their propaganda were much more professional. Paul Ferdonnet, who was the French equivalent of Britain's Lord Haw Haw, broadcast from Stuttgart; he seemed to know all the French details of personnel, who they were, and where they were stationed. 'He continued during this period to throw out provocative questions as to why France wanted to fight in the first place, claiming that Britain would fight to the last Frenchman, providing tools and machines, but not themselves. It was an effective propaganda weapon which worked well.'[10] There is little doubt that as dysfunctional as Goebbels was, his propaganda war was clever. Ferdonnet and Lord Haw Haw were tools he applied well, claiming that 'Lord Haw Haw's name is on everyone's lips.'[11] The French and British saw through the propaganda, but it was a thorn in their flesh. It was a two-way process in so far that Goebbels was concerned that 'large sections of the Wehrmacht are still tuning into foreign radio stations'.[12]

The Phoney War was a victory for the Germans because of the French inability to command this strange period effectively or realistically. A French general staff captain called André Beaufre wrote, 'It was a period of decay, probably caused by the excess of the effort during World War I.'[13] In the background of the Phoney War this was a realistic assumption, and frequently commented on by Brooke.*

When the Phoney War abruptly ended in May 1940 the passivity was to be shattered by the sheer volume of military force. 'It is impossible to overestimate the impact of the eight-hour aerial bombardment that preceded the German crossing. Nothing had mentally prepared the men.'[14] The Phoney War had not primed them for action, and during February when many French and English soldiers must have wondered why they were there in the first place, they were suddenly brought face to face with the reality of a military battle against a professional and experienced German military.

There had been a distinct failure of high command in allowing this deep passivity to creep into the fighting forces. This was witnessed on the Siegfried Line, where the American journalist Abbot Liebling had watched with incredulity the inactivity of what was regarded as the front line.[15] France seemed preoccupied with potential war elsewhere in Scandinavia, which Alan Brooke called the 'wild goose enterprises', looking for conflict anywhere else but on French soil.[16] This almost led to a wilful neglect of the main forces in northern France; there was a feeling that war in that countryside should not happen. Writers of the day Arthur Koestler and Jean-Paul Sartre spent much time in their literary works on the desertion of the junior French officers and the reluctance of soldiers to fight. This desertion and unwillingness to engage in combat should be placed firmly at the feet of the top command, who failed to recognise the dangers of the long months of growing passivity. The neglect of their soldiers during the dreary and cold winter, and especially the wintry doldrums of February, amounted to a failure by the high command, most especially amongst the French leaders.

## Brooke's Phoney War

Brooke embarked for France from Southampton on 28 September with his mobilisation appointment No. 1000 as commander of II Corps, which he knew was untrained by his standards, poorly equipped, and which at the last moment had been designated to join the BEF. At this stage it consisted of two divisions of the 3rd and 4th Infantry, the latter led by General Norman Johnson and the former by Montgomery. There had been no time for any significant training, and they were simply shipped out with the idea they could be trained in France. He purchased a large bundle of small leather-bound books from a shipping line, which he utilised as his personal diaries. This diary was to be his method of communicating with

---

* André Beaufre (1902–75) was a French army officer and military strategist who became Général d'Armée before his retirement in 1961.

Benita, and time and time again details of war, comments on leaders and events, are interspersed with love messages to his wife.

The diary was, however, to prove much more than this: as noted earlier, these diaries have caused in their time a high degree of tension not least because of his forthright criticisms of Churchill and other figures of some standing. There are passages in the diary which are extremely critical of Churchill's meddling in strategy and his interference with army generals. Brooke's criticisms did not stop with Churchill, but they included Eisenhower, George Marshall, and Field Marshal Sir Harold Alexander. On the other hand, he admired Dill and even Stalin, though he appeared to have some insight into Stalin's barbaric behaviour which became more widely known in the postwar years. Stalin was more admired by Brooke for his quick thinking and military strategy. Nevertheless, these diaries he had originally purchased to stay in touch with Benita, provide some interesting and intriguing insights, not least because as a major military figure it was his way of easing the tensions which he felt in himself, but could not express publicly. He was no longer the sensitive child, the sporting subaltern game hunting in India; he had experienced the bitterness of the Great War and suffered the personal tragedy of losing his first wife. He was now a highly regarded professional soldier expected to do his duty, to set an example to others, and concerned with the possibility that he might have to send more men and friends to their death; a pestering thought which always worried him.

In his initial war diary entries he expressed the sadness he felt because he was leaving Benita and almost immediately the sense of 'the awful futility of it all proved by the last war!'[17] For Brooke it carried a feeling of *déjà vu*, which was both sad and misleading.[18] Brooke like most others thought it to be another war of trench attrition and no one at this stage could have envisaged the sheer energy and drive of the German attack to come the following year. Leaving Cherbourg, he travelled to GHQ where his fear of a Great War repetition was enhanced by hearing that both Corps were to be sent at once to the Belgian border. He knew it was a political move to be there, but he also knew that the men needed at least 'one and half month's training'. On the 29th he recorded his words in a conversation in which he noted that in war they should all expect the unexpected; in this he was prescient in his forecast.

On 30 September he was entertained by a French Colonel Marchal, and he found to his delight he had hunted at Pau. Soon his diary entries became somewhat cynical, with realistic appraisals and comments on French 'slovenliness, dirtiness and inefficiency' and visits by various people including the Duke of Gloucester, wondering whether 'they would all pull their weight??' Brooke's repeated use of question marks and exclamation marks underlines many of his thoughts and reflections.

These opening lines were to be repeated throughout the Phoney War: a serious discontent at the state of the French military, and a critical view of other commanders and leaders, resulting in many seeing him as a moaner; on the kinder side 'General Pownall recorded Brooke as a pessimist'.[19] He had been born in France, his first language was French, he liked the French; he was also a British senior military officer proud of his tradition. However, none of this stopped him from expressing in his diary, meant for Benita, the truth as he regarded the situation. It would be all too easy to call him a cynic, but he was with his background a realist, and as a senior commander in charge of men and responsible for their well-being, he had every right to be critical of the circumstances and what was happening around him. He was not necessarily correct in all his observations and sometimes he may have wrongly appraised some people, but in his diary, he was blatantly honest, and often in public when he felt it was required. As a senior commander he was undoubtedly correct in stating what he thought to be the truth; he was not a socialite, or a yes-man, but a person who took his responsibilities and duty as his top priority. Many people may not have appreciated him for this attitude, but it was his views which brought him into a high degree of prominence, and he would emerge as one of the leading military men in the British army.

He found himself in France with poorly trained troops, because the war had suddenly been declared based on the promise to 'honour a guarantee to Poland and nothing less than a complete change in the nature and direction of German policy' was demanded.[20] In many ways the guarantee to Poland was almost a futile if not an immoral gesture. The British had assured the Poles that if the Germans carried out their threat of moving into Poland then they would instigate a bomber offensive, and the French promised that they would attack Germany within 15 days. There is little doubt that these immoral promises had made the Polish government, and some of its people, somewhat confident if not complacent about the German threat.[21] 'The British Chiefs of Staff were entirely opposed to the guarantee to Poland given in March 1939,' probably because they held a more realistic appraisal than the politicians, whom, it could be argued, at least took a moral stand.[22] There was simply no way the Western Allies could at this stage do anything to stop Hitler's invasion into Poland; the Allied guarantee was no salvation for that country. The French did nothing, and the British followed the same policy by bombing Berlin, but with pamphlets. As Private K. S. Karol a teenage member of the Polish army, later noted, they felt they had been 'betrayed by all sides: by the Western powers, by the Russians and by our own government which has already bolted to Romania'.[23]

As in the Great War the initial British contribution to the continental land army was almost insignificant. The British had provided four divisions and even when the number was eventually increased to ten it was too small to offer any strength, and the British knew that with these insignificant numbers they had to place themselves under French command. Brooke was aware of the situation which was to dog him for the next eight months, being his sole experience of high field command on active service. He was acutely aware of the deficiencies in the French command, often portrayed as the suffering from a hardening of the arteries based on the victory of Verdun, and the belief they would fight the same type of war and win. The French under General Maurice Gamelin only envisaged the one plan: that the Germans would attack through Belgium and possibly the Netherlands; nothing else was considered. As General Pownall had observed, Brooke was a pessimist, and Brooke was right to be so. Brooke was also somewhat justified as he studied the quality of their allies and their plans, and with good reasons to think this way. Throughout the Phoney War he was to comment both on French command, British leadership, and the narrow-mindedness of the French plans.

A Franco-Belgian Alliance had been signed between King Albert I and the French after the Versailles Treaty in 1920. King Albert I died from a mountaineering accident in Belgium in 1934, and his son, Leopold III, lacked the political understanding of his father. Leopold was concerned about the growth of German militarism, and he viewed France as impotent. In October 1936 he had revoked the earlier Treaty in order to return to a neutral state: 'Leopold III did not inherit the full measure of his [father's] wisdom and moral courage.'[24] It should also be noted that 'the Belgian forces had deteriorated so markedly by 1936 that it could not even man the fortified areas east of Liege with trained troops'.[25] This was a major concern and would cause Brooke to feel angry with the Belgians as well as the French, but, on the other hand, which Brooke rarely mentioned, the British had also been complacent about the continental situation. The Phoney War may have felt comfortable for civilians at home, but it gave no sense of stability which was a cause of deep frustration for Brooke and many others.

Brooke's experience during October, expressed through his private diary entries, was to be characteristic of his thoughts and work until the German invasion in May 1940. For most of the month he visited troop sites, and on the 20th in pouring rain he toured Montgomery's defences. He wrote that 'a lot of work has been done under very trying conditions, and defences are taking definite shape.'[26] Despite some ups and downs with Montgomery, Brooke always appreciated the professionalism of the man, and often stood by him when he blundered or was indiscreet and undiplomatic; which Brooke had to manage too often. Later Montgomery would cause political mayhem with his egotism, but he was always guarded by Brooke from this point in time, because Brooke remained, as it was once claimed, 'forever awed' by Montgomery's calm and skill on the field of combat.[27]

Three times during the month he had to engage with Prince Henry, Duke of Gloucester noting on the first occasion that his visitors 'were not good at going away', but on the third visit he was pleased that the royal visitor had met his son Tom, also serving in France, in another area. It was not the only 'royal' time because Gort asked him to write to the king who liked to hear from 'his' generals. He was also asked to attend to a visit by the Duke of Windsor, noting that he 'was accompanied by Howard-Vyse who had instructions against his [Windsor] endeavouring to stage any kind of "come-back" with the troops out here.'[28] This was a curious note by the non-political Brooke who had been trusted with this confidence. There was, in the early years, concern over the Duke of Windsor's behaviour and views, but Brooke never mentioned these issues in his diaries; it was not part of his professional remit.

He had been in France less than a month when he had become concerned at the situation; he expressed his unease to General Pownall that attitudes were 'half-hearted' and that may have been the reason why Pownall later called Brooke a pessimist. Brooke thought GHQ far too large, he was critical of the Belgian king demanding neutrality, found the French top commander 'rather tired', believed that Gort had not realised the seriousness of the situation, complained about the shortage of barbed wire, and later the lack of sandbags which were all used up in England. He was, however, a highly professional soldier who had fought the Germans before, and twice in October he made comments about German military efficiency. He was a realist who had quickly spotted the lack of appropriate preparation by the British, and his gathering serious doubts about the French allies continued to expand. As the Phoney War months passed Brooke's criticisms would increase in number and depth, but the later military onslaught in May would prove him correct. He had a wider perspective; apart from being concerned that some French communists had talked to the troops, he was aware of the political danger of being drawn into Belgium, and that the Germans might invade on the excuse there were internal problems.* There was one moment when it was rumoured the Germans were coming, but this rumour was to happen every month for the next eight months.

Throughout November the rumours that the Germans were coming persisted almost daily until in the second week when Brooke wrote, 'I still have grave doubts as to veracity of this forecast.' He was an anxious man because of his sense of responsibility, which was later emphasised by the possible threat of Operation *Sea Lion*. During this part of the Phoney War he was concerned at a personal level because he was still uncertain about II Corps training, and on 28 November decided that his anti-tankers were still untrained.[29] The social side continue to irritate him as he was on the second day of the month obliged to have another lunch with Prince Henry with too much food, and hoped it would be the last such meal. He never enjoyed over-indulgence in food or drink, and this sense of puritanical distaste would last throughout his life, being frequently mentioned in his diaries, especially later in visiting Russia and Stalin.

He was obliged to help arrange a visit for the king, and he had to entertain Hore-Belisha whom he found looking tired. He opposed the minister's idea of sending troops out to France to train for political reasons, telling him that it was bad for them, bad for the BEF and the French. At the end of the month he was informed by Gort and Ironside that Hore-Belisha had returned to London claiming that the

---

* Following the Ribbentrop-Molotov Pact the French Communist Party not only lost members but were persecuted by the French government as potential traitors. Later Stalin instructed them to resist, probably because he was concerned about German strength.

BEF had become the 'laughing-stock'.* It was little wonder amongst the various reasons postulated for Hore-Belisha's unpopularity that the senior commanders were irritated by him, and Brooke especially was always suspicious of meddling politicians who, in his experience, lacked experience of war at the front. Many other later commentators noted that Hore-Belisha was attempting the necessary reforms in the army, and some, probably quite rightly, detected a degree of anti-Semitism in Hore-Belisha's critics.

As always, Brooke continued to visit the various posts, meeting Montgomery on several occasions and addressing him in his diary as Monty. It was during November (23rd) he had to dress Montgomery down for a writing a vulgar letter to the troops about avoiding catching venereal disease; this letter had led to many complaints. Montgomery had a belief that official brothels would cure the problem, which within the traditional British army was considered an appalling 'stepping out of line'. Brooke told him off but refused other requests to have the letter withdrawn on the common-sense grounds it would undermine Montgomery's authority. There is no doubt that Brooke thought highly of his subordinate, noting that he took the official 'telling-off' well, but writing that 'it is a great pity that he spoils his very high military ability by a mad desire to talk or write nonsense.'[30] This was going to be a difficult relationship because Montgomery was egotistical, lacked diplomacy, derided the Americans when they later arrived, and would cause all kinds of crises. This problem would increase with Montgomery because, as Alexander noted, 'Montgomery wanted to have complete independence of command and do what he liked.'[31] Brooke stood by him in the years ahead because he saw in Montgomery a professional commander, but whether he was correct in this has long been debated.

When Brooke met General Alphonse Georges, he was surprised to find a French officer whom he appreciated and who inspired confidence, but his criticisms of most of the French commanders grew by the week. He even thought their ceremonies were not up to the mark, and he wondered whether they were 'firm enough as a nation' for the coming conflict, and thought they had done little in their defence preparations. His sense of depression with the French increased, as did his critical approach to Gort as the weeks passed, believing Gort was caught up in minor detail and failing to see the broader picture. Brooke thought little of the proposed plans, realising that a dash into Belgium would leave him with serious flank problems. He found Gort almost impossible as a major commander describing him as a 'queer mixture, perfectly charming, very definite personality, full of vitality, energy and *joie de vivre*, and gifted with great powers of leadership. But he just fails to be able to see the big picture and is continually returning to those trivial details which counted a lot when commanding a battalion.'[32] As already mentioned, historians have disagreed over the British figure of General Gort; as noted earlier, Julian Jackson cast him in a

---

* Gort had been CIGS, but he was replaced by Ironside so Gort could command the BEF.

rather poor light, fussing about how to wear tin hats, and Alistair Horne painted a different picture of a brave and steady leader, but qualifying this praise by referring to his limited intellect.[33] Brooke's friend Dill tended to agree with him, and Gort was well aware that Brooke and Dill regarded him as inadequate, and found that Brooke radiated too much gloom and often contemplated his replacement. When Kennedy was in France during this fraught period, he knew that Gort was aware of these criticisms from Dill and Brooke, but Kennedy believed Dill and Brooke understood the situation better.[34]*

Brooke liked Gort for his loyalty and sense of spirit, but Brooke was a realist, and despite his sense of friendship from knowing Gort for so long, Brooke was a pragmatist and always understood the professional qualities of the German military. Brooke was to demonstrate all his life that he was capable of exercising sound judgement and understood the nature of a command position, and he recognised that with the overwhelming odds the BEF faced, Gort was failing to focus on the prime issues. Nevertheless, when the crunch arrived in May of the following year it was Gort who saved the BEF from extinction with sheer willpower, by moving rapidly back towards Dunkirk as the only resort for the long-term survival.

Brooke was frequently aware of his sense of responsibility in holding the lives of men in his hands. As he visited the various HQs and posts interviewing his officers, he expressed his deep concern (on 16 November) that he felt that 'terrible feeling' that it might be his orders which would be 'instrumental' in sending them to their deaths. He regarded many of these men as friends and found this aspect of the war command a heavy burden. This was the human side of Brooke, and it stood him apart from many of those commanders, who sought glory and reputation despite the human expense their plans might involve. Brooke also managed to keep his sense of humour for which he had been known as a subaltern. On 4 November he had assisted in a pillbox experiment where he and eight other high-ranking officers had assembled in the chosen pillbox, and fired off an anti-tank and Bren gun through the narrow apertures to measure the amount of accumulating toxic gases. He described the assembled officers as 'expensive white mice' which if the experiment had gone wrong would have 'assisted promotion considerably'.

The last month of 1939 witnessed the incoming cold and general discomfort of the weather which was to last for several months. It would prove to be one of the coldest and dreariest winters on record, and the neglect of their soldiers during the grim and cold winter, and especially the later icy doldrums of February, was a failure by the French high command. For Brooke it was a short month because of

---

*   Major-General John Kennedy served as Commander of the 52 Royal Artillery Division in France, then on his return became Director, and from October 1943 to February 1945 was the Assistant Chief of the Imperial General Staff. He and Brooke were close friends and confidants, and this relationship was much helped by their common love of birds.

Christmas leave, but December was filled with his usual routine of visits, reflections on poor preparation, sad memories as he visited places he recognised from the previous conflict, and entertaining important visitors.

On 1 December the CIGS appeared, and Brooke showed him the prepared defence lines north of Lille, met Montgomery and the reserve position, and wondered whether all the good work would lead to the downfall of their political critic Hore-Belisha. King George VI arrived on 6 December and Brooke showed him around, had lunch with the king and General Giraud, and was then concerned as the king slept in the train as it passed by the expectant and waving troops. Ten days later Brooke was looking after Prime Minister Chamberlain, showing him selected areas and having another lunch. In between these high-level social and political duties, he continued his rounds of inspections, visiting critical areas with Montgomery, checking Harold Franklyn in the 5th Division, and studying Montgomery's proposed manoeuvres if there were a sudden order to move into Belgium. On 15 December Brooke studied the defences on Mount Halluin, and there heard the tragic news that four officers had been killed and others seriously injured while preparing an anti-tank mine. It raised the question for Brooke as to how safe these mines were to handle; sadly, as he observed, the men who could explain what had happened were all dead.

His uneasiness about the immediate future never deserted him, and time and time again he found himself being worried about the anti-tank ditches. He had on the second of the month read carefully about the German campaign in Poland, and he started to understand the critical growing importance of the tank.* He realised that the ditches which were being prepared were far too shallow and not wide enough. The tanks had developed a long way since 1918, and the German tanks would be one of the overwhelming factors in the looming confrontation. He remained concerned at the French lack of preparation, especially on 9 December when he had visited the French 51st Division. On the other hand, he was impressed by the French commander of the 42nd French Division, but with Dill, he remained critical of those working in GHQ.

Just before he took his Christmas leave, he visited a section of the Maginot Line which reminded him of 'a battleship built on land'. He saw it as a stroke of genius and a brilliant achievement, but he wrote that 'I consider that the French would have done better to invest the money in the shape of mobile defences such as more and better aircraft and more heavy armoured divisions than to sink all this money into the ground.'[35] Brooke knew Gamelin was fixated on the probability that the Germans would invade through the Low Countries, and he could not be persuaded to consider alternatives. Gamelin believed the massive Maginot Line would hold the

---

* During this month he also read about the Battle of Bovines fought in 1214 between Phillippe Augustus of France and King John which Chamberlain had enjoyed hearing about; but it was far removed from 1939. Brooke had a deep interest in history.

rest of the French borders. The Maginot Line was the 'fort of all forts', 'the shield of France', the ultimate in a Verdun-type defence, but although it led to self-satisfaction, the fort did not stretch far enough, and its spiralling cost meant France 'neglected the remainder of her forces in order to pay for it'.[36] Brooke had another tour the following month, and although he admired the engineering he never changed his mind. For him it was a purely static defence, but he noted the most dangerous aspect 'is the psychological one, a sense of false security is engendered, a feeling of sitting behind an impregnable iron fence.'[37] Brooke was aware of the issues involved and later his criticisms would prove justified. The French, for financial reasons, had stopped building the fort at the Belgian border, leaving them vulnerable. It was a mistake, but English historians should recall that the English Channel cost nothing.

On the family side Brooke had looked for his son Tom in the early part of the month only to discover his regiment had moved, but he caught up with him on the 17th where he found him busy but happy. He had, however, forgotten his seventh wedding anniversary until a letter arrived from his wife. His response was quick, naturally, but heartfelt, writing that 'I never realised that such happiness could exist on earth...and I thank God from the bottom of my heart for having brought us together.'[38] He left France on 23 December ready for what he described as his 'ten days in paradise.'

## CHAPTER 4

# 1940

The autumn of the year 1939 had witnessed serious upheaval in the European scene, and across the world there were rumblings of a sinister nature in the Japanese and Chinese conflict, and most countries, especially America at the beginning of 1940, wondered what the New Year would bring. In January, the war between Russia and Finland continued to rage, but for many people that seemed so far away as to be inconsequential. For the political leaders amongst the Allies there was the traditional fear of the growth of communism, and the continued threat that this combination of Russian communism in league with fascist Germany could be a lethal cocktail. There was also a high degree of surprise in the way a tiny, sparsely populated country like Finland managed to fight back in its defence. Hitler was especially interested in this aspect, not so much because of Finland's reaction, but the perceived weakness of Russian military forces.

The Phoney War continued during one of the coldest winters on record. While the British limited their efforts to patrolling exercises and digging trenches, the French, with Gamelin's ingrained defensive policy, did next to nothing which was to have an appalling effect on the morale of the French army. The Germans, preoccupied by their Eastern exploits in Poland, encouraged the Phoney War, and indulged in psychological attacks using their skilled propaganda. Hitler's aggressive stance was somewhat restrained by worried military commanders and questionable logistics, but the chief cause for holding Hitler's ambitions back in the West was the poor weather, which Brooke rightly presumed to be the case. There was a genuine and understandable nervousness about the future. While Chamberlain remained prime minister, no bombs were dropped on Germany, and the French military did little more than meander close to the German border. For his part Chamberlain retained his belief that the war would be just as devastating as the Great War and follow the same pattern. In November he had written to his sister stating that 'I have a hunch that the war will be over before the spring. It won't be by defeat in the field but by German realisation that they can't win.'[1] In this statement there is a distinct element of pure gullibility, and a continued underestimation of Adolf Hitler's hold over a powerful nation like Germany. In the September of 1939 when Leo Amery had questioned

Kingsley Wood, the secretary of state for air, about bombing the ammunition works at Essen, or setting the Black Forest alight, he had been told that there was a reluctance to do so because it involved private property. The New Year of 1940 would witness the end of such civilised niceties, and the beginning of a total war where any form of humane restriction or civilised behaviour would become totally irrelevant. During the Phoney War and the opening months of 1940 there were still many who hoped that the war would die a natural death. It was to be a forlorn hope and as mentioned, the real reason for the continuation of the Phoney War was to be found in the extremely bad weather during the winter of 1939–40. On 17 January, a profoundly serious cold wave had struck Europe and even the River Thames froze, while in Finland the temperature dropped to an unbelievable minus 45 degrees Celsius; even Goebbels constantly complained in his diary about the cold in Berlin.

For the French and British it was a time of nervous anticipation marked by some who believed in eventual victory, while others wondered whether declaring war had been a horrendous error in the first place. On New Year's Day, Monday 1 January, the British age of conscription was designated as 27 years of age and later would be raised again. Basic food rationing was started (8 January) with bacon, butter and sugar, and much more would soon follow. True to human nature it was decided that 'secrecy should surround the announcement of any commodity that was to be rationed for the first time to try to prevent a rush to purchase and hoard'.[2]

A week later the British government took control over the meat industry, which was for a liberal democratic society built on free capitalism, a warning sign that times were changing. Later in the month Scottish soldiers were told that kilts were too dangerous to wear because of the threat of poisonous gas, although pipers and drummers were excluded from this command for some extraordinary reason of tradition. The use of wood was restricted, and women were asked in the following July not to wear high heels because of the use of such a valuable commodity. It must be noted that nobody was sure of the future, and near the end of the month many children who had been evacuated in a sense of panic had started to return home. In anticipation of the worst scenario, the British even approached the Italians about purchasing war planes, but the Germans quickly put a stop to such a possible trade arrangement. Uncertainty about the future was rife and permeated every level of life. Even in America Roosevelt watched with the same growing uncertainty and speculated how it could touch upon that continent thousands of miles away. In his New Year State of the Union speech on 3 January he referred to what was happening in Europe, and he spoke of the necessity to increase the budgets on national defence.

## Brooke's January onwards

Brooke's main concern in January was the wintery condition which had brought to a halt the necessary work with concrete fortifications and defence measures; apart from this problem he found it uncomfortable as most of the BEF would have done. Brooke only mentioned this aspect of those living under canvas once; to him this would have been a part of the soldier's lot. His continuous visits took on a more serious hue, and the issues which he had to deal with became more critical. He carried out his traditional inspections on the 3rd Division Front (6 January), next day back in the Halluin area, and three days later inspected the 53rd Light AA Regiment which was intended to protect French power stations, where he found himself drinking champagne and nibbling biscuits in an office. He was also having to tackle leadership problems, such as an interview with the head of the NAAFI who did not impress him; he found the Indian Mule Company badly housed, and the Cypriot Mule Company where the officers did not speak the same language. He discovered that the 6th Argyll and Sutherland MG Battalion was commanded by a Shaw Stewart 'who struck me as being no use at all. A good unit being spoilt by a bad CO. Shall arrange to have him changed.'[3] He also inspected the 1/7 Middlesex MG and decided their commanding officer had to go. On top of all these hard decisions he had to talk with the prefect of Lille regarding the murder of a Frenchwoman by a British soldier. He was in the unenviable situation brought about by his senior position of having to make tough decisions which were essential, not only for the conduct of war, but for the safety of the soldiers. On top of this and NAAFI problems, he had the huge embarrassment of dealing with a murder case; the war had not started on his front, but the strain of everyday life was immense.

On his return in early January he had been pleased with a new pillbox mounting which he had designed for the anti-tank gun, and the prototype was precisely what he had required. A week later he was checking the effect of machine guns on bricks (often used in pillboxes) but on 14 January was woken up at 3.30 am to an alarm that the Germans were expected. This was all a result of what has often been called the Mechelen incident.

It was at this critical time that at Mechelen in Belgium a significant accident occurred. Major Erich Hoenmanns carrying laundry for his wife, had given a passenger seat in his aircraft to a Major Helmuth Reinberger; while flying they had met an area of high fog and missed the Rhine, and having inadvertently turned off the fuel supply switch they were forced to crash land in Belgium. Reinberger was committing an unforgivable mistake in so far that he was carrying plans for an operation, *Fell Gelb* (Case Yellow). He tried to burn the plans, but at the last moment a Belgian officer saved some of the burnt documents from destruction; he kept it quiet and convinced Reinberger that they had all been destroyed. The Belgians informed the Dutch and the French, but it was too much of a risk for the German security to believe that *Fell Gelb* had not been compromised.

The plans disclosed that they were vaguely like the original *Schliefflen* plan of the Great War, and this incident caused three reactions. First, Hitler delayed *Fell Gelb* while considering the ramifications. Secondly, Gamelin appeared to be correct, which confirmed his belief in himself, and thirdly, the Germans revised their plans. It has been said that this Mechelen incident was good for the German military, but there has been some debate as to how far this was true.

As for the British, who according to Brooke were in an understandable state of severe war nerves, they simply found it too incredulous that the Germans could make such a mistake. Brooke wrote:

> We came to the conclusion that the whole affair looked like a "plant" on the part of Germany. It was not likely that officers would fly over Belgium with a plan of this kind in their possession. It seems probable that the whole affair was staged with the object of trying to induce Belgium to call on France and England for military support in the face of such a threat and thus provide Germany with an excuse for violating the frontier.[4]

This was a reasonable deduction by Brooke, but the fact remains it was simply a mere blunder by a German pilot, unusual as that may appear.

The days of the Phoney War were marked by the problem of Belgium, France's immediate northern neighbour, and an entire book could be devoted to the machinations of the Franco-Belgian relationship in the twentieth century. Unlike Turkey and Spain, Belgium was too close to the heart of Europe to avoid a potential conflict there, and its declaration of neutrality was a hopeless gesture. Belgium was occasionally referred to as the 'cockpit of Europe' because of its geographical position. Speculation is not called for in history, but an invasion by Germany through Belgium made more sense according to the view of the French military command, than attacking the Maginot Line or penetrating the Ardennes. Hindsight clearly indicates that the defensive nature of the French command made anything else feel unlikely, and the British were too small in their contribution to make their views known, of which Brooke was all too aware.

Brooke met an admiral of the fleet, Sir Roger Keyes who was the special liaison officer to the Belgian king (who he addressed as *Mr X* in his diary). King Leopold was now considering asking whether the French and British would come to his aid; the disclosed documents from the plane accident appeared to have at last raised his awareness of the critical geographical position of Belgium and the German intentions. Brooke wondered whether the plane accident had been organised by the Germans to activate this line of thinking and give the Germans the excuse to attack through Belgium. He had the foresight to see that the open countryside of Belgium would lead to 'the open warfare nature which would suit German forces', but the Allies would have a shortened front with 18 Belgian divisions. Brooke was acutely aware of German military efficiency noting the formidable nature of the River Lys as a barrier, but also commenting that 'the Boche with their efficient bridging equipment would have little difficulty in negotiating it unless opposed by a strong defence.'[5] He tried during this month of January, when the war of nerves over the timing of the probable German attack was rapidly building up, to find out from a visitor called Dewing, from Military Operations at the War Office, more about the prosecution of the war. He learnt that the general belief was that it would be a victory in three years, but having read of the German success by combining ground and air forces, Brooke made the understandably cynical remark that they were neglecting the possibility of 'losing it in one year'. Brooke was astute enough to weigh the potential dangers realistically, and his views were uncomfortably prescient. His understanding of the smallness of the British with their BEF contribution, the staid thinking of the French high command, the inefficiency of many French senior officers (which he was trying to eradicate in the BEF) and his regard for German military was realistic. It gave him the reputation of moaning and being a pessimist, but he was the one man at this stage who could sense the dangers of defeat, which set him perpetually on his guard, and his fear of German military power justifiably remained with him for a long time. He was sensible enough to realise that the German military would somehow thwart Hitler's precipitate attack in the middle of a bitterly cold winter, but it was for him and many others a time of nervous tension wondering when the Germans would make their move.

Amongst his personal asides to his beloved wife were notes about yet another visit by Prince Henry, the dismissal of Hore-Belisha which he had correctly speculated on the month before, and the ongoing problem of having to suffer another tooth extraction. He had to say farewell to one of his senior officers, General Sir Harold Franklyn whom he described as 'a more attractive type of individual than Montgomery'. There is little doubt that Montgomery had Brooke's support because of his perceived military ability, but Brooke would always understand that at times Montgomery could be arrogant and too egotistical. There is a hint throughout the diary that whenever Brooke addresses Montgomery as Monty, he is on the better side of Brooke. On 24 January Brooke found time to attend the gala performance of the film *The Lion has Wings,* which, unknown to Brooke at the time, was later to be a jibe used by some French commanders including General Weygand as the British fled to Dunkirk, namely that the British army was a lion with wings when it ran towards the sea. January was just another month in the Phoney War but Brooke could feel the tension rising, and he worked assiduously at all the necessary tasks, not least in trying to ensure the best officers were in place; he retained his doubts about Gort and GHQ.

When Brooke noted in his diary on 1 February that 'the thaw continues…a nasty wet and foggy day' he inadvertently summarised not just the weather typical of February, but for many people the nature of that month in its many aspects during 1940. The Phoney War was dampening the spirits of all those involved. For the soldiers it could hardly have been drearier, and many wondered whether there would ever be a military conflict in Western Europe. The war remained a mystery to most people, including many politicians. It was not the best of months for Brooke who had no mail and no letter from his wife, around whom, he wrote, 'turned the hub of my day'. He had to entertain the president of France, Monsieur Lebrun, cheered up when his son Tom appeared one day, then suffered more dental problems when he broke his dentures.

> Brooke had a meeting with Gort who had detected problems with the Green Howards and asked Brooke to investigate the situation. Brooke noted that Gort would have been happier in leading a battalion into battle. Brooke was constantly seeking out officers he thought unfit, and he described the divisional commander of the 22nd Division as 'a fire-eater with curled up moustache constantly acting, and I should think unreliable and useless'.

If Brooke were having to pursue the continuous task of sorting out senior officers, it was in February that his fear about the future increased. He was aware that in London they were talking about other theatres of war, ranging from Finland to the Balkans and back to the Scandinavian countries. For Brooke it was a repeat of the previous war, with the same 'string pulling…contemplating wild projects' and with 'history repeating itself in an astonishing way'.[6] He admitted that it filled him with gloom, and the gathering political opinion that the Germans would not attack during spring prompted him to write that 'personally I hold diametrically opposed views'.[7] Brooke, who read his Bible daily, may well have recalled the verse that it is 'in the spring of the year, the time when kings go out to battle'.[8] More to the point he was annoyed at the possible recall of some divisions, some held in reserve, others not being sent, and noted that Gamelin had not been kept in the picture.

On 16 February he was visited by the new secretary of state for war, Oliver Stanley, along with Field Marshal George Milne. Brooke being Brooke made the most of the opportunity and questioned the secretary of state about his views of 'weakening the BEF' at this vulnerable time. Brooke pointed out that the front in France was the one place where the war could be lost. Brooke was of course right, both from the French and British point of view. It appeared to Brooke that Stanley tended to agree with him, but Stanley was a politician who then added that he felt that the Germans would not attack this year. It would take little imagination to envisage Brooke's response as an experienced commander who had fought the Germans. He wrote in his diary: 'I told him I had no doubt whatsoever, and looked upon it as a certainty,' also noting that Field Marshal Milne tended to agree with him. This would not have raised politicians in Brooke's regard, and it would often be a cause of aggravation to him when politicians suddenly became experts in those areas in which they had no formal training or experience. Brooke had the feeling that the War Office regarded the Western Front as a 'stalemate' but Brooke clearly understood that the war, which was now six months in duration, had not actually started in army terms. 'Stalemate' is a chess term and means neither side can win either through lack of material or because the only possible move cannot be made by being in check; in this analogy the Germans were still putting their pieces on the board and the so-called 'game' had not started. Brooke recognised this and noted that his lord and masters 'may well have a rude awakening!'[9]

During March there were a few minor skirmishes on the front line, and on 5 March, he heard that two men had been killed in a bombardment when some local shelling had taken place, followed by light automatic fire. Brooke visited the area and was somewhat concerned 'that the two section posts did not seem to have put up all the resistance that might have been expected'. Nearer the end of March, he travelled to Metz where there had been a patrol encounter, and he was more pleased with the action in so far that that the Lancashire Fusiliers had killed five Germans and captured one. His main concern was with the overall picture; he felt more satisfied that the Finnish War had started to end, and he decided that it was a good thing that the 'wild goose enterprise' had almost finished, and reserve troops could be returned to where they were really needed. He gathered that the Swedish government had refused the Allies access which given their proximity to the Russians and Germans was a realistic approach. The Finns under Baron Carl Gustaf Mannerheim had fought bravely, but Brooke was correct that it would have been a useless foray for the British and French at the very time when the Western Front could suddenly open. He was cynical enough, or rather realistic enough, to note that 'I wonder what wild scheme maybe given birth to next,' a comment which many could argue was prescient.[10] He was pleased that III Corps would be returned to France where they were needed. He wondered what the German reaction would be to the Russian effort, not knowing that Hitler was somewhat bemused by the Russian forces' weakness exposed in their fight against such a small country. It is now known that Hitler thought he recognised a serious weakness in the Russian military, which was probably true, but as always he underestimated Russian resources, and the problems of fighting in bitter wintery conditions against men who were accustomed to that type of climate.

March was another month of this Phoney War with Brooke travelling around on his persistent tours of inspection, pleased with 'Monty' but ever aware of the greater picture, the singular component of his thinking which made him a reliable senior figure to many observers later in his career. He was a central figure at Lens where a service was held in memory of the dead from the previous year and the last war, and he gave a speech in French which was broadcast on radio, which he enjoyed hearing, and he hoped his beloved wife had also heard his broadcasting efforts. Twice this month he attended major church services and was impressed by the sermons and the liturgy, and there is little doubt that he was taking his religious feelings more and more to heart. It was not a good dental month for him as he had his remaining three teeth extracted and had to be fitted with new dentures, which he amusingly described as 'real soldiers' dentures'. He had experienced constant toothache and lumbago; the latter he managed to resolve, but painful teeth, as for most people, were an aggravating nuisance. He saw his son Tom who looked well but had eaten something which disagreed with him; this was probably the onset of a problem which in the coming months would cause Brooke deep concern. The weather continued to be cold and wintery, and at the end of the month he visited the Corps Prisoner Detention Centre where he addressed the 'malefactors' as he called them, reflecting the word used in the Authorised Version of the Bible to describe the two thieves hanging on crosses either side of Christ.

The diary is a mixture of his observations of the overall strategies, a detailed analysis of what was happening within his area of command, comments on the weather, his teeth, and his family. His character is fully revealed in this private diary to his wife, and it exposed not just the reality of the day in France during the Phoney War, but also paints a remarkable picture of Brooke the man.

During the month of April, the military effort, political machinations, and the news headlines revolved around the invasion of Norway and Denmark. The capture of Denmark was finished in a matter of hours; it was as senseless for the Danish to resist as it would have been for Cornwall to resist an aggressive Britain. The Norwegians were never entirely certain which country would invade them first, and it is claimed (with some likelihood) that when King Haakon of Norway was told that the invasion had started, he had asked which country had arrived. It was not just a question of Swedish iron ore. The Germans had become fixated on Norway because they were aware of the Allied interest in the area, and they also needed a longer coastline to the Atlantic if they were going to utilise their Kriegsmarine with any effect. The infamous fascist Norwegian politician Vidkun Quisling, apart from giving his name to the notorious vocabulary of unpleasant connotations, had added a more sinister touch to the German invasion. His ideology was dangerously close to that of the fanatical Nazi Alfred Rosenberg, and almost immediately there was talk of a Scandinavian SS unit, the SS *Verfügungstruppe Standarte Nordland.** The Scandinavian features were viewed by many Nazis as close to their racial image of the pure Aryan. The fair hair and blue eyes were Nordic features; ironically, these characteristics were not shared by any of the Nazi elite.

Although the Norwegian battle would roll into the next month, it was evident even during April that the entire episode was transpiring to be a disaster from many perspectives for the British and French. The Allies had proved to be too aggressive without the means or the appropriate planning, but the Germans lost huge chunks of their naval force having been obliged to use most of it transporting troops, and in skirmishes with the Royal Navy. The British generals appeared to show a lack of leadership, and it was the Royal Navy, although under constant attack, which managed to inflict the greater damage. The whole episode had been

---

\* Alfred Ernst Rosenberg was a Baltic German theorist and influential ideologue for the Nazi regime. Having been introduced to Hitler by Dietrich Eckart he held several important posts. Many considered him a key author for such policies as racial discrimination, anti-Semitism and *Lebensraum*; he was hanged at Nuremberg in 1946. Quisling was executed by firing squad at Akershus Fortess in Oslo on 24 October 1945.

encouraged by Churchill, but it was to be the prime minister, Chamberlain who paid the price in Parliament. Churchill, as always, was playing the cultural British strategy of attacking the peripheries of the enemy because British land forces would need considerable reinforcing to meet the Wehrmacht in a direct clash on the continent mainland.

For Brooke, this startling month began in the usual fashion, especially being unaware of German intentions. He was pleased to collect a new set of dentures which cost him nothing, and he sardonically observed that it was 'wrong to look a gift horse in the mouth'. He even records times when he had a haircut, underlining the personal nature of his diaries, which have otherwise proved invaluable as an insight into the man and the war for historians.

From the second of the month he had a week's break, but as he prepared to set off to see Benita he paused to reflect in his diary as to whether there would ever be a time when mankind would cease from war, and whether 'we will reach this high standard of evolution in Europe'. The first time he mentioned Norway in his diary was on his return from Dover where he noted that two leave boats had been withdrawn and he speculated they were being used in Norway, but he was more alert to the spreading rumour that the Germans were preparing to enter Belgium. It was the old question as to when the Belgian King Leopold III would allow the Allies into the country, which Brooke described as 'the race to Belgium'. On his return he was caught up with discussions about appointments and the replacement of some officers. As events unfolded in Norway Brooke reflected on the Italians 'rattling the sword in the scabbard' regarding it as a bluff, but the next day he admitted they were in fact looking more aggressive. He was also somewhat disconcerted on 18 April when he heard his close friend and confidant Dill had been ordered home to take up the position of VCIGS, ruminating on the better possibility that he would soon replace Ironside. Brooke had to admit that Dill's departure left him feeling somewhat lonely.

For him life was again the accustomed routine of the Phoney War, inspections, being pleased at the construction of some 90 new pillboxes, joining Prince Henry to hear Gracie Fields singing to the troops, and trying to resolve what he called a 'flutter in the dovecotes' because the Duke of Windsor had been invited to watch a football match when he was no longer the commander-in-chief of the Middlesex Regiment. On Sunday 21 April, he watched the French strolling around in their 'Sunday best' and reflected that the war seemed for them far distanced. The war was being fought in Norway, and Brooke makes little mention of this mainly because his pre-occupation was France which he knew would be the critical area. He did, however, note in his diary on 24 April, that the news from Norway did not sound good, writing that 'I don't like our prospects there,' believing the Allies would be pushed back into the sea with heavy losses.[11] He was correct in this observation. Looking back, he must have felt that he had been living in a surreal world because he was being ordered to sit for a portrait by the official War Office artist, a Mr Eves. Brooke thought it would be a good portrait since he had heard that when working privately, he charged £1,500 a picture. It might strike the modern reader as somewhat curious that with Scandinavia embroiled in war and the threat of invasion on the continent, the War Office was building up its library decorations.

At a personal level Brooke was concerned about his son Tom also serving in France. He had noted the previous month that he had not looked well, and on 25 April Brooke was informed he was suffering from appendicitis. He visited him nearly every day because it transpired that the appendix had burst, causing peritonitis, and as the weeks passed, he needed another operation for an abscess, requiring morphia and a blood transfusion. On his visits Brooke found Tom looking seriously ill with his eyes sunk deep in their sockets, and he appeared to be hovering between life and death. Brooke was an emotional man in family matters, as his diary perpetually reminds the reader with his loving references to Benita. He must have felt deeply worried for his son, and he visited him almost daily and received constant phone calls on his condition. In his diary he reports on this personal drama in a very 'matter of fact' way which causes the reader to wonder whether he was doing this for Benita's sake, or whether it was 'just his style'; the general conclusion must be that it typified Brooke's way of expressing himself, namely 'to the point'. It does indicate that his diaries were written in a formal style, and it needs the reader to catch the occasional word or expression he uses to detect the extremely sensitive human being inside the uniform.

During this personal family trauma, being Brooke, he continued with his duties. He attended some searchlight trials and AA gunnery and was not impressed. His many movements and posts during the interbellum years were paying sound dividends with his accumulated experience. He was not just a curious general on a visit; his oversight of the TA in Britain had given him some considerable knowledge of this type of work. Later, during the night of 9 May, when German planes had flown overhead, the searchlights and guns attacked, but Brooke was told that it was without results. The system had little opportunity at this stage to be tested, because this type of operation needed the actual fighting more than mere rehearsals to make any significant progress.

He met the Canadian defence minister, a Mr Rogers, and later a General Odlum (Canadian 2nd Division) whom he described as a 'political general' which, in Brooke's style of language, was intended to be disparaging. On 1 May Brooke received orders from GHQ to change plans: the role of Corps II would change to that of Corps I, which involved Brooke in a massive amount of administration work and reorganisation. Brooke made no diary comment on this sudden change in planning, he just did what was required. Ten days later, in the early hours (3 a.m.) of 10 May Brooke was woken with the news that Belgium was being invaded. It was necessary to initiate the 'D Plan' which was to move as rapidly as possible towards the River Dyle, east of Brussels.˙ He quickly made time to see Tom, thought the plans were working like clockwork, but knew it would take some eight days to move the whole Corps forward. The Phoney War had ended.

## May 1940

On 10 May Prime Minister Chamberlain resigned after a series of parliamentary attacks, and instead of his own political party's hopes Churchill, and not the anticipated Halifax, formed a national government. This sudden turn of events started at the same time as the Germans launched Operation *Sichelschnitt* starting with the surprise crossing through the Ardennes which were thick with woods, steep gradients and twisting roads, regarded by many as impossible, by others as far too risky. In 1938 the French had carried out a map exercise with the Germans crossing within 60 hours, which was about the time it took them in 1940; nevertheless, from the German point of view the plan 'was a gamble with high stakes'.[12] This move surprised everyone but Brooke, who had predicted the outcome of this German radical thinking, namely that their (three) Panzer Divisions would thrust forwards.[13] Brooke had long accepted the potential for the tank in battle. He may have been somewhat conservative in his thinking about tanks, but he had taken on board how effective they could be in the right hands. One historian wrote that Brooke was 'not noted a tank enthusiast and regarded in some quarters as an unimaginative Horse artillery man averse to mechanization'.[14] This was a sweeping and merely popular view of Brooke, because it reflected his very early days and even then Brooke was prepared to learn and adapt. He also knew from previous experience that the Germans, with their Prussian background, were reliable soldiers led by a highly professional officer class. The German success was not so much by numbers and armoured forces, but 'more an attitude of mind, and the understanding of manoeuvre' unlike the conservatism of the Allies.[15] It has often been claimed with some justification that the key general in their military arsenal was von Seeckt, who was long dead. During the interbellum years he had led a team of the best military officers to rebuild the German military, using speed, mechanisation coupled with airpower, and above all surprise. As the month progressed even the Germans were astonished at their success, and Hitler took it on board, looking like Napoleon once did, for a knock-out blow.

For his part Brooke studied with interest the way the Germans used their airpower. The dive-bombing Stuka with its whining siren (brought into production by the air

---

* As noted, the French operated Gamelin's Dyle Plan which had failed even to contemplate the crossing of the Ardennes; thus, the Germans drew the Allies towards the north-east.

ace Ernst Udet) had a powerful and damaging psychological impact on its victims.* Later it would become an easy prey for the Spitfire and Hurricane, but as a support system for the troops it was a first-class innovation in terms of ground battles. By the end of the month Brooke had grasped the importance of this type of airpower, and the danger of well organised tanks supported by infantry. Brooke was amazed at Guderian's success, and the theory of the interbellum years may have caused him to reflect that perhaps Fuller and Liddell Hart had been closer to the true value of tanks than he had been, though this possible thinking by Brooke is pure speculation. By the end of the month he was even more uncertain about the French military; he had been convinced for a long time that it was weak and lazy, but in the turmoil of this month he also thought many of them were cowards. This was perhaps somewhat unfair, but the ordinary French soldier was badly led by weak officers who showed many signs of panic.

It soon became apparent that the German plans were not just going to be a movement around the Allied left wing as in 1914, but a direct thrust through the Ardennes by armoured forces, and then crossing the Meuse between Dinant and Sedan. The idea was the British and French would advance towards the Scheldt and the Dyle, and the German *Schwerpunkt* (the focus) would break in behind them. There had been some Belgian intelligence suggesting this, but there were reams of intelligence information reports, some of which could not be trusted, some were confusing and some correct but changed at the last moment; it is always easy to have the benefit of hindsight. General Georges had been concerned about such a manoeuvre and had expressed his apprehensions, but General Gamelin considered himself correct in all matters and forecasts.

On 10 May as noted above Brooke under instructions moved towards Belgium following the D Plan where the British were expected to hold the position at the River Dyle. General Corap with the Ninth Army stood at the Meuse which was where the *Schwerpunkt* of Operation *Sichelschnitt* was to fall. Brooke was always critical that the GHQ remained at Arras, in a post just south of Lille; this major body should have been closer to the centre of activities, though given the speed of the Germans there was not much they could have done about it in the circumstances. Brooke had never been happy with the D Plan as he believed it an error to move from prepared defensive positions and meet the Germans in open warfare, of which they had already had recent experience and were adept to its demands.

The next day on 11 May Brooke crossed into Belgium, what he described as 'the promised land', and was driven to Sotteghem which was to be his advance HQ. When he arrived, he heard there had been some bombing, and his AQMG (adjutant

---

* Göring had promoted an old friend, Ernst Udet (with a previous career of stunt-pilot, filmmaker and described as a 'hard-drinking *bon vivant*') to the position of chief of Luftwaffe's Technical Office. Udet was not competent for this office, committing suicide in 1941 because of the strain.

and quartermaster general) had been killed by a bomb. Montgomery informed him that Belgian troops had fired at them, mistaking them for Germans; such was and is the confusion and reality of war. Brooke then received the order that he was to fill the gap between the Belgian forces and Corps I, which he considered an impossible situation demanding major movement by Belgian forces. Brooke travelled to find out what was happening, mainly because now his position was dependent upon Belgian forces which had never been part of the original plans. He met Roger Keyes who organised for him a meeting with King Leopold, and although he found the king pleasant enough, he was continually contradicted by a French officer who at first did not realise that Brooke spoke excellent French. He needed the Belgian forces to move, but the French officer objected every time, and Brooke decided it was useless speaking to the man, because 'he was not familiar with the disposition of the BEF and seemed to care little for them'. He abandoned the conversation and talked to a General Chamon who said he would raise the matter with General Georges. Brooke was staggered by the number of refugees on the road, pleased with the RAF support, but was somewhat critical about the Belgian army.

This was an exhausting month for Brooke, at times kept awake by AA gunfire, and almost too tired to write his diary. He did learn to his satisfaction that there was an agreement reached for his 3rd Division to relieve the Belgian 10th Division, which was probably the result of his hard work and negotiations the day before. It was not to be that relevant as the Germans, after a mere few days, were making rapid progress, which was already causing a sense of panic and confusion, and communications were poor. Brooke had to find his way to the embassy to use the phone to track down Pownall (CGS), but he failed because he and his staff were already on the move. Roger Keyes requested Brooke to persuade Gort to meet the Belgian king; Gort, when seen, was evidently totally unaware of the issues surrounding the king of Belgium. This was part of Brooke's criticism, that Gort failed to see the 'broader picture'. During these fraught days Brooke heard that Tom was holding his own, but he heard no more news about his son until after Dunkirk. This was an added burden to all the mayhem happening at that time.

15 May was significant because pieces of news from the flanks were disturbing as contact was made with forward German units, and Brooke learnt that the French were having trouble in the south, and more seriously Corap's Ninth French Army had broken on the front south of Dinant, and the Germans had penetrated at Sedan and Mezières. General Gerd von Rundstedt had been unbelievably successful; it was a brilliant and decisive move by the German army. It was later known that even Hitler had been concerned at the speed of advance. There was the danger, as Brooke rightly perceived, of being encircled by hostile forces.

The French First Army was under intense pressure and it was clear that the French, the largest army in the world at that time, were not coping. The Belgians according to Brooke were weak (though this was not entirely true), and the Netherlands were already occupied thus releasing more German troops for the fray. Brooke knew that his flanks were both in danger, and it would be a difficult task extricating them. This was only five days after the battle had started, and Brooke expressed himself as feeling gloomy; but he never gave up hope, claiming that 'right must conquer wrong', and wherever he went he had a reputation for spreading confidence, even in retreat. The next day the retreat under Brooke's direction was underway as they withdrew towards the Scheldt, and by 18 May he had established a temporary HQ at Dendre. He met an old friend, Michael Barker who did not seem to be coping and Brooke was somewhat critical about his poor reactions, though later he realised that his friend was suffering from a nervous breakdown. This colleague was not the only one to suffer from this problem, because the sudden onslaught and collapse of the Allies was so totally overwhelming many French and British officers and soldiers simply could not cope; Brooke was internally a tough person and continued to exude a degree of confidence, which benefitted many around him.

Brooke travelled out into the area, where he was to be further stunned by the flood of refugees on the road, compounding the problems of movement and communications. Annoying as it was it is possible to detect from his formal diary writing that he had a degree of sympathy for their plight, later writing that 'they are a most pathetic sight, with lame women suffering from sore feet, small children worn out with travelling but hugging their dolls, and all the old and maimed struggling along.'[16]

In the early hours he checked the defences along the Scheldt, and then attended a GHQ for a Corps Commanders Conference, which he described as a 'momentous one!' It was disclosed that the French were going to attempt a counter-offensive, and Brooke and others realised that if it failed the BEF and others would be cut off and probably encircled. It was mooted that the general scheme would be to move towards Dunkirk. Brooke's priority was to keep the unity of the BEF, and on his return he was anxious that the 3rd and 10th Divisions had arrived safely; it took to the evening before this concern was resolved by their return. Brooke noted that II Corps had covered some 150 miles in nine days.

It was clear at this stage that they were surrounded by overwhelming forces and staring disaster in the face. He met Montgomery and later Alexander to discuss a withdrawal scheme, only to find that in the retreat men had been obliged to swim across the canals and leave much valuable equipment behind. Even the CIGS had flown out from Britain to discuss the immediate future. Montgomery's 3rd Division had established its lines, but Brooke noted they were somewhat thin on the ground. He was told on the 21st that Gort would be calling in, the same hour he heard the further disastrous news that the Germans were at the coast and near Boulogne. There was some discussion of breaking through to the French in the south and fighting with them. Brooke preferred this to withdrawing to the coast, but he knew this would be difficult, and being a realist, he knew some form of retreat was necessary because of the possible encirclement by German forces. He had always held the German military in high regard, and during these fraught days noted in his diary that 'there is no doubt they are the most wonderful soldiers'. The major point of the various conferences was a withdrawal towards the coast. Brooke was not one of those commanders who stayed still and waited for news, he was always prowling around to see for himself, and with his team he did a reconnaissance of the canal line through Lille. After this he returned to hear that General Giraud (commanding the Ninth French Army) had been captured, and that General Billotte had been seriously injured in a car accident; he died a few days later. By 23 May, less than a fortnight after the Germans attacked, Brooke was noting that 'nothing but a miracle can save the BEF and the end cannot be very far off.' It was so bad that he later admitted he even thought about destroying his diaries. He had managed to withdraw his troops to what he called the old frontier lines, namely where they had started before the rush into Belgium. His main concern apart from being surrounded was that the Germans would push through the Belgian border in pursuit because, in his opinion, the Belgians were not fighting.

Bad and disturbing news appeared continuously. He heard the Germans were now established on the coast in the regions of Calais, Boulogne, and Abbeville, and pushing towards Béthune and St Omer which was uncomfortably close to the rear. He was also told that he had a change of divisions as the muddle of organisation caused by the onslaught was becoming close to sheer mayhem. On 25 May he was told that the breakthrough to the French was still under discussion; it appealed to him, but he thought it unlikely. Either prospect of cutting away through to the French or retreating to the beaches for an evacuation seemed too hazardous, and the ordinary soldier manning temporary posts must have felt completely confused if not bewildered.

Brooke realised that II Corps had become the left wing of the BEF, and there was a widening gap between the Belgian and British forces with a probable attack in the rear. The Belgians through Sir Roger Keyes asked for a counterattack, which theoretically would have been useful, but under the dire circumstances, it was barely feasible. Any form of joint Franco-British attack was called off for self-evident lack of resources and non-existent reliable communications, and a decision was made not to destroy troops in futile gestures. Gort, quite correctly, was beginning to see that evacuation was the only viable option for the long-term future of the BEF, and even the safety of Britain.

On 25 May the news came through to Brooke that the Germans were crossing the Belgian border. Brooke travelled down to Ypres to see if the Belgians were defending the area, but as a force they were not evident, and he checked the canal line for a defensive position. He only just escaped being trapped on the wrong side of the canal as the bridges were blown, and several times he had to resort to jumping into ditches to avoid the bomber planes. At a GHQ conference on his return the instructions had become loud and clear; the only option was to evacuate from the beaches. Brooke immediately set about making the necessary plans to take his troops through the mishmash of confusion, knowing that it was going to be, in his words, a 'hazardous enterprise'. Brooke's leadership during this critical month did not go unnoticed, and Churchill in his war history noted that the battle-line from Comines to Ypres was where Brooke and his II Corps 'fought a magnificent battle'.[17] This was where Brooke had quickly and skilfully rushed his II Corps in to fill the gap caused by the Belgian collapse: he was described by a historian of the Dunkirk episode as 'the more ruthless General Alan Brooke', a personal commodity which was going to be in demand over the next few years.[18]

On 21 May British armour had attacked the Arras heights and although the day started well it eventually failed. The Belgian government had moved to Bruges, and such was the success that *Grossadmiral* Raeder directed Hitler's attention to the possibility of invading Britain. Hitler had always regarded Britain, which he called 'a tough opponent', as the main threat.[19] At Château de Vincennes near Paris, Weygand explained to Reynaud and Churchill his anticipated plans. It has often been claimed that Weygand appeared to offer a glimmer of hope, but by now the proverbial dice had been cast. The French also applied considerable pressure for more support from the RAF. Reynaud had asked for ten fighter squadrons, but 'Churchill with Dowding's warning fresh in his ears explained that to strip Britain of its defences would be disastrous. He reminded him of the terrible losses the RAF had suffered trying to bomb the Meuse.'[20]

The Belgians were reluctant to retire further west and the British were obliged to evacuate Arras, creating highly significant gaps in the Allied lines. The Germans could hardly believe the speed of their own success, and on 23 May von Rundstedt ordered a temporary halt to the German advance for the necessity of re-grouping; this singular action was to give space and time for the evacuation at Dunkirk. A good deal of nonsense has been speculated on the nature of this decision, some even claiming Hitler admired the British and wanted them to escape. However, the Germans needed to regroup, and 'the area of canals and ditches around Dunkirk was not good panzer territory. Why not let the infantry move in rather than armour has often been asked? The British tank attack near Arras, followed by a small French V Corps action on 22 May had worried German headquarters.'[21] It was a decision that saved the British, providing them with the opportunity to escape towards Dunkirk. This 'moment of salvation for the Allies was, once again, owing to a controversy between the German "progressives" and "traditionalists"'.[22] It was Hitler, who for military reasons and these reasons alone, confirmed Rundstedt's order.

Two weeks after the start of the battle on 24 May Boulogne and Calais were under attack. Many soldiers would have been captured or killed, but the off-shore destroyers helped fight the German land guns and rescued many.[23] Boulogne was taken the next day, and the remaining French, British and Belgian forces were now surrounded; the Allies rapidly fell back towards Dunkirk.

On Sunday 26 May, the Belgian government requested that King Leopold III leave the country, but he refused.* The famous Operation *Dynamo* prepared to save the surrounded British army was sanctioned at 7.00 p.m., and started the next day with massive support from the RAF. At 5.00 p.m. Leopold offered to capitulate but Hitler wanted unconditional surrender, which typified his style of leadership and exposed his political intentions. Leopold signed the surrender on 28 May without consulting the Allies, and the Belgian Cabinet repudiated his action, but there was no longer a Belgian army; this decision became a point of serious contention. The Belgian king was criticised and some French felt betrayed at Britain's proposed departure, although many French soldiers fought well to enable this to happen, and many went to Britain with the British troops. Unbeknown to Brooke, a German order to stop the armour on the line of the canal running from Gravelines through St Omer to Béthune would give him breathing space. The Germans, Brooke had discovered, had penetrated the 5th Division front elsewhere, and he spent 27 May rushing around issuing his orders and advice.

Throughout the Phoney War Brooke had become more and more disillusioned with the French military, the high command, the officer class, and the badly led soldiers. It was not helped on this day of tearing around when a dead body was pointed out to him, and when he asked who shot him Ronnie Stanyforth, one of his military assistants replied 'Oh! Some of those retiring French soldiers, they said he was a spy, but I think the real reason was that he refused to give them any cognac.'[24] Brooke regarded this as indicating the breakdown of French discipline. There is little doubt that there were heroics and cowardly behaviour by every nationality, and after the British had left France, the statistics indicate that the French soldiers fought well against overwhelming odds. However, it seems that Brooke may have been right in so far that the French soldiers were not led by sound officers. Agnes Humbert of the later resistance related her observations of a French general pleading with fleeing refugees to let his car pass by as he fled, and she further observed a group of six soldiers with not a single weapon between them, and carrying only a frying pan.[25] An internationally renowned medieval French historian, Marc Bloch, who was an officer in the French call-up and later died in the Resistance, wrote that he 'blamed the ruling class, the military and the politicians, the press and the teachers, for a flawed national policy and a weak defence against the Nazi menace, for betraying the real France, and abandoning its children.'[26] Whatever the reasons for the collapse of the French army, which will always be debated, Brooke's observations appeared to be somewhat sweeping but at times uncomfortably close to the truth.

---

\* This stubborn refusal eventuated in him becoming a German prisoner, which had postwar political ramifications.

On 28 May as reports arrived that a German column had entered Nieuport (Nieupoort), which was only 20 miles along the coast from Dunkirk, Brooke went on a frenetic tour of all his senior men, calling in to see his commanders Martel, Haydon, Montgomery and Ritchie and then moved his headquarters to Vinchey; it was no wonder that he had little sleep. During the retreat Brooke was 'noted for his command and vigilance' especially during the battle to close the gap left by Belgium's surrender.[27] When the Belgians laid down arms it had left Brooke's II Corps in danger of collapse and capture, but he had organised a series of intricate and clever manoeuvres to avoid such a disaster. His outstanding field-command skills were already being noticed by others, as they would be during the retreat and evacuation at Dunkirk; it was later suggested that without Brooke's efforts there might not have been a Dunkirk. Later some American critics would suggest that his sole field experience was one of retreat and evacuation, which was somewhat unreasonable under the circumstances.

On 29 May he received orders from Gort that he was to return to Britain which he could hardly believe, and he went to see him asking (perhaps even demanding) whether this was an order. Gort established it was and that he was expected to form a new army. Brooke never questioned orders once he knew that they were real, but he claimed time to ensure the perimeter defences of his divisions were in place. When he heard that the Division Lourde Motorisée had received orders to go to La Panne for embarkation, he was furious because it would leave part of his front exposed and the roads would be further jammed. He told the liaison officer 'that if even a General disobeyed my order and I caught him I should have him shot!'[28] Did Brooke really mean this – was he saying that he 'would be shot' or was 'should' used in a suggestive fashion? Brooke was an angry man at the disasters surrounding him, and he was made more so by orders to return to Britain. He never said this directly, but this is the implication in his outburst.

The next day on 29 May he once more inspected all four divisions to check their defences, and he was pleased he had managed to extricate them 'out of the mess we were in' and organise their arrival to this point. Before he embarked, he gave Montgomery charge of the Corps, replacing him with General Anderson and Anderson with General Horrocks. According to some accounts of Montgomery, Brooke had tears streaming down his face; given Brooke's character he may well have been sad, but tears would be unusual, and in his memoirs of the occasion Montgomery wrote Brooke was sad, but there is no mention of tears.[29] He visited all his commanders to say goodbye, and he wished them well. Brooke arrived at the beach at 7.15 p.m. to be rowed out to a waiting destroyer; they left in the early hours and arrived in Dover at 7.15 in the morning. In all the retreat manoeuvrings and 'the operations covering the evacuation from that port in 1940 Brooke displayed consummate ability' which would be recalled in *The Times* obituary some 23 years later.[30] On that day, however, he was tired from sleepless nights, he had being working non-stop, avoiding bombs, had yet another toothache, and no idea where his son Tom was, whether he had recovered or was still ill, whether in France, a prisoner of war, or even in England. Once ashore he could hardly believe the sense of peace in Britain compared to the last three weeks in France. He met his old friend Admiral Sir Bertram Ramsay and then drove towards London through the beautiful and peaceful countryside of Kent, a memory he always treasured. Later, many fighter pilots having been engaged in fierce conflict would write of returning home and seeing a game of cricket being played below them in the peaceful English countryside; this was Brooke's experience at ground level.

## More Evacuation

He slept for over a day to recover from his exhaustion, was thrilled to see Benita, but felt somewhat depressed at the defeat across the Channel. On 2 June he set off to the War Office to try and discover what was now expected of him. He met his old friend Dill now the CIGS, who informed him he was expected to 'return to France and form a new BEF'; he described this as 'one of my blackest moments'. It must have struck him that back in Britain they were totally unaware of the circumstances existing across the Channel. He knew beyond a shadow of a doubt that the French were in a state of total defeat, and Brooke had witnessed that Weygand had been no improvement on Gamelin, and the French army was disintegrating. He also knew that the Germans were a powerful military force, and however corrupt the Nazi machine was, their army and Luftwaffe were well officered, well prepared and were at this stage virtually unstoppable. It must have seemed to Brooke to be an act of sheer madness to be ordered to pick up the remnants of home forces with limited materials, to return to France for what he rightly perceived would be another disaster. He had left a defeated France, a struggling and exhausted BEF scrambling off the beaches, and in England the army was wide-spread and in general chaos. He met Anthony Eden, the secretary of state for war, whom he found 'charming and sympathetic' and told Eden that his proposed mission had no value at all. He informed the minister that he was not commenting on the political nature of the argument, but he wanted Eden to understand the military perspective which clearly forecast a definite disaster. Eden may have been sympathetic, but the orders stood, because he would have known that the instructions emanated from the new prime minister Churchill, giving Brooke no choice. He ruminated that he was being used as a political requirement by the British government in a forlorn effort to keep the French going, and demonstrate that the British were still with them. He was undoubtedly correct in his thinking, and there is no question that when the Armistice was later suddenly declared, the British army would have lost a massive number of now experienced soldiers and officers.

On 11 June he was required at Buckingham Palace where the king awarded him the KCB for his services in France. It must have felt like an unreal world as he had returned from a massive military defeat. Although the British characteristically turned the defeat and Dunkirk evacuation into the next best thing to a victory if not a divine miracle, it was realistically a downright disaster. However, Brooke's efforts in organising his troops, both in planning and defence and then skilfully extricating them from total disaster, had not gone unnoticed. The king's award acknowledged this, but the military chiefs and politicians were also beginning to realise that Brooke was a highly dedicated military officer. What they had yet to realise was that he was also capable of understanding the wider picture of events, and they would discover very quickly that he was a man who obeyed orders, but who was not timid and would express his views strongly; Eden may already have detected this feature.

On 12 June, a mere fortnight from his arrival back from France, Brooke was setting out again on what he called a 'dirty little Dutch steamer' with nearly a hundred Frenchmen on board. The vessel could only make 12 knots, there was no food on board, and on arrival the boat was instructed not to enter the port until notified. Brooke was furious and regarded this as a disgrace, which 'I propose to let them know in no measured terms'.[31] He had just settled down to sleep when a small boat was sent to collect him by the Cherbourg commander, a Gervase Thorpe; the situation was not helped as it was pouring with rain.

The next day he drove to Le Mans, and once again he observed the problem of refugees packing the road as he hurtled along with what Brooke considered to be a dangerous driver. He was somewhat disconcerted to discover that there were still some 100,000 BEF still in France. He also learnt that the major 51st Highland Division had been forced to surrender the day before. This important division had been sent to help guard the Maginot Line even before the Germans had even started their invasion. They had been forbidden by the French command to retreat beyond the Seine, and eventually had no choice but to surrender. Brooke would have found this whole episode a salutary reminder of the danger of troops under the command of another power, and one for which Brooke had little respect.

On 13 June he set off to see Weygand and travelled some 170 miles on the one day. Given the refugees, the danger of sudden Stuka attacks, and that the cars of that generation were not as comfortable, safe or fast as cars of today, it must have been exhausting. He had earlier on that same day discovered that relationships with the French were somewhat tense, and he had worked out there was little hope of them managing to hold on against the German onslaught. He was given an appointment to see Weygand the next morning at 8 a.m., where he found the French commander looked 'tired and wizened'. Weygand was also suffering from a stiff neck having sustained an injury in a recent car crash. Brooke was told by Weygand that Paris was virtually evacuated, and the proposal was to hold Brittany starting from Rennes, and Brooke had to collect all his troops at Le Mans with this intention in mind. Brooke then travelled to meet his old acquaintance General Georges to tidy up the details. Brooke had been bemused by Weygand complaining that the current scenario was a sad business for his military career. Brooke naturally found it somewhat strange that this leading figure in the French military was more concerned about his career than the disaster falling upon his country. It did not take long for Brooke to deduce that both Weygand and Georges held serious doubts in the projected Brittany redoubt policy, not least because of the serious lack of troops and material. Even before the project was in motion the French generals held little hope of success, and Brooke could see no promise of victory at all, only disaster. The French historian Henri Michel put the situation succinctly: 'Weygand made no secret of his pessimism to Alanbrooke; he called the stronghold a "romantic idea" and confessed to him that the French Army was no longer capable of organised resistance.'[32] Brooke then sent Howard-Vyse back to Britain by plane to explain the sheer hopelessness of the planned campaign.

Early that same evening Brooke phoned Dill and asked him to stop sending Canadian troops over to France, which Dill had already done. As CIGS, Dill was having to deal with the political as well as the military situation. Brooke further explained to Dill he was convinced the Brittany enterprise would be a total disaster. Dill probably agreed with him and told him that those troops not under French command should start being organised, and those Canadian troops which had arrived were to head towards Brest ready for evacuation. That same evening Dill called again from 10 Downing Street (though it transpired that Brooke thought the call was coming from the War Office), informing Brooke that Churchill thought it necessary to help the French. Brooke's reply was a straightforward retort of 'What the hell does he want?'. Churchill then spoke to Brooke, to his utter surprise, having not realised the prime minister was present and listening in to the conversation. Churchill informed Brooke that it was important the French felt the British were in full support. Brooke's reply pulled no punches as he informed the prime minister that a corpse could not feel anything. Churchill then asked Brooke if he had cold feet, which was not only a cheap comment to such a man, but by Brooke's own admission it came close to making him lose his temper. Finally, Brooke persuaded Churchill that he was right, and this was enough for Brooke to start organising the evacuation as rapidly as he could. In his own personal account of this telephone conversation, Churchill claimed Brooke phoned him because he was regarded as 'obdurate'; such a call was highly unlikely if not impossible to conceive, but Churchill admitted that 'after ten minutes Brooke convinced him he was right'.[33] Brooke would in the ensuing years complain bitterly about Churchill's propensity to interfere in field command, and it was on this very issue that their long-term relationship started. Pug Ismay gave the interesting insight that Churchill, who was never known to let a friend down, simply did not want 'to default on the French'; it was more the emotional and political rather than military factors which dominated Churchill's mind, and these factors would be repeated again and again during the war years.[34]

It was not as clear cut as Brooke would have liked. He gave out orders for British troops to leave French command and start heading towards Cherbourg. Another phone call from the CIGS ordered that two brigades of the 52nd Division should not be re-embarked for political reasons. Dill probably added the word *political* to let Brooke know whence these contradictory orders were arising. Brooke was furious as he understood this was a waste of valuable time and shipping. He also pointed out that they were being bombed, and men's lives were in immediate danger; this made some leeway with Eden and Dill. Brooke reflected that Wellington was lucky the telephone had not been invented in his lifetime as a soldier.[35]

On 16 June Dill gave the final go-ahead, and Brooke asked his men to ensure the Royal Navy and not the French did any mine clearing at Brest, mainly based on the reasonable fear that an armistice could be declared at any moment. Another phone call from Dill set Brooke's temperature rising again, because this new instruction ordered that those British still fighting alongside the French Tenth Army were to continue to do so until the French stopped. It was a frenetic time, and not helped when Weygand claimed Brooke was breaking a signed agreement. There had been no official agreement between the French and British governments, and Brooke decided whatever the criticism he would continue to act his way to save British troops. There was a strong precedent for his action, in so far that when the French had asked for more fighter planes they were held back for the defence of Britain; Brooke was saving soldiers who might soon be needed for the very same reason. He also had a phone call from the RAF Commander Barratt stating that too many RAF personnel were still in France, but Brooke assured him they would be embarked with the 60,000 Brooke hoped for the next day.[*]

An important day for Brooke was 17 June because it became clear that the French Tenth Army was in full retreat, so 'Jimmy Cornwall' (General Sir James Marshall-Cornwall) extracted his troops to head for the designated ports. Brooke observed that Dill was under the impression that he was of some political importance with the French, but Brooke noted he had no connections with them whatsoever. Brooke sent orders to the commanders of Cherbourg, St Malo, Brest, St Nazaire and La Rochelle to continue embarking the men at high speed. As he was organising this Brooke heard again from Dill who informed him the French had stopped fighting. Brooke would have been aware that Weygand and Pétain were looking for an armistice, but it was clumsily presented and poorly timed. As soon as there was even talk of agreement, and before any concrete arrangements with the Germans had been organised, Pétain immediately took to the radio and announced on 17 June 1940, that 'with a heavy heart I tell you today that it is necessary to stop the fighting.' It

---

* Sir Arthur Barratt at that time was commander-in-chief of RAF France.

was not for another two or three days that any contacts with the necessary German channels were even established. As a result of this ill-conceived and badly timed statement, it is estimated that of the one and a half million prisoners taken by the Germans, most were picked up between Pétain's speech and the actual armistice many days later; the broadcast had given the soldiers the impression the war had finished.[36] It was a total disaster for French soldiers, but at the very best it clarified the situation for Brooke.

He was also brought news of the sinking of the *Lancastria* taking troops home, a liner with an estimated 6,000 troops on board. It was estimated but never confirmed that somewhere between 3,500 and 5,500 lives were lost. There were some 2,447 survivors but the number who died will never be known. This commandeered Cunard liner had a normal capacity of 1,300, though some authorities state it was 2,200 including a 375-man crew. Under the circumstances of the day the captain was understandably ordered to take on more people regardless of international limitations. More lives were lost than the total on the *Titanic* and *Lusitania* together, and it was placed under an official D Notice.* The news eventually broke, but for many years there was an official silence.

The next day Brooke boarded an armed trawler called the *Cambridgeshire* where one of the crew was suffering a breakdown because the vessel had been involved in rescuing survivors from the *Lancastria*, and the tragedy had unbalanced the man; in Brooke's words of the day 'he had gone mad'.† It was a slow and dangerous journey back, what with minefields, the constant danger of air attack, and choppy seas. During this journey Brooke reflected on what a mad week he had experienced, writing in his diary that it had been a time 'to try and relate political considerations, with which you are not fully informed, with military necessities, which stare you in the face, it is a very difficult matter when these two considerations pull in diametrically opposed directions.'[37] Brooke had understood the political wish to assist a crushed ally, but he immediately recognised the necessity to bring the remnants of the British army back for home defence. As he stepped ashore, he 'thanked God for allowing us to come home again'. Brooke was one of the senior commanders, but he had witnessed first-hand, as in the Great War, the experience of bitter conflict.

By 20 June he was back in the War Office with Dill and facing a degree of criticism because so much military material had been left in France. This seemed somewhat churlish given that he had carried out a major enterprise within a week, saving thousands of lives (probably in the region of 160,000), returning with 300 guns, while putting

---

* This was the usual method and was often referred to as a D Notice, established in 1912 and revised in 1993 as the DA, the Defence Advisory Notice, namely official amnesia for public or military security.

† The HMT *Cambridgeshire* (FY142) was an anti-submarine trawler which later saw action in Operation *Neptune* which was the naval operation associated with D-Day Normandy.

his own life at risk. There had been serious contentions over Weygand's denials that he spoke to Brooke about the imminent failure of French arms, but Brooke was a meticulous diary keeper and known for his critical attitudes, but not for lying.

## Southern Command

On his return, Brooke had little free family time and was concerned about his son Tom, who had been safely evacuated but was still seriously ill and in need of blood transfusions. He would later recover and return to duty, but it took time and naturally it weighed heavily on Brooke's mind. He was informed by Dill that he was taking charge of Southern Command for the defence of the realm. With many troops killed or taken as prisoners of war, and lost resources and weapons, as *The Times* noted, 'this was a position of serious and indeed daunting responsibility.'[38] He took a few days to recuperate and write up his reports, and had a one-to-one lunch with Churchill who questioned him closely about the situation in France. This would be the first of many meals he would share with the prime minister, with whom he would often disagree and become angry, but he always admired him as a worthwhile leader in conflict. He recognised in Churchill a man who refused to accept defeat and who opted for the high stakes. There would be times when the prime minister, from Brooke's point of view, interfered too much in military matters, especially personnel, but Brooke was democratic and recognised that the prime minister was in ultimate charge. Hitler and Stalin could not be argued with even by their most senior military commanders. To disagree with Hitler meant immediate sacking, disgrace by trumped-up Gestapo investigations (as with Generals von Fritsch and Blomberg), an obligation to commit suicide as with Rommel, or execution. Churchill had a strong will and was difficult to argue with because of his powerful personality, but he was democratic, acknowledged that others had a point of view, and being a parliamentarian was able to step back, recognise the value of another viewpoint, and eventually accept the fact he might just be wrong. Churchill realised that he needed to be surrounded by strong men of purpose, and this lunch with Brooke was undoubtedly Churchill's way of looking for such men.

By 26 June Brooke was once again moving rapidly around his immense area of concern, checking the available resources and manpower, visiting Bulford and Tidewell, checking the Australian contingent at Amesbury (he noted they would need at least another month's preparation for action) and generally trying to come to grips with the lack of resources following the defeat in France, and army impoverishment in the interbellum years. The LDV (Local Defence Volunteers or Home Guard) had been formed prompting a bemused Brooke to ask in his diary: 'Why do we in this country turn to all the old men when we require a new volunteer?'[39] He even questioned whether he was too elderly; he had been aware that both Gamelin and

Weygand were very or even too old for their tasks. He was deeply concerned at the shortages in the army, and spoke to Paget about the circumstances of the new situation with occupied France, just across the Channel, and the lack of resources to defend the islands from an invasion; he compared it to a state of 'nakedness'. He explained to Paget he needed a new Corps HQ, another division, armoured units, and the right to call upon bomber squadrons.*

It was a precarious time for the country, of which Brooke was all too aware. Hitler was making overtures about some form of peace settlement, if only to rid himself of an enemy in the West while he looked to his East European projects. Hitler was conscious of the vast dominions and colonies Britain could call upon, the possibility of inducing America into the conflict, and the annoyance of the Royal Navy's strength. There was, as Hitler eventually came to realise, no hope of any form of peace with Churchill at the helm.

Above all there was the growing and relentless fear of Operation *Sea Lion*, which preyed on Brooke's mind constantly.† Hitler had clearly indicated the invasion, there were preparations but no carefully prepared plans, and Field Marshal Kesselring noted after the war that *Sea Lion* may have been contemplated, but was never realistically considered, quoting the historian Fuller in support.‡ General Fritz Manstein had a slightly different view: 'Hitler would have preferred to avoid a life-and-death struggle with the British Empire because his real aims lay in the East.' This was not just Manstein's view, but was shared by many other senior military leaders.[40] However, the threat was real enough, and had it been carried out instantly following the Dunkirk retreat it may or may not have succeeded (a continuous debate to this day), but it would have caused considerable damage and horror. However, during the summer of 1940 the German E-boats attacked convoys, and such were their speed and tactics of surprise, the response against them was often minimal; more to the point during June they were often seen off Dungeness and the Romney Marshes, one of the proposed and suspected landing places for the proposed Operation *Sea Lion*. There was a genuine and understandable anxiety in Britain that the invasion could happen at any moment, and Brooke felt this deeply because of his immense responsibilities, and his growing knowledge of the lack of defensive requirements. This fear never left Brooke; he was all too aware of German military proficiency, which was understandable, expecting the event to happen at any moment. Brooke was correct to be concerned because, despite the later claims of Kesselring preparations

---

* General Bernard Paget was his chief of staff, and later became a senior army officer. He commanded the 21st Army Group from June to December 1943, and he was commander-in-chief of the Middle East Command from January 1944.

† Operation *Sea Lion* were the German plans for invading Britain.

‡ Kesselring Albert, *The Memoirs of a Field-Marshal* (London: William Kimber, 1953) p.58; in Hastings, Max, *All Hell Let Loose* (London: Harper, 2011) p.81 where it is claimed that Kesselring preferred an attack on Gibraltar, rather than England.

were in hand, with 13 divisions assembled to be the first wave across the Channel, backed by two airborne divisions. The final figures for this operation amounted to 41 divisions, nine Panzer and mechanised divisions, and, as Brooke always suspected the target was the south-east coast stretching from Folkestone to Bognor. British intelligence was generally reliable, and the threat was kept under constant review. According to Hitler's directive of 1 August, the order was to be ready for starting the operation on 15 September. It was later cancelled, two days after the launch date, because the first objective of control of the skies had not been attained. Despite Göring's boasting the Luftwaffe would rule the skies, the RAF, with some incredibly brave young men, ensured the Germans did not hold dominance over the Channel or the skies above the British beaches. Even later, when the threat appeared to have subsided, Brooke remained alert because he knew, like many others, how volatile and unpredictable Hitler could be. In early July and during the next three months, Brooke devoted every working moment and nearly all his spare time in preparing for this dreaded event.

By 1 July he had established his new HQ at Wilton House (near Salisbury), but became more and more appalled at the shortage of trained fighting men. German planes had attacked Portland, Weymouth and Bristol, and Brooke became more and more convinced that the Germans were preparing for the invasion. He was alert to the fact some of his men had been utilised to take over French ships in British ports and assume control. This was a contentious move and resented by many French people, which along with the sinking of the French fleet did much to tarnish the relationships between the two allies. This resentment by the French was understandable and marred relationships in the postwar years.

Brooke spent his time and considerable energy racing around his vast area checking defence measures and observing the senior officers; he was determined to have the best men in the right places. He was impressed in the Oxford area which covered the south Midlands, describing it as a 'good show', but he was once again concerned at the lack of men. He was not so impressed with Plymouth which he found somewhat 'sketchy', and he decided the commander of the south-west had to go – he was far too old amongst other problems – and within a few days he was replaced by a man called Allfrey. For many subordinates Brooke may have appeared somewhat tough if not ruthless, but Brooke, not known for being a 'mean person', had to put the demands of the defence of the country first. If he found a perceived weakness in command, he had no choice but to be merciless. It was this quality in a time of crisis which made him such an important officer because of his ability to understand men and their likely performance.

He also visited the Chemical Warfare Training Establishment near Andover (Porton Down), a means of warfare he would one day consider if German troops tried to make it ashore. Brooke was perpetually on the move inspecting areas, resources, and commanders. On one occasion, having been called to London to see Eden, he had called in at his home in Ferney Close to see Benita, but discovered she was out; amongst all his commitments this domestic mishap was unfortunate for a man dedicated to his wife and family. One historian commented that 'a remarkable feature of Brooke's war thereafter was the amount of time he was able to spend at home.'[41] This was far from the truth as the years unfolded, but he was sensible enough to find recuperation at home when he could, which was not that often, and was able to do so only because his duties were from this time largely based in Britain.

## Commander-in-Chief Home Forces

A summons to London on 19 July proved to be significant because Brooke heard the news that he was to be replacing Ironside as commander-in-chief of home forces. Ironside was to be made a field marshal, and Gort was to be inspector of training. Brooke was stunned by the news, writing: 'I find it hard to realise fully the responsibility that I am assuming. I only pray to God that I may be capable of carrying out the job. The idea of failure at this stage of the war is too ghastly to contemplate.'[42] His diary indicated that the enormity of his task at this vital time, with the critical nature of the assignment, dominated his thinking more than the elevation of his personal position of importance. He later admitted in his diary to Benita that he was all too conscious of his own weakness in the task, yet he somehow had to demonstrate a sense of confidence wherever he went. When he had witnessed senior French commanders break down in tears, he knew that this personal element from a fraught commander sent the wrong message to all subordinates. He had been chosen because 'his record stood high' and in France he 'had acquitted himself with singular firmness and dexterity in circumstances of unimaginable difficulty and confusion', according to Churchill.[43] Brooke threw himself into the task with vigour, wanting to succeed because of the need for national survival, and undoubtedly because being human there was always the ambitious element. He demanded a great deal from his officers and their men, insisting on long, demanding exercises which could last several days, to be carried out in all weathers and often with 30-mile plus arduous marches. His recent combat experience had underlined the importance of such training.

Churchill's immediate response to his new appointment was not reassuring as the prime minister told Margesson, his secretary of state, that Brooke did not appear 'to be up to the level of discussion', which Dill had overheard and warned Brooke.[44] It was the start of a see-sawing relationship, and later in a Minute to David Margesson, reporting Brooke's acceptance as CIGS, Churchill wrote: 'He is a combination of wisdom and vigour which I found refreshing.'[45] It was always to be an 'up and down' relationship, and there were some who thought Brooke should not have been appointed because 'he was considered to be of all British soldiers of his generation the most likely to shine in the field'.[46] It was because of Dill's quiet warning that Brooke came up with the *Victor* exercise This was based on how to deal with a possible invasion which was more appealing to Churchill, who shared and discussed the plans with Eden and Clement Attlee. Brooke was convinced that the *Victor* exercise was valuable in revealing their strengths and weaknesses as they speculated on invasion points in Norfolk, Suffolk and Kent coastlines, and the problems of Germans seizing power stations (Neasden) and the Metropolitan Water Works.[47]

Brooke's new headquarters were in St Paul's School, but he was unimpressed with the site which had little furniture and few basic comforts. He was bemused that Ironside had left him a Rolls-Royce as his car, but not a single note on the nature of defences. He was aware that Ironside had preferred a static defence with trenches, pillboxes and concrete tank traps, but Brooke preferred a mobile structure, with designated units ready to launch an offensive attack on the projected points of invasion. He shared this view with Churchill, and Brooke's sense of relentless duty and his military views were probably the reason for him being given this major task. He investigated such tactics as using searchlights to illuminate the beaches which might be utilised for the invasion, and then attacking them with the mobile forces. Later, Rommel would share the same policy, demanding that invading troops be hit before they crossed the shoreline. Brooke made a priority of meeting all his new staff, spoke to the head of the SIS, and when asked to attend Chequers to his relief he managed to evade the engagement. He rarely enjoyed the socio-political meals at Chequers, where drink flowed abundantly, and late hours were the norm. He visited the Cabinet War Office where he would be stationed if the invasion started, and on 22 July Brooke dined with Churchill and found him 'full of the most remarkable courage, considering the burden he is bearing. He is full of offensive thoughts for the future.'[48] That Churchill was full of 'offensive thoughts' would have been music to Brooke's ears as this was his form of defence. His relationship with the prime minister over the next few years would be a rollercoaster of emotions and heated arguments, but he never lost his admiration for Churchill. Six days later Brooke would spend time with Churchill in the Cabinet War Office which became all too realistic as there was an attack on Dover with a destroyer sunk, and a furious aerial battle in the skies overhead.

He used Hendon many times in taking flights to visit the north, starting with York, and then the night train to Edinburgh to inspect that area's preparations. Brooke was aware that the army and air force were to be the main defence, but he was less certain about the Royal Navy who were informing him that they could not safely bring their larger warships south of the Wash. Brooke was unhappy with this thinking, but there seems little doubt that in this view Brooke was being somewhat unreasonable. The Admirals were unquestionably considering the manoeuvrability of their battleships and the need for air cover, but they had been happy to send destroyers to Dunkirk, and in the event of a genuine emergency they may well have used their considerable strength. Having experienced the war in France only a few weeks before, Brooke was sharply aware of the fighter planes, and he made sure he had open lines with the RAF. This problem of the three services acting independently was a cause of concern for Brooke, especially in this type of emergency. The imminent threat of invasion, the times they were then living through, needed and demanded better coordination. In a democratic society the top man was the prime minister, but Brooke often worried that Churchill would not be the best overall military commander: he took high gambles, risks and played for high stakes. The Germans had resolved this issue of overall command with the OKW which combined the various services, but fortunately for the Allies Hitler presumed he knew best as the military mastermind, which he was not; at least Churchill could be challenged.

At the end of the month he was invited to visit King George VI, who asked him if he would appoint Prince Henry as a liaison officer; he had held this post under Lord Gort. Prince Henry was sometimes called the 'unknown soldier' because he carried out a series of diplomatic and military duties during the war. Brooke also met the Polish leader Władysław Sikorski to discuss the deployment of Polish troops. During this month of July Brooke, as he had assumed top command with his usual fervour and sense of duty, was plunged into the melee of trying to coordinate, organise, and increase the limited resources and manpower available. When he had arrived as chief of Southern Command he had a single Corps HQ, one regular division (the 4th) and two TA divisions, with a vulnerable coastline stretching from Sussex to south Wales; now he had responsibility for the whole country. He had received letters of congratulations, many of which commented that 'it was bound to come', which was true enough; but for Brooke it was a duty which weighed heavily upon him, not that he would ever expose this except in his private diary for Benita's eyes only.

During August Brooke's life was one of unbelievable frenetic activity, dashing the length of Britain to the north of Scotland and to the west; using plane and train, he relentlessly pursued his task of inspecting defensive measures and the commanders. He would often fly from Hendon to save time. In the second week of August he went to Norwich and visited the coastal regions around Great Yarmouth, to Harwich, back to Stanmore to meet Dowding to discuss the use of fighter planes, followed by a series of conferences at the War Office, a Chiefs of Staff meeting (COS), then down to Sheppey, the Isle of Thanet salient, and along the coast to Rye. Next day he was in the Hastings area which enabled him to see his son Tom, hospitalised in Eastbourne, then to Brighton and Hove. He inspected the Canadian Corps, watched a tank demonstration, and took a deep interest in a secret projected anti-tank obstacle. In these opening days of August, he travelled thousands of miles and held at least 15 meetings, which for many men would have simply been too exhausting with the added sense of national responsibility.

On 10 August he attended the secretary of state for war, Anthony Eden, with two issues on their agenda.* The first was the LVD (Home Guard) with which Brooke was never entirely happy; he was correct to be sceptical. There is little doubt that many would have fought bravely had there been an invasion, but it would have been a waste of life against professional German soldiers, and as such no real reliance could be placed upon them except in guarding and monitoring local areas. Later in August Brooke was 'unimpressed' when Pownall (Inspector General Home Guard) presented his report. The second item on the agenda came as a greater shock when he met Wavell, the commander-in-chief of the Middle East. The decision to build up forces in that area would one day be regarded as far-sighted, but for Brooke the main understandable concern was the British Isles which needed to be defended first and foremost. According to his War Office colleague Kennedy, Brooke had told him that he hoped 'we should not "raid his orchard" any more to reinforce the Middle East.'[49] Brooke had long stretches of coastline to guard with too few men and limited resources. Most people living in the summer of 1940 would have agreed with him. He noted in his diary that: 'I had this critical time, to agree to part with one Cruiser Regiment, one Light Tank Regiment and One Army Tank Regiment!'[50] At the end of the month he inspected a New Zealand division based at Aldershot and was 'very much impressed', but worried that they were being prepared for the Middle East. It was, as he noted later, a substantial part of his defence force, but this decision was above his pay grade and it had to be accepted. He was, however, somewhat angry with Baron Beaverbrook who according to Brooke was building up his own private army, including armoured vehicles, to defend his factories. As Brooke wrote, 'What would happen if the main battle were lost?' These vehicles were small armoured cars dubbed 'Beaverettes' and mainly put at the disposal of the Home Guard.

Brooke was never comfortable with Beaverbrook, especially after meeting him at a social level at Chequers which he did a week later. On 17 August he was invited with Charles Portal, Pug Ismay and Duncan Sandys to join Churchill at Chequers, where he noticed that Beaverbrook poured himself whisky after whisky, noticing his 'monkey-like hands' reaching out for ice-cubes. 'The more I saw of him throughout the war, the more I disliked and distrusted him. An evil genius who exercised the very worst of influence on Winston.'[51] This distrust or distaste for Beaverbrook was not just Brooke; Jock Colville noted in his personal diary earlier that he had heard that Beaverbrook wanted to resign from his post in aircraft production where he had done so well. It was because Beaverbrook claimed he was having difficulty with the Air Ministry. Colville was somewhat cynical, suggesting that Beaverbrook wanted to leave at the height of his success, but whatever the reason, Churchill simply refused. On 8 July Churchill sent a note to Beaverbrook on how the British might win the

---

* Anthony Eden would stay in this post until the end of 1940 when he would be transferred to the Foreign Office.

war; he could only see one way based on the fact that Britain had no continental army to take on German military might, and that the best way was 'an absolutely devastating, exterminating attack by heavy bombers from this country upon the Nazi homeland.'[52] There were many people who shared Brooke's views regarding Beaverbrook, but Brooke by his own admission hated the late-night drinking sessions, and often the company; Brooke was not a puritan but he lived a different lifestyle, and compared to Churchill he was an 'early bird' and not a late-night man. Churchill appreciated Beaverbrook because he had at least brought a sense of vitality and determination to the essential plane producing industry.

Halfway through the month it was reported that the Germans had been spotted embarking in Norway, provoking a rumour that they might invade from the north, which Brooke noted in passing. This would have been, he must have speculated, a highly dangerous course because of the Royal Navy's presence in the northern seas. Brooke always considered the south-east of Britain as the likely area, but he flew off to the West Country where he observed that his replacement of the previous commander with General Sir Charles Allfrey was working, and the defences were proceeding well. Later he flew up to Middlesbrough and inspected the northern defences. Nearer the end of the month he checked the coast around Scotland, but he must have known an invasion in the north was too risky for the Germans to contemplate.

His new command may have brought him extra work and responsibility, but at least it brought him closer to home, and he found time to call by Ferney Close where he could catch up with Benita and the children. He was also able to take the occasional meal in his club, often meeting with his cousin, Lieutenant-General Sir Bertram Sergison Brooke, whom he knew as Bertie, and who was commanding the London District. He was someone to whom Brooke could talk freely and in the knowledge his cousin was safe and secure. The only other person he felt able to do this with was Dill, and this secrecy which Brooke had to maintain made his diary to Benita a blessing for future historians. As he made his way towards his flat, or the club, or Hendon, he was all too aware of the increased bombing over London, the growing intensity of the battle for the skies, all of which must have portended preparations for the invasion.

This instinctive feeling Brooke had that the invasion was imminent remained with him most of September and beyond. Had the British had a deep cover agent inside the Hitler circle this would have confirmed that Brooke had every reason to regard 15 September as the key day. He might also have relaxed more had he known, as mentioned above, that the Luftwaffe failure to gain control of the skies had led Hitler to postpone the invasion. Cypher work and studying coastal observations were important activities, but everyone, including Churchill and Brooke, was aware of Hitler's volatile nature. Brooke asked himself whether the increase of ships and concentration of Stuka formations was a 'bluff to hide some other impending stroke?' Given the lack of precise knowledge of Hitler's plans, Brooke was right to be relentless in his pursuit of defence measures, and to ensure that his political masters and other authorities were made alert to the dangers. The intense bombing of London was for many a clear indication that the Germans were trying to create confusion as part of their preparations. Brooke was keenly aware of these attacks, describing London as looking like Dante's Inferno, and one night, having dined at the Orleans Club with his cousin, he counted some 60 bombs within their area of central London. It was typical of a man like Brooke to count the number of bombs while dining. Afterwards he took a stroll to the Army and Navy Club as the bombs fell, and realised he was not wearing a tin hat as the splinters were falling about him. It could be claimed Brooke as the top defence man should not be exposing himself to such dangers, dining in a central club, wandering the streets for a stroll, but Brooke by his very nature would have been impervious to such thoughts.

Early in September he experienced a better night at Chequers, even though dinner did not start until 8.45 pm, and they had to wait for Churchill to come down from one of his habitual rests. Churchill was in an excellent frame of mind, and they indulged in war games with Churchill playing the role of Hitler with various proposals about how to invade, and Brooke indicating how such a plan would be countered. Although he was not in tune with Churchill's social habits, late nights and drinking, and regularly disliked the company, he saw more of the sociable side of the prime minister and there was often plenty of laughter. Churchill often dressed in a blue siren outfit which reminded Brooke of a child's romper suit.

Various peaks were reached with information, and rumours that 'today was the day', and on 8 September there was an air of certainty that the invasion would start either on the south-east or the East Anglian coast. On that day Brooke still managed a visit to Benita and family at Ferney Close, commenting that he needed more professionally trained men at his disposal. He later wrote that during this time he felt more responsibility than at any other time in his life; it was almost 'unbearable' and weighed on him 'like a ton of bricks'.

Mid-way through September Churchill suddenly raised a concern about the guns in Dover, so Brooke and Dill joined the prime minister's train to Shorncliffe, examined the defences at Dungeness, and had lunch with Bertram Ramsay in Dover. Brooke had raised the issue that in his opinion it would be the south-east which would be the selected invasion area (after the war the plans for Operation *Sea Lion* confirmed that he was correct), and 16 reliable divisions were placed in the vicinity; Churchill observed that as far as Brooke was concerned they were 'well poised and deliver as might be required; no one was more capable'.[53] As Churchill did this tour Brooke noticed how popular the prime minister was with the public he encountered. Churchill had hoped to watch an aerial battle overhead, which either did not happen, or was too high to see; the German bombing intensified between Plymouth and the Thames, then fell strangely quiet, which Brooke found somewhat 'ominous' like the quiet before the storm. On the day of the proposed invasion (15 September), not that Brooke knew the precise date, he ruminated on the vulnerability of the length of the British coastline, twice as long as what the French had to defend with some 80 divisions, whereas Brooke only had 22. He wrote that he found it hard to maintain 'the hopeful, confidant exterior which is so essential to retain the confidence of those under one and to guard against their having any doubts as regards final success.'[54] Brooke understood the importance that those in command had to imbue others with a high degree of confidence. He never stopped in his pursuit of inspections, checking vulnerable areas, and looking for weak command situations.

Freyberg his New Zealand general, bade him farewell before travelling to the Middle East. On 13 September Mussolini's troops had started to invade Egypt, which was all part of the Italian dictator's imperial ambitions in North Africa, and to demonstrate he was co-equal with Hitler. For Hitler it was to be a minor area of interest, but later, with Rommel's incursion to rescue the Italians, this theatre of operations became of greater significance.

More to Brooke's immediate interest at this time of national survival was when he heard that the Americans, through their various contacts, had warned the British that an invasion was going to happen within the next two weeks. It is now known that this was not the case, but it was either deliberate misinformation percolated by the Germans, or more likely a mere rumour from diplomatic gossip circles. It was another month of frenetic activity, but at least Brooke managed to see more of his beloved Benita with his children on Sundays, and he found time to wander over to Savile Row to order a new uniform for winter. He had been obliged to attend many meetings, especially Chiefs of Staff. His month had started with such a meeting to discuss the defence measures in Dover, Cornwall and even the Scilly Isles, as well as the essential defence of aerodromes. By the end of the month he was growling in his diary that 'this organisation works surprisingly slowly considering there is a war on'.[55] He was constantly concerned about the need for a combined command for defence mentioned above, which he considered essential. He had already developed suspicions about the Royal Navy, and he was now concerned whether the RAF would pay enough attention to the army requirements. As noted, in Germany this had been achieved by the OKW, but in general terms the German land forces had Luftwaffe units (known as *Luftflotte*) attached to zones corresponding to army areas of activities. Brooke was an army officer and singularly minded in his bias towards the land forces; he was right that there had to be some workable combination, but whether a single guiding figure was the best solution was and remains somewhat contentious.

As the winter months settled in Brooke continued to dash around checking and rechecking areas and commanders for improvement. It was clear to Brooke that the remnants of the army he was trying to build up and not to lose to the Middle East needed toughening up. He wanted them to be able to take on the strongest enemy in any conditions of weather, terrain, and at any time of day and night. He therefore needed to know that the commanders and senior officers thought and behaved along the same lines. He had always supported Montgomery who felt the same way. There were times when he had to be ruthless and even dismiss old friends, but he was not a hard man and tried to do this duty in an explanatory way to ease the task. 'One commander who had been replaced left Brooke's office in tears, but he could only say as he left the room "what a wonderful man!" Brooke in the fullest sense, was a man of sympathy.'[56] As with any reliable leader in his situation he had to put the needs of the country first despite friendships and old acquaintances. His activities involved not just inspecting but inspiring others, running intensive training exercises, holding conferences, and having discussions about the nature of developing modern war. He did not always replace commanders if he thought some correction or change of policy was all that was required. In early October he held a long discussion with Guy Williams (commander-in-chief Eastern Area) because Brooke was unhappy with his 'units' disposition'. Brooke felt these divisions were not getting out to train enough, and he was deeply concerned about the Isle of Thanet salient needing more protection. After the session Brooke decided that 'now it should all be satisfactory'.

Most of the forces from Australia, New Zealand, South Africa and India were serving in the Middle East. Brooke had the Canadians under General Andrew McNaughton and he was not always happy about their training and efficiency. McNaughton later complained that Brooke was prejudiced against him for matters dating back to the Great War, but this again was unlikely. Brooke was only interested in efficiency and often referred to McNaughton as an old friend, although he would have constant problems with him and many doubts about his ability as a commander of forces.

He met and never changed his mind about Charles de Gaulle and remained suspicious of this French leader and many of his team. This was understandable given de Gaulle's general manner and demeanour, but also a little unfair in so far that de Gaulle's first natural interest as a Frenchman was in the well-being of France. Churchill had given de Gaulle shelter and prominence but grew to distrust him, and later the Americans would detest him. In England de Gaulle's support came from Eden, but one of his biographers noted that de Gaulle was aware that men like Alexander Montague Cadogan and Robert Vansittart thought little of him and that 'Alan Brooke was not much impressed'.[57] There was also a degree of distrust with many of the French, not so much because of Marshal Pétain and Vichy France, not even the collapse of the French army, but the way the British had taken hold of their ships, naval and merchant, and, as noted, this was later heightened by the near destruction by the Royal Navy of the French fleet.

Brooke appreciated the men of the Polish army, undoubtedly because they were tough fighters, as they would one day prove, but he mainly respected Sikorski. It was helpful to Brooke to have Sikorski to keep him informed through his various contacts about what was happening in Eastern Europe; in October Sikorski was able to inform Brooke that Stalin was uneasy about what was happening in Germany. Later, Brooke would also welcome the Polish General Władysław Albert Anders, when he had been released by his Soviet captors.

At the beginning of October while in the middle of an inspection tour he was summoned by Eden, and heard he was going to lose the whole of the 1st Armoured Division by the end of the month. This would make him short of a hundred cruiser tanks, and although Brooke made no further comment it is not difficult to imagine his frame of mind, or his conversation at dinner with his cousin Bertie that same evening.* This month of October started with the hope that the invasion had been dropped, but Brooke wondered whether the Germans were preparing some other surprise. It was a matter of working in the dark. From the sublime to the ridiculous Brooke found himself 'attacked by the Secretary of the Jockey Club who wished to carry on with the Newmarket Race Meetings as if no war existed.'[58] Curiously, and probably not the intention of the Jockey Club Secretary, it may have been best for people if normality could be maintained as far as possible for the sake of public stability. However, faced with the national threat from Germany, Brooke's reactions were understandable.

Brooke revisited Scotland but found air transport more difficult. Hendon had been badly hit with 27 aircraft destroyed; on the way back from Scotland with fog banks it was dangerous; and the same with a trip to the west, and often planes were unable to take off. Even at home in London there were dangers from bombs and on one dinner engagement at the Berkeley, he and his guest were asked to shelter in an inner room because a time-fused bomb had landed in Piccadilly Circus. Another dinner engagement at Chequers proved to be of more interest because Churchill spent the evening discussing the possible course of the war, and the failure at Dakar.† He wrote of Churchill again that 'he has a wonderful vitality and bears his heavy burden remarkably well'.[59]

In October he was also invited to Windsor Castle where he had lunch with the king and queen, whom he found charming, and the two young princesses. The king wanted to know about air defences for the castle and the safety of a trip to Norfolk. This was not pure self-interest by the king, but the safety of the royal family within the public consciousness was more important than the Newmarket race meetings. His other meetings tended to be the Chiefs of Staff where the shortage of ammunition and intelligence was often high on the agenda. The shortage of weapons was one

---

\* The cruiser tank (cavalry tank) was a British tank concept developed in the interbellum years to function as a modernised armoured and mechanised cavalry.

† On 11 September, the 11th French Squadron departed for Dakar backed by the British they failed on 23–24 of the same month, because they met the resistance of some French naval vessels who had arrived earlier. The question of information leakage by the French caused some concern.

thing, but lack of ammunition another, and great strides were made to rectify this sorry situation pushed forward by Brooke. In a minute from the COS meeting of 12 August and in the War Cabinet, Brooke 'was able to report that small arms ammunition had been issued on a considerably increased scale for training purposes, and this should have a reassuring psychological effect on the men in the front line'; Brooke was always conscious of the morale of troops.[60]

He visited Thanet again – it was the area which concerned him most, and it was not helped by receiving some disturbing information that the Germans were accumulating troops along the Scheldt. Brooke wondered whether they would hazard crossing the Channel during October, but he could not dare take the risk that they would not. He was also informed that wireless intercepts were confirming this information, and that there was a build-up of ships in Rotterdam. Brooke immediately requested the bombing of Rotterdam harbour.

This new tension set Brooke into philosophising in his diary, writing 'why human beings must behave like children at this stage of the evolution of the human race is beyond me'. He then decided that after much suffering human beings may learn 'that greater happiness can be found in this world by preferring their neighbours to themselves'.[61] It was a week of tension, more Chiefs of Staff meetings, and he met Stewart Menzies the head of SIS, known as 'C,' and wondered whether the sudden inactivity by the Germans was 'the lull before the storm'. He even wondered if Hitler's visit to Franco was to detract attention from the invasion. As it transpired it was not and Franco's meeting, as far as Hitler was concerned, was a disaster. The last two weeks of October were fraught with this renewed threat of invasion, something which was Brooke's duty to take seriously. Having received the information he could hardly be expected to offer the defence he had pondered, that if the invasion took place, that he could not excuse it by saying 'I thought it unlikely.'

The battle lines were slowly changing in emphasis, and at the end of the month the Chiefs of Staff meeting, this time with Churchill present, was mainly about freeing destroyers to hunt down U-boats in the Atlantic. It would take a long time for Brooke to accept that the invasion was no longer a threat. Fog and bad weather frequently stopped Brooke using aircraft during the remaining months of 1940, and it was unlikely that the Germans would risk crossing the Channel in winter with weak air cover, but even on 17 December there were more rumours that a German invasion was imminent. Brooke was conscious of this threat, and two days later he met Sholto Douglas (commander-in-chief of Fighter Command) to discuss the way fighter planes would be used. This was Brooke's only mention of a winter invasion and despite intelligence received, he continued his routine, probably sure that the wrong weather conditions made it improbable.

During these winter months he was able to spend more time at Ferney Close with Benita and the children, even taking time to fill the coal store. Any other senior commander would have used assistance, but Brooke was a homely man and enjoyed the domestic scene. It would have made a strong comparison with his military life where he had many assistants. The bombing continued to such an extent that Brooke tended to note in his diary the 'quiet nights', writing that 'it is a queer life knowing that bombs are being carted about the sky over one's head and may be released at any moment.'[62] He was personally disturbed when bombs fell close to his much-loved Orleans Club, which during the winter months was destroyed. This had been his favourite dining area which he shared with his cousin Bertie, and on 19 November, he dined with Bertie at his flat in Chesterfield House. He found his cousin, as mentioned earlier, not only excellent company, but somebody he could speak with confidentially.[*] He visited some of Bertie's defence systems and was pleased with what he saw, and often wished he could promote his cousin to be commander of a Corps, but Bertie, he knew, was ageing. The bombing was disturbing for him, not least when the Naval and Military Club was hit, and he considered himself lucky because he had often stayed there overnight. During the middle of November, to sleep better he had moved into the Headmaster's house at St Paul's, where he was away from the noise and immediate danger. He took an interest in a new method of bomb disposal, watching a demonstration of using plastic explosives to detonate bomb-casing to find the time fuse, without blowing the bomb up. It was on this occasion he met Lord Suffolk who oversaw the exercise, a man he described as a 'queer specimen' because he did not fit with Brooke's image of a regular army officer.[†]

Churchill was also concerned about the bombing, suddenly worried that following the Coventry raid (14 November) the Germans might try and pinpoint Chequers during a full-moon period. He moved his retreat area to Ditchley Park (near Oxford) which was owned by the wealthy Conservative MP Ronnie Tree. Colville thought it generous of Tree, and he considered it must have been something of a trial when Churchill arrived with such a vast following. It must have felt like a medieval king arriving with his entourage.[63] Brooke found himself there many times, and as at Chequers, he was always concerned about the late hours and over-indulgence. The bombing touched upon everyone's lives, from Churchill and Brooke to Buckingham Palace, and more pertinently to people's homes, especially those living close by to

---

[*] It has been somewhat cynically claimed that Bertie's 'chief wartime function seems to have been providing shooting facilities for his ornithologically inclined cousin' (Nick Smart, *Biographical Dictionary of British Generals of the Second World War* (Barnsley: Pen and Sword, 2005), p.45) which seems with Bertie's other duties somewhat unfair.

[†] As a matter of curiosity Lord Suffolk came from the Howard family, and until 1917 had been Viscount Andover, and earlier in the year during the retreat from France, he had helped organise some French nuclear scientists and heavy water to be brought back to Britain. Brooke mentioned their joint nickname of the 'Holy Trinity' which applied to Suffolk, his secretary and chauffeur who both assisted him in this dangerous task. He was often given the nicknames of 'Mad Jack' or 'Wild Jack', and Herbert Morrison once described him as a 'remarkable young man'. The following year on 12 May all the 'Holy Trinity' were killed when defusing a new and complex bomb device.

their work in the East End of London and many other ports. Bombing was a major part of everyone's existence, but there was a quiet truce at Christmas.

At the beginning of November, he had spoken to General Corap who was the chief liaison officer working with the Poles and Czechs. Their disposition and potential use for fighting were important, and as mentioned earlier, Sikorski's knowledge of Eastern Europe was informative. Events during these last two months of 1940 were ominous in the eastern area. Between 20 and 23 November, Hungary, Romania and Slovakia all signed the Tripartite agreement. Yugoslavia and Bulgaria would follow in March, but after a coup d'état Yugoslavia withdrew just before that country was invaded along with Greece. As Brooke summarised in his diary at the end of the year, it was impossible to try and predict 'what course this war would take'. He had attended the Lord Mayor's Lunch at the Mansion House and listened to Churchill giving a speech, which mainly related to Roosevelt, who had just been re-elected for his third presidential term of office. Brooke did not refer to the American situation at this juncture, but he must have realised by now Churchill's hopes and anticipation that America would eventually join Britain in the conflict. Brooke was aware like everyone else that Roosevelt had promised the electorate that American boys would not be sent to Europe, but at the end of December Roosevelt made the promise that the 'USA must be the arsenal for democracy'.

Brooke was more than aware that although it was impossible predict the future course of the war, the pace of events was increasing. He had lost valuable resources to the Middle East and Mussolini had invaded Greece through Albania. Churchill had argued the case of sending British troops there, prompting Brooke to write: 'Why will politicians never learn the simple principle of concentration of forces at the vital points, and the avoidance of dispersal of effort.'[64] This would be the same strategic argument which would later lead him into confrontation with Eisenhower. Brooke often complained during his time in France that Gort had failed to see the wider picture, and this criticism could be levelled at him failing to see the ramifications of what was happening in the Balkans, and in the wider global picture as it developed. On the other hand, Brooke's duty was the defence of the British Isles, and this was his consuming passion. It may be that Churchill was correct in showing a sense of unity with those fighting the same enemy, that Mussolini could be kept in his box, that it could lead to a wider dispersal of German troops, and many other reasons. It was to lead to disaster once the Germans later took an interest, obliging another evacuation, and the battle of Crete.

Brooke was more aware of the home dangers, which as commander of the Home Forces was understandable, taking an interest in weapon development, especially in the invention of a new type of mortar. He was also attempting to create new divisions to replace those going overseas, and with the intention of strengthening the army so severely damaged first by lack of input during the interbellum years, and then by the destructive results incurred during the Battle of France. He was also modernising his own views, taking an interest in the development of parachutists; he suggested the best training for such men could be in Canada. The Germans had already demonstrated the use of the best possible trained soldiers suddenly arriving from the air, and Brooke watched a display at the beginning of December when 32 men dropped from four planes at 500 feet, and apart from one twisted knee injury, they arrived safely and ready to fight. He watched with Montgomery a demonstration using an armoured division, working with a motorised division with an armoured battalion alongside parachutists. He had seen this work for the Germans and realised it was a sound attacking offensive. Brooke like many others was concerned with the need for innovation in military matters, which caused Churchill on one occasion to be 'aggrieved at Brooke's and Dill's hostility to one of his proposed promotions, namely the return of General Hobart to high command, "Remember," he told Dill, "it isn't only the good boys who help win wars. It is the sneaks and stinkers as well."[65] For traditionalists such as Dill and Brooke, Hobart had too much of a short temper and could be hot-headed and too individualistic, but it was generally acknowledged he was good on technical matters. Later Brooke, like many others, would be grateful for Hobart's inventive tanks, and on this occasion, Churchill was more astute than his top military men.[*]

At a personal level Brooke was concerned about Dill, whose wife had suffered from a stroke, and Dill was also finding it difficult to cope with Churchill. Brooke noted that these two men were poles apart, Dill being too refined for the 'gangster transactions of politicians'. Brooke believed that Beaverbrook had poisoned Churchill's mind against Dill, and that his friend had also suffered from the Hore-Belisha debacle. During December Brooke met the Canadian envoy to Vichy France, and he probed him about Pétain and asked about French reaction to the sinking of the French fleet at Mers-el-Kébir (3 July 1940). Brooke would have discovered that naturally many of the French were almost regarding the British as the enemy after the destruction of their fleet, and that the Vichy government was drawing uncomfortably close to the Nazi regime.

By the end of the year, as Brooke wrote his final observations for 1940, he ruefully noted that 'Dunkirk will take its place amongst the many examples of disasters due to political mis-appreciations of the requirements of war.' There seems little doubt that Brooke was also thinking of the loss of resources and men towards the Middle East, something which he would one day fully support. On the last days of December, he had managed to find some freedom by going on a pheasant shoot.

---

[*] See Chapters Seven and Eight when Brooke was pleased to inspect Hobart's work.

## CHAPTER 5

# 1941

## Home Defence

If 1940 had been an anxious year for Brooke with his sense of responsibility, this tension in his life would intensify over the coming year. However, as he noted in thinking about the course that the war was taking, he admitted he had no 'sound thoughts', but by the end of 1941 the overall picture would have a little more clarity. Russia and Germany were both totalitarian states, and for the SIS to gain reliable information from inside either country during these years was difficult, if not impossible. It would have cheered Brooke and Churchill considerably to have known that at the end of 1940 Hitler would issue his Directive 21 (18 December) ordering Operation *Barbarossa*, the invasion of the Soviet Union. When it started on 22 June 1941 with a declaration of war against the USSR by Germany, Italy, Hungary, and Romania, although appearing initially successful, for the more discerning it was a suicidal act. Near the end of the year on 7 December Pearl Harbor would be attacked, and Churchill would declare war on Japan immediately. The situation would be further aided by Germany and Italy declaring war on the USA on 11 December. Brooke continued to be conscious of home defence, his personal responsibility, watching events in Greece and the Middle East, but the broader picture was to establish a possible light at the end of an exceedingly long, dark tunnel.

Before all this occurred, for Brooke, the year started as the previous year ended with a continuous round of plane, train and car travel to every corner of the British Isles. It is easy to gain the impression from his diary that he felt able to spend more time at Ferney Close, simply because he was based in Britain. Several times he mentioned being at home doing carpentry work, working on his camera, and making brass fittings to build himself a tripod; his love of nature and capturing it in pictures never left him. In early January he was given a new office near the Cabinet War Room (under the Office of Works) which he thought was well fitted out, bomb proof and, he wrote, generally excellent, with one fault, namely 'its proximity to Churchill'.

Brooke dedicated himself to improving the Home Army and defences, giving more talks, several conferences on using combined forces such as parachutists, armour, gliders, bridging methods, and as he noted 'instilling a little more offensive spirit into the army'. It was a matter of modernising an under-resourced army and thereby giving its men and officers a sense of confidence. Some believed Brooke was looking to the future, which of course he was, but during these months he was mainly concerned with defence, because he believed the invasion remained a distinct possibility. Brooke had always believed that the best form of defence was attack, a strategy often employed by chess players. It was therefore no surprise that in a Chiefs of Staff meeting he raised the issue over the lack of ammunition, causing Churchill to complain to Dill that Brooke was far too critical. This was the 'pot calling the kettle black' but Churchill was a politician and any criticism was rarely received graciously by that occupation. Defence of the realm totally absorbed Brooke's mind, and he had an argument with Admiral Tovey as to how the Home Fleet would be used in the event of an invasion. In March he had a meeting with Air Chief Marshals Portal and Freeman to discuss who should be Brooke's link with the RAF, and he was not satisfied with that meeting. Brooke and Portal became good friends with their common love of fishing and nature, but Brooke always wanted the army to have more aerial support than Portal seemed willing to give, and Brooke often contemplated setting up an army air support system.

He also had continuing difficulties with the Canadian McNaughton who complained that during the exercise Canadian troops had been misused. Brooke had felt obliged to split the Canadians and put one of their divisions in another Corps which broke convention and the constitution, according to McNaughton. Brooke managed to calm the Canadian down and settled the matter 'amicably' but privately noted that McNaughton was short on 'strategic vision' and he had not understood that 'extreme emergencies' took precedence. Later, in April, Brooke travelled down to Lewes to see the Canadian 1st Division, and he was 'rather depressed at the standard of efficiency'; he could see the soldiers were good, but he had serious doubts about some of the commanders. Even in mid-June on a visit to see Canadian troops in Horsham he remained unsure about McNaughton's ability as a commander, and worried about the Canadian officers. He knew that McNaughton was good in 'matters of science', but he was appalled at his ability as a commander.

Brooke tried to use every meeting and contact to enhance the defence system, worrying about the refugees who had been hampering communications in France, about evacuating the seaside towns in the south, and the problems of coastal holidaymakers who did not appear to realise 'there was a war on'. He met the minister of fuel and oil to discuss the possibility of setting the sea alight around invading troops, and he was disappointed that it all depended on the weather, and that waves could disrupt this defence. He even spent time with the minister of agriculture on how to neutralise potential landing grounds against enemy parachutists, gliders and planes without causing too much disruption in essential food supplies. He had already visited Porton Down, and he was prepared to use gas despite its risky nature.

These months of early 1941 remained frenetic for Brooke as he relentlessly pursued all possible avenues of defence. Between 20 and 25 January he held a major home defence exercise which tried to cover every possible scenario. He carefully watched reactions and looked out for weaknesses among his commanders or within the system. It struck him that the Eastern Command, which hitherto had been controlled by one commander, Guy Williams was too vast an area for one individual, because it covered the coastline and hinterland from the Wash to the Thames, and beyond nearly as far as Portsmouth. Nor was Brooke entirely convinced that Williams was doing the job well; he mused over the fact that Williams was an engineer, and as such turned more towards defensive measures, when Brooke had always suggested an offensive strategy. He later noted in March that Williams was 'lacking strategic and tactical flair'.[1] He started to work on some changes, considering keeping Williams in the northern sector, deploying Paget (his chief of staff) in the south and replacing Paget with General Budget. He had some criticism over Budget who had suffered a nervous breakdown during the Dunkirk episode, but Brooke believed Budget had overcome this problem, and he knew why it had happened in the first place. Later in April Brooke would have a 'painful' interview with this old friend Guy Williams, who wanted to refuse the order to go to New Zealand to look after their defences. It was obviously not even a promotion upstairs, and he must have felt that he was being exiled to the other side of the world.

There were other areas of concern, and Brooke decided he had to change local commander Freddy Carrington in Scotland with a Bulgy Thorne, and he replaced him with Montgomery to guard the dangerous south-east corner. For Brooke it was a matter of constant surveillance to ensure the best commanders were in place and living up to his expectations. In early February he met the Home Guard commanders in Kent and Sussex; he knew they had a part to play, but very much like the television series *Dad's Army*, he noted that they were 'a grand load of patriotic retired officers'.[2]

Brooke continued to dread the invitations to Chequers, and on 2 February (when he met Frederick Lindemann, Churchill's scientific adviser), he gave them a lecture on the recent Home Defence exercise. The prime minister struck Brooke as pleased, but he felt that Churchill was also critical, pointing out that the Home Fleet and Fighter Command lessened the threat of invasion, implying, Brooke thought, that Churchill thought the fear of invasion was being built up too much. It may well be that Churchill was right, and with the benefit of hindsight he was, but Brooke had been charged with Home Defence and he was not going to be found lacking on his watch. He found some comfort from Churchill's implied criticisms by talking to Dill; both men thought along similar lines. Working with Churchill was going to be a steep learning curve for Brooke and many others. Churchill was an extremely unusual prime minister, if not a unique personality, and the times were equally exceptional. Later Brooke had to speak to the king on the exercise (codenamed *Victor*) which was a more pleasant experience. The king always showed an active interest in military matters, and Brooke was also still meeting the king's brother Prince Henry. He stayed with the prince on 17 March while inspecting the Kettering area, always found him charming but 'not easy to make conversation with' and discovered that Prince Henry felt bitter about Gort. Brooke also knew that as far as Gort was concerned, he found the royal prince 'got on his nerves'.

It is easy to gain the impression that Brooke was overly critical and perhaps too sensitive. If he overstepped the mark, he tended to acknowledge it with later entries in his diary. In March at a Chiefs of Staff meeting chaired by the admiral of the fleet, Sir Dudley Pound, Brooke described him as 'the slowest and most useless chairman one can imagine. How the prime minister abides him I can't imagine.'[3] As he defended Budget over the nervous breakdown incident, once he understood what had happened, so he later retracted his harsh views on Dudley Pound when he discovered the admiral was seriously ill. Two days after this meeting Brooke had the opportunity to meet Roosevelt's envoy to the Balkans as he was passing through to return to America: Colonel Donovan who was later to become the head of the American OSS, Office of Strategic Services. Undoubtedly Brooke heard some interesting information, but he must have gained some cheerful anticipation that the American president was pro-active and wanting to understand the situation in Europe.

On 13 March he had to pose, of all things, for photographs for the National Portrait Gallery and the magazine *Illustrated*. It was reflective of the time in France when the War Office wanted his picture painted by a professional artist. It gave Brooke time to think, and on the same day he was pondering what the Germans would do next, and he came to a prescient conclusion noting that 'I would not be surprised to see a thrust into Russia.'[4] It would take a few more months for the truth of his personal prophecy to be proved accurate, and a few more weeks before intelligence information started to point in this direction.

In late March he attended a Secretary of State meeting at the War Office to examine the prime minister's directive on the role of the future army. This may possibly have arisen over Brooke's clash at Chequers regarding the *Victor* exercise mentioned earlier, and Churchill always held strong opinions, but at least he wanted them discussed, unlike Hitler and Stalin. Brooke found the whole paper 'hopelessly adrift' and he managed to convince others in the room to 'crush' Churchill's presentation. Dill at this time was in the Middle East, while Brooke in Whitehall, missing his personal and intellectual friend, could not wait for his return: 'I am longing to have him back,' he wrote. When Dill returned, he organised for a further 60 cruiser tanks to be sent to the Middle East. Brooke described this as an 'appalling blow' but later admitted it was the right decision. It was again Brooke's broader picture, which was somewhat limited by his current role of defending the home territory.

It must have struck Brooke as he toured the Isle of Wight at the beginning of April that there was a widening perspective in the war, especially when he heard that Benghazi had been lost (2–3 April), observing that the troops which had been sent to Greece had weakened the Tripoli front. The month of April ended with another visit to the dreaded Chequers; Churchill was due to give a radio broadcast, and so the meal did not start until 9.30 p.m. and they were kept up until 3.30 a.m. It was a typical soirée, but Brooke was learning to keep as silent as possible and not rattle the great man; he had to be on the road again next day, only five hours after they eventually retired.

During May, Brooke started to attend a series of meetings which were dubbed the Tank Parliament. In the first such meeting on 5 May he met with other significant figures, including the controllers of production, to discuss the urgent need to produce tanks as soon as possible. The meeting was held at 10 Downing Street, and Brooke found it useful that those industrialists who designed and produced the various tanks, met the military men who drove and fought in them. Brooke found these meetings useful, but there were moments of frustration, mainly based on Brooke's demand that it was critical to produce many more spare parts than they intended. This pragmatic insight by Brooke was to prove in time to be all too true. Churchill wanted, as Brooke observed, just the whole tank image for 'front window' presentation. This was an ongoing frustration for Brooke who was still arguing his case in late June, noting that lack of spares was later going to cause serious problems. In early June Brooke visited the Birmingham factory where they were made, and earlier he had gone to see for himself a new 35-ton tank, which he personally drove and amusingly, and no doubt to the concern of others, chased a pheasant through the scrubland test-site. The Tank Parliament discussed many aspects of the war, and Brooke admitted that at one meeting in May (on the 13th) he had become 'a bit heated' over the issue of the Air Ministry's lack of cooperation regarding support for the army. He was pleased that Churchill supported him in his views, and because of this there was a degree of better liaison between the air and land forces over the months ahead. Although Churchill and Brooke were often clashing, after one Tank Parliament in late May when air-cooperation and anti-tank weapons had been on the agenda, Brooke described Churchill as a 'most wonderful person', writing that he was one of those 'Human Beings who stand out head and shoulders above all others'.[5] These sudden outbursts of praise for the prime minister were a characteristic of Brooke's reflections, and continued throughout the war even when he was at loggerheads with his political master. He was, for example, horrified only a fortnight later when Churchill was pressing for two major fronts in Libya and another in Syria, when Brooke was understandably concerned about the lack of manpower. Brooke was making a pertinent point about having trained soldiers on the ground. In Germany, the one-time army officer and now Luftwaffe Field Marshal Kesselring often argued for the importance of airpower, but always acknowledged that it was 'feet on the ground' which won battles and wars. As noted earlier the interbellum years had seen the British army suffer the most from lack of resources and attention; the conscription age was always being upgraded, but the shortage of foot soldiers and ammunition was a continuing problem.

Despite all the pressures and chasing around the country during May and June, Brooke's notes and letters indicated he was finding some release through his passionate love of ornithology. In the late winter months, he had been busy building up and creating new camera equipment, and during the spring when birds were nesting, he took every opportunity to watch and photograph his feathered fascination. On a trip to Scotland he took time off to visit Lord Kitchener's memorial on the sheer cliffs at Marwick Head, five miles east of Dounby in Orkney, where he watched a peregrine falcon on its nest. It is easy to speculate how his various accompanying officers regarded this hobby of their commander, standing around on the top of sheer cliffs while Brooke watched with such keen interest some bird sitting on a nest. Some may have enjoyed the break, listened to Brooke's excited commentary, and there were probably a few winks and grins at their commander's sudden joy over his feathered friends. Later a naval vessel would take him to the famous Bass Rock (in the outer part of the Firth of Forth in east Scotland) where he spent hours photographing gannets. The navy later (12 June 1942) took him to the Farne Islands in pursuit of his hobby, but he missed his step and disappeared (for a time) under the water with all his equipment.[6] It would not be difficult to imagine the fright this would have given to some junior naval officer watching such a high-ranking commander in his care vanish from his boat. At home he would photograph blackbirds and starlings, and as noted earlier, found time to chase a pheasant in a tank. There is no doubt that this hobby helped keep his head above water during these turbulent years, as did Ferney Close with Benita, and the children who also gave him hope, reassurance and comfort. It is sometimes amusing on reading his diary to launch from global events into the life of an owl or great tit. Later, on critical trips abroad he would always find time to watch local birdlife and comment on what he had seen; it helped the human personality to emerge from the uniform respected and feared by so many.

Brooke was always meeting interesting and significant people from whom he gleaned many insights. With the secretary of state, he met the new American Ambassador John Gilbert Winant at the Ritz. Brooke was favourably impressed with the new man, and later in the war they came to know one another well. Winant had succeeded the appeaser Joseph Kennedy, and he stayed in this post until the end of the war. As a man he supported the beleaguered Britain and undoubtedly influenced Roosevelt, knew Churchill well (and Churchill's daughter and family) and he was generally appreciated for his support of the British. Brooke ate in the best places, lunching with Prince Henry and Sikorski at Claridge's, where he heard more about Eastern Europe from Sikorski's spies. The head of the SIS preferred to call them agents, but Brooke as always used direct language and went straight to the point, referring to them as spies. What caught his immediate attention at this meeting was when Sikorski suggested that the Germans were planning to attack Russia, if only because it would detract German efforts from Britain. He spoke to a Brigadier Inglis, recently returned from Crete, to learn more about German fighting tactics and methods, especially their use of airborne troops. Later he listened carefully to Mountbatten about his naval experience around the Crete disaster. He was always attentive to news from 'ground level'.

Brooke's main concern was home defence, and he was planning with the necessary London authorities an exercise, but news from Greece, Crete, Syria and North Africa clearly indicated the war was taking a new and wider direction. Brooke was resolving his problems over the matter of air-cooperation, but he was disturbed when he heard that the secretary of state was thinking of replacing Barratt with 'Stuffy' Dowding, whom Brooke considered to be a 'doubtful advantage'. Barratt had seen first-hand the way the Germans had used their airpower when he was in France with the RAF. Brooke was

General Władysław Sikorski (Martin Belam)

also suffering the same doubts about the navy, and after a Commanders-in-Chiefs meeting he wrote that it turned out 'in the long run mainly to be a meeting of moth-eaten old admirals'.[7] He seemed to hold them, unfairly, in the same light, if not contempt, as he regarded the 'retired patriotic officers' of the Home Guard.

On 22 June, the stunning news broke that Germany had invaded Russia (Operation *Barbarossa*). Brooke had once reflected on this possibility when having his photograph taken, and as mentioned above, Sikorski had revealed it, and the SIS had regarded it as likely. By the time it happened it was generally widely known that this event was possible, and only Stalin refused to believe it would happen. Nevertheless, when it occurred it came as a shock. Brooke admitted that at that time he and many others did not think Russia would survive for long, and Brooke thought it would be over by October. Because of his personal responsibilities, Brooke wondered if the German invasion of Britain would then be revitalised, hoping the winter months would at least hinder such an event. Operation *Barbarossa* had employed excellent military tactics; untold numbers of Russian prisoners had been taken, an estimated

12,000 tanks destroyed or captured, and the German Wehrmacht appeared to be almost invincible. In addition to this the Russian struggle against Finland seemed to indicate their military was weak, and Russian military strength had not been helped by Stalin's vicious purges in the mid to late 1930s. When Brooke heard the news, he realised that at least it gave him some breathing space, an opportunity to build up the army, and to think more offensively, perhaps with an eye to overseas. Brooke's diary and letters clearly indicated his singularly directed mind, dedicated to home defence. The sinking of the battleship *Hood* and then the *Bismarck*, the mysterious arrival of Hitler's deputy Hess, Crete, Greece, and even the Middle East and Syria are barely mentioned. It was not that he was unaware of these events, but they were for him less critical than the island defence, which dominated his diary during these months.

Brooke was right to consider the danger of the winter months in terms of warfare, and it was in Russia that the weather was to count as German forces ground to a halt on the outskirts of Moscow. Brooke was like so many others in thinking the Russians would collapse, and only the more astute realised the enormity of the Russian demography, landscape and potential resources which would eventually succeed and win the European war. The British military attaché in Moscow, General Mason-Macfarlane would later write to Brooke informing him that in his opinion 'the Russians would hold on and hold out in spite of great difficulties'.[8] Brooke found this difficult to believe and he was not alone in his views: respect for the German military was high, the Soviet Union was regarded as another pariah state, but Hitler's megalomaniacal nature had launched him on the road to national and personal suicide.

During the summer months of 1941 the Wehrmacht assisted by the Luftwaffe made headline success with their progress into Russia. Although Brooke knew this would give breathing space for the British to consolidate, as he watched the German success there was the constant fear in his mind that the invasion of Britain was still likely to happen in due course. He continued his routine of inspections, making notes of officers who had to be replaced, at one time noting that 'I now have a despatch case full of stuff to get rid of', the 'stuff' being senior officers.[9]

On one occasion he was flown by a pilot who limped, and only when he landed was Brooke astonished to learn that the pilot only had one leg; he did not seem to have been aware of Douglas Bader who flew fighter aircraft with no legs, and was taken as a POW the month after this diary entry. He was equally bemused watching a parade at Broome Park which used to be Lord Kitchener's home. He was, being Brooke, more fascinated by his arrival at home to find a wryneck and green woodpecker nesting in his boxes, and he decided to set up a hide to photograph them.

He was constantly planning conferences and exercises. The one mentioned earlier, an airborne exercise over London, was causing problems, and raised Brooke's temperature. Eventually it sent him spiralling into a diatribe against politicians and even questioning the value of democracy. Brooke had been asked to explain why he thought the exercise was necessary, when he had hoped he was at last making progress. However, his *bête noire*, Beaverbrook, poured 'vitriolic' criticism on the plan, and Attlee expressed concern that it would create widespread public fear. Attlee may well have been right, and some members of the public, if not warned beforehand, might understandably have seen this as enemy action making the situation hazardous. Brooke was furious, writing that politicians were always terrified by public opinion. Brooke was right and so were the politicians; most of them did and still do fear a hostile public reaction, but the public voted them in, and both politicians and military were there to defend the public, the mass of the nation. He was a very angry man and produced his own vitriol, writing that 'the more I see of democracy, the more I doubt our wisdom of attaching such importance to it!'[10] Later, in a calmer frame of mind, he retracted this view, explaining that he had at that time little experience of dealing with politicians, and wrote that Churchill was almost a dictator, just 'humouring Parliament and the Cabinet'. There was a degree of truth in this, but Churchill was aware many times during the war that an angry House of Commons could topple him. However, his singular style of leadership tended to be accepted by consensus because of the crisis, and the proof of this occurred in the victory year of 1945 when he was promptly voted out of office.

This proves to be a valuable insight into the nature of Brooke's diary keeping. It is widely accepted that Brooke was not a communist or a fascist, that he was democratic, respected the parliamentary system and recognised the prime minister as his natural boss; but one night, fed up to the back of his teeth, he simply protested, and put his deviant thoughts and vitriol into writing. He was not making a public statement, not really writing what he generally believed, but just letting off steam in a bad-tempered moment late at night. The fact that he left it in his diary underlines the integrity of the manuscripts.

His fury was rekindled the next day when he became angry with Attlee again, writing that 'dealing with frocks' was never easy.* Brooke decided that in reality it was 'impossible for soldiers and politicians ever to work satisfactorily together, they are, and always will be, poles apart.' When Eden proposed sending help to Russia Brooke decided that there had to be a move away from democracy, to 'another form of government'. This was another outburst by Brooke at those who could curb or challenge his ideas, but when he later saw the brutality of the Nazi fascist dictatorship and experienced Stalin's version of communism, he may well have considered democracy to be weak, but he knew there were no better alternatives. He probably calmed down two days later when he was happily photographing a sparrow hawk, the only bird of prey which cannot be used for hawking sport. He had to play the

---

\* 'Dealing with frocks' was the old expression for politicians who often dressed in frock coats while the military were generally known as the 'brass hats'.

part of the politician himself, as a month later he had to sit in his office to hear from Prince Henry about his plans to go to Gibraltar and the Middle East, meet an American general, have a meeting with Dill, see the king on RE matters, and meet an Andy McCullough to discuss protecting Oil Board installations. Undoubtedly, he would rather have been inspecting troops, checking their officers, watching a demonstration, or photographing a sparrow hawk, but he had responsibilities and a higher authority demanding this of him, as did politicians.

He was obviously in a contentious mood on 17 July as he watched an exercise with bombers cooperating with the army and he thought it was 'good', but adding the line he never expected 'real cooperation' because they were too independent. He cheered up two days later when a Mr Thomas showed him a model of a Bofors gun mounted on a tank, which had been his idea, and Churchill supported his pleas for an extra 100,000 men.[*] At the end of the month Brooke was reminded how popular some politicians could be when he went with Churchill to meet some of the troops, noting that he had 'an astounding reception' and 'his popularity is quite astonishing'. On 22 July Brooke paused and realised he had held this post for one year and two days, and from his own meticulous records worked out that in that time he had flown some 14,000 miles and travelled by his or other cars a further 70,000, but he did not mention his many train journeys. He may have reflected during this moment of contemplation that although Churchill was a democratic politician, he would always be more popular and better known than any single military person.

Even though the enemy was occupied in a war against Soviet Russia there remained the persistent fear of invasion, with rumours that the Germans were gathering more landing craft, and they had enough troops for a parachute drop. It prompted Churchill to warn his military to be prepared, offering the thought that 'the first hour is the only hour that matters and the first ten minutes are the minutes that matter most', and asking Brooke to consult the air staff over this issue.[11] A few days later Churchill turned up with the ditty '*Let everyone, Kill a Hun,*' and suggested everyone should be armed even with a pike or mace, and then asked if Brooke could look into this and come up with designs for such weapons.[12] Brooke never mentioned this in his diary; it was apparent that he had other pressing matters on hand than investigating medieval weapons for the romanticised views of Churchill.

It was for Brooke a challenging life of duty, a time of anxiety and often frustration. He depended on Benita and his children to keep him sane, but when he went back to Ferney Close and they were away, he described it as 'feeling like an empty shell'; he did snatch other moments of peace, fishing on the Tay, and the next day shooting grouse and hares. He met a person whom he described as an interesting Polish officer when meeting the Poles with their new tanks. He mentioned no name, but it has

---

[*] The Bofors was a 40 mm gun often just called the Bofors, and it was an anti-aircraft autocannon designed in the 1930s.

been suggested by some that it was probably General Anders, newly released from Russian captivity, who was to be of considerable military importance later. However, this speculation may be off the mark, and it was probably not Anders because in later April 1942 when he met Anders, the diary indicated it was for the first time. Brooke always had a great respect for the Poles and their military contribution.

August had its tensions, and Admiral Roger Keyes whom he had met in France, was now in charge of combined operations. This was undoubtedly supported by Churchill's idea of 'punching the Nazi on the snout' by preparing the now well-known use of commandos.* Brooke objected to the policy from the very start, feeling that such units should be part of the army; in his own words he 'made no progress with Keyes': both men were stubborn. Later in September Brooke heard of a joint planning effort to produce a 'mad scheme' for a feint attack on the Cherbourg salient to relieve pressure on the Russians. Later he visited Keyes at the Combined Operations Centre at Inveraray where he felt the training was too stereotyped. He watched a night exercise with men approaching in boats, but he found it too noisy, and could hear the approaching voices. He was never happy with this experiment, believing that commandos should not be 'divorced' from the army, but that each regular division should have its own unit of such men. He was conservative in his approach, but as he recognised that highly trained parachutists were necessary, so were commandos; it was for Brooke simply a matter of the army having control. He was first and foremost a senior general of the British army.

At a Chequers meeting the same month Churchill took him aside and explained his plans to launch an intrusive type of attack on Norway. Churchill was desperate to take the fight to the Germans, but Brooke was more interested in the home defence; that was his specific task. It was not a contentious meeting; undoubtedly Churchill had understood where Brooke stood, and Brooke wrote that Churchill was 'in a very good mood and very pleasant to argue with'.[13] Brooke was also pleased that Churchill was backing him against the reduction of forces from which the home defence was suffering. Brooke had held a conference with senior commanders a few days before, which concerned the problem of reduction and organising the troops ready for the winter months. It was only September, but the temperature was dropping, and Brooke was disappointed that the king at an excellent parade in Newmarket complained about feeling cold.

---

*   Admiral Roger Keyes had a strong naval background, was elected as a Conservative MP, and appointed as liaison officer to Leopold III of Belgium and then as the first director of combined operations. Colville, Churchill's secretary, had a low opinion of him (John Colville, *The Fringes of Power*, (London: Hodder and Stoughton, 1985) p.318) and Admiral Pound wrote claiming 'I firmly believe that the only thing he cares for is the glorification of Roger Keyes.' (Philip Zeigler, *Mountbatten, The Official Biography* (London: Collins, 1985, p.154). But Keyes was a determined servant to the country, and his death came as a result of visiting an American ship under attack by the Japanese: he died from smoke inhalation at home in December 1945.

Brooke was incredibly happy with a new trench-digging machine which could create an anti-tank ditch of nearly three-quarters of a mile in an hour. He was also busy preparing the *Bumper* exercise which would be the greatest hitherto and would be held all over the country. The purpose was to give the senior commanders an idea how to handle mobile divisions, to look at an expeditionary force, and to test the defensive measures, all of which for Brooke were more important than feint attacks on Cherbourg. He was pleased with the way the armoured divisions were making progress, but he was less certain about the ability of some commanders to handle them. It was a constant problem for Brooke finding the right commanders; many of them were too old and not up to date.

In America they used to joke about the British military as Colonel Blimps, but Brooke often had the same feeling, content with them in the Home Guard, but not in senior positions in the British army. The caricature of the Colonel Blimp was widespread, prompting George Orwell to return to his suspicions of some elements of the upper class when ruminating on treachery in the higher command; he did not believe it was widespread but thought it existed only 'in the pro-fascist element of the aristocracy and perhaps in the army command'.[14] Orwell believed the only hope was 'getting the whole thing into a new class basis'; it was all a matter of what he called 'unblimping'. He continued this theme by asking the question as to why England with one of the smallest armies in the world still had so many retired colonels. Orwell was famous for his left-wing views, and he would not have been surprised had he read Brooke's outburst against British democracy, but Orwell may have been perceptive about the reliance having to be placed on 'old timers'. Brooke often pondered the lack of good officer material, and he ruminated on the probability that the best had been killed in the Great War, appeasing his mind that the politicians had the very same problem, and that the retired colonels were not the pick of the bunch.

At the beginning of October Brooke was presented with another problem, which was the prime minister's growing obsession of attacking Hitler in Norway at Trondheim. The only reason which Brooke could elicit from him for this plan was that Hitler had unfolded the map of Europe starting in Norway, which was where Churchill said he wanted to 'start its refolding'. Brooke was concerned that this was a madcap idea, but the American historian Gerhard Weinberg has suggested that it could have been valuable, and that the Germans were worried about such an attack.[15] Given the long sea route and the complexity of amphibious landings Brooke was probably right to oppose the policy, and Weinberg, for once, wrong. Churchill, however, with his usual demands wanted prepared plans within a week, so with Dill they had to make their way to Chequers to meet Dudley Pound, Portal and Attlee. In the years to come Churchill would often come up with ideas which the COS rejected, and, as Liddell Hart once noted, there were never occasions when Churchill overruled the COS decisions, but he certainly tried to manipulate them.

There is a suggestion that Churchill tried to use Brooke to out-manoeuvre the COS Chiefs, but Brooke found himself in agreement with them.

Brooke argued against the scheme, pointing out, quite reasonably, that such was the distance the troops would not have the support of airpower. This could mean a repeat of the previous disaster, and for Brooke it was sheer folly. The Chiefs of Staff ruled out the scheme as impractical, but Churchill was not a man to drop his ideas easily. Brooke was given charge of the plans and had to appoint a commander for the attack, but as far as Brooke was concerned it was sheer recklessness. He made it clear that he would need to call meetings of the commanders of the navy and RAF and they would have to cooperate; he was assured this would be the case. He personally thought it was 'a good deal of wasted time' and was more interested in the nationwide Exercise *Bumper*. Despite the prime ministerial pressure, he still found time and enjoyment in building a goat-cart for his two children, Pooks and Ti as he called them: Ti (to him) was his son Victor and Pooks was Katherine, his daughter.

The day after his home visit he held a conference on the Norway project, managed to attend Dill's wedding, and talked about Exercise *Bumper*. with Montgomery, because there was to be a major conference on this subject two days later.* He was summoned at first to Chequers, but it was changed to 10 Downing Street to discuss the Norwegian plans, which Brooke still found unfavourable and a waste of time. Churchill was unhappy about Brooke's views on the policy and the plans, many of Brooke's criticisms based understandably on the lack of air-support. Churchill complained that instead of studying detailed plans Brooke had 'submitted a masterly treatise on all the difficulties'. Brooke found the meeting like an 'unpleasant grilling' as Churchill demanded answers and evidence to every point raised, but later added that it 'was a good experience for what the future held'.[16] It was not to be the only time Churchill would suggest such ventures which Brooke thought 'mad', and Churchill's critics often point out that Gallipoli 1915 and Norway 1940 had been similar disasters of Churchill's making.

Brooke relieved himself of the experience by watching an exercise designed to raid the French coast at night; the men had to wear blue goggles because to them it was darkness, and not the sunlight the observers were bathed in. Brooke found it a good exercise and was somewhat impressed. However, the Norwegian question would not go away. The Canadian McNaughton turned up in Brooke's office and informed him the prime minister had asked to see him about Norway, and McNaughton was curious to know if Brooke knew what the matter was all about. Brooke explained the background surmising that Churchill was going to turn to the Canadians, which McNaughton would, he hoped, oppose. When McNaughton returned to Brooke as requested, he looked 'ghastly weakened', acknowledging that he had been beaten into agreeing to study the plans. Opposing Churchill was never

---

* Dill's first wife had died from a series of strokes mentioned earlier, on 22 November 1940.

easy; even the strongest characters found his forceful personality difficult to handle. McNaughton, to Brooke's relief, told him that he had already communicated with the Canadian prime minister warning him not to agree. As Brooke observed, Churchill was tenacious, and he was constantly battering at the door for agreement from the military for his sudden ideas.

Near the end of October Brooke started to hear rumours that Dill was to be replaced as the CIGS, probably, he suspected, caused by his *bête noire*, Beaverbrook, whom he suspected of influencing Churchill. It would appear though that Dill and Churchill were temperamental opposites, and they were simply out of tune with one another. The growing animosity Churchill felt towards Dill continued to rise, and in September 1941 Colville wrote in his diary that 'incidentally he [Churchill] has now got his knife into Dill and frequently disparages him. He says he has an alternative CIGS in mind, i.e. Brooke…he went on to say we cannot afford military failures.'[17] Brooke and Dill had become personal friends, and more to the point Brooke admired Dill's intellect, his grasp of military concerns, and his ability to understand the wider picture. Brooke could not understand why Dill was being replaced on the grounds that he had reached the age of 60, when Pound was 64 and Churchill 67 years of age; he recognised this as a mere excuse. The rumour was that a senior officer, General Pile, was to take his place, and when Brooke heard that another officer, General Nye, had spent time with Beaverbrook this deepened other suspicions; it must have felt like operating in the old Byzantium or Borgia courts. Brooke liked Pile in so far that he was a sound officer, but felt he was not right for CIGS.

On 26 October Brooke was back in Chequers which proved to be a long night, with Churchill dressed in a colourful dressing gown, reminding Brooke of Joseph's coat in the Old Testament. As October turned to November, Brooke watched an impressive airborne display and saw what such a unit could do. He also noted that Mountbatten was to take over from Keyes as adviser to Combined Operations, and at a conference he held a discussion on the withdrawal of tanks for the Middle East and Russia.* As always Brooke suspected Beaverbrook of interfering. He visited Devonshire House where wireless interception in those early days was being carried out. He thought it was very good but suspected they still had a 'long way to go to catch up with the Germans'.[18] Most historians would agree with Brooke as it seemed evident that the Abwehr tended to have the upper hand during the first two years of the war; but this soon changed.† He also enjoyed what he called Churchill's 'Christmas present' by being offered the use of his own train, which he found not only comfortable but useful.

---

* The word 'adviser' was used because Keyes had clashed with the COS, seeing himself as directly responsible to Churchill and not COS, so they gave the title adviser rather than director; see Philip Zeigler, *Mountbatten, The Official Biography* (London: Collins, 1985) p.154.

† The Abwehr was German military intelligence, run at this time by Admiral Canaris.

## Appointed CIGS

In the meantime the chatter about replacing Dill was increasing, and apart from Pile the name Paget popped up, which Brooke described as a potential 'tragedy and a definite step towards losing the war'; another name was Nye whom Brooke considered a 'good officer but too junior'.[19] According to Kennedy, Churchill listened to Dill who thought Brooke was 'too narrow'. Kennedy believed this view was 'perhaps well-founded at that time, but Brooke was eventually to develop in a quite remarkable way as so many good men when given responsibility.'[20] In the end Dill supported Brooke as the best candidate with the help of Margesson, with Kennedy later remarking, 'I thought the politicians did not, perhaps, realise what they had taken on, for Brooke was tough and impatient.'[21]

Brooke was invited to Chequers again on 16 November in the company of Mountbatten, Pug Ismay and others, but Churchill later in the evening took him aside and informed Brooke he wanted him as the CIGS. Brooke described how he met the question with silence which Churchill misconstrued; when Churchill had once been asked if he could serve under Halifax, he conveyed his negative answer by silence. Brooke was silent because he felt sad about Dill leaving and he had enjoyed overseeing the Home Forces. He disliked being the man who pushed Dill out, and he had self-doubts as to how he would handle Churchill, but he was also, like all men, ambitious. Churchill broke the silence with 'Do you think you will be able to work with me? We have so far got on well together.' Brooke had no issue with Churchill because he respected him, but he knew it would be a rough ride as the Norwegian project had recently demonstrated, knowing that there would be times when he would have to withstand the 'storms of abuse' thrown at him. He would be launched from the domestic Home Forces into the vast global scene, and he wrote that 'the consequences of failures or mistakes are a nightmare to think about'.[22] He knew it was not the best of times as Britain still stood alone, and unlike Brooke, Churchill was impetuous, and there was in Brooke's opinion still a possibility of invasion. He accepted the post, and when Churchill left his room, he admitted that although he was not an 'exceptionally religious man' he fell to his knees and prayed for help. This was a duty he felt he had to do, adding in his diary that there was 'no sense of happiness simply because I was at the top of the ladder'. The other two Chiefs were not overwhelmed with delight at Brooke's appointment because they had found him 'too abrupt, over forceful and tactless' let alone being 'hawk-faced'.[23] In his six-volume war history Churchill tended to make few personal comments on Brooke, as noted in the Introduction, making more references to him when he was a field commander in France, but he added the telling line on this appointment that Brooke 'stayed with me to the end'.[24] Churchill's secretary and confidant John Colville later wrote that 'to take Dill's place at the War Office Churchill chose a man of tougher fibre and less compromising disposition', noting that Brooke had worked with Dill and Gort in France and 'he had the better brain'.[25] Colville also added the interesting note that 'Brooke liked business to be conducted in an orderly fashion and Churchill, as often as not, was the reverse of orderly', not a prescient view because this was a postwar observation, but nevertheless, true.[26]

Brooke had been right to be suspicious of Beaverbrook because he had tried to influence Churchill to consider Nye, and it was Dill who had dissuaded the prime minister. Not everyone agreed with Brooke's appointment, and Portal thought that Brooke would be too abrasive, often stating 'I disagree' and snapping his pencil, but in times of crisis this sort of challenge from informed people was often needed. Later Portal would change his mind, but he, like others, often found Brooke somewhat tactless. However, even when he was made chairman of the COS, Brooke never tried to override the other two chiefs; like him they had both experienced the nature of combat within their spheres of expertise, and both men were tough and experienced. Brooke could be tactless, but he was not attending some social dinner party. He was welcomed to the post by many, some possibly serving their own needs, others genuine. Brooke always replied, even when answering a letter to an assistant cook in the Merchant Navy, almost in terms of the intimacy of two colleagues.[27]

Paget and Brooke were due for a week's leave, but Churchill intervened, and Paget was asked to stay on duty while Brooke had the rest of the month to return home and recuperate ready for the gigantic tasks ahead of him. As a young subaltern in Ireland and India Brooke barely changed ranks for years, merely passing his captain's examinations, but the Great War and the next had accelerated his promotion to the top, based on his professionalism, his sense of duty, his sheer dedication, and simply being a strong and tough character who would be able to work alongside, and if necessary challenge Churchill, despite the tension it would cause. Later Churchill would note their habitual 'ups and downs', writing that during Brooke's long tenure as chairman of COS in which 'he rendered services of the highest order, not only to the British Empire but to the Allied Cause…these volumes will record occasional differences between us, but also an overwhelming measure of agreement, and will witness to a friendship I still cherish.'[28] Sometimes these agreements would be few, and the friendship was strained both during and after the war, but it was, as Kennedy observed, good fortune that Brooke was thick-skinned compared to Dill who was sensitive.[29]

## CIGS and COS

The position of the COS and CIGS developed more significance as World War II started.[*] It became much more than an advisory body as the War Cabinet was

---

[*] In brief, the British became aware during the 19th century that the Prussians had an effective centralised system of army control, not reliant on the localised regiment system. In 1907 the

Chiefs of Staff, 1943 (IWM TR 2839)

reborn, and thereby part of the supreme directory of military operations, which had not happened in the Great War, and the wider global aspect of World War II made it essential. There were in 1939–45 greater permutations of strategy right across the globe; this had all been part of Brooke's training at the Imperial Defence College. The question has often been asked as to where the genius and impulsive Churchill, who relied on instinct, would have been without the relationship with Brooke, known for his professional approach to strategy. In short, when Brooke had the backing of the COS, Churchill felt obliged to listen. Even so he always paid attention to Brooke's views even when he disagreed; it was built into the nature of the COS and the CIGS structure.

principle of an Imperial General Staff was adopted following an Imperial Conference, and in 1909 this was broadened to include a 'Chief'. It was somewhat lost during the turmoil of the Great War but reborn in the interbellum years. It had basically indicated a professional elite; the Prussians wearing a broad red strip down their trousers, in the British army the 'red tabs' made their appearance. The chief was a *primus inter pares* and became an adviser to the secretary of state for war, and professional head of the British army.

There is one special aspect of strategy which needs to be understood, which was shared by Churchill, Brooke, and other significant figures in high command. It is sometimes referred to as the 'strategic culture' namely the ethos appertaining to a nation, and it is 'critical to understand how nations view, consider, and react to national security threat' based on their culture and experience.[30] All countries have a different approach, usually influenced by their geography, history, their immediate previous experience, and their own culture and attitudes. Britain as a small island situated off the west coast of the European mainland, with larger and more powerful continental countries, had for the last millennium successfully defended its shores from invasion by the existence of the English Channel and its use of sea-power. Britain had (and still retains) a unique system of a constitutional monarchy, and during this period, it held in these years a massive global empire, depended on trade and the naval force, often referred to as the Senior Service, which was of paramount importance, and for centuries had the command of the seas. Britain's safety as a nation both in security terms and economic survival depended on the sea. Liddell Hart noted the importance of the link between the necessary economic demands of a small island with a large population and its maritime power. To survive Britain needed constant imports and the control of the seas guaranteed this necessity. This naval-economic relationship had long been considered a critical component. On the other hand, the British army, as old and traditional as it was, tended to be used more as a police force governing the empire. It was this factor which led to the 1938 situation of the British army being so small and widely dispersed around the globe.* When, historically, continental problems emerged, the British maintained a tradition of aligning themselves with another power or manoeuvring powerful alliances, and were always content to send a smaller or token force across the Channel.

Sir Michael Howard wrote that the 'command of the seas and maintenance of a European balance were in fact, not alternative policies…but interdependent…as Britain formed a tradition of strategic organisational coordination.'[31] There is little doubt that 'Brooke was wedded to the traditional British strategy of weakening Continental powers by blockade and peripheral operations, carried out in areas where the enemy found it most difficult.'[32] Before and after the Napoleonic Wars the truth of this policy can be discerned.

This was precisely what Brooke would later hope for in the Mediterranean and Italian theatres of operations. After the invasion of Sicily more than 40 Axis divisions had to be withdrawn from other fronts, and the number of German divisions in Italy rose from 12 to 18, to say nothing of the demand on Luftwaffe resources, according

---

* 'It has often been said the British Army does not exist, that it is in fact only a loose federation of military tribes…this is usually in order to explain its peculiarities to American military colleagues and is said only half in jest.' See A. J. Trythall in David French & Brian Holden Reid, *The British General Staff, Reform and Innovation, c.1890–1939* (London: Frank Cass Publishers, 2002) p.119.

to Bryant, who alluded to this cultural strategy without mentioning the term or understanding its significance.[33] The concept of a British cultural strategy was imbued subconsciously into Brooke and many others, and it was, given Britain's size and status as an island, a sober pragmatic viewpoint. This was later epitomised by clashes with the Americans, with their developing cultural strategy, who envisaged the destruction of Nazi power through a direct route to Berlin. British cultural strategy looked to bombing, blockading, and wearing away the enemy on the periphery until the enemy was weakened by this policy, along with the powerful allied Russian land forces, before an invasion of France dared to be contemplated. When Brooke was elected chairman of the COS, he was *primus inter pares*, and despite the ups and downs of the three services they all tended to retain this traditional and cultural strategy.

One of the first tasks for the COS, and Brooke in particular, was to prepare for a continental war of different proportions, with the problems of a small volunteer army against the mass conscripted army of Germany, and 'a practical military preparation being reconciled with political detachment' and how it could be deployed on the Continent.[34] The army, as mentioned, had policed the empire – indeed with the navy won the empire – but now had to change roles. 'The General Staff demonstrated a high level of independent judgement and professional common sense in dealing with an uncertain and politically sensitive set of variables' as times rapidly changed.[35]

The three distinct services in the COS structure were expected to co-operate, not least because of the need to win the war for their country. As such these men and the various committees became the main engine for the control of the war and as the years passed, they became more critical. During the war years the COS was frequently associated with Brooke who was the long-term chairman, but they were not widely known by the public. There were many sub-committees and staff, and later the chief of Combined Operations (now Mountbatten) frequently joined, and although there is no perfect way to conduct the mayhem of war, this machinery worked well most of the time. Mountbatten's inclusion in the COS was not welcomed by the other members, and Pound wrote his objections to the prime minister.[36]

Later there was a Combined Chiefs of Staff in Washington (CCOS) and Dill would become the resident British member. This COS system would have been unthinkable in Germany which had its OKW, but Generals Keitel and Jodl would never dare question Hitler, and field commanders who did were soon in serious trouble. Churchill may have fought with the COS, and it was never easy when the British and Americans met as the Combined COS, with manoeuvrings by both sides. However, there was at least the scope to raise questions, put forward new strategies, to do so with good intentions and not be hampered by fear of arguing the issue with the political leaders. Later, in the spring of 1942, the Americans drew up a confidential memo on the three British chiefs, describing Brooke as a 'suave, intelligent, politico', Portal as 'having lots of ability imbued with offensive spirit... interest in creating tremendous and essentially British airpower', and Pound as 'a tired old gentleman, straightforward, quixotic, an eminently successful naval officer of the old school'.[37] This was a reasonably astute appraisal. The COS met every day, sometimes twice, and an estimate indicates that during the war years they met nearly two and a half thousand times.

## Brooke as CIGS

Brooke's main task was regarded as twofold: he had to think along the lines of grand strategy on a global basis, and secondly keep a tough watching brief over the army. He was overseeing the rapid expansion of the British army after its appalling reduction in the interbellum years, organising its modernisation which was so desperately needed. There was a third skill demanded of him, namely his communication abilities with other commanders and politicians. In his obituary many years later *The Times* wrote: 'He possessed a gift for lucid explanation and exposition which was an invaluable asset at international conferences and also enabled him to succeed in the task in which so many soldiers have failed of talking convincingly to the politician.'[38] The writer of this obituary was correct in many ways, but it was never an easy or straightforward task, especially given Brooke's propensity to speak his mind, and demonstrate sometimes too bluntly when he disagreed with other points of view. It would lead to moments, as Brooke had predicted, that he would clash with Churchill, a man with whom he could become furious but whom he always respected. Churchill, being Churchill, often wrote to commanders in the field asking about what was happening and asking for their plans. Churchill regarded this as the prime minister's right, but he often warned the field commanders that they had to keep the CIGS in the same picture. Leading politicians had the right to dictate the overall strategy for the military who were the servants to the nation, this did not infer, as Churchill often did, that they had the right to interfere in the minutiae of military command structure.

There is no doubt as the years unfolded that Brooke could be tough and sometimes hard on subordinates whom he thought lacking in depth, especially the more senior men. When he made an appearance, people were alert to his presence, and 'he did not induce relaxation'.[39] He was quick in language, in thought, and expected others to be the same. This was probably why he was so often angry with Admiral Dudley Pound when he was the chairman, who was well known for taking his time. Above all Brooke always had a sense of necessary urgency, and he was expected to understand the wider nature of the war and in the necessary detail. This sounds easy in theory and with hindsight, but in the turmoil and mayhem of sudden or gathering events it needed a man of considerable military and intellectual stature.

December 1941 was a highly significant time for world events and for Brooke. Dill was due to give up as the CIGS on Christmas Day but from 1 December Brooke took over the reins, pausing on the 25th to note that he was now officially the CIGS. On 7 December, the Japanese attacked the Americans at Pearl Harbor and Churchill declared war on Japan instantly, clearly delighted that this event would forcibly draw America from its isolation. This major event was heard by Brooke over the radio, and the potential ramifications were so immense that Churchill immediately made plans to fly to America with his CAS (Chief of Air Staff), and Brooke managed to persuade Churchill to take Dill with him, and leave him there as their representative. This took some considerable persuasion as Churchill was not overly fond of Dill, but as events were to unfold it was a sound proposal. There was also the added burden of how to keep the Australians from withdrawing their men from the Middle East, and from taking their cruisers back for the protection of their own homeland with the Japanese threat emerging, which was quite logical. Brooke's work now placed him at a quite different level; instead of worrying about gun placements on the south-east corner of Britain he was thinking about Hong Kong, and he made the percipient observation that Singapore was likely to fall. His diary and letters were always from his angle of events, and as broad as they had now become, they reflected his main concerns, or what he deemed to be the priorities, which dominated his writings. The fact that the Red Army had launched a counter-offensive, the German military machine was indicating some of the first signs of faltering, and Field Marshal Walter Brauchitsch had resigned and Hitler had made himself commander-in-chief of the army went unobserved, because the main issue for Brooke was Eden's proposed visit to Russia and what gifts he should take with him. Even the information that Germany and Italy had declared war on the Americans (11 December) went unobserved, although Brooke would have recognised the potential significance of these events. It is a reminder that although Brooke's diary is a useful tool for historians, it was not and never meant to be a history book.

Brooke was naturally consumed in his efforts by trying to cope with a much broader picture than the Home Front Defence had required. It was fortunate that he was the sort of person who held a watching brief on wider events, and his friend Dill had always kept him in touch with the global scene. He had previously discussed with Dill the possibility of America joining the war, and the need not to provoke the Japanese who were clearly seen as a serious threat to the British colonies in the Far East. Prior to the events of Pearl Harbor, Halifax was sending back reports that his conversations with Roosevelt were going well, and Churchill, as is well known, had maintained a steady and growing friendship with the American president. As noted above, in early December Brooke's main concern was Eden's proposed visit to 'Uncle Joe Stalin' and what gifts he should take with him. There were many differences of opinion on this meeting, with Churchill suggesting the 18th and 50th Divisions should be offered to the Russians for their southern front, a gift of the newly developed tanks, even aircraft, all of which Brooke was unhappy about. Eden was desperate to take gifts, Churchill wanted him to take much, but Brooke was uncertain, having decided that North Africa and keeping the Mediterranean free for naval and shipping communications was essential. Had troops been sent to the Eastern Front, where life was cheap and thousands of men lost daily, it would have had serious ramifications on the political front. The British public were accustomed to their troops fighting British battles, not being used as a military-political gift.

Only a few months before Brooke had been sceptical about losing forces to North Africa and the Middle East, but now his perceptions of priorities were changing. Historians will long debate the policy of the British in North Africa and later Italy, some seeing it as essential and others as diversionary. This is not the subject of this study of Brooke, which merely observes that his promotion to the senior role changed his perspectives. He had been the caretaker of national security; now he was responsible not just for home defence, but all the wider dimensions on a global basis. It also marked the beginning of a turbulent relationship with Churchill, of whom Brooke wrote that 'planning strategy was not Winston's strong card'; this was to be a persistent tension for years to come.[40] During the discussions about what gifts Eden should take, Brooke noted that Churchill simply lost his temper, closed his file, and walked out of the room; Brooke described it as 'pathetic' but put it down to overwork.

Two days before he heard about the Japanese attack, Brooke had decided to meet the various military attachés. He had found the Japanese looking somewhat 'gloomy' and on hearing the news of Pearl Harbor, he made the laconic remark that he and his fellow chiefs had wasted time meeting them, because 'the Japanese had done it for them' – that is, they had brought a potential major ally into the war. Churchill went into action at once, making arrangements to travel to America, which at first Roosevelt resisted, but it went ahead, and trying to convince the Irish leader Éamon de Valera to join the war; he would never be successful with the Irish.* Brooke was rightly concerned that America, under threat from the Far East, might withdraw the resources which had been arriving in Britain, because of the need for the nation's own defence.

There were a series of frenetic meetings to discuss the immediate future and the necessary reactions. Churchill was working out who to take to America with him, and Brooke was 'to be left in the saddle' at home, as chairman of the COS, with Attlee as acting prime minister. Brooke accepted this role but was unhappy about the situation. There was the concern that the Japanese had control of the seas, and Churchill insisted that the battleships the *Prince of Wales* and the *Repulse* should be dispatched to the East at once, where they were instantly attacked by aircraft and sunk. As Brooke noted, to all effect the British had lost their customary control of the seas. There was some anxiety over Churchill's health; he had been complaining

---

\* Éamon de Valera was an Irish patriot who kept Ireland out of the war, although many Southern Irishmen volunteered to fight with the British. De Valera shocked the world when on Hitler's death he went to the German Embassy to sign the book of condolences. He knew there would be ramifications but 'even he was taken aback by the international outcry'.

Charles de Gaulle in Conference (Musée de la libération)

of pain, which caused Brooke concern, because despite the tensions and conflicts he recognised that Churchill was the man for the moment.

He had to see de Gaulle, whom he described as 'a horrible specimen', and the issue of Madagascar was discussed with a concern that the Japanese might invade that island. Plans were studied, and Brooke was concerned because de Gaulle demanded to help, which Brooke saw as 'an encumbrance'; he also had to cope with Duff Cooper's criticisms of General Percival's defence plans for Singapore. The Far East was a major point of concern when on 20 December news arrived that Hong Kong was half-invaded, and on Christmas Eve the news broke that it had fallen. Brooke was also concerned about Churchill's machinations in America, with his various schemes for co-ordinating the war which Brooke described as 'wild and half-baked'. Brooke believed there had to be a global organisation, and not dividing the world into small areas of concern, with Wavell suggested as being responsible for huge swathes of the Far East; this perspective always dominated his thinking even into the immediate postwar months. He was also busy trying to persuade the Australians not to return home and to understand the broader global picture. Brooke was looking for a unified and singular control centre, while Churchill was at least stirring the action and firing on all cylinders.

Brooke noted on Christmas Day that he was now officially the CIGS, worked all day (having a break at Ferney Close on the 28th) and in the quieter moments reflected on the increased enormity and importance of his work. The Japanese attack, Germany's declaration of war on America, and news that Russia was beginning to hold against the German attack, marked this month as a possible turning point from despair to hope. Russia showing signs of halting the Wehrmacht, and Hitler's inane declaration of war, meant Britain was no longer alone.

## CHAPTER 6

# 1942

## Taking up the Reins

At the beginning of the New Year Brooke moved into a new flat at No. 7, Westminster Gardens, where he stayed until the end of the war; its proximity to the centre of command was essential. His ADC (aide de camp) was a Barney Charlesworth who even supplied some of his own furniture to make the place comfortable for Brooke. It is clear from his personal notes that Brooke was fond of this man, whom he could talk with openly because he was as 'tight as a clam'. He and Barney were to become close personal friends. He had always found his cousin Bertie an ideal trusted outlet, and he felt much the same with Charlesworth; Brooke needed someone with whom he could let off steam, which was also the impetus behind his diary keeping for his beloved Benita.

He met Eden on his return from Soviet Russia and was fascinated to hear about Stalin's drunken dinners with his senior commanders; later when he experienced the same situation, he was less certain about the more amusing aspect of these drink-sodden gatherings. He also heard from William Tennant, the captain of the *Repulse*, and was informed that the Japanese aircraft had spotted his battleship at 11 a.m., and within an hour and a half it had been sunk. The growing importance of aircraft in warfare, even at sea, was not lost on him and others. The global aspect of the war with the Japanese belligerence had caused many to consider the safety of Madagascar as mentioned, but also the island of Timor which the Australians had occupied to the annoyance of the so-called owners, the Portuguese. Consideration was given to asking the Americans to occupy the Falklands, but there was the nagging concern that they would take control, and later hand the islands back to Argentina. The overseas colonies and empire still preoccupied the thinking of many powers, especially Britain, and America, a one-time British colony, held a deep suspicion and distaste of empire building by the Europeans.

During this month of January, starting on the 3rd and discussed at the Washington Conference, various forms of command spheres were mulled over, the main one being ABDA, standing for American, British, Dutch and Australian interests, projected as the way forward with Wavell being made responsible. Dill was unhappy about Wavell's projected appointment because he thought there were soon going to be a series of impending disasters. Whether he was concerned about his friend Wavell or that he would not cope, is not clear. Brooke was somewhat critical of this broad picture, feeling Burma, which had a long border with India, should not have been included, but he thought it should have been linked with ANZAC making it a single unit; he raised this with Churchill once he returned. Life was hectic, with Attlee looking for a new commander-in-chief for India; the Canadian troops, of whose leadership Brooke had been so critical, were still a growing concern; and he met Harry Crerar about its future organisation. Amongst all these administrative decisions which had to be made, he asked that wireless intercepts should become wider to listen into Japanese sources, he met the Northern Ireland prime minister to discuss the projected arrival of American troops (they arrived on 26 January), and the possibility of an Ulster Force moving into Eire in the event of an invasion. Whether he was thinking in terms of Ireland (Eire) being invaded, or Britain, or both, is not clear. George Orwell in his war diary thought the Germans might invade Eire, but with the dominance or rather the German fear of the Royal Navy, this was an unlikely risk.

Churchill returned from his American visit on 17 January, and the next day Brooke was invited to dine with him and Mrs Churchill with their daughter. It was a pleasant experience, and afterwards they withdrew to discuss Churchill's apprehensions about Singapore, giving Brooke the opportunity to raise his concerns about the importance of Rangoon and Burma generally. They both recognised the significance of Singapore if they were to wage any form of successful war in the Far East. A week later he was called to Churchill's bedroom, where he was wearing a red dragon type dressing gown, looking like a 'Chinese Mandarin' with a huge cigar in his mouth, surrounded with piles and papers and notes. Churchill needed to discuss their views on the question of ABDA mentioned above. At the next Chiefs of Staff meeting this was raised, but Brooke was once again annoyed that Dudley Pound seemed to be incapable of seeing the problem. As this was taking place Churchill won a vote of confidence in Parliament with a staggering victory of 464 to only one dissenter.

The wider picture, however, did not feel good with Benghazi lost again, and Singapore looking dubious regarding its safety. As he reflected on the situation in the Middle East, he became more concerned about General Claude Auchinleck's ability; he had always considered him a sound man, but Brooke thought that he too often chose the wrong type of men to serve him. Brooke was especially concerned by a staff officer called 'Chink' Dorman-Smith who, Brooke felt, was clever but not tuned into the demands of war. He was also aware and deeply worried that Rommel always seemed to have the upper hand and knew precisely what the British were planning.* In the confusion of war it was sensible to have a man like Brooke with an overview of what was happening, even if at times he appeared tactless and somewhat critical; the war was not just about promotions and demotions, but national survival. In all this toil and tribulation Brooke still enjoyed a day at home 'glass blowing' with the children.

Churchill was refreshed and renewed after his American trip, which was later referred to as the First Washington Conference, and sometimes the Arcadia Conference (a name often associated with pastoral paradise and in Greek mythology the home of Pan), because it at long last fulfilled Churchill's wish of having the Americans on side, being able to discuss a joint strategy; the meeting remained secretive over its intentions and plans. As noted above, Brooke had not gone on this occasion, having been left to take care of matters at home, but this precluded him from involvement in matters of major decision making. It also gave time for Dill, whose next task was to act in the role of British ambassador in military matters, to come to know Marshall and most of the American leaders. Marshall and Dill became close friends, so close some were concerned that Dill may have started to see matters all too much from the American perspective, or to use the expression used at the time, that he 'had gone native'. This was not entirely true, and because the Americans liked Dill so much, they were prepared to listen to him, and he carefully kept Brooke and Churchill informed during the coming years. Brooke's suggestion to Churchill that Dill was the right person for this post paid huge dividends; his work was invaluable in maintaining a sense of Anglo-American unity.

The most important aspect of this conference was the eventual agreement that Germany was the principal enemy and had to have priority. This would have been one of Churchill's great achievements because not all the senior American commanders agreed with this proposal, and it produced the invaluable Combined Chiefs of Staff (CCOS) which tussled out the long-term and necessary global strategies. The British promised to strengthen their forces in the Far East, and the Americans, perhaps half-heartedly, came to terms with the British over North Africa, and even the possibility of invading Sicily. The Americans would send some troops, establish bomber bases and a combination of resources, which was behind the uncomfortable ABDA agreement. However, the Americans never lost their suspicion of Churchill's love of empire, and they remembered Gallipoli as another time when Churchill tried

---

* What Brooke did not know was that a US military attaché in Cairo, a Colonel Bonner Frank Fellers, was sending constant reports back to General George Marshall in Washington. These were comprehensive reports including locations, casualties, intentions, and plans; what he did not realise was that the US diplomatic code he was using had long been broken and accessed by the Germans. Until Fellers was removed in July 1942 his information was unbelievably valuable to Rommel. This was a mishap and not the work of a traitor.

the 'soft-underbelly' approach. They always wanted to punch directly into Germany and foresaw 1943 as the year they could cross the Channel and head for Berlin. This would be a later headache for Brooke because he was a hard-nosed realist, a pragmatist, imbued with the British cultural strategy, and knew that this would take time and huge resources.

As the year 1942 opened Brooke had managed to make the Home Defence more reliable; he was building up the army, and pressing for more and more resources and manpower. In the Middle East they had built up a formidable armoured force, and thanks to the colonies and dominions they had more men there than Brooke could have dreamt possible a year earlier. The British army in North Africa, now known as the Eighth Army, was under Cunningham, but he was replaced by Ritchie, probably because he was suffering from sheer exhaustion.

Taking the fight to Germany directly, as the Americans wished, could still only be done by bombing. Airpower was becoming more and more critical; it had demonstrated some early potential during the Great War, but technical development had made the military power of the plane of growing importance. The Germans had utilised its Luftwaffe in a simple and direct fashion which became known as *Blitzkrieg*: the elimination, stage by stage, of each and every obstacle which might frustrate the freedom of movement of the ground forces. It was an art of war, which attributed to any airpower almost every possibility except that of occupation of enemy territory. 'It was ideal for the type of continental warfare which the German High Command had planned.'[1] It was also claimed by the German Luftwaffe commander Wever that if there were to be a war against Czechoslovakia the Douhetian use of airpower could break the enemy's will.*

All these points were valid, as Brooke understood; bombing could destroy industry, possibly break a nation's willpower, and could assist ground troops which was Brooke's main intention. The Germans had deployed tactical bombing, hitting ports and industrial complexes, but such was the state of bomb-aiming devices it appeared more like strategic or carpet bombing. From 1940 strategic bombing was assumed to be the role of airpower which the Allies quickly adopted; it remains a contentious issue to this day, but Brooke was watching the nature of war changing rapidly. It has been noted that 'at no stage did Kennedy, Brooke or anyone else in the decision-making reaches of the High Command ever employ humanitarian considerations among their reasons for why the aerial bombardment policy was mistaken.'[2] Later the main concerns tended to relate to the high loss of life amongst aircrew, the financial implications and resources, and the possibility that air attack would be better deployed in support of military operations on land and sea. Attempts at tactical bombing of oil installations, railway communication and factories for ball-bearings and war materials were severely

---

* Manstein, after the war, wrote that he did not believe Douhet's theory of winning by strategic bombing, pointing out that neither Britain nor Germany succumbed; see Erich von Manstein, *Lost Victories* (Minneapolis: Zenith, 1982) p.158.

hampered by the lack of development in precision bombing. It appeared that Marshal Sir Arthur (Bomber) Harris was not that popular, and the COS could have ordered him to change policy. 'They never did.'[3] It had become a total war of retribution, hatred, national survival, and the desperate need for final victory ruled out humanitarian reasoning.* This was later typified by Harris when he wrote about Churchill's worry about bombing French civilians prior to D-Day Normandy: 'I couldn't give a damn if I killed Frenchmen. They should have been fighting the war for themselves.'[4] The hatred was visceral, and the normally forgiving Churchill when he saw the damage created by an aerial mine in Wandsworth, exploded with 'we should castrate the lot of them' and there will be no talk of a 'just peace'.

However, as noted, men like Field Marshal Kesselring and Brooke knew that to win there had to be army boots on the ground. Brooke was also equally aware of the battle in the Atlantic with the U-boats attacking the convoys, as essential major resources and troops poured across from America to Britain. There was now a renewed hope in so far that America and Russia were fighting the same enemy, but the Far Eastern theatre had made the situation somewhat darker. Brooke was Europe orientated, and he understood that the Germans knew probably better than anyone else how to conduct a war with well-trained professional soldiers and excellent commanding officers. This year of 1942 offered some hope, but Brooke knew that it was never going to be easy, and he was correct.

During February the devastating news of the fall of Singapore (15th) came through, the Australians for the first time in their history were in danger with the bombing of Darwin (19th), and Java was under threat as was Malta in the Mediterranean. The possibility of losing the key port of Singapore led to serious political challenges over the efficacy and fighting spirit of the British troops, and when challenged by politicians in the Cabinet meeting, Brooke admitted he found it hard to 'keep his temper'. It was not helped by Churchill who joined in the attack and who asked, 'Have you got a single general in that army who can win battles, have none of them any ideas?'[5] Brooke was furious about this approach as he found it detrimental in a time of crisis which could lead to a loss of confidence. Churchill himself had to face a questioning Parliament over Singapore. There was a lack of sensitivity by the politicians in this issue, as sitting in a Whitehall office was hugely different from the experience of soldiers thousands of miles away fighting for their lives against an horrific onslaught, by a dedicated and vicious enemy. To the bitter end the Japanese soldiers were to prove to be difficult opponents. This left Brooke in a foul mood, and he was unnecessarily rude to Ernest Bevin, but they made it up over dinner and Brooke found Bevin to be a 'very great man'. Brooke knew well that he was too capable of exploding, and he often resolved the problem later with a sociable meal with his opponent of the moment.

---

\* During the early stages of the Cold War the Soviets criticised the West for the carpet bombing until it was made clear that it was often done at Soviet request.

Brooke seemed to have parrots on his mind as he reflected on the Cabinet when they were discussing the question of Lend Lease – he described it as something like a 'parrot house' and the next day at a COS meeting wrote that Dudley Pound 'looked like an old parrot asleep on his perch'.* There is little doubt that under these pressures Brooke was becoming somewhat cynical. Hardly a page in his early diaries passes without a vitriolic line about Dudley Pound, which was to cause him considerable pain when he later discovered his colleague was seriously ill. He was sometimes unforgiving about some of the people he met. When he had lunch with various Allied force commanders, he always enjoyed the company of Sikorski; he met the American General Chaney freshly arrived from the American troop base in Northern Ireland; but when Brooke saw de Gaulle he once again described him as an 'unattractive specimen'. The Americans soon disliked de Gaulle immensely.

Later in February Churchill reorganized his Cabinet and Brooke's *bête noire* Beaverbrook was no longer included. Brooke could hardly conceal his delight; he described this as a 'Godsend' and a 'blessing to be rid of Beaverbrook'. A day later he was back on this subject reflecting on his 'general relief at the riddance of Beaverbrook'. Brooke was by nature a conservative person, and just as he had started to appreciate the secretary of state for war, he was disappointed to find he had been replaced by a James Grigg; he was 'sorry to see him go'. He was not insensitive, as previously noted, but most men under intense pressure, and especially those who hold strong views and have important roles, tend to react in the same way. As the years progressed, he grew to like Grigg and they became personal friends, but Brooke was always wary of change. He liked Auchinleck but was wondering about his ability; he was also sad to have to write to his beloved cousin Bertie and explain he had reached the age of retirement, and was immensely relieved when Bertie accepted his letter in 'good heart'. As a matter of curiosity Bertie later served as Britain's Red Cross commissioner with Allied Liberation armies in 1943–45, and although born earlier than Brooke, outlived him by some five years.[6]

Brooke was receiving correspondence from Auchinleck who was complaining that cavalry officers were not fit for purpose in armoured vehicles, and the cruiser tanks were mechanically inferior to those of the opposition. Brooke did not disagree with this, but he knew that tactical and operational doctrine came first, and this was Auchinleck's prime responsibility.[7]

There were some policies which Brooke had been uncomfortable with such as the ABDA theme, and he was right in so far that after the disasters in the Far East it was soon put aside. Later in this month he observed that the pattern was becoming clear with the Americans looking to the Pacific, and the British to the Middle East,

---

* Lend Lease was signed on 11 March 1941 and finished in September 1945. It was the granting of free resources for which the Americans were granted leases for army and naval bases, and territory during the war. Canada had a similar arrangement called Mutual Aid.

India, Burma, and the Indian Ocean; Brooke always liked clear command areas. This area of British interest coincided with much of the old British Empire, but Brooke believed that over the previous ten years he 'had an unpleasant feeling that the British Empire was decaying' and 'we were now on a slippery slope'. He was of course correct in this, and despite Churchill's later efforts the empire would disappear after the war, to be replaced by the better system of the friendlier Commonwealth.

Even at this stage in early 1942 he was gathering doubts about American motivations and intentions. He attacked Portal and Dudley Pound on their return from the First Washington Conference for acquiescing too much to American plans. Brooke believed 'the Americans are rapidly snatching more and more power with the ultimate intention of running the war in Washington' and he thought that Portal and Dudley Pound eventually came around to his viewpoint. From the historical benefit of hindsight Brooke may appear somewhat parochial in his thinking at this stage, but the Anglo-American power tussle would grow, and American dominance grew simply because of their immense military power and resources. Churchill had the good sense to recognise this, unlike the Nazi leadership, who tended to underestimate America's potential. Militarily the American army was not that strong at this stage, and their navy had been weakened by Pearl Harbor, but their industrial output and their demographic capacity was immense. Churchill had rightly perceived that only with the USA as a partner could Britain achieve survival and eventual success. With the benefit of historical hindsight, it was Russia who basically won the European war, but they also benefitted from American industry and the British Merchant and Royal Navy. At the end of this month Brooke was somewhat downcast when he heard that 72 Hurricane fighter planes were being sent to Russia, as a the result of Beaverbrook's visit who according to Brooke, wanted to 'pour everything' in their direction; and all Britain received from the Russians, Brooke claimed with some justification, was 'abuse'. Brooke's views may have been parochial, but he was a man of his times and he was totally committed to the British cause, as was Churchill.

Brooke had several concerns during this month, not least with the fall of Singapore which even caused him to question the fighting ability of British forces; Churchill was not allowed to do this according to Brooke, but it had given Brooke cause to ponder. He was also concerned about shipping losses, bringing supplies from America, and wondered at one stage if this factor might be Britain's 'undoing'. He was also disconcerted that the German pocket battleships the *Gneisenau*, *Scharnhorst* and *Prinz Eugen* had escaped Brest with the loss of 40 British aircraft to Germany's 20. The picture was looking bleak, and Brooke described this period as the 'black days'. The events in the Far East, and their ramifications, caused Brooke to feel that Europe and especially the Middle East had fallen somewhat into the background.

The collapse of Singapore had faced Churchill with severe political problems, and Brooke had to explain to the Dutch military that the Australians would not be taking Java, which was under threat and invaded at the end of the month. Burma was also looking in danger and with its almost thousand-mile border with India, the situation appeared grim. It was being decided whether to send Alexander out to take control, not least because Rangoon (now Yangon) was looking precarious. None of this was helped by the sense of panic in Australia, which had never been attacked before and had suffered a bombing raid on Darwin (19 February) as their 7th Division was sailing near Java to return home.

Brooke had to think and plan at all sorts of levels over a global basis. His first task was to understand and construct a long-term strategy for the Allies, which demanded an intangible and almost abstract set of thought processes, and like a chess player on a time clock had to think of as many variations and possibilities as he was able, narrowing down the possible to the probable. It was fortunate that he had followed Dill and had made a study of the wider scene, always enjoying Dill's talks and insights into the global picture. Brooke, as well as having to sell his proposed policies and ideas to his senior colleagues, Churchill, and others in the Cabinet, now had to use his powers of persuasion to tackle the Americans. This was never going to be an easy task. Brooke believed the Mediterranean operations were critical to keep the Suez open for Far East communications, and to stop the Germans invading for their oil resources. Many of the Americans interpreted this as Britain's route to India and the empire, and Marshall, Brooke's American equivalent, thought the Mediterranean theatre was intended to move troops away from their main purpose, which was a direct attack across the Channel to help the Russians.

Beneath the surface there were two Mediterranean strategies: Brooke's version was to clear the Mediterranean for shipping then take Italy out of the war by invasion. The second version consisted only of Brooke's first part, what has often been called the 'arterial strategy' of keeping the seas clear of the enemies. This even had Marshall's support and encouraged him to agree to invade Sicily to 'make the Mediterranean more secure for shipping'.[8] Brooke already had his eyes on mainland Italy, but the arterial strategy was working, and later in May 1943 Admiral Karl Dönitz informed Hitler that 'it must furthermore be kept in mind that the Anglo-Saxon powers have gained two million tons in shipping since the Mediterranean was cleared'.[9] It has been observed that the 'arterial strategy made the most sense of the North African campaigns,' and there was 'no desert war' but a fight along the coast for ports and aerodromes.[10] Brooke would not have agreed with this perspective at the time.[*]

Brooke was also conscious that the American Admiral King still led an influential Pacific lobby of dealing with the direct threat against America, the Japanese.[†] Selling

---

[*]   Cunningham worried Brooke by stating, in the arterial debate, that the Mediterranean was secure without invading Sicily, that it was 85 per cent secure at the time and Sicily's invasion would make it 90 per cent secure; Marshall used the naval argument of 5 per cent to opt for Operation *Husky*.

[†]   Admiral King, like many others, believed the Japanese had to be continuously on the defensive, otherwise they could strengthen the islands which would be the road to Japan and its defeat. See Gerhard L. Weinberg, *A World at Arms, A Global History of World War II* (Cambridge: CUP, 1994) p.642.

his long-term strategic views was never going to be easy for Brooke, and he would need his very forceful personality to prepare his many persuasive arguments. Brooke, as mentioned, knew that a second front across the Channel could not be achieved in 1942 or 1943 without a serious reduction of German resources, and he hoped that the Soviet Red Army would suck the life out of the Wehrmacht. He knew that blockading was not going to win the war; it was Britain which was being blockaded. On the other hand, the traditional naval blockade was also a perpetual threat to Franco and helped keep Spain out of the conflict, but it would not subdue Germany to the point of surrender. This was equally true of bombing which might weaken German industrial efforts, but in the end it demanded, as noted before, the army with 'boots on the ground' to succeed, and Brooke realised that only time would allow Operation *Bolero* (build-up of American forces in the British Isles) to be ready for a serious second front; this was one of the many reasons he was worried about the U-boat conflict.

In addition to this planning and preparing an overall strategy and persuading others of its value, he had to deal with current operations which needed rapid appraisal; in chess terms this was called Blitzkrieg chess where the time on the clock is limited to a few minutes. If commanders made mistakes it was Brooke and Churchill who took the blame. Percival in Singapore was criticised, and Churchill blamed; Auchinleck was in retreat and was coming under Brooke's scrutiny and facing Churchill's criticism, but it was Churchill and to a lesser extent Brooke who were at the sharp end in political terms. This was an exhausting job description and it was not going to become easier.

During March the Russians were fighting a bitter war on their front, and the Japanese had landed in New Guinea, (8 March); Auchinleck was causing problems for Brooke, and the only hopeful military action on the Western Front was a Combined Operations raid on the French port of St Nazaire (Operation *Chariot*) when a commando attack was planned with the Royal Navy to blow up the one dry dock able to accommodate the *Tirpitz*.* Brooke does not mention this because for him it was merely a minor tactical blow.

One of his major problems this month tended to revolve around Auchinleck and defending this general from Churchill's anger. Churchill had prepared a draft note to Auchinleck which was full of 'abuse' but Brooke and the members of the COS skilfully reworded and toned it down before transmission. They had heard that Java and Rangoon appeared to be heading for disaster, which would signal

---

* This raiding party rammed an old destroyer (*Campbeltown*) into the dock entrance where it later blew up. This raid involved some 611 men, of which 169 were killed and 215 became POWs. It was later learnt that the Germans had some 5,000 troops in the town, which would indicate Brooke's concern that a larger raid on the French coast would be easily resisted without the Germans having to withdraw troops from Russia. Five Victoria Crosses were awarded for personal bravery during this brave action.

the end of ABDA, but Churchill was made more furious by the lack of attack in North Africa; he always wanted positive action. Brooke was never happy whenever Churchill interfered directly with commanders, usually based on the grounds that any politician, despite his past personal experiences, cannot necessarily know what that commander is facing in the field. On the other hand, Brooke was still concerned about the influence of Auchinleck's staff officer Chink Dorman-Smith. To counter this problem, he arranged for General Richard McCreery, one of his finest divisional armoured commanders, to go out and join Auchinleck, only to discover later that McCreery was totally ignored. A few weeks later Churchill asked Auchinleck to return home for discussion, but he refused, suggesting that Brooke and the CAS should go to him. Brooke dreaded what reply Churchill would send. Brooke was finding the matter aggravating, not least because he was gathering doubts about Auchinleck's control of the situation. He already had to stop Churchill replacing this man with Gort and then Nye, both of whom Brooke held some serious doubts about. Eventually, near the end of the month, Churchill agreed that the North African offensive could be delayed until 15 May. At the end of the month, which always sent Brooke into a more reflective mood as he looked back, he expressed his habitual concern that the army was too short of good officers.

Another typical tension raised its head again over the relationship between the three services. It arose initially at the beginning of the month with the suggestion that there should be a single or supreme commander in Ceylon, but this was opposed by both the navy and the air force. A week later it arose again around the issue of how the army or navy could call upon the RAF, and again it did not make any further progress. There were the usual clashes with Portal. Brooke knew that for the RAF, bombing Germany was their main priority, and they were busy building four-engine bombers and finding the necessary crews. Such was the belief that bombing was important, it was often thought that it was not simply a way of weakening the enemy but of winning the war, and the use of ground troops would be a thing of the past.

On 11 March the prime minister read a document newly arrived from President Roosevelt suggesting new spheres of command, but Brooke was certain that it was the American method of driving Australia, New Zealand and Canada into American arms, to help 'bust up the empire'. Brooke was always suspicious of the Americans, but he realised that Australia and New Zealand were not overly happy with the situation as it appeared to be developing.

At the time (first week of March) when Churchill was contemplating visiting Stalin to discuss war boundaries, and Eden was nervous that the Russians might make peace with the Germans, Brooke was suddenly told that he was to be chairman of the COS in place of Dudley Pound. He was somewhat nervous about this because technically it should have been Portal's turn to hold this position. This decision was probably arrived at because Portal was some ten years younger than Brooke, Pound was still in active command, and there was little question that Brooke had the best strategic brain. When the COS met again two days later, Brooke was relieved to find on his arrival that Dudley Pound, for the first time ever, had arrived earlier and ensconced himself in Brooke's old seat, and both he and Portal 'played up very well'. He was 'deeply grateful' to Dudley Pound for making the transfer so easy; there is no questioning that Pound belonged to the old and respected class of 'gentlemen'.[11]

However, Brooke was not so pleased with the arrival of Mountbatten as head of Combined Operations, because the COS as a body did precisely this type of work. He did not even like the title since he believed operations should always be regarded as combined. Mountbatten was to attend only a couple of times a week when larger problems were being discussed. Socially Brooke found Mountbatten good company, but in terms of military professionalism he believed Mountbatten 'frequently wasted both his time and ours'.[12] When the suggestion arose about occupying Madagascar, Mountbatten had suggested it could be done with four battalions, which Brooke knew was totally inadequate. Mountbatten's service had been in the navy (even in this role he has had many critics over his service at sea, and his rapid promotional rise) and he was pontificating on army numbers based simply on coastal raids. There had been a great deal of discussion, undoubtedly prompted by Churchill, about raiding the French coast to give the Russians breathing space; Churchill used to call this a 'punch on the snout'. At one stage there was a discussion about a raid on Bayonne France, and Mountbatten suggested Cherbourg, and had to be dissuaded by the other members. Churchill and Mountbatten tended to think along the same lines with a high degree of romantic military ventures. The debate on raiding France was going to be a protracted affair, and stirred up, according to Brooke, by Beaverbrook's press. Time and time again Brooke argued that they only had ten divisions available, and such were the number of German troops in France they would not have to withdraw any men or material from Russia. His arguments were correct, but he had the impetuous Churchill and Mountbatten to contend with, the former being the most difficult.

In a discussion with Lord Milne, Brooke gathered that this peer thought that Churchill's political time was coming to an end, and that he would probably be replaced by Stafford Cripps. This was not based on Churchill's longevity (though he had occasional worrying pains) but the gathering criticisms about the conduct of the war. Brooke made no further comment; he was an admirer of Churchill most of the time, but not of politicians. In his reflective meanderings at the end of the month, he returned to his old complaint that 'democracy is at a great disadvantage against a dictatorship when it comes to war'. He based this mainly on his perception that petty party politics and jealousies blocked progress, and politicians had little to no knowledge of military matters. He concluded by wondering whether 'we shall muddle through this time as we have done in the past'.[13] The next day, as April began, Brooke reread what he had written the night before, and admitted that 'I was liverish', which was probably true. He summarised his concern as a matter of choice between 'pulling through or sinking', which had made him downcast.

## The Americans and British

April 1942 was a major month in terms of the British and Americans waltzing together with plans for the immediate future, the smaller British partner out of step but pretending the dance was going well for the sake of necessary harmony. Brooke recognised that the British forces were widely dispersed all around the world, and that drawing some of them home for the American plans for an immediate second front to help the Russians, would mean defeat elsewhere. He also knew that the Germans had too many available forces for the Allies to cross the Channel in a direct confrontation, as it would lead to a total disaster. Brooke's main problem was that many of his colleagues were more obliging, and it was not helped that from the time that Churchill had stepped ashore in America, he was so effusive about the alliance that he had probably promised too much. When Marshall and Hopkins (Roosevelt's close friends and advisers) arrived during this month Brooke liked Marshall as a man, but he remained constantly concerned about what he considered his lack of strategic foresight. The problem for Brooke was he was aware that somehow the Allies had to stay in harmony for a successful outcome. Brooke knew they only had 48 divisions at the most and was staggered to hear the Americans were thinking of that year (Operation *Sledgehammer*) to initiate an invasion, or at least in 1943 (Operation *Roundup*, later called *Overlord*); the first to establish a bridgehead, the second to crush Germany. Brooke was a pragmatist and knew this was a fantasy; it was what he referred to as 'castles in the air'. Brooke's colleague Kennedy possibly prepped by Brooke, responded to Marshall's criticism that wars cannot be won by being defensive, by pointing out that 'our information was that the Germans were in a position to concentrate 30 divisions against us there, without taking a single man from the Russian front.'[14] British intelligence at this time would have been better informed than the Americans, and the benefit of hindsight clearly indicated Brooke was correct in his thinking, not least because of the other problems such as the Japanese threat against India, Burma, Ceylon and possibly Australia.

The Americans had just appointed Douglas MacArthur as the supreme commander in the south-west Pacific and they were feeling confident, even though on 9 April American troops had to surrender on the Bataan Peninsula. The Doolittle raid on Tokyo took place on 18 April, but these were pinpricks in a growing and successful landscape for the Japanese.* Brooke was all too aware of the Japanese

---

* The Doolittle Raid (sometimes known as the Tokyo Raid) happened on 18 April 1942, with an attack on Tokyo; it was the first air operation to strike at the Japanese archipelago, and served as an act of retaliation for Pearl Harbor. It did little damage but was a psychological boost for the American public.

danger, that Auchinleck was struggling in North Africa, and that the critical island of Malta was under constant attack (the island was awarded the George Cross on 18 April) and in imminent danger of invasion. In this global backdrop Brooke was more than happy to have the Americans onside, but knew their approach had to be more carefully planned and monitored. At the first COS meeting of the month he was angry with Dudley Pound because the admiral, as far as Brooke could see, was refusing to cooperate with the Americans in the Pacific and Indian Oceans, and most of the eastern fleet appeared to be turning west. Brooke knew the Americans were essential, but inexperienced at this time following a long period of determined isolationism.

In naval matters Churchill had made it clear he wanted the French battleship *Richelieu* destroyed, but Brooke and the other COS members were less certain about the ramifications. There was a great deal of uneasiness about the way some Vichy government personnel were pandering to the Nazi regime, the sensitivity about the Free French, the French North African colonies, and thereby the safety of Gibraltar. Despite this Churchill was insistent, but the situation was relieved when the *Richelieu* stayed in harbour. On 18 April, the news came through that Pierre Laval, known as a collaborationist, was back in power, which also threw doubts on occupying Madagascar.*

The House of Commons and others were making loud noises about the conduct of the war, because of the apparent lack of success, and forgetting that the Battle of Britain had stopped Parliament from being under Nazi control. It was not an easy time and just prior to the arrival of the American visitors, Brooke had experienced a difficult COS meeting with various arguments given to attack occupied France if only to give some relief to the Russians, which Brooke knew it would not. After this difficult meeting he drove to Hendon to greet Marshall and Hopkins with their staff. The next day Marshall attended the COS meeting and there was a long discussion on starting a second front. Brooke realised that although the Americans were on the way they were not enough in numbers for such an enterprise. He watched and listened to Marshall, and later he wrote, 'I liked what I saw of Marshall, a pleasant and easy man to get on with, rather over-filled with his own importance. But I should not put him down as a great man.'[15] Brooke came to this conclusion when he heard of the plans for 1942 which he thought were 'simply too fantastic'. Brooke was, however, bemused to watch Marshall suffering the long late hours which Churchill kept. He gathered that Marshall only saw Roosevelt once a month, noting that 'I was fortunate if I did not see Winston for six hours!' Brooke was probably more reserved or restrained than usual over the American preparation of plans, if only for the sake of ongoing harmony, but he could not see the sense of going on the offensive too early.

---

* Laval was executed by the French after the war, perhaps unfairly, because his collaboration policies were always based on French survival.

However, on 13 April there was another joint meeting at 10 Downing Street with Hopkins and Marshall in attendance at the Defence Committee meeting. Brooke described this as a 'momentous meeting' because it concerned the American proposals of an offensive in 1942 and greater action in 1943. Beneath his pose Brooke must have felt somewhat angry and cynical, later writing, 'They have not begun to realise all the implications of this plan and all the difficulties that lie ahead of us.'[16] He could hardly believe that with the Japanese in the ascendancy, the dangers in India and the Far East, the German threat of finding oil resources in the Middle East, the problems in North Africa, the shortage of supplies with the U-boat war, that this could be considered a serious project. Brooke knew Marshall was good at raising armies, but believed his American friend had 'no strategic ability'. He was contemptuous that this was supposed to help Russia, and more so when Marshall's idea was a landing and creating a bridgehead, but with no policy or plans where to head afterwards, even if the operation were achieved. Marshall's lack of formal military training made it clear to Brooke that the Americans had no idea of the dangers in crossing the English Channel, and his 'stunted strategy' made such discussions impossible.

Brooke was not helped with the knowledge that the public tended to be equally eager in hoping for such action, as did some of his colleagues. Both Churchill and Brooke had to be politically sensitive towards the Americans and their plans. It was generally understood by the Americans that Brooke was against the concept of launching an attack across the Channel, either as a major offensive or even for forming a bridgehead on the Cotentin coast, sometimes known as the Cherbourg peninsula. This was not entirely true; Brooke was more concerned about the timing. He knew that the Russians had first to weaken the German military, that resources including shipping had to be greater than was then achievable, and some careful logistical planning had to be undertaken. Brooke and Churchill were acutely aware that if Russia collapsed or made some form of treaty with the oppressor, then the British Isles would again be threatened, and they needed American support and troops to survive. Unlike many Brooke had never forgotten that Stalin had once been an ally of Nazi Germany; he knew Russian success was critical, but he never trusted them entirely. In one of his presentations he held up a prepared map of the European battle area, showing the vast Russian front of some 1,500 miles and compared it to the proposed Cotentin line which would be 20 miles in length. He hoped that by doing this he would be able to illustrate how ridiculous such a second front would appear. Nevertheless, he knew that he had to tread carefully to avoid a situation when the Americans might 'give up' and turn their attention towards the Pacific, where the American public interest tended to focus. It was clear from his diary he thought little of Marshall's proposals and his strategic thinking, but he could not say this bluntly or publicly. As Churchill's personal secretary noted above, Brooke was not always able to conceal his emotions, he was not good at dissimulating, and Marshall would have been aware of Brooke's feelings. Brooke and Marshall were two very different men although they shared many human qualities. One of Marshall's biographers wrote that 'those who did not know Marshall were apt to think of him as a cold lofty man, but compared with the hard, distant, lofty Field Marshal Brooke he was a ball of fire.'[17]

Generally, the Americans were suspicious of Churchill and the British, especially in terms of their empire, and their obsession with the Mediterranean as part of their overall policy. There was, perhaps understandably, a growing Anglophobia with some of the Americans which would later develop rapidly among some of their field commanders. General Albert Wedemeyer, who was one of Marshall's planners at this stage and Marshall's chief consultant, stated his perceptions of Brooke in an open and frank way.* Wedemeyer, who disliked Brooke, wrote that he:

> talked in a low measured tones and was cautious as he commented upon the American concept as described by Marshall. The British were masters in negotiating, particularly were they adept in the use of phrases or words which were capable of more than one interpretation… no expressed opposition to Marshall's ideas at this first meeting, just polite suggestions that there might be some difficulties…what I witnessed was the British finesse in its finest hour, a power that has been developed over centuries of successful internal intrigues, cajolery, and tacit compulsion.[18]

He was correct in so far that the British, led by Churchill and Brooke, were doing their best to be polite because they needed American power, but wanted it to suit their strategy which they genuinely believed to be the best.

When the Americans had gone it must have felt like something of a relief, and Brooke visited Bletchley Park to watch the innovative code deciphering, and he noted the 'wonderful set of professors and genii'. He heard from Sikorski that the Germans were preparing a new offensive, and he wondered how he gained this type of information because it was the first time he had heard about these plans. There followed a series of discussions on the threat to use gas if the Germans deployed it against the Russians (on 26 April an Anglo-Soviet Treaty had been signed), how to destroy the Luftwaffe to give Russia help, and the occupation of Madagascar came up again in the light of Laval's return to power.

On the personal side of his life Brooke was pleased to be nearer home, and often Benita would join him in London for lunch. There was less time for birdwatching, but the following month of May he spent a day photographing blackbirds. One of his children and Benita also had some unpleasant earaches caused by mastoids which caused him concern, but they both recovered. In May in between the COS meetings he managed to 'nip' out with Benita and buy Ti (Victor) a pushbike, and later helped Benita catch a swarm of bees, which was

---

*    Later Wedemeyer served in the Far East and China where he became more ardently anti-communist than anti-British.

highly painful, having to extract some 20 plus stings from her neck, which then gave her a high temperature.

His life was simply busy with the machinations of politics and military in an accelerating war. He met the Polish General Anders and discovered that the Poles were divided over whether to build up their forces in Britain or the Middle East, and he tried to persuade Churchill to appoint Gort to oversee Malta. He ended this frenetic month discussing with Churchill, after the usual late dinner, all these issues, not least the bombing of the battleship *Tirpitz*, whose very presence hidden in Norwegian waters would cause panic and later the virtual loss of the PQ17 convoy (4 July 1942). All these momentous areas of concern were daily life for men like Brooke and Churchill, but there is little doubt that Brooke's main concern above and beneath these daily issues was keeping the Americans onside while trying to curb their over-enthusiasm, which Brooke was certain would lead to disaster.

The events during the month of May summarised Brooke's busy life. Allied forces occupied Madagascar, British troops withdrew from Burma, Corregidor fell to the Japanese, Rommel attacked at Gazala, the first thousand-bomber raid took place (30 May) and Sydney Harbour was bombed. During all this activity, the debates over the Air Ministry's seeming lack of cooperation continued, with the added anxiety, for Brooke, of the American wish to dash across the Channel in a precipitate offensive which he knew would end in disaster.

Early May revolved around the attack on Madagascar, with Brooke noting that Churchill appeared 'cheerful' because there was an offensive taking place. Madagascar, a French colony, had declared itself Free French after the collapse of France, but after the sinking of the French fleet at Mers-el-Kébir, the island had taken on a Vichy administration. Brooke could never understand why the invasion of Madagascar had to happen, although he had to help in the planning; he was aware that the Germans had pressed the Japanese to take the island, but he did not think they would, and he was more worried about Laval's reaction, with which Churchill and Eden appeared unconcerned. Vichy France (which had bombed Gibraltar) was virtually at war with Britain, though there was never an official declaration of war, and this situation persisted until Hitler eventually occupied the whole of France. Brooke was concerned that the Madagascar Operation *Ironclad* did not seem to go well at the start, but it worked, and the major ports were taken after some initial fighting. The South African prime minister pushed for the whole of Madagascar to be taken, though Brooke never mentioned this fact, and it was handed over to the Free French again, by Eden's pressure and to the joy of de Gaulle. Brooke quietly objected to the Free French but he never explained his thinking, and it may well have been his deep distrust of de Gaulle. When the matter was discussed on the first day of the following month, he noted that Eden's support of de Gaulle 'may lose us the war'.

Australia's demands for their own defence were causing some concern, and they had questioned the policy of 'Germany first'. Brooke always found this difficult to understand, which may seem unfair; it was a huge continent but with a small population in isolated areas, and very much alone, along with New Zealand, and uncomfortably close to Japan. Darwin had been bombed, and at the end of May Sydney Harbour suffered the same fate. It was later revealed that the Japanese had considered occupying Australia, but eventually decided it was not worth the effort and risk. The American navy was reasserting its presence (the Battle of Midway would start at the beginning of June with the loss of four Japanese carriers to the Americans' one) but the Japanese threat appeared all too strong. On 12 May Brooke had an uncomfortable meeting with the Australian politician Evatt whom Brooke thought was creating a blackmail situation. Evatt threatened to withdraw Australian divisions from North Africa, just at the time a major battle was anticipated, if the Americans did not supply more aircraft for Australian defence. America was not being so generous at this juncture, because their industry was building up its own forces, which given their previous lack of preparation was understandable. Brooke in formal meetings and over lunch tried to explain to Evatt the global picture, pointing out that a failure in North Africa and Europe would leave Australia more vulnerable. It was a fair point to make, but the Australian would not be convinced, and this must evoke some sympathy. To Brooke it seemed small-minded, as if the rest of the world did not count, but each politician and soldier nearly always puts their own country first.

The Americans had placed General MacArthur as the supreme commander in that part of the Pacific, and he was adopting the policy of what had often been dubbed island hopping: taking island by island, drawing closer and closer to Japan. It was going to be a slow process, which appealed to Brooke's strategic way of thinking, but this area of activity was fraught with danger.* Many of the British, as well as a growing number of Americans, demanded European activity to help the Russians – not out of any altruistic motives, but because it was apparent that the Russians could bleed the Wehrmacht to death. Brooke understood this, but he wanted the battle in North Africa to succeed because he was certain that cross-Channel offensives needed considerably more time.

The German offensive in the East had restarted, just as Sikorski had informed Brooke, that Molotov was passing through London to America to try and convince the Western Allies to start the second front, for self-evident reasons. Brooke noted that Marshall was already changing his mind on the 1942 proposals of a bridgehead in France, causing Brooke to note that 'it was a rod made by Roosevelt for his own back and of his Allies' backs'.[19] Brooke knew the invasion would have to be planned

---

* Brooke always thought very highly of MacArthur, but he moderated this personal appraisal when he met him much later.

and hoped it would be done with more appropriate timing; he started once again the discussions on a supreme commander, and hoped that the Americans had really decided that Operation *Sledgehammer* was dead in the water. His experience in France during 1940, in Brooke's opinion, gave him a better understanding of the Germans than the Americans, and this factor always influenced his strategy. A few Americans, as mentioned above, saw him only as a master of retreat and evacuation.

There were times when many have regarded Brooke as overly cautious and a blocking device, but Brooke was more than aware that a misconceived plan or its timing would cost lives and threaten disaster. At the beginning of May he was involved in a discussion over a suggestion of an attack on Alderney, one of the Channel Islands; quite why this should have had any bearing on the war is difficult to imagine, and to Brooke sounded like a 'fruitless venture' which he managed to persuade the COS to reject. It was as pointless, Brooke believed, as Churchill's continuous pressure to attack Norway which would have had no strategic value. The plans to raid the French coast continued with a major operation called *Imperator*, and a smaller attack on *Dieppe* codenamed Operation *Rutter*. The Dieppe raid was discussed, and Brooke was somewhat concerned that Mountbatten and Churchill were showing too much optimism, and they were discussing 'lodgements' along the French coast; both men seemed to be underestimating the power of the possible German reaction. Every time Brooke discussed this issue with Churchill, he seemed to understand what Brooke was trying to say, but kept turning to Norway as another possibility; it is little wonder that Brooke felt so frustrated at times, or in his words, 'liverish'. These discussions of attacking France were always on the agenda, and on 27 May, almost in passing, Brooke mentioned that at one of the meetings on how to attack the French coast, Eisenhower, the American DMO (director of military operations) attended; he would have much to say about Eisenhower in the ensuing years.

On this day Brooke was more concerned about North Africa where Rommel had started an attack and a major battle was underway. He knew much depended on the outcome and was concerned about Auchinleck. Earlier in the month Auchinleck had complained about the number of tanks arriving. Brooke was angry about these anxieties of his field commander, and he felt that Auchinleck had no idea of the problems the convoys were experiencing, especially with the attack that Malta was suffering. Brooke believed the main issue had to do with strategy; as always, he had serious doubts about Auchinleck's ability in this area, and thought he was not helped by his staff officers. He was also having doubts about Ritchie whom he thought was not 'big enough' for the task. Auchinleck had already made Churchill angry by once again demanding to postpone the attack from the agreed May date to July or August. Despite his own doubts Brooke suggested to Churchill and the COS they should listen to Auchinleck because he was the man on the spot; this was always a major policy of Brooke to take the word of the commander in the field, but he was suffering some personal doubts in this case. There was a Cabinet meeting on

Auchinleck, and Churchill produced a draft note to the general, but Brooke and the COS redrafted the text and in its toned-down format it was accepted by the prime minister.

On 13 May Brooke met Charles Hambro who had taken over the Special Operations Executive (SOE), and he was asking for Colin Gubbins, who had freshly returned from Russia. Gubbins was to become a well-known name in this area of activity. Later in the same month Brooke ruminated on the thought that the SOE and SIS should be under one umbrella. This had once been the policy, and in the Great War these activities had been mixed up with such characters as Sidney Reilly, but Churchill had insisted SOE had its own existence.* The prime minister was in many ways right and Brooke wrong; it was self-evidently clear that the two had different objectives, and the deciphering and information intelligence were rapidly becoming of prime importance; it could be said that in this sphere Brooke's strategy was misplaced. Although being a traditional soldier of the old school, Brooke valued the work of the intelligence services, and always supported them. The head of SIS, known as 'C', was Stewart Menzies, and it was well known that Churchill constantly pestered him for information to the point of exhaustion. One historian noted that 'Churchill refrained from trying to issue operational orders, and when briefly tempted was firmly brought to heel by Sir Alan Brooke.'[20] Brooke barely mentioned in his diary the work of the intelligence services, except in the immediate postwar years when he was concerned about political interference. In the official history of the secret services it was clear that Brooke was on the fringes, but he was trusted. There had been some internal dissent over the quality of Menzies' leadership, with the curious note that 'Edward Beddington, the Deputy Director/Army in SIS [from 1942–44)] was worried and agreed to work with Menzies on condition that he retained a right of direct access to CIGS, Sir Alan Brooke.'[21]

The Joint Intelligence Committee (JIC) was chaired by the Foreign Office through Victor (Bill) Cavendish-Bentinck who was never happy with Brooke, thinking Portal was the best of the COS. Brooke had 'persuaded himself that the Germans retained a "mass manoeuvre" uncommitted to the Eastern Front, which might still invade Britain...it was widely thought that successive War Office Directors of Intelligence were too eager to tell the highly opinionated army chief what he wanted to hear.'[22] Brooke relied on his instincts and awareness of German military strength, and he was often correct. Later in November 1943 Brooke himself complained that the JIC often underestimated the enemy's military capability, which as Max Hastings wrote 'was half true. Brooke should instead have acknowledged that the chronic problem for the Allies...was that the enemy consistently displayed superior combat skills to those of Anglo-American armies, even when the latter had more troops'

---

* Sidney Reilly was known as the 'ace of spies' during the Great War; he was an adventurer, eccentric, and had worked for the SIS who were always worried about what he was up to.

and overwhelming forces and Ultra.[23] From his experience in the Great War, and in France 1940, Brooke had long acknowledged this factor and had often been criticised for doing so too much.

The debate on bringing relief to the Russians by invading Europe was constantly under review. The Russians had asked for three million gas masks, which was a huge order and the convoys to Russia were exceedingly dangerous. Such was the difficulty that on 18 May there had been a debate on the safety of one convoy, and the lack of air support, the prolonged argument causing Brooke to question whether an Army Air Command was necessary. Against the advice of the COS, Brooke demanded, with Churchill's support, the convoy should make the journey. Whenever Brooke, in his more 'liverish' moments thought dictatorship was preferential to democracy, he may have thought differently with Churchill influencing the advice of COS. The debate between Brooke, Portal and Pound over air support was at times heated, and Brooke considered the Air Ministry as 'too divorced'.

On 20 May Brooke found himself in Ireland for a variety of reasons, and when driven by Colebrooke, his old home, he wrote that 'I felt as if I were in a dream'; the times and his circumstance had certainly changed, and his home setting stirred some memories and reflections. When he returned to London, he met Vyacheslav Molotov, the Russian minister for foreign affairs, and experienced his first drink-sodden all-round toasting and boisterous meal at the Russian Embassy, which, he wrote, 'gave him the creeps'. He was there with Churchill, Eden, Cripps, Bevin and Attlee, and described Molotov as an 'unimpressive sight', yet he detected a 'distinct ability and shrewdness' in the man. Molotov was a clever man, and shrewd as Brooke observed. He had survived the various Stalin purges, and held important positions in Soviet Russia, later disappearing into the background during Khrushchev's time after the war. More to the point, as the months unfolded it was becoming clear to all observers that Russia was taking the major brunt of the European war, indicated by the sheer number of dead and casualties on both sides. The number of German divisions fighting in the East dwarfed those in Western occupied Europe to the bitter end, but the Allies, as Brooke knew, still needed to build up their forces as fast as possible, not least because for the British and Americans the war was more global.

In June Brooke visited America for the first time in his life, the Battle of Midway was successful for the American fleet, the Germans launched their summer offensive (codenamed *Blau*), and to their horror Churchill and Brooke learnt of the fall of Tobruk while in the White House. Despite these momentous events Brooke's life was one of plans, meetings, and although he does not say so, it was a time of manipulating the Americans to the British way of thinking.

Mountbatten had been sent to America to explain why second fronts based in France and Western Europe would be disastrous if too early, and Churchill and Brooke listened carefully to what had been said from that meeting. When Mountbatten had turned up for his consultation with Roosevelt, which lasted many hours,

Wedemeyer, who as noted above was highly cynical about the British and their motives, would have preferred an American officer to have been present to check what the British 'were up to'. He was right on this occasion because Mountbatten would be conveying the British concern that there were not enough landing craft to launch Operation *Sledgehammer*. Roosevelt was a secret admirer of royalty and Mountbatten was the right man to go. Churchill, with Brooke's help, perceived that this cross-Channel expedition needed more force, and he decided that he and Brooke should go themselves for a series of meetings. Churchill told Brooke it was necessary because it seemed that 'Roosevelt was getting a bit off the rails'. Mountbatten gave the interesting insight that Roosevelt and other leading Americans believed that Russia might collapse at any moment, and then a Western invasion would have more problems with the influx of battle-hardened Eastern Front soldiers. Roosevelt was also eager that American ground troops should be fighting the Germans before the approaching their presidential elections. The British understood this because if Roosevelt lost and was replaced by Republicans and isolationists the ramifications could be disastrous.

Prior to their departure to America, there were the usual rounds of proposed plans, ranging from the Western Front to recapturing Rangoon, occupying north Norway, and capturing Spitsbergen. In addition to this the news from North Africa continued to be worrying, and Brooke was concerned that Ritchie, whom he had arranged to assist, was being 'out generally manoeuvred' by Rommel. On 16 June Brooke was suddenly informed by Churchill that they were about to fly to America within days. He was somewhat startled at the speeding up of these events because he had been in the process of ordering lighter clothes and uniform, knowing the weather in Washington would be hot. He complained that this meant he had wasted his coupons. Had Brooke been the leading senior general in the enemy camp, or any other country, he would not have had to worry about coupons, but Brooke was always honest. As a man of deep integrity, he would not abuse the system by using his power and influence, and at the end of the war he and Benita were not that well off. It was to be a month when his family life was limited; he missed lunch with Benita because of Churchill's hurry, and he had spent only one day at home photographing a mistle thrush.

## Talks in America

They travelled by a large seaplane across the Atlantic, internally improved to make the journey as comfortable as possible, taking with them their key staff. It was by today's standards a long journey (some 26 hours), but as Brooke noted at least they had beds and a toilet. No doubt Brooke found it an interesting experience, and he observed Churchill was almost excited, especially when they spotted far below a convoy making its way through the Atlantic perils. Churchill always liked to be near the scene of action which was to cause deep concern as D-Day approached in 1944. During this long journey he and Churchill had time to discuss their plans with the Americans to make sure they were coordinated in their approach; though, as Brooke anticipated, this would be more a problem for Churchill than himself, because the prime minister often suddenly developed his own ideas and could be impulsive.

The American experience was novel for Brooke, there was considerable socialising, and although he was staying with his old friend Dill, the first evening he was expected to dine with Lord Halifax. It was a critical time politically because the British knew that they had to keep the Americans onside, yet explain why they appeared to be reneging on previous agreements. As an overall picture, the British had to clarify why they thought the idea of crossing the Channel to establish a foothold ready for invasion in 1943, was too risky with the limited forces available. They also had to convince the Americans that the battle in North Africa was critical for oil and communication necessities in the Mediterranean, and that knocking Italy out of the war was essential. The Americans always had their doubts about this and were highly suspicious of British motives. Whether an attack on Italy was justified was questioned as a future project, and to this day historians who explore the overall grand strategy are also divided on this matter. On the other hand, the British at this juncture held a better appraisal of German military strength, had the experience, and tended to be more realistic about timing than the Americans, who always appeared to be in a hurry.

On 19 June Brooke addressed the Combined COS (CCOS) and presented the British argument and points of view. This task was never going to be easy, and generally Brooke was never able to convince Marshall that North Africa and Italy were part of the necessary plan for the ultimate blow, which was the invasion of France. Brooke emphasised the points of the British strategy and stressed the importance of Operation *Bolero* which was the rapid build-up of American power in Britain. He argued that at least the British Isles were secure, leading to the later quip that Britain became a massive aircraft carrier for the Americans off the west coast of occupied Europe. The American secretary of state for war, Harry Stimson, had presented a paper which reflected Marshall's views that all forces should be concentrated in the one spot, namely the Western Front. Brooke liked Stimson as a man, found him 'charming', but already knew he was 'one of the strong adherents of breaking our heads in too early operations across the Channel' – and he always supported Marshall.[24] The concentration of forces in a critical area would once have been Brooke's type of policy, but the circumstances surrounding a premature invasion in 1942 were very different. Brooke had to counter these arguments with his appraisals, and Churchill had to do the same with Roosevelt. It was equally difficult convincing the Americans that Operation *Gymnast* (later called *Torch*), the invasion of French colonies in north-west Africa, was necessary, but they found some leeway because Roosevelt felt it was essential that the American army should be 'bloodied' and gain experience.

Brooke as a man could be authoritarian, and there is little doubt that some of those listening to his lecture delivery style, and his personal conviction when he always made it clear that he was right, often felt a degree of resentment. Brooke certainly lacked what may be described as an appropriate sense of tact and diplomacy, and he had none of the charm which endeared Dill to the Americans. On the other hand, it has been thought that 'American regard for Brooke increased as, at meeting after meeting, they got to know him better and appreciate his skill and his professional expertise'.[25] Brooke was a dedicated and highly professional military officer with experience of two major wars against Germany, and despite his authoritarian approach his listeners would have gleaned that he was a man who had to be taken seriously.

When Brooke met Admiral King, who was still demanding that Japan should be the primary target, he was impressed by the naval man's military approach, liked him, and found they both shared two mutual issues. The first was the problem of airpower co-operation, and the second was that they were both concerned as to what their respective political masters were 'hatching'. Churchill and Roosevelt were holding their own military and strategy talks at Roosevelt's private residence called Hyde Park. Roosevelt was a political giant but he had no military experience at all, and as Brooke noted, Churchill considered himself as something of a 'military genius' stemming from his ancestor Marlborough; for Brooke and Marshall these two political leaders were a risky duo.

There was continuous shuffling between military views and strategies, and it was not helped by the private conversations between Churchill and Roosevelt; both Brooke and Marshall were concerned as to what they were possibly concocting next. It was a continuation of a game of chess in which one side was always trying to deploy the board in their favour, but the British, cunning as they could be, were the mendicants desperately needing American support and so playing the game, while trying to manipulate the Americans to their strategy. Brooke and Churchill knew that an early cross-Channel invasion could be disastrous, and their North African plans seemed the only way forward. The Americans often thought these strategies were only meant to distract them from France, and even the official 'historian of British Grand Strategy for this period, J. R. M. Butler described it as the Day of the Dupes,' but of the 15-odd times Churchill had visited America this was the critical one because of this success.[26] Whether the Americans were manipulated, even misled, remains a point of contention, with Wedemeyer later writing 'the insincerity of the British about *Bolero-Roundup* was ultimately to be exposed long after the war, when Sir Alan Brooke confessed that the promotion of Operation *Gymnast* was specifically designed to stall the cross-channel operation scheduled for 1943.'[27] Marshall was certainly unhappy and believed that Roosevelt and Churchill had conspired against him. It was certainly true that the British wanted Operation *Bolero* (American forces in Britain) at full pace, but they wanted to fight to the last Russian before British and American troops invaded France. The Americans were eager, and in Brooke's opinion, too eager to move beyond Churchill's policy of delivering the occasional punch on the nose, setting Europe ablaze, bombing, and taking Italy out of the war. They wanted to head directly for Berlin, and although the British may understandably have been regarded as devious, their sense of timing was undoubtedly more accurate. This time it was not just a matter of British cultural strategy but a matter of precision timing for ultimate success.

As they drew near to the end of the visit Brooke was hoping for a quiet day with his friend Dill, but he received instructions to join Churchill and Roosevelt for lunch at the White House. He was embarrassed at the immediacy of the summons because he was not appropriately dressed, but on apologising to the president he was immediately set at ease by Roosevelt's humour and pleasantness. He also discovered that as a boy Roosevelt had met his father Victor Brooke at Hyde Park many years before, which was a stunning surprise. According to Churchill's account the president was pleased to meet Brooke because of this past family connection, and that Brooke's 'personality and charm created an almost immediate intimacy which greatly helped the course of business'.[28]

As referred to earlier, this social chatter ceased as soon as Marshall entered the president's office with a piece of pink paper which announced the fall of Tobruk. It came as a shocking surprise to Churchill and Brooke, who had not anticipated this disaster. It must have been extremely painful and embarrassing to have this news delivered in such a venue. Pug Ismay recalled that Churchill, unusually for him, winced, and there was complete silence eventually broken by Roosevelt, who 'in six syllables epitomised his sympathy with Churchill, his determination to do their utmost to sustain him, and his recognition that we were all in the same boat: "What can we do to help?"' he asked.[29] Brooke also recalled the sense of sympathy from the American president and even from Marshall who offered to send out men and armour to North Africa. Brooke recognised this as pure kindness because the American soldiers he felt were untrained for such an immediate venture. Later Brooke watched some American troops in an exercise, and thought the elementary basics were good, but was 'less certain' about their 'higher training' which he thought would have to be learnt in the 'hard school of war'. His feelings were apparent to the Americans who cynically noted that 'the birdwatcher in Brooke was more impressed by a Kentucky cardinal [a striking red bird with a black mask and emblem for Kentucky State] than he was with the training of the men'.[30]

After the White House meeting Hopkins drew Brooke aside into his bedroom and explained to him the reasons why Roosevelt thought the way he did. Brooke was always impressed with Hopkins, who held no official position, but was highly influential, playing a major and successful role within the American administration. After the formalities, the British team enjoyed a small recreational tour where Brooke was bemused when the Americans kindly invited Churchill's butler along; he enjoyed the refreshments, with perhaps too much alcohol. On the flight back Brooke mused over the various Americans he had met, he liked them socially, but also had reservations about their military ability. He also recognised that his friend Dill was doing a brilliant job in America. He found the flight again awe-inspiring, especially when he looked down as they crossed his old home at Colebrooke. In his conversations with Churchill, Brooke realised that Neil Ritchie's time had come, and the angry Churchill wanted him replaced. Back in the reality of 10 Downing Street the Dieppe raid was discussed, and Churchill was proposing a personal flight to North Africa; Brooke thought he would like to go, as Churchill suggested, but he would rather not do so in the prime minister's company.

## Back in Britain

Brooke's hopes and wishes were never entirely fulfilled: the debate with the Americans continued, his wish to travel to the Middle East looked promising for a time, but first it had to be delayed by the Americans announcing they intended to visit Britain, and then Churchill deciding he too would visit the Middle East. The first El Alamein battle started on 1 July and on the 4th the disaster of the PQ17 convoy (mentioned earlier) was discussed along with its ramifications. Brooke was unhappy about the American plans but irritated and angry that there was home pressure by the politicians to start a second front. He wrote in his diary that 'one might think we were going to cross the Channel to play baccarat at Le Touquet'.[31] He was frequently annoyed by politicians who suddenly considered themselves military experts, and none of them considered the ramifications of sending six divisions to fight 20 to 30 German ones. He always found Eden, Bevin and Stafford Cripps especially obnoxious. He was suffering a long-term problem with politicians, who because of their position of authority, assume they know more than dedicated experts, an issue each generation to this day too often experiences.

Brooke had to see the king who wanted to hear all the news, and he was then called to a late-night talk with Churchill who was preparing a speech for the Commons the following day. He heard a day later (2 July) that the address to the Commons, which Churchill had tested on Brooke, was successful; in fact, Churchill had to survive a censure motion in the Commons which had questioned his leadership. At least Brooke never had to suffer these problems even if he did have his critics. Later that day he dined with Eisenhower at the Dorchester because Eisenhower had replaced Chaney as the new American general. In his usual blunt fashion Brooke noted that Eisenhower made no 'great impact' on him, and later added the additional note that had he been told about this man's future 'I should have refused to believe it.' The internal conflict between Brooke and Eisenhower would reach ugly proportions, based on Brooke's view of Eisenhower's perceived lack of strategy, and his ability as a field commander. Later Eisenhower would exact a degree of retribution in his own postwar reflections. He later referred to some questionable private conversations he purported to have had with Brooke, which the assiduous diary keeper Brooke never mentioned. One was the occasion when Brooke suggested that the cross-Channel invasion should be abandoned and let the Russians do the job, and Brooke believed the Russians would return to their borders once the war was over. Brooke never opposed *Overlord*, but was concerned about its timing, and he had a better understanding of Stalin's long-term aims than Eisenhower, especially during the war years. Brooke was also supposed to have told Eisenhower that 'if another war happened, we would entrust our last man and last shilling to your command'.[32] Given the general understanding of Brooke such a conversation was simply unbelievable. Eisenhower found Brooke and especially Montgomery difficult to handle, and with the benefit of hindsight he deserved some sympathy. Brooke always found fault with Eisenhower, but mainly in his diary, as they could converse in a civilised and courteous manner. Montgomery was another issue, and most pertinent was Gort's observation about Montgomery stating, 'he was not quite a gentleman', he was not one of us, and with some justification. There are those who believe that this was Montgomery's strength, but it caused too many problems with and for Eisenhower.

The growing concern, apart from keeping the Americans onside, were events in North Africa, when Churchill expressed the fear that Rommel was making enough progress to reach as far as Cairo. Time and time again Churchill wanted Auchinleck replaced, and several times, as in the past, the COS made desperate attempts to modify Churchill's wired transmissions to the general. Brendan Bracken, Churchill's personal adviser, had privately spoken to Brooke about dissuading Churchill from his desire to go to the Middle East, probably for safety reasons, and Brooke was more than happy to comply for that as well as other motives. Annoyingly for Brooke, Leo Amery's son arrived from the Middle East and informed Churchill and Brooke that the prime minister must go to boost the falling morale amongst the troops. Churchill was pleased with the compliment, but Brooke found the young man like 'a cheeky young pup', questioned him and thought the message of low morale came from idle chatter in the messes, and called him a 'bar-lounger'. Brooke was especially irritated when at a Cabinet meeting Churchill ran down the Middle East army in a 'shocking way', but Brooke was finding that to support Auchinleck was an uphill struggle, not least with his own increasing doubts. The prime minister persisted in asking why the 750,000 men in North Africa were not fighting, as it seemed that only 100,000 were in the field of direct combat. Brooke noted that Churchill seemed unaware of the sheer vastness of the North African area over which the conflict was taking place. Later in the month Brooke had a 'sad' interview with General Ritchie who had been summoned home. Brooke felt his old friend, who had served well in France, had not been given the best of orders, and he told him to take over a Home Division for a time, then he would give him a Corps. This he did later and so kept his promise. Ritchie's removal did not help the North African enterprise, and by the end of the month it was clear that Auchinleck's attack had been repulsed; Brooke was naturally concerned but Churchill was furious.

Churchill never gave up his desire to attack the north of Norway, and McNaughton saw Brooke because he had been asked once again to study a plan for the Canadians to carry through this project, which Brooke considered a useless policy and unnecessary in the overall strategy; he was, many observers since agree, correct in this line of criticism. It was in Brooke's view 'impractical' and he explained this to McNaughton. The political interference by Churchill in military matters Brooke had understood would be an issue. He recognised this from the start of their working together, probably from the time he had furiously challenged Churchill over the phone about the lack of sense in losing men in the Brittany redoubt in June 1940. Later in the month, McNaughton returned saying he needed five divisions, 20 squadrons and a large fleet; Brooke was astonished at these requirements, but he probably realised that McNaughton had taken his advice by coming up with these impossible demands.

At a Cabinet meeting in the second week of July the problem of the PQ17 convoy disaster was discussed. When the convoy PQ17 scattered it was because it was believed the *Tirpitz* was at sea, and the convoy was ordered to disperse and was virtually destroyed (possibly up to 75 per cent). This had been the order of the admiral of the fleet, Sir Dudley Pound, and it appeared that he failed to heed his own intelligence sources, which had indicated that the silence on the airwaves, and lack of general wireless traffic, seemed to imply the battleship *Tirpitz* was not at sea. Whether Brooke was aware of this at the time was unlikely because his vitriol towards Pound knew no bounds. It was a 'stormy meeting' but it was finally decided to stop sending convoys through the perilous Arctic waters. Brooke would have supported this because he tended to believe that in 'terms of resources Britain was committing too much to the Russians'.[33] It was a tough decision, and later in the month the Cabinet had to deal with an abusive letter from Stalin demanding the restarting of convoys, as well as a second front; both would happen, but later, in what the British tend to call 'due process of time'.

Brooke had his *bêtes noires*, amongst them Pound and de Gaulle, but during this month he added another and noted that Mountbatten was 'assuming wild powers to himself again'. He tended to like Mountbatten at a social level, but Mountbatten's sudden elevation from captain to the COS had not been the best of moves, and most historians shared the same doubts as Brooke. Brooke was, however, learning how to deal with Churchill, asking him during a pleasant garden moment over a drink whether he could go to the Middle East via Gibraltar and Malta, and Churchill consented; later Brooke thought he might add India to the list. He knew that to ask Churchill for something was never sensible if he were in a bad mood, because he rarely changed his mind. Brooke was greatly relieved he could travel by himself to see what was happening, but he was frustrated when he was asked to delay because the Americans were coming to Britain. He was trying to work with the Atlantic cousins, and he had just had a dinner at the Ritz with Eisenhower and many other attendant Americans. He had watched Americans training in Northern Ireland, but he was dreading this visit because he and Churchill knew they were crossing the Atlantic because of the British refusal to follow their agreed plans.

Marshall was the one who wanted action in Europe, Admiral King wanted the Pacific as the priority, and mercifully Harry Hopkins tended to agree with the British; it was an unusual mix and Brooke described it as a 'queer party'. The Americans arrived by plane, but the weather was so bad Churchill sent his train to take them to Chequers. It did not start well because Marshall ordered the train to London where he had fixed a meeting with Eisenhower; Churchill was furious. Brooke was personally pleased because it avoided 'another Chequers' meeting'. Marshall was determined to demand Operation *Sledgehammer* for taking the Cotentin peninsula, and Brooke pushed forward all the problems. Not least amongst these was the German ability to move forces around Europe with considerable ease, and muster bomber and fighter aircraft at this stage. Hopkins was present and Brooke was suspicious as to what was happening in the American camp. Hopkins was Roosevelt's close friend and adviser, and with the elections approaching, as mentioned above, the president preferred that American soldiers were fighting Germans, in what he perceived to be the less dangerous area of North Africa. The British at least had the American president on side.

As far as Brooke was concerned any 1942 cross-Channel operation was dead in the water, and even the year 1943. This type of military activity, as far as Brooke was concerned, largely depended on the Russian situation. It was clear that Marshall wanted a rigid plan, but Brooke was dumbfounded as to why his American counterpart failed to see the self-evident problems. The American troops which Brooke had seen for himself were newly trained, and they would be pitted against highly proficient and battle-experienced Wehrmacht troops. The proposed plan was an amphibious landing and the Germans could reinforce the point of attack much more quickly than the Allies. There was also a shortage of vessels which would remain that way until the Mediterranean was free, and if Russia collapsed there were thousands of experienced and toughened troops who could move west rapidly. It also struck Brooke that Marshall had no concept of the dangers of crossing the English Channel, especially during the winter months with an amphibious landing, which also worried Churchill. In July 1941 Churchill had told Eden that the medals on his chest marked the Dardanelles, Antwerp, Dakar and Greece; Churchill had been responsible for all these failures, and he could have added Norway and Crete, but he at least recognised the inherent dangers of amphibious landings and evacuations. For his part, Brooke had a completely different sequence of future events, which first included the 'liberation of North Africa', though he meant by this phrase Allied occupation. The next was to open the Mediterranean which would free up shipping, and to remove Italy from the war, and then, and only if Russia survived the onslaught, to look to invading France and then Germany. Brooke knew from bitter experience that the Wehrmacht and

Luftwaffe were powerful and disciplined forces, and they would never be easy opponents as the future years would prove.

The arguments were long and varied in many directions, with, as Brooke wrote, Admiral King sitting there 'like a sphinx' hoping that the Pacific would soon be placed at the top of the priority list. The Americans presented a draft memo which suggested an attack on the Cherbourg salient, to be followed by a full invasion. They decided they would need to speak to Roosevelt. It was a head-on clash of policies, but amenable, and that evening they all had, according to Brooke, an enjoyable dinner at Claridge's, but it would be surprising if there were not some subdued tensions at their dining table. There may have been many frustrating and annoying times for Brooke, but he always managed to eat in the best places.

The next day, 23 July, was his 59th birthday and it started with his usual 'difficult' COS meeting. The good news seeped through that Roosevelt had replied and agreed that the 1942 Western Front was off, and he was in favour of invading north-west Africa. Brooke does not mention it, but it was highly likely, as mentioned above, that Hopkins was again exercising his influence; Churchill was probably not so surprised. The fact that an immediate attack on the Continent had been nullified must have been music to Brooke's ears, especially in the American acceptance of the north-west African operation. The Cabinet was divided, but Brooke managed to persuade the majority to his common military sense of thinking.

## Middle East

Brooke had not had much of a personal life in the early summer; he only managed two visits to Ferney Close, had a couple of lunches helped by Benita popping up to London, and was having another portrait painted by an Oswald Birley. He realised that with Benita off to Cornwall and him going abroad, it was to be another long separation.

Now these Anglo-Americans issues were resolved, at least for the time being, Brooke was able to concentrate on heading towards North Africa, something he was desperate to do to examine the situation first-hand. The news was that Auchinleck was facing more problems with his attack which unsettled Churchill. He attended the last COS meeting only to learn from Portal, to his absolute horror, that Churchill had changed his mind and that he would be following Brooke to North Africa, and he wanted Brooke to accompany him on a visit to Stalin. Churchill would have undoubtedly have taken Brooke to Russia anyway, but he had also received a letter from Stalin with the sentence 'the presence of the Chief of the Imperial General Staff would be extremely desirable'. Brooke may or may not have been privy to this letter.[34] This request made Brooke somewhat 'liverish' as he prepared to fly from Cornwall to Gibraltar. He also noted that he had better take a new diary because he could not afford to crash into enemy territory with the current one in his possession.

He had thought about this in the Battle of France, and again he had to realise the potential danger of his thoughts and insights which he committed to a personal diary. It was a risky matter keeping this sort of diary but of great joy to future historians.

During August, on the global scene American troops had landed at Guadalcanal, Operation *Pedestal* had brought a convoy through to a besieged Malta, the Dieppe Raid had transpired to be a total disaster, and at the end of the month the Battle of Halfa started as Rommel tried to break through the British defence lines guarding Egypt. For Brooke it was a vastly different month, travelling some three and a half days by plane, visiting Gibraltar, Malta, the Middle East, Teheran and Moscow. There were difficult moments of conflicting viewpoints for Brooke having to confront various problems, restraining Churchill, and being offered a new post which caused him pause for thought and a life-long self-questioning. The Anglo-American debate transmuted into a Russian confrontation, while the American concerns now centred on Operation *Torch*.

On the first day of August Brooke had a tour of Gibraltar, and he was amazed at the way the Rock was used for safety cover, and that a road had been driven through the natural gigantic edifice. He then flew to Malta and landed in the dark, because it was dangerous for the pilot to be up and about with enemy fighters in the vicinity. When he arrived, he was concerned about Gort who was living off the same rations as those imposed on the population, and Gort travelled by bicycle having to carry it himself across bombed sites. Brooke was worried for him, but it certainly indicated Gort was a man of strong social principles. He stayed with Gort and took a tour of the island and was shocked to see the damage in Valletta harbour, where the sheer destruction gave him memories of the Great War. He shared possible future plans with Gort in the hope it would cheer him up, because his old commander believed he was deliberately being kept in a backwater. They spotted a German plane, but it just passed over. Malta was a vital island in the Mediterranean, and it impinged in a critical way on the North African conflict, because of the essential communication links it provided.

The year 1941 had been a crucial time for supplies being sent to Africa; in August some '35% of supplies and reinforcements were sunk and 63% in October' which caused serious concern.[35] Malta was like a port in the middle of the sea, or put more succinctly by Rommel's adjutant, 'Malta probably has to be occupied first, as we cannot leave the English on our flank.'[36] Throughout January Field Marshal Kesselring had continued an intensive air attack on Malta, but he later wrote that the island needed to be captured. Kesselring was never ordered to invade, and this failure to occupy Malta would prove to be a decisive factor in the Mediterranean campaign. Rommel would become one of Kesselring's scapegoats, Kesselring complaining in his postwar interrogation that Rommel kept changing his mind about Malta.[37] It was a matter of timing: in the *Rommel Papers* it is clear that Rommel believed 'Malta should have been taken instead of Crete'.[38] Later Rommel was to write,

'It had actually been intended that Malta should be taken by Italo-German parachute and airborne forces…but for some unaccountable reason our High Command abandoned this scheme.' The truth is that Hitler was simply not keen; to him it was just an island, but he misread its importance. In many ways Gort was on the front line.

After leaving Malta, Brooke landed in Cairo almost at the same time as Churchill arrived in his plane. He was met there by Robert Corbett, the CGS (Chief of the General Staff), whom Brooke thought was 'a very small man', both in size and personal stature. A few days later Brooke ensured Corbett was

**Cairo Conference,** Lord Mountbatten present (US Army)

replaced, and was further convinced he was right when Corbett, who was only 54, asked to retire. Brooke thought little of this attitude and was pleased that Smuts had arrived at the same conclusion. This inability of Auchinleck to select the best men was, in Brooke's opinion, becoming one of his chief weaknesses. Brooke did, however, meet Field Marshal Jan Smuts on this expedition, and he thought very highly of him. Churchill admired Smuts and often relied on his observations and insights, and most people were impressed by him. Churchill's secretary Jock Colville thought that if Churchill were killed this man could make a fine prime minister even if it caused some problems. He became so obsessed with this notion, that he wrote to his mother in the anticipation she 'should put it to Queen Mary' with the idea 'of filtering it to the King' who chose the prime minister.[39] It was not that often that Brooke would meet someone he immediately admired.

As soon as Brooke and Churchill came together, Brooke knew it was going to be a contentious time because the prime minister was complaining about the lack of action, and wanting Auchinleck to remain commander of the Middle East, and to place Gott in charge of the Eighth Army. Brooke was not impressed by General William Gott (nicknamed Strafer) whom he considered somewhat 'too tired', perhaps somewhat unfairly.* It was during these initial discussions that Brooke's own future was raised, as Churchill, frustrated by Brooke's continuous objections, suggested he should take over the command. Brooke's response was to argue that

---

\* It was Gott's aggressive and impetuous personality which probably appealed to Churchill. Eden had served with Gott during the Great War, and in this case, despite Auchinleck's and Brooke's views, Eden's proposal appeared to win the debate.

he had not been trained in 'desert warfare' which was an odd defence, because Rommel and Montgomery (whom Brooke had in mind) had had no such specific training. Brooke later wondered whether he had missed one of life's opportunities, because on looking back he had found overseeing II Corps in France during action an exhilarating experience, and better than the 'friction and frustration' of working with Churchill. It would certainly have been an unusual moment in terms of British military history. Even later in life Brooke pondered on this opportunity, and if he had taken the offer, he 'might well have been in the position of the national, indeed international hero that fell instead to his protégé Montgomery'.[40] Later at a social function in the Dorchester, Smuts claimed it was him who had suggested Brooke for this post of command. If Churchill had pursued this (he may have used it as a threat) he would have lost one of his best advisers. Brooke was not an opportunist like Churchill, he was never prepared to gamble, but he was a realist and calculated every proposal. Nevertheless, in hindsight it has been suggested that perhaps Churchill was 'being disingenuous with Brooke...he may have offered the post because he wanted a more malleable CIGS...and perhaps Brooke did not accept it for that reason.'[41] It is almost impossible to conceive that Churchill would select his CIGS for a subordinate post, and it may have been a passing moment of anger at Brooke's stubbornness or his sheer frustration at the lack of action. On the other hand, Churchill's suggestion that Brooke took on the command may not have been a testy suggestion. Churchill wrote later that CIGS 'whose duty it was to appraise the quality of our generals, was my adviser. I first offered the command in the Middle East to him...and I knew that no man would fill it better.'[42] Brooke had proved his ability as a field commander in 1939–40 France, and he would often reflect over whether he had made the right decision.

Brooke was not always easy to 'chum with' as Churchill knew. Brooke commanded the respect of his fellow senior officers because of his sheer professionalism, 'but rarely' as Grigg noted, 'did he arouse affection, for he was insular and rarely offered friendship, regarding subordinates as cogs in the machine.'[43] This may have sounded somewhat harsh, but Britain at this stage needed a 'machine' or a power-hub in order to win through a dangerous period in its national history. Brooke tended to relax with Dill and Wavell because of past experience and respect for these men, but had his contemporaries read his personal asides in his diary to Benita and the family, they would have found his loving and affectionate expressions hard to believe. Junior officers may have been less surprised. He was a forbidding character, and it is difficult to find any official photograph of Brooke where he does not appear stern, and most men stood in awe of him. Brooke was also aware that he was one of the very few who could act as a restraint on Churchill's sudden whims and precipitous ideas for immediate action; this was a major role for Brooke as CIGS, and it may be that even Churchill recognised this aspect. Most senior commanders probably knew how he protected them as men in the field of combat; even Montgomery had felt his sharp rebukes earlier in France over the venereal disease letter, but he knew that Brooke supported him. He had supported Ritchie even though there were question marks, and Brooke had also spent months defending Auchinleck although it was an 'uphill struggle' and he was having his own doubts. Churchill may have felt annoyed at Brooke for objecting to his grand ideas, but he must have known his value as the most respected CIGS, and it is difficult not to conclude that Churchill's suggestion was a clever political threat. It had been Brooke's persuasive and forthright lecture-type addresses which had brought the Americans into line with British thinking; he knew his job.

The discussions on the Middle East were important, they involved safe sea communications and the area of Abadan for its oil resources, and it was at least an attack on German and Italian forces. Churchill wanted Gott to take over the Eighth Army and Brooke proposed Montgomery as the best choice. In the end the conflict was resolved by Gott being shot down by an enemy fighter, which had stumbled across Gott's transport plane. One of Churchill's complaints had been that Montgomery was too far away, but Gott's sudden death stopped this argument. Many officers would have been surprised that in his diary Brooke wrote, 'I feel so sorry for Mrs. Gott,' as he obviously felt for her; he was not the automaton that so many believed. Brooke was encouraged when Auchinleck agreed that Montgomery would be the right choice for the Eighth Army, but he worried that Auchinleck would interfere too much in Montgomery's command. Churchill was also arguing the case for Jumbo Wilson, who Brooke thought too old, but later he recognised the fact that his judgement was wrong. Brooke retorted to Churchill's pursuing Gort and Jumbo Wilson, by suggesting that Eden always chose old Green Jacket officers. The next day they visited El Alamein and met the commanders, especially those overseeing the Australian and South African troops. The choice of commanders and senior officers was Brooke's constant nightmare, not helped by Churchill's interference as he regarded this as the prime minister's right. As noted by Andrew Roberts, 'it is hard not to escape Sir Alan Brooke's conclusion that the brightest and the best British soldiers had been killed in the First World War,' but adding the pertinent comment that this 'fails to explain why the Germans were so good' in the Second War.[44]

When they returned Churchill rushed into Brooke's quarters while he was still dressing, excited at his 'new ideas'. He had decided to split the Middle East into two commands divided by the Suez Canal; to the east would be called the Middle East, and the west would be the Near East. He suggested, again, that Brooke be the commander of the Near East with Montgomery commanding the Eighth Army, but because of all the reasons Brooke had reflected on before, especially his ability to restrain Churchill like no other could, he refused, and Churchill accepted his decision. Smuts and Churchill talked and arrived at the decision that Alexander would take over the Near East, and Auchinleck the Middle East; Brooke found this more acceptable. The Cabinet had been wired over the issues, and it transpired that they only objected to the nomenclature, and it was agreed that the name Middle East be retained west of the Suez, and Near East would be known as the Persia and Iraq Command.

Auchinleck took the suggestion very badly and could see no sense in the new structure, and he declined, expressing the wish to retire. This reaction caused Auchinleck to go down in Brooke's estimation, regarding it as 'unsoldierly' and behaving like an 'offended film star'. Brooke later wrote that 'I have lost all confidence in him as a commander, he is bad in the selection of men to serve him and has a faulty conception of modern war.'[45] Montgomery later weighed in characteristically and unpleasantly, claiming that 'Auchinleck should never be employed again in any capacity', but he used Auchinleck's major plans claiming them as his own.

Churchill also decided that he wanted Alexander in charge of Montgomery and the Eighth Army, and Brooke had to spend time with Churchill explaining the nature of army command. When Alexander arrived, Brooke was somewhat devious and rushed into the privacy of the toilets to find and warn Alexander of Churchill's 'mad thinking'. Later Brooke had to see Auchinleck who was in a 'stormy and unpleasant mood' which was not helped when Brooke had to explain to his old colleague that they had lost trust in him. It was, Brooke noted, a difficult moment, but he was pleased that eventually they parted on good terms; Auchinleck would at least have been aware that Brooke had long supported him against the prime minister's constant criticisms and demands.

## To Russia

The next stage of this tumultuous month was the long and dangerous flight to Moscow. They travelled in three Liberators which were not designed for passenger comfort, and Brooke had a bed set up for him in the bomb racks. They stopped in Teheran and enjoyed a meal under an old-style traditional Persian tent. The next day Churchill's plane took off for Moscow, but it was not so straightforward for Brooke as his plane developed serious problems and had to return to Teheran. This time Brooke and his party were taken in a Douglas aircraft which was much more comfortable and with a Russian crew, landing at Baku for fuel. Brooke was pleased to spot an eagle below them, and he studied the Caucasus as they flew over; he looked for defence lines which he could not see, arriving in Moscow at 8.30 in the evening. It was to be a vastly different experience from America, and there they met Stalin and Molotov, whose main agenda was to press for a second front immediately. Stalin accused the British of breaking their word, lacking courage, not realising the importance of the Russian front, and only giving the Russians the equipment which they did not need themselves. Stalin even accused the British of being frightened by the Germans. It was, as Brooke noted, a period of continuous abuse. Typically, Brooke blamed Beaverbrook for making too many promises from his earlier visit. It would not take long for Brooke to realise this was down to Stalin's character more than anything else. At one time Brooke believed that Stalin's abuse was deliberate to uncover Churchill's character; Stalin was described as a 'smiling tiger in a tea shop'.[46]

Brooke and Churchill had to repeat all the arguments they had used in the American debate which was not an easy task. The Americans had used cogent arguments such as the concentration of forces, a short sea passage, and Brooke had used all his logic to counter these views. The Russians were less easy to cope with, and they demanded yet more urgency. They were under intense pressure from the German military, and they needed German resources to be occupied elsewhere. Again, Brooke may have appeared too cautious both to the Americans and Russians, but above all he was a realist, and understood the limited British resources.

Brooke was much taken by the image Stalin presented of himself, noting that the two leaders, 'Churchill and Stalin, are poles apart as human beings, and I cannot see a friendship between them such as exists between Roosevelt and Winston.'[47] He often accused Churchill of being impetuous and he was right, but he was equally astute about Stalin, observing that he was a 'man of facts and a realist', later adding that 'Stalin is an outstanding man but not an attractive one, with an unpleasantly cold, crafty, dead face…but a quick brain and a real grasp of the essentials of war.'[48] Some of Stalin's better generals may have disagreed over Stalin's military ability, but Stalin was above all crafty and cruel.

The Soviet leader's social life did not appeal to Brooke; noting the amount of caviar and vodka which was always available was pleasant enough, but when he had to attend a banquet in one of the Kremlin's state rooms, Brooke was astonished at the serving of 19 courses (mainly oily fish) and the endless toasts until he felt sick at the sight of more food. He had to propose a toast which he offered to the Red Army and then he was left alone.

More interestingly he watched a display of the new rocket mortars which he thought would be useful. This was the device later dubbed as 'Stalin's organ', but when they later asked for information on this weapon there was never a reply. He also met the Polish General Anders who was back in Russia, rounding up Polish soldiers who had been prisoners, and moving them towards Persia. Later he had a private meeting with Anders who kept tapping the tabletop with his cigarette case, telling Brooke that if he made this noise they could not be overheard; Brooke had at this stage no idea that tables and rooms were cleverly bugged, but he may have suspected this that this was a possibility. Anders explained there were many prominent Poles, including high-ranking officers, he could not trace – they had simply disappeared without explanation, and he suspected they had been eliminated in some Siberian camp. Time would prove this claim correct when the Katyń massacres came to light. As Brooke looked around Moscow, he reflected that if the place indicated the value of Bolshevism 'we must certainly look for something different'. The fact was that it reflected a totalitarian state which was as corrupt as Nazi Germany; Brooke may have reflected that his ill-tempered personal diatribes against democracy were mistaken.

Brooke was concerned about the Germans forcing their way through to the oilfields, and he asked General Voroshilov about the defences across the Caucasus.* Voroshilov informed Brooke he lacked permission for a such a study, but later he was told that the place was covered by defences, prompting Brooke to write he was 'told a complete pack of lies'. Brooke had only just flown over the area, and with his trained eye he had seen nothing, and later ruminated that it was fortunate that Hitler was fixated on Stalingrad and not pushing to the south. Russia was not a trip Brooke enjoyed, feeling as if he were in an alien place, even when compared with his recent trip to the unfamiliar desert regions. As they flew back he looked down during this long haul over the Holy Land, saw Galilee and thought 'about Our Lord walking on water' and probably, thinking of miracles, prayed that the Alexander and Montgomery combination would work. He met Wavell and explained that the Iraq and Persian Command would be attached to India, and he was told Rommel appeared to be preparing to attack. He gained this information from wireless intercepts, but he did not mention this Sigint (Signal Intelligence) in his diary in case it fell into the wrong hands.

When he was at the Embassy, he picked up the information about Dieppe and the total disaster of the raid. The Dieppe raid had begun life as Operation *Rutter*, but had been cancelled in July, chiefly because it involved so many personnel knowing the details making the security risk dangerously high. Montgomery and others advised that it should not be revived as an operation solely on these grounds. Despite this warning the operation was revitalised under the name of *Jubilee*, and it had been launched at 5 a.m. on 19 August 1942. It involved over 6,000 infantrymen, a huge number of Royal Navy vessels, and a substantial contribution by fighter squadrons. Less than six hours later the raid was abandoned with the most appalling losses. The Canadians constituted the bulk of fighting men, and out of 6,086 men a total of 3,623 were killed, wounded, or captured, a staggering 60 per cent. 'It was the sort of event that on the Eastern Front was a daily occurrence' but in the West was unacceptable.[49] The debacle was contentious, and Mountbatten's role was questionable in causing this disastrous fiasco. Mountbatten always claimed it as a victory, a 'tester' for D-Day, and many historians to this day still believe the veracity of this claim. However, when Andrew Roberts described this view as 'tripe' he was closer to the reality: it was a trumped-up excuse.[50] The lesson of attacking a major port without intensive intelligence or naval and aerial bombardment, and lacking secrecy, did not need so many Canadian deaths at Dieppe to make this self-evident point. Brooke, who had fought with the Canadians at Vimy Ridge (April 1917), recognised it as an

---

* Kliment Voroshilov (1881–1969) was a prominent Soviet military officer and politician during Stalin's time. He was one of the original five Soviet Union Marshals, and a political survivor. He died in 1969 and was placed in the Kremlin Wall.

appalling disaster, and its only real lesson as far as Brooke was concerned was this tragedy acted as a warning against crossing the Channel without appropriate and extensive preparation. When sometime later Brooke was critical of Mountbatten's planning at Chequers, it led to a confrontation with Mountbatten who was furious, and he wrote to Brooke that he wanted an investigation. This never happened, and Mountbatten's official biographer believed Brooke 'mollified' his subject 'and there is no trace of a written reply'.[51]

## Home Again

Brooke met Jumbo Wilson and informed him of his fears that the Germans might try and penetrate the oilfields, after which Churchill made a 'secret slip away' to fly home followed closely by Brooke. The area was infiltrated and monitored with enemy spies, and it was essential that these 'agents' were kept in the dark when Britain's top command were flying within the range of enemy fighters. At home Brooke expressed his joy at seeing Benita again, and then discovered that new tensions with the Americans were now focusing on the plans for Operation *Torch*, the invasion of north-west Africa. He was approached by the Duke of Gloucester who wanted Brooke to employ him. Brooke found this embarrassing because he had worked with him in France, and he did not think he could maintain the necessary pace. He had to meet the king who pressed the same issue about his brother, but he was glad the monarch and Gloucester did not push the matter and it slipped away; Brooke's silence on the issue was enough to register with the royal family. On the last day of the month he wrote that he had a bad COS because 'I bit the First Sea Lord, and felt depressed the rest of the day having bitten a corpse.' He felt bad about his views on Pound later, but their unpleasant existence in his diary reflected the veracity of his diary when studied in later years. He also heard that, as predicted, Rommel had started his attack. The Middle East and Russia had been a quite different experience for Brooke, but life at home followed the same pattern of the previous months.

September continued with a battle royal between him and Churchill, somewhat disconcertingly for Brooke, because he gathered from Churchill's doctor that he was worried about the prime minister's heart since his last American visit. The doctor had informed Brooke that Churchill was once again thinking of flying to America to sort out the *Torch* problems. Brooke agreed he would suggest otherwise, but he warned that if he went there alone, he would need to take a politician. In this diary entry he revealed that he was by nature democratic despite his occasional criticisms about the system. Brooke offered military advice, but he knew that when it came to grand national strategy an elected politician had to be present. Ambassador Samuel Hoare had arrived from Spain and was warning of the ramifications if north-west Africa were invaded. Franco had his own ambitions in that area (as Hitler was also aware) and the Spanish non-involvement was important. It was a constant concern, but Franco, who was dependent on overseas resources, knew that the British Royal Navy could blockade his country with ease, and the Americans might stop the essential imports. Although Franco believed Hitler would eventually succeed, he was more concerned about his personal grip on Spanish power.

The proposed American plans were causing some concern, and a meeting was called at Number 10 with Eisenhower, Admiral Ramsay and General Mark Clark, whom Brooke met and liked, but who in time would become egotistical and an embittered Anglophobe. They and others met to discuss the problems. Even when plans had been agreed there were the usual disagreements as to how they should be operated. Marshall wanted to have one landing at Casablanca, but there were concerns over the well-known high levels of surf in that area, and Brooke suggested two invading points, one at Casablanca and another at Algiers, and then suggested that they move rapidly eastwards to cut off German and Italian supply routes. How far Vichy France would cooperate and whether Franco would react were the current concerns, and eventually Roosevelt and Churchill waded in with their own ideas. They finally decided on several landings, but Brooke was correct in suggesting moving eastwards as soon as possible, because as soon as the landings eventually occurred, the Germans might arrive in huge numbers at the Vichy-controlled airfields in Tunisia, which they eventually did. There is no doubt that when it came to forward thinking in military operations, Brooke was amongst the absolute best. There was debate over who should be the commander in charge, and Dill reminded the British that because the American dream of *Sledgehammer* was dead in the water, they should propose an American for the post. At first Brooke and Churchill considered Marshall, but eventually Eisenhower emerged as the man of the moment. Churchill decided to send Eisenhower, Mountbatten and Ramsay to America; he asked Brooke if he wanted to go, but Brooke (whom Churchill probably wanted on hand) told him 'Dill would do a good job.'

Churchill had once again become fixated on an attack in north Norway, having mentioned it to Stalin who liked the idea. Stalin would have appreciated anything so long as it drew the attention of the German forces. Brooke's reaction was immediate, pointing out that this venture would be hampered by lack of shipping resources because of the reinstated Arctic convoys, and the necessity of preparing for *Torch*. There was always the risk that in the winter months some 80 vessels could be ice-trapped in Archangel. The next day Brooke held a COS meeting to make sure everyone was of the same opinion. Churchill was to remain unmoved and later sent for the Canadian McNaughton with the idea of sending him to speak with Stalin. McNaughton was not happy about the proposal, and he quietly sent a staff officer back to Canada to explain the situation to his own politicians. The reply was an outright negative response to Churchill's proposal which greatly upset Churchill. He spoke to Brooke about the refusal, who was quietly delighted with the Canadian answer. It was a difficult task for Brooke dealing with the mercurial genius of Churchill who was so upset that 'tears streamed down his face'. Churchill explained he was only trying to win the war, and at times felt he was the only one with any ideas on how to achieve this goal. This sad anger by Churchill had its effect on Brooke who wrote that 'he is a wonderful mixture, but one never knows what mood he will be in next'.[52] Brooke was correct in his observations. Churchill by his own admission suffered from bouts of depression, which he called his black dog days, and he was not just prone to angry outbursts but more than capable of losing his temper, and often stomping out of the room. This downright refusal by the Canadian prime minister at least had the result that at long last Churchill gave up on the Norwegian venture.

Brooke had taken a few days' break on 19 September to go grouse shooting on the moors. While he was enjoying this relaxation, a dispatch rider arrived asking Brooke to make immediate contact with the prime minister using a safety scrambler phone. It was for Brooke an irritating intrusion as far as he was concerned, mainly because he had to abandon his leisure and be taken to the nearest aerodrome at Catterick. Once there he discovered that Churchill was speaking of a message sent by Alexander delaying an attack in North Africa. Brooke had not seen the message, and the next day he had to arrange for this correspondence to be sent to him by yet another dispatch motorcycle rider. Churchill in the next call petulantly demanded why Brooke was unaware of the strategic developments, and Brooke informed him that Churchill had agreed with him that he could take a few days' rest to shoot grouse. Brooke pointed out that there was nothing urgent in Alexander's message, and a delay by the commander in the field had to be respected. Brooke later noted that he always found it annoying and disturbing when the prime minister constantly pursued him, even when he was having a day's break away at Ferney Close or elsewhere. 'For his part Churchill showed little understanding of the sensitivity and tension concealed behind Brooke's austere nature,' and he was not interested in fishing, shooting or that Brooke may have had a family life.[53] The strained emotions between these two men may have seemed palpable at times, and their relationship was to fluctuate wildly over the ensuing years, but there remained a deep underlying mutual respect. Had Churchill and others read Brooke's personal letters to his wife and their loving affectionate nature, they would have seen a glimpse of the real man, but there is the possible speculation that Churchill had perceived this personal dimension of Brooke. As it was, because of Brooke's nature he tended to be a lonely man, who admired in his own way Churchill, and who was always terrified about Chequers which Churchill relished so much. They were two different men but sharing the same goals, and despite the endless quarrels and disagreements, they may have understood one another better than the diaries suggest.

There was, during these months, an 'office' type Machiavellian plot fermenting. The secretary of state for war, James Grigg, whom Brooke admired, quietly complained to Brooke that Duncan Sandys, the prime minister's son-in-law, whom Brooke did not appreciate, was 'snooping' for Churchill, and Grigg suspected that Sandys was after his job. Brooke was immediately concerned, and he wrote that if Grigg were supplanted by Sandys he would have no choice but to resign. There may have been some substance in Grigg's fears because Brooke heard that Sandys had complained to his father-in-law, and he was peevish that Griggs was not giving him enough responsibility. A few days later Brooke spoke confidentially to Eden about the situation; he promised he would investigate the matter. In October Churchill warned Brooke that if Grigg handed in his resignation he would accept it, which concerned Brooke because he now considered Grigg not only as a friend, but as one of the best to hold that vital post. Brooke never knew how Eden handled the situation, but it worked, and Grigg remained in this post for the whole war, while to everyone's relief Sandys was moved away from the War Office. Sandys was not the only one jostling for a position, and the Duke of Gloucester arrived to tell Brooke that he had acquired a position in the War Office, with Brooke noting in his diary it was not an easy job, suggesting he may possibly have been behind the appointment. Apart from grouse shooting and occasional visits to and from Benita, Brooke had little personal time, but he was pleased to see his eldest daughter Rosemary (who was a subaltern in the ATS) at home for a day. Later in the month both Brooke and Benita enjoyed a meal together only to be struck down for a couple of days by what sounded like a mild form of food poisoning.

The Russian front was increasing in its ferocity, but in Britain the main concerns centred on the problems of shipping, the preparation of plans for the *Torch* arrangements, and North Africa generally. As noted above Alexander was delaying the attack which was, naturally, upsetting Churchill who always wanted action at once. This led Brooke to write later that 'unfortunately Churchill always wanted to stick his fingers into the pie before it was cooked' even though after Rommel's attack he was 'back where he started'.[54] As with Auchinleck, Brooke spent time and energy redrafting Churchill's angry messages to Alexander, often with the backup of the COS. Brooke advised Churchill that the commander in the field had to know that he had the prime minister's confidence. Brooke also had to argue with Churchill's idea of sending tanks to Turkey. Brooke knew that the tanks were essential for the North African terrain, but Churchill was also doing his best to keep Turkey out of the war; it was, as Brooke knew, a risky gift. In Madagascar, where the fighting in the interior had continued, along with the wrangling between the Free French and Vichy which had been torturously grinding on, it appeared to be resolving itself favourably. Brooke had met de Gaulle when he was leaving Downing Street and who was self-evidently in a bad mood. Brooke later heard that de Gaulle was setting off to give a broadcast, but Churchill had ordered the BBC to switch him off if he departed from the agreed script.

Brooke also heard, somewhat disconcertingly, that MI5 had tapped into a telephone call which appeared to be disclosing information about the *Torch* operation. He was even more disturbed about this piece of information when he was summoned to Churchill on 1 October where, in his words, 'he found him in bed with Duff Cooper (not both in bed!)'. He was told the tapped phone call seemed to indicate that Kennedy, his DMO, was the guilty party. Brooke instantly made his way to his officer's flat where he discovered he was ill. It soon became clear that it was not Kennedy, and later the culprit transpired to be a man called Hannon (SOE) who was too free with his chatter. Britain was not inundated with spies or agents, but it was still too risky to have valuable information talked about on the gossip circuit. De Gaulle's Free French were often accused of this, and it may have been the case that one of the French officers was a Vichy agent. Brooke also thought that Eisenhower's camp was anything but watertight. Later in the month, when Montgomery gave Brooke the date of his attack in North Africa, he asked him to keep it a secret. He decided not to tell Churchill, but he found this difficult because the prime minister was constantly requesting this precise information. A few days later he decided to inform Churchill because it seemed only right, but he impressed on him the need for total secrecy. Only two days after giving Churchill this information, Brooke discovered that Churchill had told Eisenhower and American General Walter Bedell Smith of the date, so he saw Churchill and 'I rubbed his iniquity into him and he was very nice and repentant, and said he would send for Eisenhower immediately at once to impress the necessity for secrecy.'[55] He also found Grigg had told someone else, writing in his diary 'that it is absolutely fatal to tell any politician any secret, they are incapable of keeping it to themselves.'

The COS meetings discussed the state of war as of that moment, and tried to work out the future possibilities. Malta was in a serious state because of lack of food, and the ongoing issue of air support led to some heated moments. On 5 October Churchill had tried to resolve the matter, but in Brooke's mind he failed because he did not understand the necessary ramifications of the debate with the RAF. Brooke had row after row with Portal, and once expressed his delight that Pound stayed awake long enough to support him. He and Portal had much in common in their pursuit of hobbies, they were friends, but such were their roles in the national scene, personal feelings could not be allowed to interfere in their decisions when debating issues of national security and progress. Brooke wrote that he had for a long time planned the North African front and the future way of conducting the war, but times had changed with the Japanese belligerence in the Far East and the arrival of American allies, and just as his plans started to look more viable, he could not convince Portal that bombing alone would force Germany to surrender. Göring had once claimed that he could destroy the British at Dunkirk and bomb England into submission, and Brooke was correct to challenge Portal on this issue of the efficacy of airpower. Tactical bombing could weaken industrial output, but it was, even with carpet bombing, difficult or impossible to reduce a country to surrender until the deadly arrival of nuclear weapons. Brooke's hope and fear played on him, later writing that 'the very fact that these feelings had to be kept entirely to myself made them all the harder to bear.'[56] Brooke stated this as if his attitudes and feelings were hard to detect by others.

He had lunch at Claridge's with the king of Greece, asking himself what precisely the Greek king wanted. It was a simple request that the Greek liaison officer should be given a higher rank to give some sense of dignity to the Greek contribution. He also lunched with Bullitt, the American ambassador to Vichy France, and immediately believed he could not trust him.* The same day he heard that he had been appointed ADC to the king. He seemed, however, more interested in the way information was being gleaned from German POWs by using hidden microphones and stoolpigeons. It was not brutal, but sheer cunning, and after the war it was revealed how useful this had been in collecting information in titbits of conversations, especially from among the senior German officers.†

General Clark flew that month to Gibraltar and then travelled by submarine to the North African coast, a mission which for a senior officer could have been not only risky, not only in a personal sense but because he also knew all the details about the proposed operation. He returned with the good news that Giraud (the French general who had escaped from German captivity) was happy to come over to the Allied side and leave the Vichy regime. While there the clandestine meeting in North Africa was almost compromised by the sudden arrival of the armed police and the visitors had to hide in the cellar. Brooke was somewhat bemused to hear that the British naval captain nearly gave them away by not being able to supress a cough until Clark gave him his chewing gum. Later, when the captain complained it was flavourless, Clark said he was not surprised; he had been chewing it for two hours.

The main concern at the COS meetings continued with the future conduct of the war and the plans for the North African Operation *Torch*, over which Marshall had started to suggest further changes, and how to deal with Spain if it 'turned sour' during the invasion. It was not helped on one occasion when the prime minister turned up unexpectedly and wasted their time when, according to Brooke, 'all he wanted to do was talk'. It was no great surprise that when parts of Brooke's diary became available Churchill resented some passages.

The battle of El Alamein, known as the 'second battle', started on 24 October, and Churchill, being Churchill, expected rapid news of success. This led to more tension with Brooke when he heard that Eden had told Churchill that the attack was 'petering out'. Brooke was simply furious, especially when Churchill threatened to write a note of admonition to Alexander and Montgomery. Brooke told Churchill that Eden was no expert on military tactics, even though Churchill kept reminding him that Eden had been a staff officer in the Great War. Brooke also pointed out that the foreign secretary was not the right person to consult on such matters. At a convened meeting Brooke challenged Eden on the question of

---

* William C. Bullitt had been the first American Ambassador to the Soviet Union, who in 1936 told his overseers not to send spies into Russia, because honesty would confuse their hosts. Bullitt was later ambassador in Paris and was a private and ill-informed source of information for Roosevelt, and Brooke may well have been right in his observations.

† An interesting book on this way of finding information from German officers is Neizel Sönke, *Tapping Hitler's Generals* (Barnsley: Frontline Books, 2007).

tactics and was grateful for the support of Smuts which helped resolve the issue, and 'the temperamental film stars', according to Brooke, 'returned to their tasks, and peace remained in the dovecotes.' Brooke however, admitted in his diary that he was deeply worried and concerned, and hoped that Alexander and Montgomery were up to the task.

November 1942 at long last brought significant success against Rommel Operation *Torch* started in north-west Africa, and there was a sense that a turning point may have been reached after two years of near disasters. The month started with farewelling Eisenhower and Clark, and the news that Montgomery had launched a major attack with the New Zealanders. Brooke visited the airborne division, saw the men in action, the use and loading of gliders, and for once was much impressed watching the men and their training. When he returned to London, he found Churchill in a state of excitement with the information of Montgomery's breakthrough, and he was writing letters to Russia and America with the good news. Even Brendan Bracken's apprehension that Roosevelt's election was causing concern was put aside, and Brooke tried to warn Churchill not to have the church bells rung across the country until it was all confirmed. Wireless intercepts had been picked up from Rommel's headquarters that he was in a state of retreat. It was the victory that Churchill and Brooke had been longing for, and El Alamein has since become part of British and colonial history. They estimated that there were some 13,500 casualties, but the Allies netted some 30,000 prisoners, and Rommel's troops were fleeing west, with Mussolini complaining that the Germans were leaving the Italians behind.

Regarding the prospect of Operation *Torch* Brooke noted that there seemed to be negligible reaction from Germany, Spain and France, though Hoare had raised the issue that the 'natives' might revolt against the incoming forces. Brooke heard that Giraud had arrived safely in Gibraltar and took himself off to a pheasant shoot despite the rain. On 8 November there were landings at Casablanca, Oran and Algiers, and the only bad news was, according to Brooke, Giraud 'had turned sour' and was demanding control of all the forces, and 'his personal vanity may upset some of our schemes'. The relationship with the French leaders was going to be an ongoing concern for the next few months. There was an urgent feeling that it was essential that the Allies did not find themselves at war with Vichy France, and the main and contentious leaders were Giraud, later Admiral Darlan, and of course de Gaulle, all of whom were regarded by many of the Allies as *prima donnas*.

In London they heard the news that Rommel had been driven across the border, that Spain, according to Brooke, was 'wonderfully quiet', and Churchill was 'welling over' with the success he had long hoped for. At a meeting Churchill was jubilant, but Brooke noted that the prime minister 'did not give the army the credit it deserved'. This was not entirely true because he did thank the CIGS and Grigg for their work, but Brooke later added that this was the only public occasion that Churchill ever did such a thing.

On Armistice Day Brooke laid a wreath at the Cenotaph, heard the news that Darlan had signed a separate peace with Clark, and walked home because the fog was too thick for cars. He never mentioned that on that same day Hitler had ordered the occupation of the rest of France, and the Germans and Italians simply walked into Vichy France taking overall control. Brooke's diary was not a general history of the war years, it was a personal diary, but this was a major event.

At the strategic level Hitler was probably concerned about the southern front with North Africa disintegrating before his eyes, and the news about Darlan and Giraud may well have bolstered his continuous distrust of the French. There had been times, especially when Darlan had been in control, when Vichy France had made overtures about a partnership with the Germans; Hitler had always refused such co-operation because of his deep habitual distrust of the French. The British, perhaps more than the Americans, had realised the danger of Darlan as a potential enemy; he was considered to be more dangerous than Laval, 'partly because he was the more "respectable" politician and partly because of his feelings of bitter animosity towards the British.'[57] Darlan, whose great-grandfather had fought at the Battle of Trafalgar, was a devious figure who was considered no improvement on Laval from the Allied point of view, having once claimed that 'if we collaborate with Germany…that is to say, if we work for her in our factories, if we give her certain facilities, we can save the French nation; reduce to a minimum our territorial losses in the colonies and on the mainland; play an honourable, if not important role in the future Europe.'[58] It was little surprise that at a meeting at Chequers Eden vehemently opposed Darlan taking control of the forces, which Churchill had recently considered as a possible way through the Anglo-French quagmire. More to the point the next major strategic move was studied, tending to focus on Sardinia or Sicily, with Bedell Smith, Eisenhower's chief of staff, being consulted.

Brooke was more relaxed than he had been for a long time; he picked up his beloved Benita to go on a pheasant shoot, and then heard on the 7 a.m. news that he had been promoted to GCB (Knight Grand Cross of the Order of the Bath) for his work in North Africa. It was an extraordinary way to hear such personal news, but he was more interested in hearing that wireless intercepts had picked up that Rommel's troops were in a 'bad way' and that a convoy had made its way through to Malta to bring some relief. He was somewhat disconcerted that the Tunisian front appeared sluggish, and he expressed his doubts about Eisenhower whom Brooke thought was more wrapped up in the developing politics of North Africa, as Brooke felt he had no battle experience. He later noted: 'I had little confidence in his ability to handle the military situation confronting him and caused me great anxiety.'[59] Brooke thought the discussions over Darlan were less important than clearing out the Germans; he was probably right, but his political antennae were not as astute as those of Eden. Brooke acknowledged, unsurprisingly, that the best method was for the Allied command to remain in control, especially when he heard that Kesselring, in charge of North Africa, was warning Berlin he had insufficient troops and resources, though some troops had arrived by air, as predicted by Brooke. Not mentioned by Brooke was the news that the French had scuttled their fleet at Toulon, which has since caused some to question why the British attacked the French at Mers-el-Kébir in the first place.

The end of November restarted the tussle with Churchill who was suddenly eager for entry into Europe in 1943, with Brooke claiming Churchill 'never faces realities' and he is 'quite incorrigible and I am exhausted'. Brooke had to point out to him that for such a venture it was first necessary to build up huge forces and the number of ships, again. Brooke had completed his first year as the CIGS and did not think he would last another, because 'at times life was most unpleasant', but added that although the prime minister was a hard taskmaster, 'it is worth all the difficulties to have the privilege to work with such a man.' This was a typical entry of Brooke's end-of-month reflections, and it echoed his feelings towards Churchill for the rest of the war years.

The last month of 1942 produced the usual round of problems for Brooke: the differences of opinion with the COS, mainly over the use of airpower in the Mediterranean, and Churchill suddenly wanting to reopen the old argument for a second front in France during 1943. He was obliged to sit through one COS meeting while Churchill expanded his ideas of building warships out of ice, which Mountbatten had decided was an excellent idea, but without considering that it would cost more than a normally constructed carrier. Churchill often came up with the strangest of ideas, but at least he later contributed and encouraged the invaluable concept of the Mulberry Harbour.* The only light relief for Brooke was his investiture of the GCB at the palace, a few days' grouse shooting, and being able to spend Christmas at home.

After his visit to the palace he met General Catroux leading the Free French in the Levant.† He found him interesting, and he hoped that with this sort of Frenchman the various factions amongst the French would soon dissipate, but this was, as it transpired, a hope too far. Brooke seemed to have little knowledge of the French political divisions which had been self-destructive before the war, and were persisting in the aftermath of the policies following the now-defunct Vichy government. The very next day he had lunch with de Gaulle and found him bitter about Darlan, which was understandable, but de Gaulle was also angry with Catroux. It would be much later into postwar years before the French found some stability, when de Gaulle encouraged French history to be written from his viewpoint.

---

* Floating blocks transported across the Channel to make a temporary harbour for unloading.
† Georges Albert Julien Catroux (1877–1969) was a French general and diplomat who served in both wars, and from 1954 to his death in 1969 was the grand chancellor of the Légion d'honneur.

The main issue was Churchill wanting to move away from the proposed Mediterranean projections and into France in 1943. Dill warned him during this month that Marshall was proposing the same policy. Churchill continued to press the point, arguing that it was essential to fight the German army and not worry about 'Sardines', which was his humorous and cynical way of mentioning the occupation of Sardinia or Sicily. In an argument with Brooke, Churchill pointed out that they had promised Stalin this very thing, to which Brooke retorted they never had. Brooke noted that Churchill then fell quiet, an ominous silence as Brooke realised that in a private moment with Stalin, Churchill had done just that, which made the future look complex if not difficult. None of this was helped with the arrival of Clark Kerr (ambassador in Moscow) who suggested there was a possibility of a truce or peace between the Soviets and Germany, which he later repeated at a COS meeting. Churchill once made the famous claim that Russia is a riddle wrapped in a mystery inside an enigma, and nobody could work out whatever passed through Stalin's mind. As a matter of curiosity, in 1941 Stalin had secretly considered a peace settlement which was unknown at the time. It was in General Zhukov's presence Stalin had instructed Beria to seek an early peace settlement with Hitler, even knowing and acknowledging that it would probably mean losing the Baltic States. Beria then asked Sudoplatov (his trusted henchman) to approach the Bulgarian ambassador in Moscow called Ivan Stamenov to act as an intermediary. Contrary to some historical accounts he agreed 'but his overtures to the Germans were brushed aside'.[60] Others claimed the Bulgarian never made the effort, telling Sudoplatov that even if the 'Russians had to retreat to the Urals you will win in the end.'[61] This effort was made a second time on 7 October but again to no avail. It was clear Stalin 'felt less than confident about the Red Army's defensive capabilities' at that stage of events.[62] Since that moment, however, circumstances had changed considerably. There was a welling up of pure mutual hatred epitomised by the sheer brutality of the Eastern Front; neither dictator could afford to lose face, and both sides thought they were winning. Brooke was probably correct in his belief that a peace was highly unlikely, not least because it appeared to him that the Russians were on the point of turning the tide, and he was correct.

It was not until 15 December that the COS finally produced the paper to try and defeat Churchill's sudden change of mind. Because the Germans had lost at El Alamein it had to be remembered that for the enemy it had been a token force in North Africa to bail the Italians out of their initial mess, but Brooke and his military colleagues knew how massive and battle hardened the Wehrmacht remained. Brooke's original policy was to take Italy out of the war and try and bring Turkey in; this was at least a possibility, unlike, he believed, an ill-prepared and under-resourced dash across the Channel. It was a matter, as always, of convincing Churchill. The next day the force of their prepared arguments swung Churchill around to their way of thinking, and Brooke noted that all he 'had to do now was convince the Americans and Stalin', a difficult proposal with the former and impossible with Stalin.

Brooke was also concerned about the lack of progress in Tunisia and worried about Eisenhower's ability in military tactics. He studied Eisenhower's plans for taking Sardinia, and he was appalled at the amateur approach of just working out the beach landings and not looking beyond; he compared it to Mountbatten's planning, which implied a major condemnation. Later he heard that Eisenhower wanted to postpone an attack by two months, and he noted that 'I am afraid that Eisenhower as a general is hopeless! He submerges himself into politics and neglects his military duties.' He later added a note to this criticism to the effect that he never changed his mind about Eisenhower's tactical ability, but admitted that as a supreme commander what he lacked on the military side 'he made up for by the charm of his personality'.

The problems and issues did not settle over the festive month, and he heard rumours that Montgomery was being somewhat 'sticky' over his pursuit of Rommel. He later found out that the probable source of the rumours came from Air Marshals Coningham and Tedder, 'two airmen who are typically free with their criticisms'. They claimed that Montgomery never wanted to take risks because of the growth of his reputation established at El Alamein.[*] This type of criticism was to arise time and time again, often in the American camp, but many historians have felt there was a degree of substance in these accusations. There was a heated row at the COS over Mountbatten's role and charter, and whether he should command the naval forces in the event of an invasion. Mountbatten had the support of Portal and Pug Ismay, but Brooke and Pound objected on the grounds that Mountbatten was an adviser and not a commander. Much has since been written on Mountbatten which tends to support Brooke's views.

After his Christmas break, he returned to the War Office to catch up on events, only to find that Churchill wanted to pull Alexander out of the Middle East, to replace Anderson, and to bring Jumbo Wilson in to replace Alexander. Brooke hated this political interference, and with some cause, and he also heard that Roosevelt was calling for a New Year conference in Casablanca. His last sentence for 1942 was 'This is a dog's life.'

---

[*] Montgomery, backed by Churchill in his excitement, saw this as the first British victory, overlooking the Battle of Britain – and not the first victory of many, as often claimed, but the only real land victory by Montgomery.

## CHAPTER 7

# 1943

At the start of his 1943 diary, Brooke reflected on the previous year during which there had been momentous events, mainly of a disastrous nature: the Japanese belligerence and success in the Far East, concerns over failures in North Africa, the Malta shipping losses, and the fear that the Russians would collapse. The only real advantage had been the arrival of the Americans which for Brooke introduced his own personal battlefield of argument and counterargument over strategy, and Brooke's utter conviction that his approach was the only viable one. He had underestimated Soviet Russian will-power, and rumours had started in the previous months that on the Eastern Front, the tide of German success had been halted. The year 1943 looked very different, and Brooke wrote: 'We start 1943 under conditions I would never have dared hope.'[1] Russia was holding, Egypt was safe, Malta in less danger, and he was feeling more confident in his role as CIGS. Later during this month British troops would enter Tripoli followed by the Free French, and the USAAF carried out its first raid over Wilhelmshaven. As he prepared for the conference in Casablanca (the Symbol Conference) he had to deal with his usual daily activities which included reading about problems in North Africa. He was also highly disconcerted to read about General Mark Clark, whom he had met and liked. Brooke's initial readings of a person were often well founded as he once remarked himself, but he had been wrong about Clark. This American general had been causing trouble, and it would not be for the first time, to use Brooke's words, that Clark had been 'egging on' Giraud to state that French troops would not fight under British command. Brooke described Clark as 'very ambitious and unscrupulous'. This viewpoint for many historical observers was uncomfortably close to the truth. These machinations by Clark were perceived to be his desire to take command of the Tunisian front. Eisenhower, becoming aware of his deputy commander's behaviour, instantly sacked him, and sent him back to command reserve forces in Morocco. This swift response certainly put Eisenhower up in Brooke's estimation. Brooke also had his usual COS problems, one meeting which was discussing projected landing craft for invasion purposes, led Brooke to write that Pound was asleep 90 per cent of the time, and Mountbatten, as usual, was confused over his own figures. He wrote of Mountbatten that 'he is quite irresponsible, suffers from the most desperate illogical brains, always producing red herrings.'[2] If the previous year had its fill of contentions, this and the following years would increase in Anglo-American tensions, and the debates and arguments would exponentially increase.

## Casablanca

Brooke's main concern was preparing for the Casablanca meeting; Churchill wanted to go by cruiser, but Pound told him it was far too dangerous, and the weather for flying was not encouraging. They eventually flew in Liberators and had to wear flying gear because of the cold. Naturally the whole expedition was shrouded in secrecy, due to the fact the British High Command were airborne and coming close to enemy territory. It had been hoped that Stalin would join them, but he had excused himself, explaining the Eastern Front was too busy, and, although it was never mentioned, the Russian dictator had an aversion to leaving his own territory probably for paranoid political reasons. For the same motives Franco, like Stalin, also had an aversion to flying. They arrived in Casablanca the next day (13 January) where Brooke found his hotel comfortable, and there were two villas nearby for the American president and Churchill.

The British started with Dill presenting the picture of American ideas and plans. These conferences were critical for Allied harmony and generally they tended to look successful, but Brooke always feared them because he knew he would be constantly having to battle for his own policies, which he was always convinced were the only ones able to produce eventual success. He also disliked always having to fight with Admiral King who relentlessly argued to make Japan the priority. Dill was a charming gentleman with diplomatic ability and the Americans liked his approach. Brooke, on the other hand, was austere, always blunt (at times hardly diplomatic) and when he addressed a meeting he presented as an authoritarian lecturer. However, it was clear to the Americans that he was highly professional in military matters, and they respected him for this, but above all for his personal integrity. During this conference Brooke had his work cut out persuading the Americans and many in his own camp that Sardinia was not the best island to occupy, but Sicily (Operation *Husky*). Brooke preferred Sicily because of the shorter distance to reach this massive island, as well as its closer proximity to mainland Italy. The Americans argued that Sardinia would be easier to invade, and its airfields were closer to Europe; this projected Sardinian policy was codenamed *Point Blank*.

Tunisia remained a matter of deep concern and discussion; Hitler had made it clear he wanted Tunisia to remain in German hands, and as noted, German reinforcements had been flown in to resist the Allies. The German Command was in the hands of Field Marshal Albert Kesselring, and although a Luftwaffe commander, he had started life in the army and was probably one of the most capable of commanders the enemy had, later to be a serious opponent to the Allied forces in Italy.*

The next day at the Combined Chiefs of Staff meeting, Brooke produced his overall picture of the global situation and his forthcoming plans. Marshall followed, picking up the areas which they disagreed with, and Admiral King proposed a 30 per cent effort against the Japanese and 70 per cent against Germany. Wedemeyer wrote that Admiral King was 'visibly annoyed at the British, and they shifted uneasily at this advocacy of a major campaign' not in Europe, and that King complained that he was annoyed by Brooke who spoke too fast.[3] Brooke was instantaneous in his reply by pointing out that presenting such figures was not a 'scientific way of approaching strategy'. It is not difficult to imagine Admiral King's response to being put down so harshly in public. This interchange demonstrated Brooke's earlier moods regarding the inevitable clashes with the highly respected American admiral. It was clear to Brooke that Germany and Japan could not be beaten simultaneously, and that Germany had to remain the priority target.

After this fraught exchange Brooke went birdwatching. He did this nearly every day, often in the company of Kennedy (his DMO) who was also becoming a close friend. Most mornings the two of them went for such strolls, even later in Turkey where security was more of a risk. Brooke was intrigued to see what he thought might be a rare pallid harrier. To the modern reader this might bring a smile to the face, but for Brooke it was a great release from the daily intellectual battles and tensions, and for him as a person it was essential to help him maintain his emotional balance.

In the evening of the first day they had dinner together, and Brooke was amused to observe that Admiral King had too much to drink, and became entrenched in an argument over his views on how to handle the French political situation. This social interchange annoyed Churchill, who was unaware of Admiral King's alcoholic state, not least because Churchill also consumed heavily, but he was better at holding his drink, as Stalin would also discover.

The next day Alexander and Eisenhower (brought in to substantiate the British views) gave their insights, and Roosevelt was inclined to take the Mediterranean plans on board. Brooke presented his policies in full, and in his usual fashion countered the arguments for an attack on the French coast, and probably left everyone breathless. Meanwhile the problems of French factions and leadership would not go away. Churchill had tried his hand at reconciliation between de Gaulle and Giraud, now High Commissioner of French North and West Africa, but it never worked.[†]

---

* Graham and Bidwell in their history of the Italian Campaign informed their readers that the Allies were 'facing as good a general as emerged from the German Army in the Second World War and certainly the best on either side in the Italian Theatre.' See Dominic Graham and Shelford Bidwell, *Tug of War, The Battle for Italy 1943–45* (Yorkshire: Pen and Sword, 2004) p.38.

† Later Darlan was assassinated, and Giraud was too weak when compared to de Gaulle, which the

Another interesting insight for Brooke was when he met General George Patton, whom he described as a 'real fire-eater and definite character', but he did not form a good opinion of him according to his daily diary. Later he described Patton as a 'dashing, courageous, wild and unbalanced leader, good for operations requiring thrust and push but at a loss in any operation requiring skills and judgment.'[4] The German generals tended to think highly of Patton because of his 'thrust and push' but there is no doubt that Brooke was aware of his impetuous approach. Later he would lose many men and much material in a ridiculous fiasco, when he pushed behind enemy lines to rescue his son-in-law who was a POW, and which failed on all accounts with a heavy loss of lives. His son-in-law was wounded in the fray.*

In the conference there were debates ranging from Burma to Iceland, and Brooke was aware that the joint planners were again under pressure from the 'Pacific first party'. The question of Sardinia and Sicily also took considerable time to resolve. It was not helped by Admiral King's relentless pressure, and some of the British participants who supported Sardinia, including Mountbatten, who had changed sides in this contentious debate. This would not have improved Brooke's critical approach towards the 'royal' personage. Brooke was beginning to feel desperate, but Portal, with whom he had often had furious debates, turned up with another presentation of the paper which Brooke thought was good. It was finally accepted, and group photographs were taken.

Much of this, Brooke later added, was accepted because of Dill's skills and diplomacy. There is little doubt that much of the British success was due to Dill, and although some British critics believed that Dill had 'turned native', many others believed he was a British spy in the American camp and 'sold Marshall short'.[5] This was an unfair assertion against Dill who only sought victory for the Allies. The Anglophobe Wedemeyer wrote that the British had 'cheated' by bringing too many staff, and with a carefully planned form of attack. He regarded Casablanca as a catastrophe for the Americans by allowing themselves to be dragged into Brooke's Mediterranean scheme; he also observed that unlike the Americans, the political leader Churchill and his staff met regularly. The British, Wedemeyer wrote, had specific purposes, and 'usually their aims would be related to Empire or their post position in the world of commerce.'[6] Nothing could have been further from Brooke's mind, and although Churchill was known for his love of empire, commercial interests in the postwar years would sort themselves out as far as he was concerned. Wedemeyer in his Anglophobic diatribes had overlooked Brooke's

---

Allies were obliged to accept. There have always been conspiratorial rumours that it was the SIS which organised the assassination of the unwelcome Admiral Darlan in North Africa, but no real substantial evidence.

* 'Patton, in his cavalier way, considered Brooke "nothing but a clerk."' Beevor amusingly pointed out that Brooke's estimate of Patton was more astute than Patton's description of Brooke. See Anthony Beevor, *The Second World War* (London: Weidenfeld & Nicolson, 2012) p.403.

force of personality. It may have been the case that Brooke was somewhat insensitive towards the Americans, but he was convinced that his way of thinking was sheer strategic common sense and that he was correct. He was blunt as noted, could be angry, and the Americans undoubtedly fathomed out from his facial expressions and attitudes precisely what he thought of their ideas. Wedemeyer should also have recalled that Marshall suspected, probably with good reason, that Roosevelt tended to veer towards the British point of view.

Churchill had failed to bring de Gaulle and Giraud closer, and Brooke had lunch with Giraud whom he immediately liked (probably helped by his utter distaste for de Gaulle), noting he was a gentleman and all he wanted to do was defeat the Germans; Brooke would have understood this wish. Nevertheless Brooke concluded, with a cynical or realistic view, that Darlan had ability but no integrity, whereas Giraud had charm but no ability, while de Gaulle 'had the mentality of a dictator combined with a most objectional [sic] personality.'[7]

He regarded Eisenhower, as previously noted, as limited, although he liked the man. It was agreed that Alexander would become Eisenhower's deputy with Tedder as the air commander. Brooke believed that the Americans would be 'flattered' by Alexander being deputy, but he hoped that it might bring some strategy into the camp which was desperately needed. The Americans liked Alexander because he was, in their view, more of a gentleman, more amenable and obliging, and not as obdurate as some of the British. There was at least a growing centralised command. Sardinia and Sicily remained a problem with the bulk of the CCOS against Brooke, and it was not helped, as noted, by Mountbatten who, in Brooke's views, 'never had any decided opinions of his own'. Brooke stuck to his guns and eventually won the intellectual battle. There was also a general agreement named *Anakim,* which was the codename for the plans for the recapture of Burma. At least the two sides were now closer together and Brooke noted that both the president and the prime minister were pleased about the conference. Brooke also knew that once they went their separate ways other differences would arise, leading Churchill to quip later that it was difficult to fight a war with allies, but impossible without them.

Churchill had informed Brooke he was intending to fly to Marrakesh to do some painting (he had painted there before) and Brooke hoped that he might get some partridge shooting in for a well-deserved break. He was constantly aware that Churchill liked to change plans at the last moment, and added in his diary that 'man proposes, and God disposes'. At one lighter moment in Marrakesh, Brooke found Churchill in his bedroom with his flamboyant red dressing gown in a typically Moroccan setting, with 'a cigar in the middle of his face'; he admitted he wanted to laugh and wished he could have taken a colour photograph. He also learnt that his hopes for staying there for a time were dashed, as Churchill decided they had to move onto Cairo as soon as possible. When Brooke asked about his painting Churchill replied that he could get a couple of hours in, and Brooke left in the hope that Churchill would change his mind again; he did not. Brooke later discovered that Churchill was awaiting an Eden telegram about the arrangements for a Turkish meeting.

## To Turkey, Cyprus, Tripoli, Algiers

Two days later they arrived in Cairo and at the embassy Churchill was offered breakfast, and when asked if he would like tea, Brooke was taken aback when Churchill asked for a glass of white wine, which 'he drained in one go and then licked his lips'. Brooke attended Alexander's staff meeting and told Jumbo Wilson of the new plans. He then went out and bought some Turkish delight for his children, and later heard the Turks had invited them to Ankara, but there was a serious security risk in this destination because of the German presence, and so new arrangements were being planned to hold the meeting closer to the border. The party then spent some time in the desert area, looking at the after-effects of the war. They eventually left for Adana in Turkey where they hoped to meet Prime Minister Sükrü Saracoglu with his foreign minister, and President General Ismet Inönü. The meeting took place in railway carriages and everything was pleasant and comfortable, but Brooke was worried about the security knowing there were Germans in the area. He went out to check the guards and found them 'hunkered down' trying to keep out of the rain. He had a row with Churchill's detective telling him he ought to stay on patrol outside during the night, and Brooke warned Churchill that his carriage was an easy target. Brooke knew from wireless intercepts that the German embassy in Turkey was aware of their presence. He found the Turkish idea of modern war was out of date and elementary, but they finally left with Brooke feeling that at least Turkey would be biased in their favour; Churchill had done his job well. On the last day of the month they arrived in Cyprus where Brooke was delighted to find an expert on birds to keep him company.

As mentioned, Brooke's diary was not a history, but it appears somewhat bizarre he did not refer to the news that the German Sixth Army under von Paulus had capitulated at Stalingrad on 2 February, and soon after the Red Army took Kursk. It was an isolated but significant battle, and many World War II historians claim that Stalingrad was the turning point of the war. The British would claim the same for El Alamein, but the numbers involved on the Russian front were simply vast. Brooke probably realised by now that although the Germans were far from being a danger to Russia, they were already planning a new offensive, and this may have influenced him in not jumping with too much enthusiasm. When all this was happening, Brooke was in transit with Churchill between Cyprus and Cairo. Brooke was in high spirits, and as Churchill addressed the various dignitaries in Cyprus, Brooke went with Major Hughes, the island's military commander, to look at defences and he enjoyed the views.

As Stalingrad fell to the Soviets, Brooke was attending more conferences and pleased that the Turks appeared to be joining the Allies, but he was wrong: they remained on the fence virtually to the end of the conflict when it was safer. He had not thought much of their forces (though they had surprised the Allies in the Great War) but aerodromes in Turkey would have been invaluable. They flew over the desert looking down on El Alamein, and they landed outside Tripoli to be met by Montgomery and Alexander. That night he slept in one of Montgomery's famous caravans and found it cold. They looked around Tripoli as the soldiers ensured they were safe from any dangerous locals, and they watched the 51st Division on parade as if they had done nothing but parade for the last few months. Brooke noted they were 'bronze and fit' and he had 'seldom seen such a fine body of men'. Both he and Churchill felt emotionally elated by their confident military presentation. Later Brooke wrote that looking at these men made 'victory become a practical proposition'. Brooke had often expressed a high regard for German troops because of their training, sense of duty, and battle experience; he was now looking at tough British troops who had beaten the Germans in the field of combat, and it gave him hope.

He met Oliver Leese and the New Zealand Division under Freyberg, and as they flew away, they saw a heavy bombing raid on Tripoli. Their next trip was to Algiers, though intelligence had reported that there was a danger that Churchill might be assassinated. Churchill decided to ignore the warning. Brooke knew him to be a courageous man at the personal level, and he also knew he loved being as close to the action as possible. When he arrived at the airport, he discovered that Eisenhower had sent Churchill ahead in an oily mud-covered nondescript car, because the American general was understandably nervous that Churchill was in his charge, and he did not want him recognised. Eisenhower had prepared for them to attend a lunch with other local commanders, and to no great surprise Brooke took himself off afterwards to go birdwatching. He managed to dissuade Churchill from wanting to spend another day there and prepared to set out that evening. In the end they did spend another night, simply because the plane's engine was malfunctioning. Brooke returned to Eisenhower's quarters to a warm bed, which he later discovered was comfortable because Eisenhower's ADC, Butcher, had been turned out to make room for Brooke. The next morning, they witnessed two fighters crash into one another, a sad sight they had to pass close by to take off. Churchill flew directly to Britain, while Brooke's pilot took him to Gibraltar where he was entertained, but more so by spotting a peregrine falcon around the rock. The curious aspect was that due to flight plans Brooke arrived in Britain just before Churchill.

## Back to Routine

On his return to London it was a matter of back to the usual routine, picking up work waiting for him, but more to the point, studying the paperwork he had brought with him which needed turning into 'facts and action'. The first COS was a matter of finding a date for invading Sicily, Operation *Torch*. The prime minister and American president had both expressed an interest in the timing. At the next meeting they started looking at June instead of July, but it was mainly dependent on the Germans being cleared out of North Africa by the beginning of May. A few days later Admiral Ramsay returned from North Africa, bringing the news that Eisenhower did not think the proposed dates were right, as he could not see that the Germans would be 'cleaned up' before May.

The routine work made Brooke feel he had not been away. He met Canadian leader Harry Crerar who felt the Canadians needed to fight for imperial and political reasons. They had refused to fight in the Middle East for their own political reasons, and the Dieppe raid had cost them badly through no fault of their own. It was a situation with which Brooke agreed. He found time to lunch with Benita's sister Madeline, but he was more concerned that Churchill was down with a fever, stating that 'I hope it won't be bad.' He saw Churchill that day and recommended to him that Auchinleck should not be given command of the Iraq–Persia sector; Brooke had not been impressed by his old friend. It has often been hinted that Auchinleck fell from grace because he stood up to Churchill, and Brooke was often commended for protecting Auchinleck. It is therefore worth noting that Brooke's diary clearly indicated that although Auchinleck was respected by so many, he was in Brooke's estimation somewhat falling short in his allotted tasks.

He met the new American General Andrews to discuss American reinforcements, which had not started to blossom despite the reassurances at Casablanca. He also had an uncomfortable meeting with some French leaders who wanted supplies dropped to the various Resistance groups. Brooke wrote: 'I told them what I thought of the French realisation of the true situation, and of their failure to get together to fight Germany instead of squabbling amongst themselves.'[8] This seemed a little unfair but Brooke could be quite harsh at times; he had probably had enough of the French squabbles in North Africa, and it was not until just prior to D-Day in 1944 that he saw the French resistance as being of any true value.[*] He was a traditional military man and did not understand the sacrifices made by resistance fighters and partisans. He knew himself that his outbursts could be dictated by his frame of mind, once writing that 'it seems more probably that I was in a peevish mood and childish mood myself'.[9] Later, the following month, he wrote 'and I grew peevish towards the end of the meeting'.[10] He was known as a truthful man, and these extracts clearly indicated he was honest with himself. He also had more COS problems with Mountbatten who persisted with his suggestion of an attack on the

---

[*] The French Resistance was small and divided into many groups. They were initially a passive intellectual resistance, but the communists led the way in physical attacks upon the occupiers and the Maquis developed in an *ad hoc* fashion. Much depended on local leaders, but as the war turned against Germany the Resistance in France grew fiercer, and finally proved useful prior to the Normandy and the south of France landings.

Channel Islands, which in his opinion had no strategic value, and he thought that Mountbatten was 'tactically quite adrift'.

On the 21st he received bad news from Tunisia where the Germans had inflicted a major defeat. It was, without Brooke stating it, the Battle of the Kasserine Pass. Like Brooke, Kesselring had suspected that the American troops were inexperienced. The American General Omar Bradley later inferred this in his own memoirs relating to this time, and Eisenhower admitted his troops were unprepared, and he even discovered that engineers had been ordered to dig into rock to give cover for senior officers; 'It was the only time, during the war, that I saw a divisional or higher headquarters so concerned over its own safety that it dug itself underground shelters.'[11] It has been stated that the blame for the Kasserine Pass 'must be shared by Anderson, Eisenhower and Fredendall' and led to the humiliating spectacle of some 4,000 Allied POWs being marched through Rome.[12] Eisenhower, amongst the reasons he listed for failure, noted the 'greenness, particularly among commanders' as well as the failure to comprehend the capability of the enemy.[13] It has to be acknowledged that the local commander, Fredendall, was 'a disaster'.[14] All this proved that Brooke had been somewhat justified in his critical appraisal that the Americans first needed battle experience against the Germans before crossing the English Channel. Brooke had seen in Tripoli British troops who had become battle experienced, and knew the American soldiers and especially their officers still had much to do to gain this level of fighting prowess, which they would eventually achieve through the bitterness of conflict. This battle which had caused such a setback was Rommel's effort, but Rommel was personally convinced that the Germans could not hold out in North Africa, despite Hitler's ridiculous order they should hold on, and his equally absurd demand that they must fight to the last man.

Churchill suddenly demanded to see Brooke, who was disturbed that this urgent interview was caused by the king wanting to know what was happening; Brooke felt obviously concerned that the prime minister should not be disturbed when he was still unwell. Two days later he went instead and met the king at Buckingham Palace and answered all his questions. He bumped into Hore-Belisha in St James's Park, observing he looked 'more greasy and objectional [sic] as ever'. Hore-Belisha wanted to engage Brooke in conversation when he was more interested in looking for a scaup duck. The same thing happened the next day with Hore-Belisha asking about North Africa. He met Portal and complained about the paucity of bombing squadrons in Tunisia with, as Brooke noted, the 'usual results': Portal was one man who could withstand Brooke's powers of persuasion. He then met General Browning who had suffered an injury in a glider accident, informed him he needed to take a fortnight's leave, then 'told him off' for writing to politicians, which 'he took in good heart'. After his trips abroad and decision making Brooke was back to his routine in the War Office; his reliefs were that Benita and family were close by at

Ferney Close, and his constant love of birdwatching, be it peregrines in Gibraltar, pallid harriers in Turkey or scaup ducks in St James's Park.

At the beginning of March, the battle for the *Bismarck* was a major news item, Brooke never mentioned this, but he was concerned about shipping. It seemed to him that the Americans were not keeping in line with their *Bolero* promises, and that Marshall was helping the French forces who could play no significant part in the invasion. He suspected Admiral King with his Pacific demands was a problem which would not go away, and a whole COS meeting concerned itself with this problem. It could be claimed with some justification that Brooke was being somewhat unfair on this issue as shipping was a vastly complex affair. He was almost becoming like Churchill who wanted everything done at once. He later had a furious argument, again with Portal, who wanted American airmen given priority in shipping places against Canadian troops. He met with Churchill at the beginning of the month when the Turkish situation was discussed, with Brooke amused by Churchill's statement that 'we must start by treating them purry-purry puss-puss, then we shall harden.' Trying to engage the Turkish leaders on the Allied side was a difficult and frustrating problem.

The next day (3 March) he had a French Resistance leader to lunch and this time listened more carefully to their side of the story. This leader was the aristocratic d'Astier de la Vigeries, who was with General Billotte whom Brooke had met in France.* Brooke would have been surprised to know that d'Astier regarded de Gaulle as a symbol for the French of resistance. This was an aspect of de Gaulle which both Churchill and Brooke could be charged with overlooking. They wanted to discuss the delivery of arms and explosives, and this time Brooke was more considerate. Brooke's routine continued with a series of meetings, having to see General Martel who was unhappy about being sent to Moscow as head of mission, watching Canadian troops under McNaughton who, in Brooke's view could not command an army. Later in the month he had a quiet word with Crerar about organising for McNaughton to be recalled to Canada. He had another 'heated COS meeting' over Mountbatten 'putting up wild ideas disconnected with his direct duties' and a more pleasant time with Hobart. He was questioning Hobart and asking for information about flotation, searchlights and anti-mine tanks. In the 1930s he had been somewhat critical of Hobart's ideas in the days of the 'tank arguments', but he was now fully appraised of the tank's potential, and Hobart was investigating all the different ways the tank could help the infantry when landing on beaches, and also leading the attack. At least during these early weeks in March, he was delighted

---

* D'Astier de la Vigeries was the least likely Resistance man; he had been a drug-addicted aristocrat who surprised everyone by cleaning himself up for the sole purpose of fighting the Germans and proved a courageous Resistance leader.

with the birth of two small white goats at Ferney Close, and he at last spotted the scaup duck which Hore-Belisha had caused him to miss.

On 4 March he had expected Rommel to attack, undoubtedly based on wireless intercepts, with what became known as the Battle of Medenine which started on the 6th, and the news was never good. Rommel had struck against Montgomery's Eighth Army in the south and caught him unbalanced, nearly pushing him to the sea. Ultra messages came to the rescue giving Montgomery inside knowledge, and the battle for the Mareth Line improved from the British point of view.* The Mareth Line was the old French defensive position built to protect the eastern border, and later occupied Tunisia.† It was only a series of block houses near the coast beside a mountainous area, and in that terrain any enemy was unable to conceal outflanking manoeuvres. Kesselring had demanded time and time again 'that the enemy be held up as long as possible in the area before Mareth, since otherwise the reception of Panzer-Army-Rommel will be exceptionally difficult', which Kesselring must have known would be true anyway.[15] It would take time, and Brooke became worried, but it was eventually successful. One sad piece of news Brooke received was that Julian Brooke, son of his nephew Basil, died at the Mareth Line. It is often personal news of this nature that could remind the toughest of soldiers of the bitter sadness and tragedy of war, which lay behind their higher strategies.

Brooke went down with the flu and was out of action from 14 to 24 March. When he returned, he heard the king wanted to visit North Africa, and neither Churchill nor Brooke were happy with Eisenhower's plans for Sicily. He had been called to see Churchill only to find him in the bath, which never embarrassed Churchill, who then slowly dressed as they discussed the Montgomery battle. Brooke was amused as Churchill slipped into white silk pants, which with his huge body and thin legs made him look like Humpty Dumpty. Churchill told Brooke he did not look well and told him to take a long weekend off. He dined with Churchill who was angry that he heard from Montgomery but never Alexander. This sounded all too typical of the man Montgomery busy selling himself. The prime minister was unhappy about Eisenhower and his plans, but as noted, Churchill thought they could invade Italy and Greece at the same time. Brooke felt this was nonsense, but there is a distinct feeling in Brooke's diary that his respect for Churchill was also developing into a feeling of affection.

In mid-April news of the massacres of Katyń percolated through with question marks over whether it was a Soviet or Nazi carnage in origin; many at this stage of

---

\* The use of Ultra in the front line was always risky. Rommel thought he had been betrayed, and Kesselring blamed the Italian Marshal Giovanni Meese. Dönitz, the naval man, often wondered whether their Enigma machine had been penetrated.

† It was sometimes known as the African Maginot Line which was a poor description.

events preferred to believe it had to be the Nazis, but others had serious doubts. Under the severe exigencies of war, it was brushed under the carpet mainly for political reasons and for decades it remained in ominous silence.* Brooke made no mention of this nor of the first Rising in Warsaw (19 April) being more concerned with the Western side of the conflict. He was also anxious about Burma, but there is little doubt that for him the Pacific problem with the Japanese was in another shop.

April began with an attempt to organise top staffing for the invasion of France. They had appointed F. E. Morgan as COSSAC (Chief of Staff Supreme Allied Command) to start preparing for the invasion of Europe.† Brooke remained convinced that his initial strategy of taking Italy out of the war was correct, but he knew there would always be some contention with the American allies over the timing of the French invasion, and their desire to crush the Japanese at the same time. Brooke always projected the theory that the Germans would be distracted from the Russian front, as its Axis ally Italy became the subject of Allied attention. This would never be the case, because Italy under Kesselring would prove to be a better place for defence than attack, given its terrain and weather, and a defence under these conditions demanded fewer troops than those needed by the Allies. In addition to this the Germans knew the more serious threat to their homeland came from the Eastern Front. Later Alexander would observe that 'it was the Germans, not the Allies, who were contained in Italy' but after the war he was more ambivalent.[16] It could be argued that the Germans, with fewer troops, were holding considerably larger numbers, and Alexander commented to a journalist in 1950 that who was holding who 'permitted no easy answer, then or now'.[17] Brooke's views on the invasion of Italy have caused some historical debate, but he was correct in not wanting the invasion across the Channel too early. This Anglo-American conflict over strategy would never go away. In the end the Americans would agree to look at south Italy once Churchill had agreed to May 1944 for *Overlord*.[18]

The planning for Sicily (Operation *Husky*) was causing many problems, with the usual debates between Brooke, Portal and Pound, and according to Brooke, arriving at a co-ordinated plan of action was not helped by 'Montgomery's egotistical outlook'. One of the problems on the military front was the way that some commanders built up their own egos and expanded their public images on their own value. Earlier in the month Brooke had heard that MacArthur, whose strategy he had admired, had become something of a *prima donna*, and this was to happen with many others such as Clark, Montgomery, Patton and Mountbatten, but it was a weakness which

---

* The Soviets became more open about their culpability towards the end of the century, but it was not until November 2010 that the Russian State Duma approved the declaration which blamed Stalin and other Soviet officials, no doubt thinking of Beria as the main culprit. See Andrew Sangster, *The Times, Life and Moral Dilemma of Beria* (Newcastle: Cambridge Scholars, 2019).

† Lieutenant-General Sir Frederick Morgan (1894–1967) was best known and famous for his role as chief of staff to COSSAC, and as the original planner for Normandy D-Day.

nobody could accuse Brooke of suffering from. He remained throughout the war years reserved, confident, but never projecting his own image, and never sought position or public applause. This was one of the obvious reasons why he was often known as the 'unknown field marshal'. When he was given any awards, he mentioned it in his diary in passing, or heard it on the news first, and never referred to it again.

Another problem over Operation *Husky* was a telegram to Churchill from Marshall, who thought Sicily could be invaded before Tunisia was cleansed of Germans. Brooke thought this was simply mad and spent time on the phone to Marshall explaining the dangers of having the enemy both sides of the water, and the danger to the supply lines for ingoing troops. Even to a non-military expert Brooke's argument made sense, and it is easy to speculate that Marshall wanted the operation done and dusted so occupied France could be invaded.

More cheering news for Brooke was hearing that events in Tunisia were becoming more and more encouraging, and the overall strategy appeared to be working within his proposed lines. He went with the prime minister to watch a demonstration of aircraft, and he recorded on 19 April his first sighting of the development of a plane without propellers, but driven by sucking in air and blowing it out the other side, namely jet propulsion, though he did not use this now familiar term. He also gathered that Churchill did not appreciate the plans for Burma, stating, to Brooke's amusement, that 'you might as well eat a porcupine one quill at a time'. He was probably inclined towards Churchill's views that it was best to wait for Russia to go against Japan, but that would have been a long time because, like Brooke, Stalin wanted Nazism destroyed first. Brooke knew that the navy and air force tended to be uninterested in Burma, and that occupying Burma would not bring the Japanese down. Operation *Anakim* had been proposed at Casablanca and conceived as a way of invading Burma to assist China, but was now being judged as impractical, especially with the shortage of necessary shipping. The Chindits would continue their raids, but after the war there would be questions about their high casualty rates brought about by a natural hostile environment, undernourishment, and fighting a persistent and ruthless enemy.

Near the end of the month Brooke was picking up news from Portal and Pound, about the prime minister wondering whether to go to America again for yet another conference. Brooke was concerned that on the British side of the Atlantic their plans were not yet ready, and he tried to explain this to Churchill. However, the prime minister responded by saying he intended they should travel on the *Queen Mary* liner, which was then in use as a troop transporter. They were soon informed that the liner was full of rats, prompting Brooke amusingly to note that 'the vermin became our allies'. There was also concern that the German ambassador in Dublin would probably hear of this venture. The month ended on the cheerful note that his nephew Basil, mentioned earlier, had just become prime minister of Northern Ireland.

During May Tunis was captured, and ten days later the Axis forces capitulated, American and Canadian troops landed on the Aleutian Islands, the Dambuster

Raid occurred (16 May) and the tide was turning against the U-boat. For Brooke, his main concern was the projected visit to Washington to seek an agreement on a joint strategy, known as the Trident Conference.

Before he set off, he met the French General Bouscat sent by Giraud to contact de Gaulle. Brooke wrote that he 'seems one of the better sorts', by which of course he was referring to French military commanders. He had become deeply distrustful of them during the Battle of France, and de Gaulle was everything Brooke disliked. He seemed to have a low expectation of the French and thought they spent too much time squabbling about who was in control. Most historians would agree that Brooke was probably close to the truth. Near the end of the month while in North Africa Eisenhower had been decorated with the ribbon of the Legion of Honour by Giraud, and it came as no surprise for Brooke when he heard that de Gaulle was angry about this award. When he met General Catroux he heard his mission was to bring Giraud and de Gaulle to work in harmony, but Brooke thought this would never succeed, and he was right. De Gaulle's overbearing and proud personality never went down well; Churchill did not like him and Roosevelt all but detested the man.

## The Third Trident Conference

After the meeting with General Bouscat, Brooke heard they were heading for America almost immediately. He was not happy about the expedition even though he knew it was essential, writing that 'I don't feel too hopeful…Casablanca had taught me too much. Agreement after agreement may be secured on paper, but if their hearts are not in it they soon drift away again.'[19] They did in the end travel on the *Queen Mary*, whose sheer height astonished Brooke, and they were accompanied by a Sunderland aircraft, a cruiser and ahead of them an aircraft carrier. It must have felt safe, but U-boats had created a sense of understandable fear for anyone crossing the Atlantic trade routes. Later, during the journey, they heard that a convoy had lost 13 ships but at the cost of five U-boats. The tide was turning against the U-boat and at the end of this month Dönitz withdrew the U-boats from that part of the Atlantic. There were 3,000 troops on board the *Queen Mary* (the vessel could take 15,000) who would have felt safer as they were accompanied by cruisers and planes, indicating the importance of the company on the upper decks. Nearer to the American coast the Royal Navy exchanged its guardian role, passing its charges onto American naval escorts with the company of a Catalina flying boat.

As they had passed one stretch of Northern Irish coast at the beginning of their journey, Brooke reflected that was where Benita bathed with their dog Mr Rex. While on board there were a series of meetings to discuss their plans and how they should be presented. The main concern was explaining to the Americans that invading Burma with Operation *Anakim* was unworkable. They knew that Roosevelt would not like this because he was desperate to encourage the Chinese, and he was under

Chiefs of Staff on Board SS *Queen Mary* (IWM A 16709)

the impression that invading Burma would somehow help. The meetings on board were often contentious, and at one stage during the journey Churchill managed to badly upset Wavell, and Brooke had to step in and try and placate them. When he was shaving the next morning, he heard that Wavell was going to hand Churchill his resignation. He dashed around to Wavell's cabin and persuaded him not to, explaining that if he resigned every time Churchill was rude to him, it would be a daily occurrence. Brooke managed to calm matters down and ensured that Churchill and Wavell met in a better frame of mind, so he could, in his words, 'shave in peace'. It was not an easy time for Brooke with so many contentious issues and differences of opinion, and on reading his diary later, he added that 'I think I was suffering from the last stages of flu.' He was becoming worked up about American views when all he really wanted them to do was supply more and more resources. They reached Washington in the early evening of 11 May. The next day the prime minister, in Brooke's view, gave a good opening address, followed by Roosevelt whom Brooke characteristically observed had a lesser grasp on the issues of strategy.

In an overall view this third Trident Conference was underlined by a deep sense of mistrust between the Americans and British, many of the Americans feeling they had been dealt a poor hand at Casablanca, and had no intention of repeating this implied failure again. Once again Churchill took with him a massive team which even the king's secretary Lascelles commented on with raised eyebrows.[20] Trident was 'regarded as one of the most ill-tempered and rancorous of all the wartime summits', not least because the Americans were not going to allow themselves to be bullied or dictated to by the British.[21] It was the time that although the Americans had generally accepted the British Mediterranean plans, the British faced considerable American suspicion at the mention of the Greek islands in the Balkan area. One of the major issues continued to be the precise dating of the launching of *Roundup*, now called *Overlord*: the British felt themselves bound to accept the American proposals, although Brooke was convinced it was too early. The main difference in the European theatre was Brooke's strategy of closing the Mediterranean to the enemy, whereas many Americans still regarded it as merely 'pecking away at the fringes' of Europe. Marshall told Brooke he thought *Torch* had been a mistake, and he forced him to agree that the British and American divisions should be later withdrawn from Italy for the attack on France. The Americans, now fully involved in the war, were asserting their authority simply because of their enormous contribution and resources, which was understandable.

The next day Admiral Leahy presented their view of the global strategy, which Brooke thought differed in two ways from the British point of view. The first was there was too much latitude for diversion of forces to the Pacific, and the second that they were wrong in thinking an early date for crossing the Channel would shorten the war. Brooke believed they did not have a proper grasp of the necessary strategy for the European theatre, and they had no understanding of the part Russia was playing. It must have been a relief for Brooke to have dinner with his friend Dill that evening.

The next day at the Combined Chiefs of Staff meeting the British stated where they could not agree with the American presentation. On explaining the reluctance over *Anakim* they met with criticism from General Stilwell, known as Vinegar Joe, who personally criticised Wavell, and it all resulted in total confusion. Brooke did not take to Stilwell; he knew he was a Chinese linguist, 'good in a fight', and Stilwell was something of an Anglophobe, but men like General Slim saw the better side of the man. Brooke perceived, as he had previously believed, that for the Americans Operation *Anakim* was only a matter of keeping Chiang Kai-shek in the war. After this difficult day there was a break with some tourist visiting, attending church where Pound read the second lesson, and dinner at the Embassy, where the better side of Brooke emerged as he felt a deep sympathy for Mrs Halifax who had lost a son in 1942, and another seriously injured in that same year.

They returned on Monday to yet more contention with Brooke believing, with some justification, that Admiral King was still aiming to make the Pacific theatre the subject of primary focus. The following day they were expecting to meet the

Americans to explore their point of view, but discovered their papers were not yet ready. The most annoying aspect was that Brooke had the impression that the 'Americans think we led them down the garden path taking them to North Africa' and they were not going to allow themselves to be led astray again.[22]

Brooke was depressed, at times angry; sometimes he felt a depressing despair because he could not convince the Americans 'to grasp how we were preparing for a re-entry into France through the operations in the Mediterranean'. North Africa had been a successful campaign despite its ups and downs, and they had 'netted' some quarter of a million POWs. They were also inflicting major losses at sea and in the air, and Germany was being weakened day by day. Brooke simply could not understand why Marshall could not see this, and he suspected that Admiral King was behind the problem. The next day, the 19th, was the most difficult of the conference which was a clash of opposing views; Marshall suggested the room should be cleared and only the Chiefs of Staff remained, and by doing this they found 'a bridge we could cross'.* They returned to the CCOS Meeting to present their resolutions which were based on preparing 29 divisions to invade France in early 1944, and to continue the pressure on Italy, and this helped clear the air. Brooke regarded it as a triumph because he knew the Americans privately wanted to forget about the Mediterranean. The meetings became calmer with one clash between Admirals Pound and King on the question of submarines. That day Brooke was lucky to survive because he fell over, and then rolled down 14 stone steps and was bruised all over; a less robust man may well have died. In a note Brooke observed that his old friend Dill was not well, but again his charm and diplomacy had helped carry the day, and he acted as an intermediary between Brooke and Marshall. Brooke later realised that these first observations on Dill's health had been the signs of the beginning of his end, because Dill was becoming seriously ill.

In a slightly amusing aside Brooke noted the different views. In his summary Admiral King's only thought was the Pacific, Marshall's of crossing the Channel as soon as possible, Portal's that bombing would win the war, Pound found the answer in submarines, Brooke wanted to disperse German forces in the Mediterranean, and Churchill kept changing his mind. Even at this stage Brooke was frustrated by Churchill's sudden wish to change plans by looking for aggressive landings in the Far East, but Brooke was rescued by Harry Hopkins who persuaded Churchill otherwise. Brooke wrote about Churchill that 'there are times when he drives me to desperation' which epitomised their long fraught relationship.

---

\* In this 'clearing of the room' it should be noted that the small CCOS sat around the one table, but there could be up to 60 people lined up around the rooms, from secretaries to planners and other officials. It must have been like watching a complex boxing bout. Clearing the room often became a habit and it nearly always worked. It was 'fortunate that the explosive possibilities of Anglo-American rivalry could usually be contained by dismissing the squabbling staff officers and having an off-the-record meeting.' See Michael Burleigh, *Moral Combat*, (London: Harper Press, 2010) p.341.

## Back to North Africa

In the end Brooke had his overall strategy accepted, which was something of a triumph given the opposition by the more powerful American partner. Historically many later commentators praise Churchill for this success, which given his political astuteness and personality should carry some weight, but they nearly always ignore the battle at the discussion tables so heavily influenced by Brooke, who is rarely mentioned.

On the 26th they left America and made their way first to Gibraltar and then on to Algiers. Churchill had asked for Marshall's company to North Africa, undoubtedly to impress on him the value of the British strategy. Marshall was reluctant but the president had agreed. According to his biographers Marshall managed to avoid discussing the recent debates on the journey by skilfully engaging Churchill in historical gossip, and his views concerning Rudolf Hess's outlandish arrival in Britain. Brooke enjoyed walking along the beach with Alexander, and he was concerned that Churchill had expressed a wish that the next stop should be Moscow. This did not happen, but it would have been cheering news for Churchill when he heard that Stalin had formally dissolved Comintern (Communist International). Stalin was basically doing this to keep the Western Allies onside, as he realised it was more important to crush the Nazi menace than spread communism. Stalin was no true communist in the original meaning of the word; he was just seeking safety and security in the first instance, then later political power by postwar occupation.

Churchill and Brooke in early June travelled around the Middle East meeting commanders, with Churchill quietly pressing Eisenhower to consider crossing to the mainland of Italy after Sicily.* The small island of Pantelleria had been heavily bombed by the Allies and capitulated on 11 June.† While in Tunis Brooke appreciated studying a captured German Mark VI Tiger Tank. The Allies were aware of the German ability to produce good tanks, but they were expensive, and they could not be produced in the same numbers that the Americans could roll them off their industrial factory floors. On their way to Algiers Churchill took the controls of the plane with Brooke noting it swayed somewhat disconcertingly; it would have been more disturbing had Churchill wanted to land the plane.

---

* After the war Eisenhower claimed Brooke had spoken to him about the Italian invasion, and Eisenhower had asked Brooke about the Russians occupying the whole of Western Europe if they stayed in Italy. Brooke purportedly replied that the Russians would return to their original borders. Brooke never noted this unusual conversation, and it was unlikely because Brooke had a more realistic view of the Russians than most others at that time, and he was not that naïve. Brooke was not against *Overlord*, but selective over timing. See Andrew Roberts, *Masters and Commanders* (London: Penguin Books, 2009) p.91.

† A tiny island in the straits of Sicily, 100 km from Sicily and 60 km from the Tunisian coast. It was reduced by air attacks over six days of bombing with 4,119 tons and the troops raised a white flag as soon as British troops arrived. They took 11,000 prisoners for one casualty whom Churchill claimed was bitten by a mule.

Brooke met Montgomery and decided he needed a better education in global strategy, and he noted in his daily diary that Montgomery was 'a strange mixture' and difficult to handle. He recognised that Montgomery was a 'good trainer of men and excellent in combat, but likely to commit untold errors of tact' and he knew the Americans did not like him. He was correct in this insight into this commander: the Americans may have stood in awe of Brooke, but they would later came to loathe Montgomery. He was especially detested by the American Generals Eisenhower, Patton and Bradley, as well as many others. In the final months of the war, Montgomery would cause serious diplomatic blunders with the Americans. Brooke later added that he had 'to haul Montgomery over the coals' for his tactlessness and egotistical outlook. Montgomery and General Walter Bedell Smith had what the latter thought was a gambling bet placed in jest, when he offered Montgomery his own plane if British troops reached Sousse by a certain date line, which they did. Montgomery then demanded his own Fortress aircraft and a bewildered Bedell Smith had to see an angry Eisenhower who felt obliged to agree, and so Montgomery landed up with a Fortress aircraft and an American crew to himself, which from any normal viewpoint was wrong. Brooke was unhappy about Montgomery's behaviour.

According to Anthony Eden and Harold Macmillan who arrived on the scene to join Churchill, there was some progress being made between the French leaders Giraud and de Gaulle, and a few days later a celebratory lunch was held to celebrate this so-called momentous occasion. On 3 June, the French Committee for National Liberation had been formed, and there was a growing hope of a better French leadership, but Brooke noted at the luncheon that 'de Gaulle was sticky and stiff'. The de Gaulle problem would never go away (even in the postwar years), and at the end of this month, back in England, Churchill suddenly informed Brooke that he was not going to let de Gaulle 'spoil his relationship with President Roosevelt'. As previously noted, Roosevelt never trusted de Gaulle, actively disliking him, but because of the necessity to keep the French onside Churchill had always supported him. In 1940 London nobody had known who de Gaulle was or much about him and cared even less; it was very much the same in France during the early years of the war. Nevertheless, he was the highest ranking official out of France to arrive in the English capital, and Churchill had decided to recognise in de Gaulle an identifiable possible French figurehead apart from Pétain and a necessary centre for growing French Resistance. It was to be an awkward and difficult relationship during the war, which extended across the Atlantic to an intense degree of almost unbelievable personal hostility between many Americans and de Gaulle.

They eventually arrived back in Britain at Northolt on 15 July, and it was on this day that Churchill first told Brooke that his long-term plan was that he wanted him as supreme commander for the anticipated French invasion.* He swore Brooke

---

\* In a curious note by Churchill it was clear the Germans were aware that Churchill was flying in the area, and on one occasion a 'thickest man smoking a cigar was seen entering a civilian plane'

to total secrecy so Brooke never told Benita of this suggestion, and Churchill was surprised when later speaking to Benita that she had been kept in the dark. Brooke understood the old saying that 'when you have a secret to keep you keep it a secret that you have a secret to keep'.

There followed a series of discussions and debates over potential personnel concerning the Far East, and eventually Wavell accepted the post of the Viceroyalty of India which left the gap of finding a new commander-in-chief of India. There was further discussion as to who should be supreme commander in the Far East, and Sholto Douglas' name was proposed which pleased Brooke. Unfortunately, the Americans were not happy with this idea, and Brooke noted that he would have done a much better job than the eventual successor, Mountbatten. As Brooke's first biographer noted, 'It is striking how seldom the Far East appears in Brooke's diary, his letters, his preoccupation.'[23] He was always sentimentally concerned about India which he had enjoyed as a subaltern, and was probably close to Churchill with his ideas of the British Empire. Brooke's main concern was the European scene and the destruction of Nazi Germany, which he constantly regarded as his sole mission in his professional and personal life. At the end of the month he attended a discussion on the rumours that the Germans were preparing new rockets to attack Britain; the scientists could not agree or understand how the Germans could do this, and Brooke later noted that none of them had been close to the mark. It was decided to bomb Peenemünde which indicated that the SIS gathering of intelligence had worked in identifying the centre of this activity.

Throughout his travels with the prolonged difficult discussions and moments of contention, Brooke always found time with Benita and family invaluable. When he was away from their company, he enjoyed his birdwatching, and reading a volume of an expensive series of bird books he had recently purchased. This was Gould's Book of Birds, some 45 volumes for which he paid £1,500, and later sold for twice that price, which he had felt obliged to do because of his lamentable state of poverty after the war. These books and his ornithology were a deep source of relief for him, which he described in his own words as 'an antidote to the war and to Winston'. Later in July at a dinner party he would meet a new friend called Henry Bannerman who was preparing a new book on birds, and Brooke wrote the foreword for the first volume. Bannerman would thereafter advise Brooke on camera and hide purchases, and a lifelong relationship was started. During a violent world war, it is curious and informative how a man like Brooke could find such crucial comfort in this hobby; in many ways it was essential.

July saw the death of his friend Sikorski (4 July) while flying out of Gibraltar, which he regarded as 'a terrible loss' and he felt he 'had lost a great friend'. This

---

which was possibly a doppelgänger for Churchill. That plane was shot down and Leslie Howard the actor was amongst the dead. See Winston Churchill, *The Second World War, Vol IV* (London: Cassell and Company, 1951) p.742. Various books and conspiracy theories have dwelt on this incident.

plane death caused him to ponder at Sikorski's funeral in Westminster Cathedral on the number of flights he took, and although he did not know it at the time, as noted earlier, Franco always avoided flying and it was rumoured that Stalin felt the same way. The same day of Sikorski's funeral Brooke had to fly to Norfolk to see Hobart's floating tanks, and no doubt this thought passed through his mind again as he sat in the plane. Sikorski had been a good friend and so when later in July he met his replacement Kazumierz Sosnkowski, Brooke did not regard him highly; a good friend is always difficult to replace.

At the beginning of the month the question of the Azores was under discussion as a possible submarine base, but this caused concern that Salazar (whom Brooke described as the prime minister, but who was more of a dictator) would not agree, and it might also cause Spain to enter the conflict and thereby attract German attention. There was no doubt that the Iberian islands were used as U-boat bases as were some Spanish ports, which only ceased as a goodwill amenity when Franco finally realised that he had backed the wrong side. There had been no movement by Vichy France over the North African occupation, and although Franco was pro-Germany, he knew Spain was too militarily weak to declare war. Nevertheless, Brooke, like many others, was not fully apprised of Spain's difficulties, and remained nervous that it could cause problems. France was now totally occupied, as mentioned, and was no longer a Vichy threat, not that this diminished the dangers. Roosevelt had suggested supplying guns and fighter squadrons to oversee the Azores, but Brooke thought it essential to avoid a Peninsula war at all costs, and worried that Churchill could not understand this problem; it was probably true that Churchill had a better understanding or instinct about Franco's position than Brooke.

The question of the South East Asia command occupied considerable time, with the COS pressing Churchill to challenge Roosevelt over the American reluctance to accept Sholto Douglas, which Churchill eventually declined, if only to keep the harmonious relationship with the American president. The prime minister pressed for Oliver Leese's appointment, but Brooke did not think he had wide enough experience. Later Brooke would suggest Jumbo Wilson, whom he originally thought too old, but had since changed his mind.

The question of McNaughton would not go away. Stewart, the Canadian chief of staff, was also unhappy about him, and shared this sentiment with Brooke as they discussed the various ways they could 'get rid of him'. Brooke had to deal with McNaughton personally over a Montgomery incident following the Canadian's visit to Sicily, where he had flown to see Canadian troops in action. The Canadians had at last consented to half their troops fighting in the Mediterranean area, and Montgomery had refused McNaughton permission to land. He had returned to London livid with anger, and Brooke had to spend over an hour pacifying him. Brooke could not understand why McNaughton should have wanted to land in the heat of a battle, or why Montgomery should make such a bizarre decision, or

Alexander's failure 'to sit on Montgomery' when necessary. Brooke was furious with the situation because he had worked hard to convince the Canadians to help, noting they 'created more fuss' than all the other dominions put together.

In the first week of the month COS looked at the final arrangements for Sicily, and later Brooke and Ismay had dinner with the prime minister and the king, with the latter kindly suggesting they removed their formal Sam Browne belts.* Later Brooke noted that his diary entries seemed to indicate that he appeared to spend considerable precious time at dinners and lunches. Nevertheless, he defended this by pointing out that it was not only a means of meeting different people, but it often provided an opportunity for 'off the record' discussions. After the meal with the king, Churchill held Brooke back and reiterated his wish for him to be supreme commander of the French invasion, now known as Operation *Overlord*. Churchill explained he wanted Brooke to stay on as long as possible as the CIGS. Despite their stormy relationship it was more than clear that Churchill held Brooke in high esteem, and for Brooke's part, although Churchill often drove him mad, Brooke respected Churchill and especially his determination to win. Brooke was curious that on the second mention of this possible appointment, Churchill was now thinking about specific dates. Brooke had already turned down one such field command in North Africa, on the grounds that his role as the CIGS was more critical at that point in time. He found this prospect of launching against the Nazi mainland more inviting, writing that 'I was too excited to go to sleep, when I returned home,' but he questioned himself as to whether fate would allow this to happen for him; 'it seemed too much to hope for.' In the meantime, he had to deal with Spears who thought the *Overlord* plans did not make enough use of French troops, but Churchill launched into a 'long tirade' against de Gaulle, with which Brooke wrote, 'I heartily agree.' The next day Brooke met Irwin back from his command in Burma from whom he heard there was disturbing news about the morale of British troops, and their 'inferiority complex' when fighting the Japanese.

There was not much Brooke could do about this situation except demand the commanders try and eradicate the weakness, and it was the same reaction on 10 July when news of problems with the Sicilian invasion came through. Brooke was pleased that Sicily was the target; he had fought his desktop battles against occupying Sardinia against formidable opposition, but now he felt worried that it would not work out as planned. As stated, Brooke did not treat his diary as a history book, and he tended not to comment on events as they unfolded. He often recorded that it was bad or good news from the various theatres of war, but he admitted in his diary that he felt heavily responsible. He spent the next two days at home moving bookshelves, mending Pooks' goat cart, and hoping for the best.

---

* These formal belts had been designed by a British Indian army officer called General Sam Browne to help him draw his sword, having lost one arm.

As is well known, Sicily was successfully invaded over the following weeks, and Brooke gleefully kept noting the 'good news'. However, he would have been aware of the blunders and problems, and he would have known that many of the Italians did not want to fight simply because their heart was not in the war. The most devastating aspect of the planning in Sicily related to the momentous errors made in the planned airborne drops. General Patton had arranged for four battalions of some 3,000 paratroopers to be dropped just behind Gela, to stop Axis forces making their way to the beach landings. It was to be an enormous night drop for which there had been no practice. The pilots had little or no experience of night flying, and many of the parachutist and glider landings resulted in a massive loss of life, many lost in the sea.

Many historians also point to the appalling lack of direction in the field plans. Patton headed towards the north-west of the island to take Palermo, which posed no threat, and Montgomery, thinking he could go alone, virtually asked the Americans to stand aside, but he became stuck on the slopes of the notorious Etna terrain. The overall strategy of heading for Messina, which was separated from the Italian mainland by a few miles, did not seem to prefigure in the overall planning, and the Germans had their own 'mini-Dunkirk' and escaped to the mainland, as Montgomery and Patton behaved like competitive schoolboys. This lack of direction was compounded by 'Alexander's unwillingness to take control of the campaign at its most crucial moment'.[24] Patton seemed interested in outclassing the slow-moving Montgomery into Messina, by sending a Ranger battalion ahead to ensure the British did not take control. This was not an easy task since 60 per cent of Messina was in ruins and heavily booby-trapped. The overall figures relating to casualty rates vary from source to source, but the Allies suffered more than the Germans, and it should not pass unnoticed that less than 50,000 Germans held back the Allied air and sea supremacy, and two huge well-equipped armies. At least Brooke did not point out, then or later, his hitherto constant warnings about German military efficiency, which may have tempted many other more egocentric leaders.

It has long been acknowledged that German military leadership and training were superior; Eisenhower grudgingly wrote that 'the German garrison was fighting skilfully and savagely'.[25] 'It was plain that, though overwhelming Allied superiority eventually prevailed, the Wehrmacht's soldiers had fought more convincingly than their Anglo-American counterparts' – a conclusion supported by the statistics, the evacuation and the small numbers defending.[26] Montgomery sacked his able Lieutenant-Colonel Lionel Wigram for his unfavourable report which stated that 'the Germans have undoubtedly in one way scored a decided success in Sicily'.[27] It was clear to Kesselring and his subordinate generals that the Allies would be conservative and cautious; what he never knew was how divided they were at the personal level over the campaign, in terms of both overall strategy and the tactics deployed at ground level. It has been suggested that because Marshall tried to block the eventual Italian invasion German troops had escaped, but this was caused because of the poor planning in not foreseeing the possibility of the Messina crossing, failing to take action during the German evacuation, and because of German military skill.[28]

As Sicily continued to rumble with war the COS was already studying plans to invade Italy through the Naples area (Operation *Avalanche,* near the port of Salerno) which were not considered to be that reliable. There was a need to 'knock them into shape', wire them to Eisenhower and hope that Marshall did not oppose the plan. It did not take a week before Marshall was registering his anticipated doubts, which Brooke, although he had known the criticisms would arrive, still found 'maddening'. The concerns were worrying for Brooke and Churchill who told him 'you look tired CIGS, are you doing too much', causing Brooke to note that 'a remark like that means a lot more and compensates for any extra strain'.

On 23 July it was Brooke's 60th birthday, which under normal circumstances, he reflected, should have removed him from the army's active list. However, he knew that for most of the month the COS had been struggling with the shortage of manpower, and in trying to find good commanding officers. On his birthday he was also considering that the time had come to split the Canadian forces which, Brooke wondered, might be a way to 'get rid of McNaughton'. Compared to many other commanders Brooke remained energetic, and he was thrilled and all too ready to hear the news that, in his words, Mussolini had 'abdicated'. Abdicate was not quite the right word, Mussolini had virtually been forced to resign and was then arrested. In his place Marshal Pietro Badoglio became the prime minister. Brooke also enjoyed at the end of the month speaking to a quartermaster-sergeant called Cook from the airborne division, who had fought gallantly in North Africa. Taken as a prisoner, he had then escaped and had returned to duty. This would have been music to Brooke's ears, and the type of soldier Brooke admired.

The main event in August for Brooke was the major conference in Quebec known as Quadrant, mainly concerning him because of the questions hovering over Italy, but elsewhere the tide was turning in the favour of the Allies. On 17 August Axis resistance in Sicily ceased; before this the Red Army had taken Orel (5 August) and afterwards Kharkov (23 August), and Peenemünde (the main rocket site) had suffered a first bombing raid. News was circulating through various channels that the Italians were surrendering in the Dodecanese, Crete, and the Balkans. It was nothing to do with the silly myth that the Italians could not fight, but they had long been divided over fighting alongside the Germans, in their internal contentions regarding fascism, and their civil war which re-emerged from these issues grew in intensity. For Brooke there were many other issues in the air about the continuing problem of manpower shortage, the Azores, and Roosevelt agreeing that Rome should be treated as an 'open town' to preserve it from destruction. The British were not so happy with this idea, and it could be argued that they had suffered destruction in their cities, but with the benefit of hindsight Roosevelt was making the correct decision, because Rome was a truly international city with the Vatican, an international church, at its centre.

## The Quadrant Conference in Quebec

Before Brooke set off for the cross-Atlantic trip he met Wingate to discuss the Chindits, the now famous Long-Range Penetration Groups, which he decided were worth backing. Brooke was surprised when he heard that Churchill was taking Wingate and Mrs Wingate to America, and he speculated that this was 'window dressing'. He may have been right, but it was useful as later Wingate addressed the Americans who were impressed by him and his activities. Brooke travelled up with others by train to Faslane (on Gare Loch) to the liner's berth. He was self-evidently not in the best of moods about the expedition, and he complained 'with sharp clarity' about his train berth being over the grinding wheels of the carriage.[29] On 5 August, Brooke boarded an old cross-Channel ferry out to the *Queen Mary* to travel to Canada. He was not happy about another conference, having heard that Admiral King was still pressing for Pacific priority, and that Marshall was upset

Conference at Quebec (US Navy)

because the British appeared less concerned about Operation *Overlord*. The issue of the Mediterranean theatre has occupied military and general historians for years. Arguments range from the British being far-sighted and the Americans blind, to the Americans prepared to take a better grip and get to the heart of the problem in Berlin. As always, the arguments are complex and difficult, but with the benefit of hindsight the truth was probably somewhere between the two camps. It would take much longer than expected to clear the Germans out of Italy; they were constantly fighting in the northern regions, and only surrendered a few days before Berlin collapsed. On the other hand, the only way to arrive in Europe was to land in France but given the German strength, it would have been too early in 1943. It was not easy to see the wood for the trees. It was clear that both the Americans and British were exasperated about another round of talks on their divergences of strategy, and Brooke had to convince Churchill not to talk about breaking out of Italy into Vienna or the Balkans, as he realised it would turn Marshall and the Americans even more against the Italian campaign.

At this stage Brooke knew it would be the same old arguments repeated all over again. That evening they had dinner together after a COS meeting, and the weather was 'dirty' but Brooke was pleased the liner did not 'wobble about much'. He read Morgan's plans for Operation *Overlord* and thought they were good, but somewhat optimistic. He discussed the question of manpower with Churchill, and then discovered that Churchill had appointed Mountbatten as supreme commander in south-east Asia, prompting Brooke to observe in his diary that Mountbatten 'will require a very efficient Chief of Staff to pull him through'; as his diary frequently indicated he had a very low opinion of Mountbatten. The days were taken up with discussions and committees, mainly about the cross-Channel invasion, arguments with Churchill over army command, the issues relating to Burma, in which Wingate was included, and the Washington inclinations that the invasions of France and Burma should become the main priorities, abandoning the campaign for Italy. Brooke wanted the Americans to try and grasp the truth behind the saying that 'a bird in the hand is worth two in the bush'. There was encouraging news arriving from Sicily and more discussion on ice-made warships which, according to Brooke, was one of 'Mountbatten's bright ideas' and therefore mad.

On arrival Brooke enjoyed looking at the Canadian countryside which reminded him of Scotland, and he settled into his comfortable rooms with their views, while Churchill went off to America to see Roosevelt at his Hyde Park home. The Americans had yet to arrive, so Brooke enjoyed a day with the others of driving, walking and some fishing. This was the first time he realised that Admiral Pound was not well. As they meandered together enjoying a pleasant day out Brooke could not help ruminating that 'I am tired of arguing with the Americans.' He met with Diss, a British military liaison officer, and held a COS meeting, knowing that because they were on what was regarded as British soil, he would be chairing the meetings.

Eventually, on 14 August they had their first Combined meeting, which was not difficult because it was agenda setting, and they appeared to be of one accord over the European theatre. Brooke heard from Auchinleck that there were serious floods to the west of Calcutta which could have damaging effects on the Burma campaign.

The next day Brooke had to cope with some personally depressing news. Roosevelt had told Churchill he wanted Marshall as the supreme commander in Operation *Overlord*. In his own account of this choice of *Overlord* commander, Churchill claims it was he who suggested to Roosevelt that there should be an American commander, and that Brooke 'bore the great disappointment with soldierly dignity'.[30] Whether it was because Churchill knew the Americans would demand the supreme command, because of their overwhelming majority in resources and manpower, or he was mollifying Brooke, or even centralising his importance will remain somewhat enigmatic. It has also been suggested that 'perhaps Churchill offered it in the hope that Brooke would become more enthusiastic about *Overlord* as a result'.[31] Brooke was not against *Overlord*, but just questioned the timing, and Churchill, who always had an eye on the geopolitical situation, undoubtedly wished for a British commander.

This was upsetting news for Brooke who had had enough of Whitehall and was desperate to take on a major field command post. Churchill had promised this to him three times, and he withdrew it without much sympathy. It was, as Omar Bradley pointed out in his autobiography, that the USA would be forming the most forces and it therefore had to be an American commander, which the British would have expected had the situation been in reverse.[32] Some thought it was because the Americans suspected Brooke of not being overly convinced of the necessity for *Overlord*, which, as noted, was untrue; he wanted it to succeed but timing was the key to that success. The French historian Henri Michel believed the Americans were worried Brooke would do his best to delay *Overlord*, but in the developing geopolitical power play the Americans were more likely simply asserting their authority.[33]

In the postwar years John Colville was certain that 'the Americans insisted that it [the appointment] was their preserve' and he was probably right.[34] Eisenhower in his postwar memoirs added the telling line that Churchill told Roosevelt that this American appointment 'cost him some personal embarrassment because he had already promised Alan Brooke the command'.[35] Brooke told Churchill he was disappointed; in fact Brooke felt depressed and deeply saddened, but not bitter or crushed as he is often described in some accounts, though with his later reflections the historian Beevor may have been right when he wrote that Brooke 'never really got over the blow'.[36] Churchill and Roosevelt had made up their minds, and Churchill explained that soon Eisenhower would replace Marshall, and Alexander would take Eisenhower's place, and Montgomery would be called back to take Paget's position.*

---

* When Eisenhower was confirmed as supreme commander Patton used his nickname 'Divine Destiny' based on the initials of his first two names; see Beevor, *The Second World War*, p.514.

Pug Ismay repeated a conversation he had at the time that Roosevelt would not be able to sleep at night with Marshall out of the country.[37] It came as a sudden blow for Brooke, who noted that Churchill 'offered no sympathy or regrets'. In some ways Churchill had no choice, but before he had offered the post to Brooke, he should have known that the Americans were the stronger power by far in terms of manpower and resources. There were those in the American camp who believed that neither Brooke nor Marshall should be supreme commander because at this stage men like Montgomery, Eisenhower, Patton, Bradley and Clark had already had battle experience, and Brooke's field command was only associated with the disaster of the 1940 defeat.

Marshall, as Brooke often stated, had in his personal opinion no strategic sense, and Dill tried to speak to Marshall man to man, but he returned to Brooke with the news that Marshall would not rein in if the British pressured him on too many points. The main thrust of Marshall's argument was that *Overlord* was the priority, and he was generally opposed to invading Italy.

The next day the news arrived that Badoglio had transmitted some peace terms which were based on the Allies joining the Italians in clearing the Germans out of Italy. As noted earlier this was never going to be easy because the Italians remained divided as a people. The Germans had already planned for this exigency with Operation *Asche* (originally called *Alaric*) preparing for Germans, with help from some Italian fascists, to disarm the Italian forces; they managed to accomplish this with over a million Italian soldiers within a few days. Meanwhile the Allies wondered whether the Germans would bother to defend Italy (the OKW had considered this at one brief time) but they sent Rommel to the northern Italian regions to ensure no doors were left open to south and central Europe. Jumping ahead of this proposed policy, Kesselring decided to fight the Allies from the heel and toe of Italy and defend Italy all the way up through the 'boot'. This eventually proved so successful that it gained Hitler's full support against Rommel's plans. In the Anglo-American camp the same internal struggle continued about whether to invade Italy and how far to go, Churchill telling Stimson, the American secretary of state for war, that the intention was to stop at Rome, which may have been regarded by some as misleading. Eisenhower was certainly interested in the taking of the Foggia plains with airfield facilities in that area, which were well situated for being useful in attacking central Europe.

Brooke was concerned at the American stubbornness over listening to his military reasoning. As chairman he wrote, 'I opened by telling them that the root of the matter was that we were not trusting one another.'[38] The Americans doubted the British intentions to cross the Channel, and they persisted in questioning the Mediterranean plans. The secretaries and planners had been removed from the meeting, and this always seemed to help matters along towards a sense of agreement. The number of landing craft became a major issue, not least because the Americans knew the British were retaining them in the Mediterranean despite the general shortages. However,

General George Marshall (NASA)

Brooke was having yet more trouble with Churchill over his obsession with taking the island of Sumatra, as if that could win the war against Japan. Churchill pursued this idea with the same relentless demands he had made about Trondheim, and according to Brooke, Churchill 'behaved like a spoilt child that wants a toy in the shop irrespective of the fact its parents tell it that it is no good.'[39] Brooke complained that it was impossible to run a conference with the prime minister 'chasing hares in the background'. However, because it was a closed session most of the problems were resolved. At the last moment Mountbatten asked if he could demonstrate his project *Habbakuk*, which was the idea of ice-built ships mentioned earlier.[*] They agreed, probably because to the Americans Mountbatten was 'a royal' and popular with them. He had already prepared for two types of blocks of ice to be put in the room, explaining one was pure ice, but the other was chemically treated, and when hit by gunfire would not splinter. He then pulled out a gun to everyone's astonishment, so the observers quickly moved behind him as they were hit by ice fragments, then he shot at the treated ice where the bullet bounced off and 'whistled' between their

---

[*] The inventor of a floating island or ship which was believed to be unsinkable was a Geoffrey Pyke; they were intended to be large floating ice islands rather than aircraft carriers.

legs. One account claims the bullet actually clipped the edge of Admiral King's leg, Brooke amusingly observed that the people outside the room waiting to re-join the closed session must have wondered whether the arguments had become so intense, they had resorted to their weapons.

The remainder of his time in Canada was less demanding, but he was concerned when he heard his youngest son Ti had been knocked unconscious by a car outside Parliament. Benita told him he had recovered and all was well, but it was for Benita that Brooke felt sorry for having to deal with such a traumatic crisis.

As he thought about the last few days, he had become fed up with debating with the Americans who always wanted arrangements wrapped up in 'lawyer-type agreements', but it was Churchill who mainly depressed him as Brooke later in the night reflected on the conference. Brooke wrote that he 'felt the inevitable flatness of depression which swamps me after a spell of continuous work'. He was finding it more and more difficult to cope 'with the difference of opinions, the stubbornness, stupidity, pettiness and pig-headedness'.[40] Unlike the usual Brooke he was almost feeling sorry for himself, adding that 'I could almost have sobbed with the loneliness'. and observing there were no birds to look at. Brooke was not an easy man to know (unless a bird lover) and even in the company of other military leaders he stood apart, appearing somewhat aloof, but ready to launch into his own battles and diatribes in support of his strategy. The next morning when he reread the diary entries he had made, he paused and added that 'I must have been feeling peevish.' He normally argued with Portal weekly if not daily over professional matters, but for the next few days they enjoyed one another's company fishing for trout, which was nearly spoilt by a sudden visit from Churchill. Churchill in his account of the visit to the fishermen painted a more congenial time as he and Clemmie dashed in at the last moment, giving an impression of 'chums together'.[41] Brooke was once asked by an historian 'if he had ever been tempted to take Churchill birdwatching' and was met by the immediate reply of, 'God forbid.'[42] While there Brooke even caught sight of an osprey and other interesting birds, and he was alert and interested by the proximity of wild bears. At least he found time for his ideal type of holiday.

Before returning he visited Admiral Pound and purchased a book on Canadian birds. It was to be the last time he ever saw Pound who had suffered a stroke in Washington. The admiral returned to Britain but died on 21 October (which seemed fitting as it was the Battle of Trafalgar Day), leaving Brooke wishing he could withdraw all his unkind words. Many a diarist may well have scrubbed out most of the comments about Pound, but Brooke was honest enough to leave even his bad-tempered moments for others to read, probably because they described the graphic reality of the situation. He flew back to Britain, landing in Poole, then took a train to London. On the last day of the month when he always turned reflective, he wondered how future historians would deal with Churchill. Brooke thought him a 'wonderful character, a superhuman genius, but with an astonishing lack of vision…he could see a whole strategy' and adding that 'he is quite the most difficult man to work with, but I should not have missed the chance of working with him for anything in the world.'[43] This description of Churchill outlined Brooke's turbulent relationship with the prime minister, from rage to love, from despair to hope.

## Italy and Other Problems

During September 1943 Brooke's strategy, which he had debated and pushed for over months of intense debate, started to make some progress. Reflecting American opinion, it has been argued by Liddell Hart that the invasion of Italy only took place because after Sicily it was too early for *Overlord*, and the crossing to the Italian mainland made sense. The Allies landed on the Italian coastline in the south (3 September) on the fourth anniversary of the declaration of war, and then further north at Salerno. Italy surrendered (8 September), the Germans occupied Rome, evacuated Sardinia, and elsewhere near the end of the month the Russians occupied Smolensk. Brooke and the COS studied the plans, listened to the results, and could only hope for the best. Brooke had to watch and wait like an anxious far-distant observer. He heard from Eisenhower that Badoglio was 'ratting', evidently because the Germans were pro-active and he could not hold them in check. Immediately prior to the proposed landings at Salerno there had been plans to drop parachutists near Rome, on the Italian promise they would be supported. This was a risky venture, but in order to stiffen the resolve, it was suggested that Rome could be taken by paratroopers, namely the 82nd, to which Eisenhower agreed, and Alexander felt the Italian offer of supplying trucks, ambulances, labour, fuel and rations could be trusted. There was perhaps a degree of naivety in his thinking, but Alexander was worried that if the Salerno landing Operation *Avalanche* failed, Churchill's government might fall, and a coup in Rome might save the day.[*]

Brooke in London would have been unaware of these immense risks, but he was a realist and pragmatist who knew that at times a gamble had to be taken, however, at this stage it was, as Brooke later commented, too far north, and German reaction had yet to be understood. As this drama was unfolding in Italy, Brooke appointed Pownall as Mountbatten's staff officer to counteract 'Dickie's lack of balance and

---

[*] The proposed operation was code-named Operation *Giant II*, but a shortage of aircraft meant that it would take two drops, the first with two battalions dropped at night on airfields 20 miles north of Rome, and over 200 miles from Salerno. Hindsight is an historian's assistant, but it almost exceeds belief that this proposed operation was taken so seriously; it was only called off when planes were already airborne, and then literally at the last moment by the firing of flares. Brigadier-General Maxwell Taylor and a Colonel William Gardiner infiltrated their way into Rome to gauge the situation. Given the seniority of Taylor this derring-do expedition was itself risky, most especially since both men were fully informed of Allied intentions post-Salerno. They both realised the operation was far too dangerous.

general ignorance of handling land forces.' Brooke did not mention the bungled Dieppe raid under Mountbatten's command, but it must have been in the back of his mind as his estimation of Mountbatten's ability rapidly deteriorated. Mountbatten had asked Brooke for one of his tunic buttons, and he proposed to do the same with Portal so he could carry all three services on his uniform. Brooke noted this in his diary as an illustration of the trivia which occupied Mountbatten most of the time. As various studies of Mountbatten have indicated, Brooke had seen in Mountbatten a man obsessed with his own standing and his appearance in the public eye. From the 9th to the 12th of the month Brooke had his first official leave as the CIGS, and spent his time shooting on the Durham moors.

When he returned to duty the news from Salerno was not good, and he was unhappy that after the earlier landings at Taranto and Brindisi, the troop movements were not progressing well. His immediate reaction was to note that Eisenhower and Alexander 'will never have enough vision to be big soldiers'. Churchill was still in America, and the Cabinet was led by Attlee whom Brooke was beginning to appreciate. His main concern remained Salerno over the next few days, and the fear the Allied troops would be pushed back into the sea. Typically of Brooke, his comments about an ongoing action were only mentioned in terms of 'good or bad' like a temperature chart, but never in the detail, most of which he would have been aware of at the time.

There had been unquestionably the wrong sort of euphoria about this amphibious operation. Intelligence officers had believed that because the Italians had barely fought in Sicily their response in Salerno would be even weaker, and that any Germans would retreat to northern Italy to establish defensive lines. They also believed that Salerno was the perfect hydrographic landing place with an easy approach for landing craft, when in fact it was heavily mined.* The Salerno invasion was nearly a total disaster because of a series of miscalculations about the terrain, and a gross underestimation of the enemy. Perhaps the most serious error was assuming that the Germans would move north leaving the Italians to defend. Even if Clark, Alexander and Eisenhower had believed that the German high command would follow Rommel's advice and defend in the north, their responsibility for their men should have assumed the worst-case scenario, namely that trained and experienced German troops awaited on the shoreline; Brooke had always pressed this point of German military professionalism. The armistice notice had given the impression that it was almost peace, and the serious military miscalculation was made by Clark not to bombard the shoreline which would

---

* The Germans already had 40,000 troops in the Naples area and it rapidly grew to 100,000: with the help of naval analysts Kesselring had given a high priority to this area. In preparation Kesselring brought in General Rudolf Sieckenius, commander of the 16th Panzer, with 17,000 men, over 100 tanks and 700 heavy machine guns.

cost lives. Running through the centre of Salerno was the River Sele dividing the British and American troops, and this soon became a serious barrier and weakness which the Germans quickly exploited.* At one point Clark decided to abandon the operation, and to this day on a small monument in Salerno there are two quotations carved with Clark's words, 'Prepare to evacuate the beach', and the response by Major-General Middleton: 'Leave the water and the ammo on the beach. The 45th Division is here to stay.' As noted by Alan Whicker, 'It is rare indeed for a division to castigate publicly its army Commander for considering sailing away from the battle.'[44]

It was not difficult to understand Brooke's anxiety as he read the incoming information, and he would have known that failure at Salerno would have spelt disaster for his strategy of occupying Italy. Fortunately, by the time Churchill arrived back from America (19 September) the news from Salerno was improving, Sardinia was evacuated (and it was hoped that Corsica would follow) and there was again a sense of hope. The near disaster at Salerno and Montgomery's slow progress from the south, over which the victor of El Alamein was accused of being too slow to protect his reputation, must have sown seeds of doubts in Allied minds.[†] The Germans under Kesselring and his highly professional commanders would use the Italian terrain of valleys, rivers and mountains to carry on a tough defence in a landscape which was better suited for defence than attack. Well-placed heavy machine guns on rocky outcrops could hold back thousands of troops, and Italy, although cynically regarded as a backwater by many, would see some of the bitterest fighting of the war. Despite the problems at Salerno and the evident German resistance, Montgomery appeared to be slow and too methodical in his approach, and Alexander did not interfere. Later Brooke was criticised by the American historian Weinberg, on the grounds that 'Brooke neither explained to his protégé why the Italian campaign was so important nor sent a rocket to him even while sighing into his diary that the Salerno landing "is doomed"'.[45] The first criticism cannot be justified, because Montgomery would have been aware of the importance of the campaign, especially from the British perspective. The second arose from Brooke's habit of not interfering with the commanders in the field, but such was Montgomery's lack of progress, perhaps Weinberg was correct in his second observation.

The British had wondered how many troops the Germans would have to send to Italy to justify the claim that it would relieve pressure on Russia and prepare for *Overlord*; because of the Italian terrain it was not going to be a heavy demand on German resources, especially when compared to what they required against the Soviet Union. The Allies had hoped to be in Rome very quickly, but this was a forlorn hope.

---

* Patton had spotted this weakness long before the invasion but was ignored.

† It is generally agreed that Montgomery was painfully slow, but the Germans had mined and booby-trapped the twisting and turning roads.

Brooke knew that Montgomery would soon be recalled because of *Overlord*, as he was to replace Paget on the Home Front. Paget, Brooke knew, had been good at his job, but Montgomery had experienced battle command and was considered the better man under the changing circumstances, and his El Alamein victory projected his image as a winner. Brooke had his doubts as usual, but he felt it was the right decision.

Churchill was now back, causing Brooke to have to continue his battle with the prime minister's impetuous ideas, including his incessant demands for Sumatra to be invaded, and then he had to visit the king who wanted to hear all the news directly from Brooke. His month ended for him on a very unusual and unpleasant note. Brooke had been approached by MI5 about some intercepted correspondence from Martel (who had been sent to Moscow against his wishes, see p.156 above) to a friend called Mackessie, in which he disclosed too much information, not least his embarrassing criticism of Brooke for sending him to Russia. It was suggested to Brooke that he ensured that Martel should take more care over what he was writing. This presented Brooke with a conundrum on how to manage this without revealing that Martel's personal post was being read; an aspect of war he obviously found somewhat distasteful, even if it were necessary.

During October the war raged across the world, with the Japanese cunningly declaring the independence of the Philippines (14th), Italy technically declaring war on Germany (14th), the Azores becoming an Allied base, and Russia self-evidently turning the tide. Brooke barely referred to these events, later admitting that he made little comment about the momentous turn of the tide by Russia which, he acknowledged, was critical to his and all Western strategy. Brooke was unquestionably aware of every piece of news, but his diary is personal, recording several grouse shoots and a tiny island in the Aegean Sea called Kos. This island emerged at this stage in the diaries, mainly because Kos had replaced Trondheim and Sumatra in Churchill's thinking processes, which were always demanding more action. It was another month of the battle of wits between Churchill and Brooke as the latter tried to make the former see sense, from his point of view. This task of restraining Churchill was important, but it is barely mentioned in any of the general histories, and even the better historians only give it a fleeting note, despite its relevance and importance.

Churchill was the elected prime minister, but being an ex-soldier he always assumed he had a grasp of strategy which Brooke found difficult to combat. None of these tensions were helped by the knowledge that the campaign in Italy appeared to be grinding to a halt. Brooke believed it to be because of lack of resources, but logistically the Allies were superior, especially in the air and at sea. Eisenhower had predicted that they would soon be in Rome, but this did not happen until the very same day as D-Day in Normandy in 1944 started. The first COS meeting of October therefore did not go well for Brooke, with Churchill wanting to withdraw troops from the Mediterranean for an attack in the Pacific, 'just', as Brooke observed, 'to equip Mountbatten [who arrived in India on 7 October] for

Sumatra'. Brooke noted that Churchill was prepared to scrap 'our basic strategy' and 'put Japan before Germany. However, I defeated most of his evil intentions in the end.'[46] Whether Churchill intended this is another matter; he may well have been using the politician's ploy of offering the worst possible scenario, but he had a strong propensity for coming up with sudden martial enterprises. It is worth noting the view that Churchill 'regularly drove his military chiefs frantic with ideas usually ill-timed or impractical. He possessed, however, a corresponding sense of when to step down' which is probably the better view.[47] Brooke tried to recover from this first bout of the month by grouse shooting for the next two days.

When he returned, he found Churchill still 'fluttering about Kos', the small, and for Brooke irrelevant, island in the Dodecanese.[*] Nearly a hundred Italian officers on Kos had refused to join the Germans and were executed, and the Germans had managed to retain the island against incursions. This island, along with Lemnos and the major island of Rhodes, was important for providing air cover for the Balkans; the main issue in a global war for the British appeared to be the importance of the Balkans, a policy which always invoked American suspicions. A few days later Churchill was pressing for Kos to be occupied which Brooke passionately opposed; they had enough problems in Italy without withdrawing essential resources from the main battle areas for this small island in the Aegean Sea. Churchill then switched his argument to the taking of Rhodes, which again Brooke protested about without much help from his fishing friend Portal, who seemed to support the prime minister. The next day Churchill tried to persuade Brooke with a *tête-à-tête*, which meant a walk to Hyde Park where Churchill's daughter was serving one of the batteries during an air-raid. Churchill failed to convince Brooke, but he also informed Brooke that he intended to ask Roosevelt to send Marshall to a conference in Tunis to discuss the matter, which Brooke would also be attending. Brooke returned home to his nightly diary entries, and he entered the observation that Churchill 'is in a very dangerous condition, most unbalanced and God knows how we shall finish this war if this goes on and on'.[48] Brooke was in despair, failing to understand why Churchill could not see that the Italian campaign needed everything, and that he would also upset the Americans again, who were always suspicious of Churchill's seeming obsession with the Balkans. To many Americans, for some reason, the Balkans meant empire. In a sense they were correct, because the Balkans provided a route to the Middle East and Egypt which Churchill regarded as part of the empire. Brooke thought the American suspicions were not groundless, and he worried that Marshall might think he was behind this extraordinary demand. He wrote to Dill on the matter, and two weeks later (22 October) received a reply, explaining that Dill had spoken

---

[*] This island had been transferred to the Kingdom of Italy in 1912 and was controlled by Italy until its surrender in 1943. The Germans occupied it until May 1945 and it then became a British protectorate until 1947, when it was ceded to Greece following the Paris Peace Treaty.

to Marshall, and he 'was very touched at your consideration in this matter of the Aegean, and he never doubted Brooke' as he knew from where the Balkan issue arose.[49] As it was Churchill received a 'cold reply' from Roosevelt telling him not to interfere in the Mediterranean campaign. After this Brooke had a phone call from Churchill who was upset, stating 'everyone is against me' but conceding that matters in Italy had become more pressing.

As the issue of Kos had rumbled on Brooke had attended a Polish reception where he was formally given the 'Order of the Restored Poland' by the president of the Polish Republic; he then had to attend a COS meeting, with Churchill in a 'peevish mood' over an intended meeting of foreign ministers in Moscow (19 October). The question of the dismembering of Germany after the war arose, and Smuts made everyone pause and think when he said that a year before he would have agreed, but he was now uncertain, since the West might need a powerful nation on the Soviet borders. This was far-reaching and prescient reasoning from Smuts, and it can be easily understood why he was so respected in his observations and suggestions. Later Eden would make contact from Moscow informing them that Russia was trying to find a way of encouraging Turkey and Sweden to fight against Germany. Brooke also had an interview with 'Bomber' Harris, who claimed that Russian success was only brought about by his bombing; Brooke could see that Harris really believed that bombing could win the war alone, and Brooke as a soldier could not understand this claim. He was paid another visit by the Duke of Gloucester who, Brooke noted, came 'for one of his usual visits and as usual was very nice and luckily did not stop too long'. It is not difficult to imagine Brooke feeling obliged to be correct, polite, and therefore friendly, but with an eye on the clock hoping the dignitary would soon go.

On 19 October it was another battle with Churchill who was suddenly swinging back to the Mediterranean rather than Operation *Overlord*, which Brooke naturally tended to have some empathy with, but he was well aware of the Americans' attitude and the need to keep them onside. When Churchill suggested another Combined Chiefs of Staff, Brooke noted in his diary that 'I shuddered.'

Pound, who had died on 21 October, was buried from Westminster Abbey, and as Brooke sat by his coffin, he could not help feeling that 'in some ways I envied him'. It had been a testing month for Brooke with the relentless battles with Churchill, and a depressing fear arising from the apparent stagnation in Italy. Brooke was unhappy about events there and concerned with news about Eisenhower's headquarters, and Alexander's ability to cope. He found Churchill in a better mood at the end of the month, and he tried to persuade him to grant Dill a peerage, because Dill had done so much work for the British effort. He felt that Churchill despite his promises would not respond on this matter; he tried again, but when Dill died just over a year later it had never happened, and Brooke never forgave Churchill for this omission of some appropriate recognition for his friend. At the end of this month (30 October) Roosevelt wrote to Churchill suggesting that a British deputy supreme commander for *Overlord* should be appointed, and he proposed Dill or Portal or Brooke. Churchill had never taken to Dill and this would have raised his objections.[50] It is clear from Brooke's diary entries that command changes were discussed at the various COS meetings, but Brooke was the key to Churchill's thinking, the prime minister noting in a wire to Roosevelt that 'I had a long conversation with the CIGS…as a result I am able to place before you the following proposals.'[51] This was one of the few occasions that Churchill let slip his reliance upon Brooke.

In November, the Russians captured Kiev and American forces landed on Tarawa which was their first move in the central Pacific offensive, while in Italy the war continued to stagnate. Brooke's main preoccupation during this month and part of the next was the first session of the Sextant Conference to be held in Cairo, and part two, known as Eureka, to be held in Teheran. The very idea of another CCOS was something Brooke utterly dreaded; his preparations on how to deal with Marshall were always prominent in his mental calculations. He liked Marshall as a person but professionally, as a military officer thought little of him, making one of his more peevish remarks that 'in strategy I doubt if he can ever, ever see the end of his nose'. The stress was almost too much for him, blaming himself for not managing to convince the Americans of the accuracy of his strategy, writing that 'instead to satisfy the short-sightedness we have been led into agreeing to the withdrawal of forces from the Mediterranean for a nebulous Second Front, and have emasculated our offensive strategy.' Later when he reread his diary he added that he was suffering from a bad cold at that time, and bravely admitted that he may have been near a nervous breakdown; not that any person in his company would have believed this as a possibility.

He also added in his diary a somewhat enigmatic statement given his protests to Churchill about Rhodes, namely that success in Crete and Rhodes might have good repercussions in Turkey and set the Balkans ablaze. It is not so easy to understand where Brooke stood in this matter, whether he had been eventually persuaded by Churchill, or was making as much of the Mediterranean strategy as possible. It is possible it was Brooke's political device to keep shipping and landing craft in the Mediterranean, not least because he was contemplating another amphibious landing closer to Rome. It was also clear that Brooke was a strong supporter of the fierce partisan war raging in the Balkans. Churchill knew that in his wish to take Rhodes and control the Dodecanese, he was somewhat isolated in his opinions, and later argued that controlling the Aegean would have brought Turkey into the war. As mentioned, the very word 'Balkans' always raised American suspicions, and for the only time it is not entirely clear where Brooke stood on this matter. Churchill also went so far as to query the agreed date of May 1944 for *Overlord*, which was taken as set in concrete by the Americans.

Turkey's neutrality was causing a degree of frustration, and Brooke was amused when Churchill wired Eden prior to his visit to that country, to tell 'Turkey Christmas was coming'. Later in the month they met Stalin, who made it clear that in his opinion Turkey would not make a move, and the question was best put aside. The main thrust for Brooke and COS was preparing to meet the Americans, and then the Russians, with appropriate plans and arguments. He heard that Churchill had received a telegram from the American Admiral Leahy making the 'ridiculous' suggestion that Marshall should be the supreme commander of the European theatre, combining *Overlord*, Italy and North Africa under one command. Brooke was grateful that Churchill was very much in agreement with him and returned a firm negative reply. It must have been a relief to Brooke that he was spending that evening at dinner with his bird friend Bannerman. The American situation was a cause of deep concern to Brooke having received a letter from Dill the previous month, stating that the 'American difficulties would increase', not least because hitherto they had given way more than the British. Dill reminded Brooke there was a presidential election looming, and it would be difficult for Roosevelt's success if the American voters thought he were safely contained in British pockets. The proposal that Marshall should be the supreme commander in Europe and elsewhere may well have been part of American domestic politics because Marshall was well known and popular.

Brooke established a firm line to present to the Americans, which had six fundamental points. The battle in Italy would only stop once they had established a Pisa to Rimini line, which meant postponing *Overlord* for two months. Then there was a need for centralising command in the Mediterranean, rearming partisans in the Balkans, bringing Turkey into the war, and forcing the Balkan states to sue for peace. Some historians have argued that this persistent pressure to wage war in south and south-east Europe left Hitler with the critical heart of central Europe. This was not Brooke's intention, but was based on fighting the Germans where they could weaken them, disperse their forces, and thereby take some pressure off the Russians and prepare for the Second Front in France. This was the basic theory, but whether this was farsighted or exhibited a state of Brooke-like stubbornness and short-sightedness will always remain a point of academic contention. It certainly reflected the inherent British cultural strategy mentioned earlier.

During the second week of December, Brooke was preparing himself for Cairo, attending the Cenotaph, taking in the news that the French National Assembly had rejected Giraud and Georges, attending a Cabinet meeting chaired by Attlee (Churchill was already at sea in HMS *Renown*), still trying to rid himself of McNaughton (who he thought of 'as going off his head'), and arguing with Eden over supplying Greek partisans with weapons. Eden thought that the partisans were too communist and would cause problems for postwar democracy in Greece. Both Eden and Brooke were correct in their different ways. In France, Italy, Greece and elsewhere in the Balkans the communist resistance movement tended to be the most violent and effective. When, for example, Corsica was freed the communists had ensured they were the first there to take civic control, and elsewhere they emerged as a powerful political force. Brooke wanted one thing, the destruction of Nazi Germany, and he had little time for the politics of resistance.

## Cairo and Teheran

On 17 December Brooke flew to Gibraltar, having first to rush around before he took the flight because he had forgotten his pyjamas; the prime minister had arrived in the *Renown* that evening. The Americans had not been happy meeting with the British in Cairo, not wanting the Russians to think they were colluding, and a disturbing message came through from Roosevelt that they had heard the Germans knew they were meeting in Cairo. The president suggested Khartoum, which in his diary Brooke followed with an exclamation mark, possibly speculating that the president may have been thinking of General Gordon killed there by the Mahdi's warriors in 1885; Churchill responded by suggesting Malta which had its own inherent dangers and history. It was finally decided to stay with Cairo as the venue, which was something of a relief for Brooke, who was hoping to call by Italy on the way. Brooke was also concerned that Churchill would upset the Americans, as he proposed to tell them that 'you play with us in the Mediterranean or we won't play with you in the Channel'. Brooke was right to be anxious, but it was becoming abundantly clear that with the build-up of American forces, and Russia's growing offensive, that Churchill was beginning to feel that he might be taking the role of the junior partner. It was probably during these months that Roosevelt was becoming less enamoured with Churchill, who in turn was becoming more anti-American. Churchill, according to Brooke, had little strategic sense, but he did have a streak of genius, had a better global strategy, and had led Britain when Stalin was a Nazi partner and America had remained aloof. He was now becoming the minor partner, the junior of the three leaders and he deeply resented this position.[*]

Brooke met Alexander in Gibraltar, anticipating a trip with him to Italy, but he wrote that although he found Alexander 'charming he fills me with gloom, he is a very, very small man and cannot see big...and he is oblivious to his shortcomings.' Later Brooke added that he may have been 'too hard' in the way he put this, but he never changed his mind. His diary when published years later must have made uncomfortable and angry reading for many public figures of some standing and substance. There was still the question hovering in the air as to whether Roosevelt would make it to Cairo, but this eventually came through in the affirmative.

---

[*] Curiously, in 1943 Churchill was 69 years of age, Stalin 64, Roosevelt 61, but they died in reverse order; Roosevelt in 1945, Stalin in 1953, and Churchill in 1965.

Annoyingly for Brooke the weather was poor, and he could not make his way to Italy as he had planned, but he did spend time with the American Ambassador Winant (ambassador to Britain for most of the war) while touring Malta, and was deeply impressed with his knowledge and depth of perception. They had met before, as mentioned above, and their friendship would have been sealed when Winant, on this occasion, presented Brooke with a book on American birds. Lord Moran shrewdly observed these two men developing their friendship and wrote in his diary their similarities, that 'Winant has wrestled with the world and has hidden, like Brooke, behind a curtain of his own making.'[52] *

As he travelled on 20 November towards Cairo, Brooke ruminated on the possibility that had the Americans given more support, they could have been in Rome with Romania and Bulgaria out of the war; given the clever and professional German defence in Italy this was most unlikely. He was placed in a villa outside Cairo with Dill, Portal and Cunningham and discovered the plumbing was poor with a lack of hot water. He continued his musings in his diary, that up to this time, shipping had been freed up, the U-boat menace was plummeting, Germany was being bombed, the Russians were on the offensive, Italy was tottering, and southern Europe was threatened on all sides. The main issue he considered was that the Germans had excellent rail and road communications, and they could speedily transport troops across Europe with ease; yet another vexing problem which he foresaw with *Overlord*. His main problem, as far as Brooke could see, was convincing Marshall to connect these different theatres in his mind, and thereby understand the whole strategy. For their part, the Americans wanted to cut to the heart of Nazi Germany, and they simply could not understand the British obsession with nibbling away at the outer limbs.

The Cairo meeting did not start well for Brooke who found that Chiang Kai-shek and his wife had arrived early, and for the Americans in attendance the Chinese seemed to dominate the scene and be the more important partners, which for Brooke did not make sense, because in his terms, the Chinese had nothing to do with Germany. Chiang Kai-shek's wife with her beauty and oriental split skirt revealing her shapely legs caught Brooke's attention, but the other younger men's appreciation was apparent. In his diary Harold Macmillan noticed her as well, writing that 'Madame Chiang excited great interest amongst the British, rather less, I think, among the Americans, who have by this time seen and heard quite enough of her.'[53] He later added 'I gather she gives herself airs and graces and behaves like an Empress, which did not go down very well in the USA during her recent trip.'[54] She was the only woman there, often interrupting a meeting to explain that the interpreter was not quite right, and with her excellent English frequently correcting him. Brooke was far from love struck but more

---

* Lord Moran was Sir Charles Wilson, Churchill's personal doctor.

awe-struck with her manners, which he considered to be a form of interference, and he soon took a distinct distaste towards her. Brooke found the place full of Chinese generals, and when it was his turn to meet them formally there was total confusion, because they had not read his papers, and after a postponed meeting Brooke realised that they had come to listen, and gather support. He felt they were leading the Americans down the garden path, and later added, with some sense of self-satisfaction, that Chiang Kai-shek had not managed to stop postwar China becoming communist. The final result was more satisfactory for Brooke as the Americans, to show support for China, had promised Operation *Buccaneer* (for the invasion of the Andaman Islands) which demanded landing craft which would lead to a delay of *Overlord*, so it was cancelled, and Admiral King offered some 50 landing-craft for the Mediterranean. This was essential for the proposed landings near Rome, Operation *Anzio*, and Operation *Anvil* projected in the south of France. There was the usual tussling over the selection of commanders, especially for Normandy. Brooke always wanted Montgomery as commander because he had experience of battle command, but the Americans did not like him (with good reason) and Churchill preferred, as did the Americans, the more gentlemanly and diplomatically inclined Alexander. Brooke was also relieved that Eisenhower had been selected as supreme commander and not Marshall, because although he never rated him highly, at least he had accumulated some battle experience. Generally, Brooke was in favour of a unified command, but when it was proposed that the CCOS should be extended to include the Chinese and Russians he was horrified.

The debates with the Americans were again heated, with Brooke having a 'father and mother row' with Marshall, and another with Admiral King over landing craft, but as on previous occasions, once they had cleared the room of secretaries, planners and others, they had an off-the-record session and some progress was made.

On 27 November, despite the covering mist they took off for Teheran, landing on time and uncertain as to whether Stalin had arrived. The Soviet and British embassies were near one another, and the American president was given rooms in the Russian embassy, aware that it was undoubtedly bugged. Sergo Beria, the secret police chief Lavrenty Beria's son, 'manned the recording equipment bugging their rooms, and he was surprised to overhear FDR level a counteraccusation at Churchill for trying to engineer an anti-communist government' in Poland.[55] On the more humorous side Brooke discovered there were local elections taking place, and he amusingly recalled the rumour which was spreading amongst the normal residents of that area, that all the 'international dignitaries were there to ensure the election was run properly'.

Brooke was not happy with the conference, noting that Churchill was not that well and had lost his voice, and all he heard was Stalin's constant demands that the Second Front should be started at once. It was difficult to argue the case because Churchill was not at his best, and Roosevelt was not much better, even suggesting that operations in the Mediterranean should be stopped once Rome was occupied, suggesting that six divisions should be launched into southern France, and *Overlord* start on 1 May. Stalin, in his usual abrupt way, told the Allies that the war in Italy was not pulling Germans away from Russia, and so the fighting there may as well stop immediately, and cynically telling his allies that they could take the winter off in Italy.*

Brooke observed that this was an historic occasion as it was the first time the three leaders Roosevelt, Stalin and Churchill had sat together round the same table. Brooke watched Stalin closely and concluded he was something of an enigma, but of the three he thought Stalin was the better strategist. In Stalin's opinion Hitler had shot his bolt, but Brooke detected in Stalin the politician who had his 'covetous eyes' on the Balkans after the war, and Yugoslavia and Austria, which was why, Brooke pondered, Stalin was content for Italy to cease as a campaign. He was militarily shrewd, but the political power grasping in Stalin was always prominent. It concerned Brooke that 'we were reaching a dangerous point where Stalin's shrewdness, assisted by American short-sightedness, might lead us anywhere.'[56]

In a meeting with his adversary Voroshilov, the old Russian general made it clear that for all the fighting in Italy, it made no difference in helping Russia, and it was essential that 1 May 1944 was adhered to for the Second Front. This must have irritated Brooke beyond belief, but Voroshilov and Stalin were probably justified in this statement given the manpower involved. Reliable statistics can never be fully substantiated, but research has indicated during this war, in terms of the entire population Britain lost about some 450,000 people, the USA 419,000, Germany between seven and seven and a half million, and the USSR a staggering 20–27 million. The divergence of the Russian figures indicates the sheer chaos on the Russian front. The fighting on the Eastern Front was not only the most vicious but the loss of life almost beyond comprehension, leading many Western historians to acknowledge that when the Russians claim they won the war, they were probably justified. Voroshilov's attack on Brooke for not being fully supportive of *Overlord* was met by Brooke's habitual stubbornness, pointing out that 11 German divisions could be destroyed with the proposed operation south of Rome, and no one could be certain of the numbers of Germans ready and prepared in France. Marshall came to Brooke's defence reminding Voroshilov that crossing the Channel was not like bridging a river; this sudden assistance from Marshall may have surprised Brooke. As a matter of curiosity many historians, as well as Alexander and Kesselring, later raised the question as to who was pinning down who in Italy, the Germans, or the Western Allies?

---

* Because of the wintery conditions in the Italian mountains, which had to be crossed, any offensive action was often cancelled. Alexander instructed the partisans to ease off, and this made Stalin's comment somewhat pertinent.

Teheran Conference (Oulds, D. C. (Lt), Royal Navy official photographer)

Their troublesome meeting finished with a ceremony when Churchill presented the gift of the Stalingrad sword to Stalin from King George VI engraved with an appropriate inscription. Stalin took the sword and looked at it briefly, then passed it to Voroshilov who then, embarrassingly, dropped it on the floor. There would have been some there who saw this as a bad omen.* Brooke may have been bemused, but he was more concerned with the way Roosevelt was bending towards Stalin's way of thinking, and Churchill was not that helpful. He had a sudden revulsion against politicians, writing 'I feel more like entering a lunatic asylum or a nursing home than continuing in my present job' and coming to the conclusion that politicians 'can't wage war'.[57] Brooke could hardly restrain his own venom as he watched what was happening, adding the next day that 'the more politicians you put together to settle the prosecution of war the longer you postpone its conclusion'.[58] The next day there was better news in so far that

---

\* The sword was inscribed with the words *To the Steel-hearted citizens of Stalingrad, the Gift of King George VI, in token of the homage of the British people.*

1 June was accepted rather than 1 May for *Overlord*, and it also transpired to be Churchill's 60th birthday.

That evening there was a joint celebratory mood in Russian style with toast after toast, with Stalin making some barbed quips in Brooke's direction; being Brooke, he responded with a toast a few minutes later. As Brooke gathered his thoughts, he was observed by Moran, who wrote in his personal diary, 'that his face hardened until it became stern and uncompromising; in this mood his features recall those of the Iron Duke'.[59] Brooke stood and thanked Roosevelt, than turned to Stalin quoting something Churchill had once said, namely that 'in war the truth must be accompanied by an escort of lies to ensures its security…and one's outward appearance might even deceive one's friends.' Afterwards Stalin approached Brooke and gave him an embarrassing Russian hug telling him he liked the 'bold soldierly way in which I had spoken'. Brooke could not wait to escape what he must have considered to be a bizarre situation. This was Brooke's account of the occasion; there have been many other variations.

> It was one of Churchill's entourage, General Alan Brooke, who had the worst verbal exchange with Stalin. This had happened at a banquet at the Teheran Conference when Stalin rose to accuse Brooke of failing to show friendship and comradeship towards the Red Army. Brooke was ready for him and replied in kind that it seemed that 'truth must have the escort of lies' in war; he went on to assert that he felt 'genuine comradeship' towards the men of the Soviet armed forces. Stalin took the riposte on the chin, remarking to Churchill: 'I like that man. He rings true.'[60]

Brooke's diary was probably closer to the actual words exchanged, but because he was Brooke, he was one of the very few who stood up to Stalin while most others simply acquiesced.

Overall, Brooke thought the conference was badly organised, but then each country, although allied to the others, was fighting its own corner. The Russians felt, rightly, they were bearing the brunt of the fighting, thus their insistence on *Overlord*. The Chinese were not interested in Germany because Japan was their enemy; the Americans had been attacked by Japan and wanted the Germans dealt with quickly. Brooke had once objected to tanks being sent to North Africa when it looked like invasion at home, and now had his own strategy with which his limited numbers could cope and act offensively in Italy, but he did not believe the Allies were yet adequately prepared for attacking German-occupied France. It was a kaleidoscope of backgrounds, motives and intentions. Brooke had stood firm, argued, became at times distraught as indicated by some of his self-confessed peevish comments, but for him the 'Teheran Conference (Eureka) ended in success. It required a very clear head and considerable speed and adroitness in debate. Brooke had both.'[61]

On the first day of December Brooke said goodbye to the Mr Trott who had looked after him; this host was an oriental secretary who collected bird-skins which fascinated Brooke. They flew directly to Jerusalem and stayed in the King David

Hotel and enjoyed a tour of the Holy City. Brooke took every opportunity to tour those places he had only read about, but he was more anxious about the second part of the Sextant Conference with the Americans back in Cairo, where he was due to arrive next. He caught up with Churchill to find he was not in the best of moods, and he had suggested to Admiral Leahy that Rhodes be starved into submission. Brooke was also aware that the Americans were in a hurry, which had annoyed him because they had all wasted valuable time with the Chinese and Stalin. He was probably more correct about the former than the latter. In the postwar years with the rapid development of the Cold War, at least the Western leaders had met Stalin and his cohorts and could gain, as Brooke had, some measure of his long-term plans. What Brooke did not know as he left Jerusalem was that in distant Chicago University, the first successful experiment in nuclear reaction had taken place; the atomic bomb which would resolve the Far East battle in a matter of a few days was making progress.

As the preparations for round two of Sextant were studied, Churchill was angry because Mountbatten was demanding resources for the attack on the Andaman Islands. These islands were, for a brief time, a serious sticking point. Brooke had outlined to the CCOS the necessity of concentrating on *Overlord*, and not these distant irrelevant islands, and in his usual blunt and honest way held forth on the frustrations of the day. There was an immediate major problem because the president had made a personal promise to Chiang Kai-shek that the Andaman project would happen. Brooke dined with Churchill and was told it was now formal that Eisenhower would be supreme commander of *Overlord*, but they tussled over the Mediterranean command: Alexander, or Jumbo Wilson. Brooke preferred the latter, based on the grounds that Wilson knew the Mediterranean well. The next day was described by Brooke as 'deadlock' as the president's insistence on the Andaman Islands was merely a matter of 'saving face.' It took until the day after for the matter to be resolved and Brooke was pleased ('to our joy') that eventually Roosevelt decided to cancel this promise. In the overall strategy of a global war Brooke was correct to fasten the Allied attention on the main focuses of the conflict, crushing the more dangerous Nazi power. Roosevelt then left for America, and the Turkish President Inönü who had been there for wooing purposes also departed. Brooke then listened to MacArthur's chief of staff Sutherland explain his commander's policies. There were times when Brooke would have preferred MacArthur in Europe, but he later changed his mind about this political *prima donna*.

Brooke hated political machinations and interference, and this was further exacerbated when he discovered that Macmillan had probably interfered over Alexander, because Churchill had suddenly pushed Jumbo Wilson aside. Brooke suspected it was because the gentlemanly Alexander would be 'putty' in their hands, whereas Jumbo Wilson was made of 'tougher stuff'. In his own memoirs Macmillan acknowledged Wilson 'is a good man', then added 'but I am sure I can work' with

Alexander, thereby confirming Brooke's suspicions.[62] Brooke spoke to Macmillan and felt he had the 'haziest ideas as to what the duties of a Supreme Commander were'.

Brooke saw his friend Smuts off at the airport. Smuts informed Brooke that in his opinion Churchill was not well, and that his doctor Moran thought the same. Brooke frequently fell out with Churchill over his lack of strategy, his impetuosity and interference in military matters, but he frequently paused to observe that Churchill was essential for the nation at war, and would have agreed with Moran's observation that Churchill's 'claim to a place in history does not rest on his strategy. His gifts are of a rarer kind.'[63] Brooke was genuinely concerned at Churchill's health. Earlier that day Churchill had suggested the king should be asked to make Brooke a Field Marshal, that he be awarded the coveted baton, and as Smuts flew off Brooke wondered whether it had been this South African supporter who put that thought in Churchill's head. For Brooke, these days were a mixture of serious meetings and some tourism, looking at the Carthage ruins, and meeting Eisenhower at Tunis where a further discussion made it clear that Eisenhower did not like Montgomery, and he would have preferred Alexander. It was also clear that Churchill's health was not good and their plans for visiting Italy suddenly seemed unrealistic for Churchill, who started to agree with Brooke, until he suddenly picked up that Brooke had spoken to Moran. In the middle of the night Brooke was awoken by a wandering and sick Churchill with a temperature of 102 degrees, which confirmed Brooke would travel to Italy alone. Despite Moran's concern that his pneumonia diagnosis might be wrong, Brooke wired Cairo demanding the necessary medical equipment to be sent. He also explained to Alexander that he was to stay in Italy, and he accepted it without question; as Brooke noted 'he always did what he was told' and he was 'a soldier of the very highest principles'.

Brooke then flew across the Mediterranean and landed in Bari where he watched a German air raid that night, the second of two, but he was five miles outside the port. What he did not add, or did not know at the time, was that in the first raid on Bari (sometimes called the Little Pearl Harbor) one of the ships had been carrying gas shells which created many deaths and injuries amongst sailors, military and civilians; this was kept quiet for many years.[64] Next day he flew up the coast to Termoli, carried in a captured German Stork plane ideal for flying low and known as a 'puddle-hopper'.* There he met Montgomery who took him for a ride along the Sangro River where the most recent battle had been fought. Montgomery warned him that the anticipated early arrival in Rome should be disregarded because it was going to take longer than anticipated. He also heard that Montgomery thought little of General Mark Clark who, Montgomery claimed, was not running the American Fifth Army well. Brooke left feeling somewhat depressed because he thought

---

* Because of this plane's capability of flying so low it was difficult for fighter planes at a higher level to spot its whereabouts.

Montgomery looked tired out, and Alexander was not handling the situation well enough. Having seen the destroyed houses and villages along the Sangro, he felt 'we are stuck in an offensive here and shall make no real progress till the ground dries.' It is easy to gain the impression that the planners had underestimated Italy's geography; the popular view is one of sunny beaches and ancient sites. This viewpoint related to some of the picturesque coastline and well-known antiquity, but much of Italy is mountainous, fast flowing rivers cutting through steep valleys, and bitterly cold and wet in winter. When Brooke stood on top of Mount Camino which had to be fought for, he could see Monte Cassino Abbey in the distance, a typically ancient site which by its very nature and height gave it a dominating position. It was to become a well-known scene of bitter fighting. He met Alexander again at his camp in Caserta, visited Pompeii and talked to Clark. He was not impressed, and he arrived at the opinion Clark 'seems to be planning nothing but penny packet attacks and nothing sufficiently substantial'. Just a month after this visit, as part of crossing the Rapido river offensive, Clark ignored the advice of his field officers and demanded by orders a crossing of the River Gari which led to a massive slaughter of his own men. After the bloodletting at the Rapido some officers met and demanded a postwar congressional inquiry; this occurred in 1946 and the Texans blamed Clark for being inefficient and inexperienced.* Nothing came from the inquiry, but the accusation smouldered for decades and is still debated. Generals write their memoirs and publish their diaries, more often than not as a means of justifying themselves, but the rightness or wrongness of decisions will always be open to debate; only the facts cannot be argued against, and far too many men were killed or seriously wounded in this aspect of the campaign. Brooke's diary differed; he seldom blew his own trumpet, admitted his errors, even to feeling peevish and harshly judging people, and although he comes across as assertive there is no egotistical pomposity, and no sense of apologia which is often the characteristic of postwar memoirs and autobiographies.

After his conversation with Clark, who would not have found this meeting comfortable because he was an entrenched Anglophobe, Brooke flew to Tunis, always escorted by fighter planes when over Italy. He found the prime minister with his wife Clemmie and son Randolph looking better and asking questions about his Italian visit, which Brooke answered but did not tell him how he felt about the situation. Churchill had his own news, that Brooke would be announced on 1 January as a field marshal, and confirmed that Alexander would stay in Italy, Montgomery would

---

\* The Congressional Inquiry was on 20 January 1946, less than a year after the war had finished. The men of the 36th petitioned the 'Congress to investigate the River Rapido fiasco and take the necessary steps to correct a military system that will permit an inefficient and inexperienced officer, such as General Mark W Clark, in a high command to destroy young manhood of this country and to prevent future soldiers being sacrificed wastefully and uselessly.' It was too soon after the final victory for the House of Representatives to do anything but absolve Clark: the country needed heroes.

go home for *Overlord,* and Oliver Leese would take over the Eighth Army. He also heard that Paget would replace Jumbo Wilson. He flew to Gibraltar the next day and was back in London, having been away for five weeks and travelled 13,000 miles.

Brooke was pleased with the way events had turned out. He had managed to find breathing space by pushing *Overlord* to 1 June, and the south of France he felt was 'something more plastic'. The attack on the Andaman Islands had been cancelled, his intricate command appointments had been largely followed, and his visit to Italy had confirmed his belief that more amphibious landings were required, and he knew that the Anzio landing near Rome was being prepared. He had a better and longer Christmas break, undoubtedly interrupted by some shooting or photographing birds; he probably needed this time because the following year would be just as difficult. He had met Benita and his youngest daughter at Waterloo as soon as he returned to London, but Ferney Close was their home where he was able to relax more.

CHAPTER 8

# 1944

The year 1943 had clearly indicated that the tide of war was turning, and 1944 was to confirm that Germany and Japan were losing their initial military momentum, and they were now on the defence. It was never going to be straightforward, and there was continuous conflict from those fighting on the land, at sea and in the air, and concerns for men like Brooke and his counterparts, who were directing the nature and flow of the conflict. The men fighting at the front line were constantly in danger of losing their lives, but commanders like Brooke provided the strategy which placed them there in the first place, and they often genuinely felt responsible for the lives of the fighting men.

In the first month of 1944 the Russians crossed the Polish border (4th), Operation *Shingle* started (Anzio landing, 22nd), and on 22 January the disastrous siege of Leningrad ended.* At the personal level Brooke on the first day of the year was promoted to field marshal, writing in his diary that 'when I look back over my life no one could have been more surprised than I am to find where I got to.' As noted above there was a degree of pleasure for Brooke but no signs or sense of vanity. A few days later he was discussing the plans for the Second Front with Montgomery; he and Portal, who had received a similar promotion, were congratulated during a Cabinet meeting, but he was more interested in the return of the scaup duck which had reappeared in St James's Park, which he described as 'a great event'. He said goodbye to Paget who was off to the Middle East and unhappy to be superseded by Montgomery, but according to Brooke 'he took it well'. Brooke was always pleased when senior officers such as Paget and Alexander accepted a change of command or status without too much fuss. Later in the month this was not going to happen with the Canadian McNaughton, who was furious at losing his command of the Canadian army, which Brooke had been trying to manipulate for years. In 1943 (March) there had been some war games (Operation *Spartan*) when McNaughton with the Canadian army had the task of breaking out over the River Thames to take Huntingdon, designated as

---

*  It should be remembered that Anzio was an Italian seaside town and not associated with Australia and New Zealand (Anzac).

the capital, but he left his command post for a minor exercise and failed to delegate, which confirmed Brooke's belief he was unfit for command. McNaughton had been furious that the Canadians were split between the Mediterranean and Europe, which he called the 'dispersion', and the Canadian defence minister (Ralston) had passed on Brooke's criticisms. McNaughton believed that Ralston had influenced Brooke, but unlike Alexander and Paget he was bitter about losing his command. It was not a personal matter for Brooke, but a military necessity. At the end of March this year he wrote in his diary that 'I am afraid that I have lost a very good friend in the shape of Andy McNaughton. I only hope that he may be able to realise the true situation to rise high enough for me not to lose his friendship.'[1]

The usual COS meetings were focusing on the well-known 'pilotless' plane, later known as the doodlebug, which would be used in the coming summer, and the intelligence information which was rapidly accumulating about this threat was understandably causing considerable concern. There were also anxieties about the intricacy of command positions, especially in the Mediterranean, and Churchill, still in Marrakesh, was trying to run the war from there with his relentless telegrams, which Brooke and COS had to handle. As with the scaup duck, Brooke's only relief was home life and dinners with his bird friends, Bannerman and Kennedy.

Amery was demanding that troops in Italy should be mountaineers with which Brooke had some sympathy, but this was impractical at this stage, which was why Brooke was making sure Operation *Shingle* worked, as he believed the mountain fighting in Italy could be resolved by cutting off German armies from the coast with an amphibious incursion. He was relieved to hear that 22 January was firmly established as the date for *Shingle*.

One of the more troublesome and divisive of Churchill's telegrams was the suggestion that captured Italian naval vessels should be given to the Russians. Brooke and the COS could see no military value in such an action, not least because the Soviets were not a major fighting force at sea as they were on land at this stage. As Brooke had perceived at Teheran, and probably others had already observed, Stalin was appearing avaricious for postwar power. Brooke believed this giving away of ships to be a simple personal matter, writing that 'unfortunately during moments of special friendship fomented by wine, promises were made by the powerful ones to Stalin in Teheran'.[2] He was probably close to the mark in this observation.

On 13 January Brooke had a pleasant interlude when he and his staff officer drove to Sandringham to be with the king and the royal family. He discovered they were not in the main building, but he was directed to a smaller house which they enjoyed as a family. They had tea and dinner with the royal household, with Brooke sitting next to the queen whose company he very much enjoyed. While there they went shooting on the estate where Brooke 'bagged' a staggering 748 birds (pheasants and partridges), and left with warm feelings about their hosts, describing them as 'a thoroughly closely knit and happy family all wrapped up in each other.'

On his return he met with Eisenhower, and he was relieved and pleased the American commander agreed with him on one issue, namely that Eisenhower was happy to argue for a curtailing of the south of France invasion. Brooke's equilibrium was somewhat unsettled by Churchill's return when he met him at Paddington Station on 18 January. Churchill, according to Brooke, looked better, but 'I did not like the functioning of his brain much' – meaning by this observation that Churchill was prone to uncontrolled rambling. The COS and other meetings with Churchill appeared to achieve nothing according to Brooke, and out of sheer frustration he had written 'my God, how tired I am of working for him!' Another moment of peevishness, but perhaps understandable.

## Anzio and Italy

Brooke was hopeful when he heard on 22 January that Operation *Shingle* (Anzio landings) had started, and for a few days the news sounded good. He met Eisenhower and later Montgomery over their Second Front plans, and nothing seemed to have changed his opinion of Eisenhower's ability, only conceding that the American was good at holding the Allies together, which with the benefit of hindsight was critical. He also had to lecture Montgomery on his usual lack of tact, he having managed to upset the king as well as the secretary of state. He had an interesting meeting with Churchill, who was angry about Stalin allowing *Pravda* to publish an article which had suggested the British were negotiating with the Germans. Brooke was understandably amused by Churchill's observations and the language which he copied in full in his diary: 'Trying to maintain good relationships with a communist is like trying to woo a crocodile. I do not know whether to tickle it under the chin or beat it on the head. When it opens its mouth, you cannot tell whether it is trying to smile or preparing to eat you up.' Near the end of the month Brooke visited Hobart again, and looked at the various tanks he had designed to carry out different tasks which he found most pleasing. He also heard that his eldest son Tom was about to be sent to a service unit. It had taken his son a long, worrying time to recover from the illness which had started in 1940 in France.

The month ended with the growing concern that the Anzio beachhead had remained on the beach, and Brooke noted that 'Hitler has reacted very strongly and is sending reinforcements fast.' It was not so much Hitler as Kesselring, who although caught by surprise at the landing, had reacted with lightning speed, and within hours of hearing had major troops with armour moved to the area without disturbing the battle forces around Monte Cassino. Kesselring was a professional leader of high calibre, and within an hour of the landing he immediately ordered roadblocks, informed Berlin, and set in hand Operation *Richard* which had been designed to cope with this precise type of emergency. Within one day of the landing reinforcements were arriving, and despite the bombing raids the Italian railways were still working. The German logistical strategy was efficient: by midnight on 22 January, Kesselring had assembled 20,000 troops, by 24 January it had grown to 40,000, and by 29 January the Germans outnumbered the Allies. Kesselring, with his administrative ability, moved troops back and forth where they were needed like a 'mastermind controlling reserves to Anzio and Cassino…who managed like a chess master to balance each front.'[3]

Operation *Shingle* had at first given the impression it could not fail. It was a total surprise for the Germans, and by midnight of the first day some 27,000 Americans, 9,000 British and over 3,000 vehicles had landed. Completely without foundation the BBC announced that 'Alexander's brave troops are pushing towards Rome.'[4] There had been a daring reconnaissance by a journalist and some soldiers who had in the early stages reputedly travelled to Rome and back, but within hours of the landing the next day this would have been far too dangerous to repeat. However, the Allies stayed on the beach and Brooke had to quieten Churchill down over the beach commander Major-General John Lucas, although Brooke felt that this time that 'there are reasons for uneasiness'.[*] German numbers increased significantly, and the criticisms against Lucas not moving off the beachhead started to accumulate. The situation stalemated, and as German numbers increased the Allied commanders criticised the hapless Lucas, agreeing with Churchill that he was too limp. Some argued the distance between Rome and Anzio was too long to defend, and Lucas had been made the scapegoat. Lucas later had support in the memoirs of Major-General Harmon, and Major-General Temple pointed out that 'the Germans produced seven Divisions in ten days with plenty of armour'.[5] Kesselring in his memoirs appreciated Lucas' position, but he thought the breakout was delayed too long, and this emphasised for Kesselring that he was opposed by mediocre commanders.

Such was the different advice Lucas was receiving it was little wonder he was confused, and he regarded himself as a lamb being led to the slaughter. Alexander had told him it was merely a matter of capturing Rome, and then a simple pursuit making Operation *Overlord* unnecessary.[6] However, Patton had warned him it would be a disaster, and Lucas was aware that the terrain surrounding Anzio was overlooked by the Alban Hills south of Rome, otherwise known as the *Colli Laziali*. The British Major-General Penney had been under the impression that the forces were to advance at once and control the high ground. Lucas was going to content himself with first gathering all the forces on the beachhead and building up supplies. There was confusion amongst the commanders which did not portend well. Although Ultra informed the Allies that the Germans were unaware of Operation *Shingle*,

---

[*]   In short, there have been many historical diatribes about the part played by General Lucas, most of them critical but some more supportive. There appears to be evidence that his immediate commander Mark Clark had told him not 'to stick his neck out' which he did not, but accumulated supplies on the beach while more men landed and were too easily shelled by the Germans. After the criticism flowed in, Clark eventually replaced Lucas with General Lucian Truscott.

and would be taken by surprise, it was nearly a failure: the operation had almost been a complete fiasco and Kesselring's reaction with Operation *Richard* had been too swift for the Allies.

Kesselring never knew that nearly all his orders were decoded in Bletchley, and then dispatched to Allied command the same day. Although some Allied strategies had fallen into Kesselring's hands, his own plans were focused on his perception of the Allied intentions. Kesselring's orders to General von Mackensen regarding the attack on Anzio were read by Ultra, and the historian Carlo D'Este opined this was one of the most important Ultra intercepts of the entire war.[7] In addition to this there were spies such as the American Peter Tompkins who not only pinpointed Kesselring's HQ at Soratte, but sent precise details of military movements through Rome.[8*]

For Brooke and Churchill, the first month of the year had ended with a deep concern that this latest venture looked more like an impending disaster rather than a breakthrough to victory. In the Pacific, American forces had landed on the Marshall Islands, and in Italy the first and second battles for Monte Cassino were being fought (1 and 14 February), and the Anzio beachhead remained a growing cause of concern, as the Germans pressed their attack on the unwelcome intruders. These concerns, along with the worry of the possible onslaught of the V1 doodlebugs, occupied many of the COS meetings. On the second day of the month Brooke attended dinner at Number 10 along with many others including the monarch, and Brooke was bemused that the royal guest stayed until one in the morning, which was not his usual habit. Churchill made many of his amusing quips, but the main conversation was about the progress of the war which tended to focus on what was happening or not happening in Italy.

There was later some discussion about pressing de Valera in Southern Ireland (Eire) to 'get rid' of the German ambassador. The neutrality of this part of the islands was a constant point of aggravation, not least because of its potential U-boat safe coastline. From the Irish point of view, it mainly arose because of the hatred felt by de Valera and his fellow Irish nationalists about the way the British had brutally treated them, and with some justification. Many Southern Irish had volunteered to fight alongside the British, which Churchill and Brooke knew, and therefore understood that there had to be a degree of respect for the Irish situation. Brooke held the opinion that since all the communications coming out of the German Embassy were intercepted and deciphered, that the Germans should be left alone. Curiously, at the end of the war de Valera turned up at the embassy, as noted in an earlier footnote, to sign a condolence book on the death of Hitler.

It was business as usual with Brooke having to deal with telegrams from America over the continued clash of opinions regarding Italy, somewhat intensified by

---

* Monte Soratte is a mountain ridge within the Metropolitan area of Rome City.

the fiasco on the Anzio beachhead. He had to deal with another problem about information which was revealed in intercepted letters. Later in the month there also arose the issue that SIS (MI6) had failed to keep Churchill in the loop about the fact that the Japanese fleet had moved to Singapore, which meant that the SIS Chief, known as 'C' who was then Menzies, had to be 'ticked off'. They listened to the American William Donovan (OSS) who had been at the Anzio landing, and Brooke, who respected Alexander as a friend and colleague, was worried that Churchill was beginning to see 'Alexander's shortcomings'. Brooke had felt this for a long time, but Churchill and the Americans persisted in liking his gentlemanly conduct, whereas Brooke wanted a competent strategist and commander.

To facilitate the preparations for *Overlord* along the British south coast Brooke wanted summer visitors banned, as he had once done in the defence against *Sea Lion*, and Churchill objected again. This was a typical clash between military and political persuasions; Churchill wanted the general population to be as normal as possible, Brooke was worried about the wrong people watching what was happening. The intelligence agencies of MI5 and SIS had improved, and it was exceedingly difficult for Germans and their spies to merge into the general English way of life. He also met Eisenhower and Bedell Smith at a COS meeting to hear of their requirements for *Overlord*, which he was pleased to note, tended to coincide with the COS estimations. There followed a moment of relaxation with insufficient material for a COS meeting the next day, so he dined with his ornithologist friend Bannerman and had a family weekend at Ferney Close.

Such relaxation never lasted long, and the Monday COS (14 February) meeting was dominated by the Far East. They had a session on the conditions in the Pacific where they heard that Admiral Chester William Nimitz (the fleet admiral) and Douglas MacArthur were working together, and yet they had never previously met. They also gathered that Marshall and Admiral King were opposed to one another in their plans, and that many were worried that MacArthur would stand for the presidency. Brooke would not have understood this tendency for a military man to have any desire for political advancement.* This discussion prompted Churchill to return to his plans for Sumatra, causing Brooke to write that he was showing 'his terrible failing of lack of width or depth in his strategic vision'. This occurred again a week later when Churchill on this hobby horse cunningly packed the meeting with those who would agree with him. Brooke had a heated argument with Eden for 'chipping in' on the Pacific issue which he knew nothing about, and although the numerical odds were against him, he had the support of Andrew Cunningham which was critical. That evening the prime minister invited Brooke to dine with him, and he was under the distinct impression Churchill had had enough of him

---

* MacArthur was popular in America, but in the Korean War was eventually sacked by President Truman for overstepping the political boundaries.

and he would be sacked. He was wrong, as so often with Churchill, because it was a family meal during which they discussed their children. It was probably Churchill's way of making sure that he and Brooke remained on good terms despite the heated arguments. However, Brooke noted the beginning of a difficult time with Churchill because they could not agree on how to defeat Japan. As far as Brooke was concerned there were two major Far Eastern alternative strategies, the first based on operations from India and the second from Australia. Brooke considered that fighting the Japanese from Australia was important if only to indicate to the Australians that the United Kingdom, the 'home British', cared. The trouble for Brooke was Churchill's utter obsession with Sumatra as if that island's occupation alone would defeat Japan.

Brooke had a telegram from Alexander who was unhappy about Lucas the commander on the Anzio beachhead. This prompted Churchill to want Alexander to take on the beach landing personally, and then bring Jumbo Wilson in to command the main front. Brooke had to exert more pressure on the prime minister to stop him interfering in matters of military command. Another political anxiety emerged in Greece where there was concern about the communists, and producing a situation in the country whereby the king of Greece could safely return.[*] Brooke was concerned and always remained so in believing that the Foreign Office heads were too interested in politics, which was part of their natural role. As far as Brooke was concerned this was a purely political situation, he disliked their interference, and he considered the conduct of the war was much more important. Brooke was determined, and it was the job of politicians to look to the long-term future while the military won the war. Brooke was single-minded, both a strength and a weakness. In terms of the immediate future Brooke and the COS rejected the idea of *Overlord* coinciding with Operation *Anvil* in the south of France, mainly because the Italian war had to be won first, and the Normandy landings demanded a total effort. Victory and the necessary resources to achieve this end were the only priority for Brooke. The COS pretended to accept the idea of the two invasions happening at the same time, if only to please Eisenhower who had to placate Marshall; as Brooke noted, 'What a way to run a war!' It was clear to Brooke that Marshall had next to no understanding of what was happening in Italy and the overall ramifications. He might have reflected on the possibility that Marshall did not care what happened in Italy because he considered it irrelevant. He had the impression that Eisenhower agreed with him but was 'frightened by Marshall', causing Brooke to note that 'I am feeling very weary and old and wish to God the war would finish.' There were many Churchillian madcap ideas Brooke had to deal with apart from Sumatra. One was to walk through Portugal, Britain's oldest ally, and cross the Pyrenees, which

---

[*] There was a time when Brooke suggested troops in Greece, but only to help fool the Germans in the deception plans for D-Day; see David Stafford, *Churchill and Secret Service* (London: Abacus, 2001) p.329.

Brooke had walked as a boy and knew it would be impossible, which was why he put his trust more into amphibious attacks; at least Brooke understood the potential military problems surrounding a proposed campaign.

Near the end of the month Ramsay reported to Brooke that Montgomery was spending too much time 'wandering around the troops' and not getting down to the essential planning for D-Day. Montgomery was good at visiting which some critics claimed, possibly with some justification, was because he liked the public adoration and it suited his ego. Brooke made the note that 'I shall have to have him up again and kick his backside again!' It was not a good end to the month, with Alexander having to propose a reorganisation with which Brooke tended to agree. He never stated what the proposal was, but it undoubtedly concerned the command of Anzio beachhead. Churchill was more than unhappy, writing on Anzio that, 'We hoped to land a wildcat that would tear out the bowels of the Boche. Instead we have stranded a vast whale with its tail flopping around in the water.' Brooke recorded this in his diary because this was one occasion when he totally agreed with the prime minister.

Reaching an understanding with Churchill was never easy for Brooke, and in March 1944 there was almost a position of deadlock between the COS and Churchill; Brooke even mentioned the possibility of mass resignations. This dilemma had its origins in the Pacific operations, and not the ongoing disaster in Italy. It had been anticipated that the Anzio forces would join the Fifth Army, but delay followed delay because of the inability to move off the Anzio beachhead, and the bitter ongoing battles at Monte Cassino; the German forces were fighting too well at both points of concern. The third battle raging around the ancient abbey began on 15 March; the Japanese had started their Imphal offensive on the same day. At the beginning of the month the second Chindit operation had been launched in Burma, but on 24 March Brooke heard that Orde Wingate, known for his courage and eccentric lifestyle, had died in a plane crash. There is a distinct impression pervading Brooke's writing, and the histories of these times, that there was a feeling the war was being won, but the issue was how to finish it off, and the growing death toll was immense.

The month started with Brooke and Churchill still at odds over the issue of banning visitors to the south coast, with Brooke complaining that Churchill 'waffles on' without reaching a decision. This was eventually resolved in Brooke's favour, but the main issue of this month remained the clash over the Pacific operations. It was not helped by the king asking to see Brooke's Australian strategy; Brooke was reluctant to give him the plans in case Churchill thought he was going behind his back. He had a difficult meeting with Churchill to discuss this matter, but Brooke eventually managed to obtain the prime minister's agreement that Brooke would explain to the king that they needed to hold back the plans because there was disagreement. The secretaries had to be cleared from a COS meeting (3 March) because Portal was complaining about the command of the air force under Eisenhower, but Churchill kept 'stepping in and muddling...crashing in where angels fear to tread', as Brooke wrote in his diary. The details of this cross-service debate were not discussed by Brooke, but it was the nature of Churchill's plans in the Pacific which led to the most heated and acrimonious arguments, with Brooke even mentioning, as noted above, the possibility that the COS might resign as a group, which would have been embarrassing if not catastrophic. It certainly underlined the nature of the tensions between the impetuous and often angry prime minister and his more pragmatic military team. It was not helped when Brooke realised that Churchill was playing a political game by stacking his side of the Cabinet with what he described as 'yes men'. Brooke named Eden, Attlee, Oliver Lyttelton and Leathers as the main culprits, based on the fact they knew nothing about the Pacific and even less about military strategy. As usual dinner with his birder friend Bannerman was the only sense of relief. Brooke's love for birds was phenomenal, and on one occasion Bannerman heard the RAF were going to practise a bombing raid on a Norfolk offshore island where some rare roseate terns were nesting. Brooke spoke to Portal and an alternative was found; it is unimaginable to think this of happening anywhere else in a war-torn world.[9]

The battle-lines for the conflict between COS and Churchill were discussed at length, and Brooke had to do most of the speaking because Portal did not like arguing with Churchill, and Cunningham was so angry he could hardly contain himself. The interference by the politicians infuriated Brooke, who regarded their arguments as 'so puerile that it made me ashamed to think they were Cabinet Ministers'.[10] At the Sextant Conference they had agreed with the Americans that the British would concentrate on Burma, but Churchill had never been happy with this agreement. They eventually agreed to look at Brooke's Australian plans and appeared to accept that capturing Sumatra would not destroy Japan, but the issue would not go away as far as Churchill was concerned, as Brooke would have known.

There was a lull in the Pacific storm next day as Churchill discussed with Brooke an intercept from Kesselring about the Italian situation from his point of view, which was 'interesting'. It was on this day that Churchill relented on his demand that holiday visitors could enter the south coast zone, and Brooke met Montgomery and wrote, 'He's making good headway in making the plans, and equally successful in making enemies as far as I can see.' Brooke had to spend some considerable time smoothing ruffled feathers disturbed by Montgomery. It was fortunate that Brooke had seen Kesselring's personal appraisal, mainly because a few days later he met Alexander in London with his proposed Operation *Diadem*, which was designed to break through the German Gustav defence line and open the Liri Valley.

Later Brooke picked up the rumour that the prime minister was proposing to go to Bermuda to meet the president. He felt that this was physically too much for Churchill, and he knew that Moran did 'not have the guts to tell him'. Nor could Brooke see the reason for such a visit because they had not yet reached an appropriate agreement on the Pacific issue. Moran was worried about Churchill's health, and he and Brooke were pleased when they heard the proposed visit had been postponed.

Brooke even wondered if one of Churchill's motives had been the opportunity to escape from his parliamentary worries. A few days later Churchill, typically, raised the projected visit again, this time proposing that after Bermuda he would go onto Gibraltar and onto Italy; as Brooke noted, 'that would be the end of him,' as he believed Churchill was tottering on the edge of total exhaustion and possibly ill.

There was no respite from the Pacific issue and Brooke picked up the rumour that Churchill had called a meeting of the joint planners, writing with a sense of dismay, 'Heaven knows what he is up to, and what trouble he is brewing for tomorrow.' Before the dreaded meeting he heard the good news that the Russians were doing well in the south, and reflected the Germans were now paying the price for the faulty strategy of turning south. Brooke would have found some support from his opposite numbers in the Wehrmacht, as many of his senior commanders had long doubted Hitler's sudden decision to turn south when Moscow had once been within their sights.

As the Russians fought on, Brooke and Churchill waged their own domestic conflict over the Pacific. The 'mad ideas' Brooke had feared emerged when the COS heard that Churchill 'had found another island' instead of Sumatra. Cunningham was strongly opposed because the Japanese navy was close by in Singapore, and even the Americans felt the Royal Navy was better elsewhere. Brooke was simply thunderstruck at Churchill's ideas, writing 'I begin to wonder whether I was Alice in Wonderland, or whether I was really fit for a lunatic asylum.' Brooke was beginning seriously to question the balance of Churchill's mind. At the Cabinet meeting it was not helped when Churchill launched into more relentless attacks against the army, and then produced a Pacific strategy which overrode every piece of advice given by the COS. The next day the COS met to discuss Churchill's 'ridiculous strategy' and again there was talk of mass resignation. This was a time of considerable strain for Brooke, and any reader of his diary and papers would wonder whether Churchill was losing the balance of his mind or sense of reasoning, as Brooke had suggested. Churchill certainly regarded himself as the military expert, which was patently untrue when compared to the dedicated and trained men who were his Chiefs of Staff. Churchill's life had been largely politics; as a young man he had served in the Boer War and was in the last British cavalry charge at Omdurman, but was widely known for the failure at Gallipoli. Churchill had served a brief spell in the trenches and read widely, but he was not a military expert but a clever politician, and in both areas he was impetuous. The problem in a democratic political system means that an elected person often rises to a position and becomes responsible for a major department, the Home or Foreign Offices, the Treasury or Health or Education, and many such politicians assume they have suddenly become experts overnight, as many civil servants have often testified. The minister's real job is to listen and try and evaluate the advice of experts in their various fields. Most politicians fail, but Churchill was loved by the public then and today. Brooke loved him but was also infuriated by him with his ideas, views with which many modern readers would possibly sympathise.

The Americans had some idea of what was happening in the British corridors of power, telegramming and asking Churchill to move along with the battle for Burma and to forget about Sumatra. Churchill prepared a message to Mountbatten to do both and ignore the American demands, but Brooke managed to stop this being sent. Brooke described his feelings as 'a man chained to a lunatic. It is getting beyond my powers to stop him.'[11]

This was not the only tension with America because at a COS meeting Jumbo Wilson wanted to scrap *Anvil*, and he even had a degree of support from Eisenhower and Bedell Smith, which gave Brooke some hope this might persuade the Americans. However, the American advice persisted in asking the British to unite the Anzio and the frontline forces emerging from Monte Cassino, and when they had eventually achieved this policy, suggested they were to move directly onto the defensive and head for the south of France. Brooke had never appreciated the south of France Operation *Anvil*, seeing it as clashing with the Italian campaign and detracting from *Overlord*. As always there had been continuous problems between the British and Americans over the planning of *Anvil*, with Marshall later suggesting that the British had only shown some interest in *Anvil* to secure more landing craft for the Italian campaign. Eisenhower certainly needed the maximum number of landing craft for Normandy, but not all the Americans agreed with one another. General Mark Clark in his immediate postwar biography wrote that he disagreed with Marshall and Eisenhower, writing that 'I am firmly convinced that the French Forces alone, with seven Divisions could have captured Marseilles, and protected Eisenhower's southern flank.'[12]

It was not the best of times for Brooke; he had just heard of Wingate's death, the Japanese were threatening Manipur in north-east India, Alexander was still stuck at Monte Cassino, Marshall was insisting on *Anvil*, and the only good news was that Montgomery's plans were looking good, in theory. It was a depressing time, causing Brooke to write later as he looked back, that 'if I had been told at that time that Winston would still be the prime minister in 1955, I would have refused to believe it.'[13]

During April 1944, the Red Army took Odessa and American forces landed at Hollandia in New Guinea. In Western Europe, Brooke's main concern was the Italian campaign with the battles at Anzio and Monte Cassino, being fought against the tough and professional German forces which Brooke had so often warned about, but the matters which personally preoccupied him the most were his ongoing battles across the planning tables. As was his custom he rarely commented in his diary or papers on some of the major issues which arose in the individual battle confrontations in Italy. It was not so much a matter of secrecy – there was little danger of his diaries or papers falling into the wrong hands, as had happened with Kesselring's policies and plans which had been intercepted by the intelligence agencies at Bletchley Park.

He mentioned the problems of Lucas' command ability on the Anzio beachhead, but at this stage he never referred to any of the immense problems associated by the battle for Monte Cassino, which had ground the main front to a halt for months and would take yet more time and lives to resolve. The ancient Benedictine monastery stood high above Cassino and dominated the surrounding area. The abbey was recognised not only as a treasure house with its paintings and works of art, but it had an ancient library as well as priceless artefacts: the buildings were world famous and magnificent in their antiquity. The Germans promised that they would not utilise the monastery, Kesselring gave his word, and his commanding General von Senger, who was a lay member of the Benedictine order, entered the ancient building only to attend Mass. He claimed in his book that he was the only German to enter the building once the battle started.[14]

Meanwhile the Gustav line was a series of continuing battles, but the anticipated victory on Monte Cassino was elusive and expensive in life. The French colonial troops under General Juin had occupied Monte Belvedere just five miles north of Cassino, then the Americans fought with the 34th Infantry Division, but Kesselring stiffened the resistance with the famous 1st Parachute and 90th Panzer Grenadiers. The 4th Indian Division relieved the Americans, but as a Brigadier-General Lemnitzer told Alexander, the troops were becoming almost mutinous at the ongoing slaughter. Many argued Monte Cassino could be outflanked, including Major-General Tuker and the French Commander Juin.* Freyberg, sometimes described as 'a difficult old cuss at times', remained stubborn. Tuker wrote that Freyberg 'should never have been put in charge of a corps, he had not the tactical understanding'; he nevertheless had the support of Alexander, who was noted for his loyalty to his various commanders.[15]

The German 3rd Parachute Regiment under Colonel Heillmann put up an extraordinary defence, commended by all sides to this day for his military aptitude. The German troops had dug into the mountain a few metres away from the abbey, but, as any modern tourist will note, the steepness of the mountain meant that even 50 metres away from the ancient walls the defending troops were within the shadows of the ancient parapets. Later that day Allied troops quietly withdrew, and over 400 tons of bombs were dropped on the abbey, killing many sheltering Italians and monks, and totally destroying the buildings: according to von Senger no single German was killed.†

The bombing of the abbey will always remain contentious, enabling the Germans to produce propaganda from what they described as a 'Philistine act'. A Berlin diarist wrote that 'photographs of the battle of Monte Cassino are piling up. The

---

\* Edwin Hoyt, *Back Water War, The Allied Campaign in Italy* (Mechanicsburg: Stackpole, 2007) p.159 claimed it was Tuker who asked Freyberg to bomb the abbey.

† In the morning 257 tons of 500lb bombs and 59 tons of 100lb incendiaries were dropped; in the afternoon 283 tons of bombs each weighing 1000lb.

destruction of that beautiful monastery is horrifying. What will happen to Florence, Venice, Rome?'[16] In Dublin de Valera protested and sent an appeal to the belligerent governments, and he wrote a personal letter to Roosevelt on behalf of Rome.[17]

The abbot was taken to Rome while the German propaganda machine rolled into action. Kesselring was puzzled by the tactical error of turning the buildings into a good defensive position, and it provided a rare moment when he felt he held the moral high ground. The debate will undoubtedly continue in military and history books: the Germans respected the abbey and its treasures, but they could not ignore the dominating mountain on which the abbey stood, and the non-combat zone was pointless. The Allies were right to place lives before ancient monuments, but the bombing provided excellent defensive rubble for the paratroopers, turning a conundrum into a greater problem than before. It was easier to defend from hidden locations within the rubble than in well-defined positions. Undoubtedly Brooke was very aware of these issues, but as usual he never commented, probably based on his belief it was to do with the commander in the field and not those behind their office desks. It would have been interesting if Brooke revealed what he thought about circumnavigating the area, the mistake of turning defined buildings into better defensive rubble, and the destruction of a world-famous ancient abbey; but as usual he remained silent as a matter of personal principle.

Despite the loss of life and ongoing fury of the battle, the Americans persisted in wanting to close the Italian operations, to Brooke's fury. Later in the month they continued to press that once the Anzio and Monte Cassino forces had linked, a defensive or holding strategy should be employed. All their planning in the Mediterranean revolved around Operation *Anvil* and invading southern France, which both Brooke and Churchill opposed. In his memoirs Alexander noted that *Anvil* was an American 'inspiration' using American troops and resources and 'our Allies had the last say'.[18] Alexander was correct in this later observation and the Americans had been for some time the major partner, but Brooke argued, also correctly, that there had been previous agreements with the Americans and withdrawing their troops from Italy would be a profound military error. The conflicting views remain contentious and cannot be resolved from the comfort of an armchair over some 75 years later.

## The Months before Overlord

In the meantime, the planning for *Overlord* intensified as D-Day Normandy drew closer. There were heated discussions over the pre-invasion bombing of French railway communication lines, which Churchill opposed on the grounds that precision bombing was difficult to achieve, and many innocent French lives would therefore be lost. This was the ghastly reality about the conflict of war, and although Churchill's arguments were civilised, sensitive and valid, thousands of French lives were to be lost, as the disruption of communication lines was eventually considered essential despite the human cost. This issue was not to be resolved until May, with Brooke complaining there was 'waffling about and vacillating politicians unable to accept the consequences of war', clearly indicating his own views on the subject.[19] Brooke held long talks with Montgomery over the plans, with Air Chief Marshal Leigh-Mallory about the air force preparations, and with Admiral Ramsay over naval measures. Brooke had much to add to the plans, having once fought and travelled widely in the area, but his advice on the bocage (the deeply hedged lanes and small fields of that area) was ignored, and this later caused many problems for the troops on the ground.[20] Brooke had always argued that an amphibious landing was not just the beachhead, but the immediate hinterland and the long-term direction after their arrival and emergence from the landing areas. There was considerable discussion and speculation about the German forces which might be available in Europe, Brooke being understandably concerned at the speed with which Kesselring had managed to deploy troops to Anzio in such great numbers, and with alarming speed. The COS also discussed the details of the proposed harbour equipment once they arrived on French shores; it was a massive logistical exercise which could not be allowed to go wrong, and for which Brooke felt a major responsibility. He remained apprehensive about the operation as did many others; Brooke was not convinced the Germans had run out of oil, and he always had a high respect for the German soldier's professionalism and sense of fighting morale. As an afterthought, Brooke was correct about the professionalism of German commanders; it was fortunate that Hitler thought he knew better than his professional military leaders, and he could not be argued with because of the personal safety of the would-be critics. Hitler always thought other viewpoints were a form of personal criticism and challenging his position; Brooke in his service would have been disposed of in 1940.

Brooke met several interesting people returning from the front lines and was able to learn much of what was happening from behind his desk. He met a man called Lyon who had penetrated Singapore Harbour and blown up seven Japanese ships, and the king of Greece struggling to find a footing in his home country; he talked to Symes who had been Wingate's second in command, as well as a Major Wilkinson back from Yugoslavia. It was from such meetings that Brooke was able to grasp some of the realities from the various theatres of the war; he was a careful listener, who consumed and studied such information.

The tussle over strategy with the Americans continued. They eventually and reluctantly agreed with the British, but they withdrew their offer of landing craft from the Pacific, causing Brooke to write that 'History will never forgive them for bargaining equipment against strategy, and for trying to blackmail us to agreeing with them by holding the pistol of withdrawing craft at our heads.'[21] Generally Brooke tended to like the individual Americans he met, but their corporate thinking made him at times depressed, and other times angry. Near the end of the month he was pleased to have lunch with his eldest son Tom who had been so ill during the battle for France; Tom had come up to London to collect his kit before he left for North Africa.

During May the Russians continued their remorseless battles and took Sevastopol. In Italy, on 11 May, to Brooke's great relief the fourth and final battle for Monte Cassino was started and won, the heights being finally stormed by Polish soldiers. It was also the time during which Alexander launched Operation *Diadem* against the Gustav Line. At the beginning of the month Brooke was caught up in a seemingly endless round of meetings. It started with the dominions and Brooke meeting all the prime ministers from Australia, New Zealand, Canada and South Africa; needless to note, Smuts was his favourite. On the first day Churchill gave a sweeping picture of the situation which Brooke thought was poor, and the next day he presented his picture of the European scenario. Meeting followed meeting, from discussing the synthetic harbours to be used on D-Day, to Jumbo Wilson presenting his Mediterranean plans, a major COS meeting to discuss the possible German forces in France, and casting further ahead, after the defeat of Germany which was now regarded as inevitable, how to conduct the Pacific War from Australia.

Brooke had experienced some gruelling times with Churchill, and he was pleasantly surprised when at the end of the first week of May, he was invited to see

Brooke with General Kazumierz Sosnkowski (Narodowe Archiwum Cyfrowe)

Churchill and consume some soup with him in a relaxed setting. During this time Churchill told Brooke some 'very nice things' which the Defence Committee and War Cabinet had said about him. Given the recent appalling debates and arguments he had with Churchill, Brooke was delighted to have this personal boost. He even softened towards the prime minister writing later: 'You would do anything within your power to help him carry the stupendous burden he had shouldered.'[22]

The plans for D-Day continued relentlessly, and there was a general rule that any person of rank or importance, who knew anything about the proposed invasion, should not travel overseas. This was common sense, as the Mechelen incident had proved. Brooke had to explain this necessity to General Sosnkowski who wanted to fly to the Mediterranean to sort out some Polish problems. He attended a meeting at St Paul's School where Eisenhower presented the final plans, and he came under Brooke's critical scrutiny but this time with a kinder eye. He noted that 'Eisenhower was just a coordinator, a good mixer, a champion of inter-allied cooperation and in that respect, few can hold a candle to him.'[23] Given the number of nations and nationalities involved in the conflict, a person like Eisenhower was essential. King George VI was in attendance and made a 'few well-chosen remarks' at the end. The thought of crossing the Channel even with such huge forces and resources, and even with the preparatory plans to hoodwink the Germans into thinking the invasion would be elsewhere, was understandably frightening for everyone involved, from those who were to jump ashore from landing craft and dropping from the skies, to those at the top responsible for so many lives. No one dared speculate to its outcome, no one knew the possible German reaction, and Brooke noted that 'the cross-Channel operation is just eating into my heart. I wish to God we could start and have it done with.'

He was at least relieved that the incoming news from Italy was an improvement on the previous months of stagnation. By 19 May he heard that Monte Cassino had been taken and the Gustav Line breached. It caused him to consider Marshall's proposal to close Italy down and start a defensive line. Brooke reflected on the nature of Marshall's strategy and his ignorance of Hitler's mind, which, to be fair, was elusive to most. Hitler had clearly demonstrated that he never retreated, and he expected his soldiers to attack and fight to the last man, even though it had led to disaster at Stalingrad and Tunisia with the taking of hundreds of thousands of German and Italian POWs. Based on this reasoning Brooke understood that Italy would not be finished until the last Germans had left. Brooke was correct in his summation of German thinking, or rather Hitler's demands, and in Italy the Germans only surrendered when Nazi Germany was drawing its last breath and their home front had virtually collapsed. On 23 May Brooke attended a Joint Intelligence Committee meeting and learnt that Alexander had launched, or rather ordered the Anzio beachhead breakout, and wondered whether he was too soon, but decided to stick by his policy, which he had always upheld with Churchill, to trust the commander on the front line. He was right to stand by his principles because he heard a few days later that the two forces at Monte Cassino and Anzio had at long last met. Just after hearing this news, he had a fraught meeting with Montgomery, whom he had to dress down again for meddling in areas which should not concern him; Montgomery had tried to interfere in Alexander's sphere of command, had talked to the New Zealand prime minister on 'what to do with Freyberg' and many other similar incidents. Montgomery may have been regarded as a key figure in military terms, but he always had the propensity to interfere way above his pay grade. Montgomery was often popular with his troops, but his egotistical manner and immense self-belief often proved too much for many others, and he was always fortunate that Brooke, although annoyed at these features, continued to support him.

There was a major meeting of the COS again on the questions of what Brooke described as 'Rocket Bombs and pilotless planes' with discussion on countermeasures. Peenemünde had been bombed, but the V1s and V2s which started in June 1944, the latter in September 1944, could not be totally eradicated from the air, and their sites would need to be overrun.* It was the Far East which continued to provide the most strife in the corridors of power. Churchill decided he wanted Mountbatten to have a specific operation, but Brooke was pleased to note that Cunningham was 'determined that Mountbatten was to have no control over the fleet'. This arose because Churchill, in his own words, did not want to 'be tied to the apron strings of the Americans'. The Australians had agreed to Brooke's strategy of operating the attack from Australia, and Churchill had at last started to move in this direction and away from his Sumatra ideas. Brooke had the support of the Australian chief of staff Blamey (who Brooke often suspected of drinking too much) and they started to draw together their plans.

It was Mountbatten who concerned Brooke most, not least because he had sacked General Giffard and replaced him with Oliver Leese; Brooke was convinced Giffard was the better man. Brooke thought the Pacific to be a 'tangled mess' and that 'Mountbatten is quite irresponsible and tries to be loved by all, which won't work'.[24] To wish 'to be loved by all' is a common human trait, but it had never been part of Brooke's personality, as is self-evident from his war diary entries. The question which is often asked was whether Brooke was correct in his continuous vitriolic attacks on the character of Mountbatten. Most discerning people never trusted Mountbatten: a view demonstrated by Lovat when he described Mountbatten as a lightweight cork tossed along on a sea of events. Anthony Eden had called him a 'congenital liar'.[25] 'Some reputable historians have suggested that Combined Operations'

---

* The V1s (the infamous Doodlebugs) launched their first attacks on London on 13 June 1944 with some 9,521 attacks. Their major site was overrun in October 1944, but they were launched from other sites. The V2s (rocket) were launched in September 1944, some 3,000 against Allied targets. The rockets were of immense interest in their advanced technology, and the Americans ensured that they took away to America as prisoners the scientists involved, including a Wernher von Braun who, with many other Germans, helped create the American ballistic missile system and paved the way to the moon.

efforts in this period 'reflected a psychopath at work'.[26] Andrew Roberts described Mountbatten as a 'mendacious, intellectually limited hustler, whose negligence and incompetence resulted in many unnecessary deaths…the numbers of which increased exponentially as his meteoric career progressed'.[27] 'Field Marshal Sir Gerald Templar told Mountbatten directly in the 1960s, "You're so crooked, Dicky, if you swallowed a nail you'd shit a corkscrew."'[28] Even his official biographer wrote at the end of his work that Mountbatten's 'vanity, though child-like, was monstrous, his ambition unbridled. The truth in his hands was swiftly converted from what it was to what it should have been.'[29] Mountbatten's popular image tends to be that of a competent commander and he is admired, but many historians paint a very different picture, and many lives were lost through his ideas and ambitions. It seems on wider reading that Brooke was somewhat astute in his views.

As noted, the month of May for Brooke was a time of endless meetings, slightly less fraught than the previous month, but with the additional burden of *Overlord* planning with its accompanying deep anxiety, and although there was news of success from Italy, at long last, Brooke remained as frustrated as anyone who had given so much to this campaign, but who had to stand at a distance and wait for information.

His love of his Ferney Close home and ornithology were the only elements which brought him any sense of peace of mind. In mid-May he had spent two hours in his bird hide watching a marsh tit on its nest, and he wrote that this moment 'made Winston and the war disappear in a cloud of smoke. It was like rubbing Aladdin's lamp, I was transplanted to a fairyland and returned infinitely refreshed and recreated.'[30] Most of his friends and acquaintances knew of his love of birdlife; some shared it with him, others were probably bemused that this tough and stern military officer could gain such deep pleasure watching a marsh tit sit on its eggs. Alan Lascelles, the king's private secretary (from 1943) met Brooke in St James's Park while he was watching ducks and joined him, and on one occasion at a formal dinner Lascelles met Brooke 'with whom I talked bird for the great part of the meal'.[31] In many ways it was fortunate for Brooke's sanity he had a family whom he loved and a hobby which obsessed him.

It was also during this month that Brooke was invited to the Soviet Embassy for a reception, where he was given the Order of Suvorov on behalf of the Russian people; he must have reflected that his strong words and standing up to the Soviet leader at Teheran had actually impressed Stalin.

## D-Day Normandy

Although the Old Testament phrase claims that it is 'in the spring when kings march out to war' it was in the summer of 1944 that the Western onslaught began, on 6 June when *Overlord* started on D-Day, on the Normandy beaches.[32] During this hectic month Rome fell (4 June), the first doodlebugs fell on London (13 June), the air offensive against Japan began (15 June) and the Philippine Sea Battle started (19

June). For Brooke and many others, this was a month of deep anxiety as they stood away from the fighting they had planned, and they waited as their soldiers fought in a series of deadly battles. As Brooke wrote in his diary on D-Day, it was 'hard to realise all day that whilst London went on calmly with its job, a fierce conflict was being fought at a close distance on the French coast'.[33] It must have been a strange atmosphere for Brooke, who had at least experienced battlefield conflict first hand in the Great War, and just four years previously during the Battle of France. Despite his tough demeanour at the safety of the planning tables, he at least had personal experience of what it was like to face the formidable and professional German fighting forces of the Wehrmacht, on land and from the air. It was no game of chess for him: he had planned and argued for his strategy, but he knew men and women would die, and he often looked for his inner peace by wandering around St James's Park watching the ducks. The strategy arguments still dominated his life, with the British and American conflict over Operation *Anvil*, now renamed *Dragoon*, the war in the Far East, the need to fight on in Italy and how to deal with the doodlebugs; they were all contentious in one way or another.

For Brooke, the month started with discussions on how to deal with the Americans over Operation *Dragoon* when they arrived, and Brooke knew it would not be an easy matter. He predicted in his diary trouble with 'Winston's ramblings in Sumatra, Curtin's subservience to MacArthur, MacArthur's love of the limelight, King's desire to wrap all the laurels round his head, and last but not least real sound strategy.'[34] He was also concerned that 'Mountbatten was incapable of seeing the problem' in his designated area. Brooke sounded and was cynical, but in the light of subsequent events he can be regarded as a realist. Churchill was in a state of pure excitement, expecting immediate victory in France, and that Alexander would eliminate the German existence in Italy. Brooke noted that Churchill was 'far too optimistic'. On the other hand, Brooke wrote that as a soldier he was personally aware of the imminent dangers of the weather, the complexity of amphibious landings which could too easily lead to chaos, leakage of information, controlling the situation once battle started, and for Brooke, having dealt with the officers face to face, he knew something of the individual commanders' weaknesses. In his diary he bothered to underline these thoughts to emphasise his thinking. As noted earlier, Churchill wanted to be near the action, and had wanted to go with the landing troops as an observer, but the king had dissuaded him by threatening to accompany him. Churchill never informed Brooke because he knew exactly what Brooke's reaction would be.

As the news filtered through, he heard that the airborne division action had been successful. He was undoubtedly reading of the British troops on Pegasus Bridge who had arrived by gliders, not about the American paratroopers who had been dropped in widely dispersed areas, and who only through personal bravery and good training worked their way through this potential catastrophe. He also gathered that the British beaches had been successful overall, that the Americans had taken Utah beach, but there was serious chaos on the Omaha landing site. There was some discussion whether these troops should divert to the British beaches which Brooke thought might create chaos, but again individual bravery by American ground troops eventually won through, with major casualties.

The news was widespread, and in Italy Rome had fallen to American troops under Clark, virtually as D-Day One was under way. Brooke made little comment on this, but he would have been aware that Clark had deliberately disobeyed orders for the sake of self-glorification. It has been argued that this was one of the worse blunders of the war. In this action of taking Rome, Clark had ignored Alexander's specific orders, allowing General Von Vietinghoff's Tenth Army to escape in order to march into Rome, and by this action he undoubtedly prolonged the Italian campaign for many months, costing untold lives. Clark had acted on his own impulse, and even refused to take radio calls from angry subordinates. Truscott and Robert Frederick, commander of US Special Forces, were both appalled, and Major-General Francis Tuker called Clark 'a flashy ignoramus'.[35] Truscott had demanded to speak to Clark but was informed by Brann, Clark's operations officer, that Clark was out of reach. For years Clark defended his decision, and some have tried to understand why he took this excessively misguided action, with the occasional suggestion it was prompted by Marshall.

It certainly made Kesselring's task easier, and this assisted the build-up of his historical reputation as a genius of defence. Clark's failure to close the Valmontone

Brooke and Churchill on HMS *Kelvin* off Normandy (IWM A 24024)

Gap, thus entrapping the whole southern wing of the Tenth Army and forcing some elements of the Fourteenth to retreat, went against Alexander's orders in Operation *Buffalo*, and by doing this 'he deliberately committed what must be ranked as one of the most misguided blunders made by an Allied commander during World War II'.[36] Kesselring could see what 'Clark obsessed with his private goals could not see, that it was the combination of the Allied thrusts…that posed the threat' of entrapping the major German armies in Italy.[37]

Brooke kept these judgements from his diary, and was more concerned about Normandy, which Churchill now wanted to visit at Montgomery's headquarters, with Brooke and Smuts. Before they went, they had a quick CCOS where the Italian situation was vaguely agreed, and Brooke was pleased that Operation *Dragoon* at least was in its 'right strategic time setting'. The small party crossed the Channel on 12 June on board the destroyer HMS *Kelvin*, and Brooke was amazed at the number of ships and landing craft which has now gone down in history as the largest armada ever put together. He had obviously been privy to the numbers involved, but like many others during those weeks he was simply amazed at the actual sight of the world's largest ever invasion fleet. They were met by Admiral Vian (famous for the *Altmark* attack) and went ashore in an amphibious lorry (DUKW) 'out of the sea and onto the road' where they were met by Montgomery. Brooke could not help reflecting that four years earlier he had been thrown out of France, and he would not have believed that so soon afterwards he would be re-entering with a serious invading force. Montgomery showed his visitors his plans which Brooke thought were good, and then they went onto 'Bimbo' Dempsey's headquarters.* Brooke noted that the French agricultural scene appeared in first class order despite the German occupation, but 'the French population did not seem in any way pleased to see us arrive as a victorious country to liberate France'. Generally, the French did appreciate liberation, but Brooke was experiencing French people who suddenly found their lives torn apart by the front line of war, where their lives and livelihoods were seriously threatened; they did not share Brooke's wider strategic purposes, understandably. For the ordinary local French people, it was a matter of sheer survival in the sudden brutal mayhem of battle. Brooke, however, was aware that the local French Resistance had played a role in disrupting German communication systems. From the Admiral's barge they watched landing craft passing by to the beaches and observed the harbours being constructed. Churchill found the small harbours intriguing, noting that some 2,000 tons of supplies a day were being taken ashore, and later writing that 'I dwelt on these facts as we drove or walked round our interesting but severely restricted conquest.'[38] It was limited and had it not been for Allied dominance in the skies it

---

* General Sir Miles Dempsey who had a close relationship with Montgomery. Dempsey refused to write his memoirs and had his diary destroyed, a curious demand, and a sad loss for historians and biographers.

would have been a dangerous place for the prime minister to be wandering around; he always relished being too close to the action. They returned home pleased with all they had seen, and at a dinner party at Number 10 with the king, Brooke and Churchill argued over the nature of necessary supplies to the troops, but not with the usual heat of their frequent interchanges.

On their return Brooke noted that the first doodlebugs had hit London but wrote they 'did little damage' and a few days later when it happened again, Brooke wrote 'the second time we have had this form of entertainment', giving the impression he was not taking these attacks seriously. However, on 19 June one of these flying bombs hit the Military Guards Chapel in Wellington Barracks and 'killed sixty people!'. Brooke placed an exclamation mark in this entry, not least because he heard the news as he had been reading a dinner invitation from a close friend named Cobbold who had been one of those killed in the barracks. It may possibly have reminded him of the local French reaction in Normandy from those who found themselves trying to survive sudden carnage. The next day guns and balloons were organised for London, and a week later Brooke had to jump out of his bed and consider diving under it as a doodlebug 'was uncomfortably close'.

In the meantime, the necessary meetings took place, including some relaxation of the previous rules of travelling, because the Germans now knew precisely what the Allied plans and intentions were. Some agreement was made over Brooke's plans for operating out of Western Australia and directing the attack through Amboina and towards Borneo. At a CCOS conference which met to discuss Burma, Brooke questioned Marshall as to whether Stilwell (Vinegar Joe) had too much on his plate, only to be met by an angry outburst from Marshall, who sharply responded that at least Stilwell 'got things done, and he was a fighter', implying he was different from his British counterparts. Brooke was surprised and taken aback by this response, and rather than ruin his relationship with Marshall walked away from the conversation. Stilwell was known to be something of an Anglophobe, but he was popular with his disregard for military formality and his fighting prowess was known to be formidable.* Brooke often believed that Marshall's views on the British had been coloured by Stilwell's reports. It was during this session that Brooke heard the disturbing news that Montgomery was meeting serious German opposition, which would not have helped his level of anxiety.

The arguments and meetings never ceased, and on one occasion Brooke was deeply irritated that a session of COS was taken up by petty squabbles between Mountbatten and Sir James Somerville, writing that 'it is astonishing how petty and small men can be in connections with questions of command', or he could have noted how personal egos dominated greater matters. Brooke was also concerned with Alexander's proposal to march into Vienna. James Gammell (Jumbo Wilson's chief

---

* Sadly, he died from stomach cancer in 1946.

of staff) attended a COS and planners' meeting to discuss this possibility. The prime minister with Eden and Macmillan who attended the meeting somewhat liked this idea, but Brooke regarded it as 'Alexander's mad hopes' not based on serious study, but 'the result of elated spirits after a rapid advance'. Brooke pointed out that they could not pass through or over 'the Alps in winter and the dangerous topography of the country'. The lessons from fighting through the Italian mountains and valleys should have registered, and Brooke was correct in opposing this view. This should have been reinforced by Ultra messages, disclosing Hitler's orders to Kesselring to keep fighting to the last man, as Brooke had predicted. Eventually Brooke was able to make Churchill see the sense of his argument.

They had a 'rude reply' from President Roosevelt almost instructing the British to adhere to the *Dragoon* (*Anvil*) agreements. There was now no question that the Americans held the larger forces on land, sea and in the air, and it was *their* decision, and the president made this crystal clear. However, Brooke had been right about Hitler not allowing any withdrawal from Italy, and they could not allow the Germans any respite. Operation *Dragoon* had and still has its critics. Two days after it started the Germans dismantled the French state sending Pétain, Laval and the French government to Germany, and many have argued that Operation *Dragoon* withdrew powers from the Western Front, which slowed progress towards Berlin, thereby giving Stalin greater scope for his ambitions. Brooke relieved his feelings by reflecting that at least Cherbourg was safe, that the Imphal-Kohima road was again open, and the attack on Caen had started well, though the next month was to dash his hopes about Caen somewhat.

During July, the Soviet Red Army seemed to be as unstoppable as the Wehrmacht had once been, by taking Minsk, Wilno, Lwów and Brest-Litovsk, and after weeks of fighting and high fatality rates Montgomery finally took Caen, while the Americans liberated Avranches. The tide was turning in the East and West but with a huge cost in human life. Brooke was growing more and more concerned about the V1s that he started to call the 'buzz-bombs' because of their strange noise, which when it stopped meant an explosion could be expected in the next minute. He noted that at the beginning of the month that this threat was 'assuming dimensions which will require drastic action', observing that the guns could not hit them, the balloons were useless, and

V1 Rocket (GNU Free Documentation Licence)

they were too fast for fighter planes. He was also irritated by the Labour politician Herbert Morrison because of his sense of panic. Morrison was often regarded as Attlee's heir presumptive and his main concern was London's safety and people's lives, but for Brooke it struck him as mere panic reaction; not everyone had been brought up in military conflict as a way of life. Morrison, as a dedicated politician, felt responsible for the public's welfare and safety. There was a proposal (probably made by Churchill) that small German towns should be bombed as retaliation in the hope the Germans would stop. Brooke opposed this on the valid grounds that nothing would stop the Nazi regime who would have known the mayhem they were causing. For some years, the German propaganda machine had offered the hope of 'wonder-weapons' which would win the war at the last moment, and with Goebbels' propaganda it was widely believed. The V1s seemed to increase, a flurry of them hitting central London (19 July) causing Brooke to have to dive under his bed. The bombing of the rocket sites was continuous and often effective, but it transpired there were many such sites, and the only hope was that the Western Allies would overrun the launch sites, but during these weeks they were still fighting to find their way out of Normandy. Brooke was also aware that the larger and faster V2 rockets would soon be in action. The traditional bombing planes were dangerous, but less invidious because they could be heard and seen for people to seek cover, but as with the cross-Channel shelling of Dover, these new bombs appeared without notice and created their own form of insidious fear.

Brooke's main concern was his frustration with the various campaigns for which he felt much responsibility. He spoke to Alexander about missing the chance to 'smash Kesselring's forces' which was probably referring to Clark's blunder of taking Rome instead of cutting off the German army; as noted above, a chance was lost which would cause more havoc in Italy. He was also worried about Leese not 'providing a hinge for the Eighth Army always behind the Americans and French'. In this observation there is a hint of Brooke's latent nationalistic pride appearing. Brooke also had to deal with Churchill who was angry with Roosevelt, and more so with Montgomery because operations 'were not going faster, and apparently Eisenhower had said he [Montgomery] was over cautious'. Yet again Brooke defended his commanders, and especially Alexander whom Churchill was now criticising. Brooke himself was unhappy about Alexander, but as a matter of personal principle Brooke did not see this as the due right of politicians. The Americans were especially unhappy at the amount of time Montgomery was taking to capture Caen, claiming he was being his usual overly cautious self to protect his reputation. Brooke attacked Churchill on these issues in another heated exchange, and when Churchill appealed in a War Cabinet about this accusation Brooke noted that Eden helped him by pointing out that Churchill often decried these soldiers in front of politicians, who knew little of the surrounding circumstances; this would have been unexpected music to Brooke's ears, especially coming from Eden.

As noted, Eisenhower's disparagement of Montgomery was widespread among the Americans, claiming he was slow and cautious because he wanted to retain his reputation. This specific criticism had started in Italy, if not immediately after El Alamein, and was again resurfacing in Normandy with the problem of Caen. Brooke would have been more than aware of the time it was taking to capture the key town of Caen which was an important centre for roads and railways. Montgomery had originally planned its occupation within days of D-Day One, and although Brooke never mentioned this in his diary, it had not escaped Churchill's attention. Later, when Brooke heard that Eisenhower and Bedell Smith had asked Montgomery to be more offensive, Brooke wrote to him asking him to heed Eisenhower's advice.[39]

As noted, Caen was important because it was situated at the critical juncture in Normandy where the communication system of rail and roads met. Between Caen and the coast were four panzer groups who tried to push the invaders back into the sea, but they were hampered by lack of fuel, powerful air attacks by Allied fighters and some powerful resistance, especially from the Canadians. It was the specific task of the British Second Army to take Caen. Later Montgomery claimed that the major part of his plan was to break the German army at Caen so a breakout could be effected elsewhere, but most believe Montgomery originally planned to use Caen as the breakthrough place for his own troops. There were a series of bitter battles starting on 10 June which shuddered to a halt against the German tanks and infantry. There seems little doubt, though, that the British forces were meeting the brunt of the German opposition. The next battle codenamed Operation *Epsom* was launched on 26 June, and on 18 July another called Operation *Goodwood*, with naval shelling and aerial support to help. Montgomery had claimed that this battle was 'it' but in fact he was obliged to order a retreat, however the formidably accurate naval gunfire was decimating limited German resources. Anglo-American bombers prepared the way by dropping 7,500 tons of bombs along the German front, causing massive civilian deaths, but the narrow Normandy roads and limited bridges meant a tortuously slow advance. This gave the Germans time to prepare, set traps, and wait behind hedgerows with their deadly 88 guns and other weapons. The British lost more than 200 tanks, but as devastating as this loss was the fact remains that Montgomery was winning the war of attrition, a type of war which Brooke took for granted. Brooke was pleased when British troops entered Caen on 9 July, but the battle for the area was far from finished. Later he watched a film (20 July) on the bombing of Caen which Brooke thought was 'effective and efficiently carried out'; he made no mention of French civilian deaths which were numerous, because war for Brooke was a state of affairs where victory could be the only consideration. 'Eisenhower was angry. He thundered that it had taken seven thousand tons of bombs to gain seven miles,' and this could not continue throughout France.[40]

Following on from his conflict with Churchill over the criticism of army commanders, Brooke reflected that one of Alexander's problems was that he did not understand politicians, even though Alexander read Hansard as often as he could. Politicians were a source of constant irritation for Brooke, and this cause of friction between military command and political control in a democratic society in times of emergency, was underlined in Brooke's writings, and deserving of further serious study and reflection. It must have been a relief when Brooke had to have lunch with the Portuguese ambassador, and discovered he was a keen ornithologist. Following on with his heated clash with the prime minister (6 July), even mentioned in Anthony Eden's book *The Reckoning*, he found Churchill in an improved state a few days later, and in a better 'frame of mind' about the Americans.[41]

The meeting with the COS on 12 July was looking months ahead, discussing what would happen to Germany after it was occupied. It had been projected there would be three zones with the Russians taking the eastern sector and the British and Americans the other two. The Americans and British both wanted the northern sector, based on the grounds that the Americans did not want their communication lines running through France. It was generally agreed the Americans could use the British northern sector, which the British wanted for ease of access and the ports. There was a growing concern about Stalin, their erstwhile ally, whom they suspected, rightly, of having ambitions for dominating Europe. Much later Churchill would propose the French should have a sector, not out of his love for de Gaulle and France, but to increase the Western influence in Germany.* Nearer the end of the month the same discussion was held in the War Office as to whether Germany should be dismembered at all, or converted into an ally against the perceived Soviet danger, Brooke noting that in 'fifteen years' time Russia will be a major threat', an astute and prescient observation. Smuts had suggested this possibility months before.

These were not the only discussions in the corridors of power as news came through that Amboina (an island of eastern Indonesia) had been captured, causing Brooke to demand from the prime minister that he should make up his mind about the proposed Australian strategy, over which he kept ruminating without a direct answer. This lack of a decisive response infuriated Brooke, who wrote 'I shudder to think where we are going with him as a leader. Why cannot big men know when to close their career?'[42] A comment which clearly indicated his level of frustration. A few days later was his 61st birthday (23 July) when Brooke felt more like 71, but he admitted he also had a heavy cold at the time. Nearer to home the Greek problem intensified. In Greece the resistance movement, as in many parts of Europe, had been divided between political affiliations, the Greek government in exile was losing its grip, and the Foreign Office wanted to ensure the monarch and democracy survived. Brooke

---

* When Stalin asked Roosevelt whether the French should have a zone, Roosevelt replied 'It's not a bad idea,' adding 'but only out of kindness.' 'That would be the only reason for giving them a zone,' was Stalin's firm reply. See John Toland, *The Last 100 Days*, (New York: Modern Library, 2003) p.61. Although Stalin would have understood the motivation was not kindness.

wondered whether it was right to denounce ELAS (Greek People's Liberation Army) who had fought so well. When he heard of the 20 July plot against Hitler Brooke simply wondered where it would all lead, and what would be the ramifications. He was already detecting that events across Europe were indicating an uncertain future.

World events in Europe and elsewhere suddenly took a back seat to a domestic crisis when he was called to see Churchill, who was literally foaming at the mouth in anger because he had been told that Montgomery was not allowing him to visit; he was more furious than Brooke had ever seen or experienced before. Brooke eventually gathered that Eisenhower had told Churchill that 'Montgomery did not want visitors' and Brooke immediately suspected, or hoped, this was not aimed directly at Churchill, but despite all his efforts he failed to convince Churchill of this possibility. He told Churchill he would sort matters out and immediately organised a flight to Montgomery's headquarters. Once there he took the opportunity to inform Montgomery about the criticisms of being too cautious, to warn him about Churchill's 'vindictive' nature over the visit, and he made sure that Montgomery sent a telegram offering an apology, and writing with some emphasis 'that the Prime Minister' was welcome any time. It is not entirely clear whether Montgomery had tried to block Churchill or had issued a simple ban while he was busy. When he returned Brooke had to make every effort and utilise all his powers of persuasion to stop Churchill sending a deeply hostile note to Montgomery. Later Churchill called Brooke and explained he had received a 'nice letter' from Montgomery, and he was repentant about his unjustified anger. Brooke had the distinct impression that Churchill had forgotten that Brooke had flown to France to resolve this very issue. A few days later Churchill was back to 'good form' and even told Brooke that on 'all military matters I was his alter-ego' which Brooke appreciated. The Montgomery problems would not go away, and Brooke had heard that the normally relaxed Eisenhower had been 'moaning' about Montgomery for letting the Americans bear the brunt of the fighting. Near the end of the month he was asked to attend a dinner with Eisenhower, Bedell Smith, and the prime minister which he soon gathered was organised to bring Brooke and Eisenhower more together over the 'Monty problem'. Brooke was going to have other Montgomery problems in the future, but at this moment he found it frustrating, writing, 'My God, what psychological complications war leads to…will we ever learn to "love our allies as ourselves." I doubt it.'

During August Brooke reflected in his observations on the sense of optimism which was beginning to sweep through the West. It was during this month that the Western Allies broke out of the Brest peninsula, Paris was liberated, Florence was entered, there were uprisings in Warsaw and a Slovakian rebellion, Operation *Dragoon* had started, the Turkish government broke off relations with Nazi Germany, and the French First Army took Toulon. However, Brooke's month started with the unresolved problem of the V1s and encroaching fear of the V2 rockets. As he made his diary entries at this time, it is possible for the reader to detect a touch of his sense of humour

Field Marshal Montgomery (Archives, Public Domain)

emerging, rather than his usual anger at incompetence. It is almost possible to sense his inner smile as he wrote that 'Portal loves sharing his scientific knowledge, Cherwell must show his mathematical genius, and Duncan Sandys insists on letting one know that he has a great political future." As he looked around the table, he had the distinct feeling that 'dear old' Admiral Andrew Cunningham 'sympathises with me'.[†] As he pondered the developing situation in Europe, he found the signs encouraging, and speculated the 'Boche' might draw a line at the Seine, but he wondered how they could cope with the overwhelming control of the skies and against the sheer weight of the logistical opposition.

There followed a mysterious interchange when Eisenhower informed Churchill that he had asked for Operation *Dragoon* to be cancelled, and all the available forces to be sent to the Western Front. This had been Brooke's argument ever since the operation was suggested, and it was music to his ears and those of Churchill. Brooke advised Churchill not to wire his support of Eisenhower's thoughts to Roosevelt, but Churchill went ahead only to hear the next day that Roosevelt had received no such communication from Eisenhower. This caused Brooke to wonder whether Eisenhower had 'fooled us' or whether Churchill was up to his games. It may have been that Eisenhower had simply expressed a wish which Churchill had grasped at, merely in the hope that if he contacted the president it would be resolved in Churchill's favour.

As usual the more unpleasant meetings tended to revolve around the Far Eastern campaigns, and there followed a meeting with Mountbatten when it became clear that there was little choice but continue the fighting for Burma. Churchill still returned to his 'mad ideas' about Sumatra-type projects in which Brooke noted that Churchill's arguments were 'becoming puerile', leading to another 'unpleasant day'. Churchill wired the American COS about British proposals in his own inimitable style, which Brooke concluded would mean its immediate rejection. On 10 August Churchill made his way to Italy so life for Brooke and others felt much quieter,

---

\* Duncan Sandys during the postwar period held various ministerial posts, and despite a divorce in 1960, Duncan Sandys is nearly always referred to as 'Churchill's son-in-law' as if it explained his success.

† Quite why Brooke described Cunningham as 'dear old' is curious. They were both born in 1883 with Cunningham first on the scene six months before Brooke, and strangely they both died in June 1963 within a few days of one another.

causing Brooke to reflect that his political master had 'done much for the country' and hoping that he would 'go soon' and not blemish his great reputation. It is evident from these diary entries that Brooke was genuinely convinced that Churchill was becoming more and more unbalanced. Churchill's attitudes and views were probably not helped by his sense of euphoria that the war was being won, and he still had a part to play. For his own part Brooke had a strong feeling he wanted to leave his job, be free from anxiety, and be himself at Ferney Close. He wrote that 'the making of plans is just child's play as compared to putting them into execution'. He was probably pondering that being a field commander was the real task, and he reflected on the opportunities he had missed or refused. Men like Brooke established the plans, Montgomery and Eisenhower executed them, but the hardest task was carried out by the man in the ranks with gun in hand doing the dirty and dangerous work.

The War Cabinet under Attlee discussed the news of the Warsaw uprising under General Tadeusz Komorwski (better known as Bór-Komorwski) which was a tragic event in which the Russians did nothing to help even though they were camped nearby, and even refused the Western Allies the use of airstrips to help. Brooke never recorded the thoughts of the discussion, but there must have been a recognition of Stalin's long-term intentions of occupying Poland after the war. Many of the resisting Poles had hoped for nationwide revolt now the Germans were in retreat, and 'that was to be the moment for the underground to emerge… and declare Polish independence.'[43] Stalin knew this, and thus his lack of help. It was a cynical political move by Stalin, recognised instantly by the Poles but more slowly by other countries. When a week after this meeting Brooke met the Polish General Anders, whom he greatly admired, Anders explained to him the Poles had two enemies, the Germans and the Russians, but the Germans were the ones they were fighting currently. Poland had a proud history, but the last king of Poland, Stanisław August Poniatowski (1764–95) had been given the impossible task of implementing reform while retaining Russian supremacy. On three occasions the Russian army arrived to ensure their order was maintained, and devised partition as a useful punishment. When the king appeared to support an uprising (1794–95) by Tadeusz Kościuszko, there was a third partition and the king died in Russian exile; Poland had been partitioned to death. Poland had always recalled its independent past, and it continued to develop its own cultural and historical identity, despite being subject to its militarily stronger neighbours. Nevertheless, Poland had a long history of being dominated by powerful neighbours such as the Ottomans, the Austro-Hungarians, the Prussians and Russians, and for years had been partitioned and re-partitioned, and it was not until 1989–90 that it regained its independence. Brooke recognised the effort put into the defeat of Nazi Germany by the bravery of Polish fighters; it had been the Poles who had eventually eliminated the Germans from Monte Cassino and played a significant part in the Battle of Britain, but they were poorly treated even by the Allies in the postwar period.

On 19 August Brooke flew to Naples where there was a brief conference on the future of Operation *Dragoon*, and the Mediterranean strategy from then on, which included the re-occupation of Greece. There was also news of the successful French army heading towards the vital port of Toulon which it took on 28 August. Brooke flew over the battle scenes of Monte Cassino and Anzio where the fighting had been hand to hand, where many claimed that the conflict had been as bitter as the Eastern Front, and then on to Rome where Brooke was disappointed that he could find no bird books. It is not difficult to imagine a startled Italian bookseller being asked by a British field marshal if he had any 'bird-books' at this vexed juncture in Italian history. What disturbed Brooke most was that he discovered there were serious tensions between Jumbo Wilson and Alexander, which was not only disturbing but could have wider ramifications.

He landed in the west of Ancona (where he again met General Anders mentioned above) and had a long discussion with Alexander over his plan that the Americans could leave for the south of France, while the British troops stayed to retain the front. Brooke appreciated the thought but had to explain to Alexander that it was unrealistic because of the potential logistical problems with shipping. He also had to make it clear that a drive towards Vienna was likely to fail, as attractive as the policy may have sounded. There was only the one 'viable path' out of north Italy, which in winter made such a campaign impossible. In this interchange Brooke's value as an overseer can be clearly perceived. Alexander as a field commander may have been closer to the action, but Brooke from behind his desk had a more comprehensive view, and he was not swept away by unrealistic optimism. He probably, without stating it in his diary or letters, had a man-to-man talk about the Alexander and Wilson clash. The latter was busy preparing what was called Operation *Manna*, organising a division to embark for Greece. Brooke had warned everyone that before this happened the Germans had first to be fully cleared out of Greece.

Brooke flew back to Naples then on to Gibraltar followed by his flight to London. As he read his papers and enjoyed the views he thought how 'the news of the German decay on all fronts continues to be almost unbelievable.' He returned to a difficult COS meeting which discussed Eisenhower's plans to take total control in Northern France, which Brooke believed could add another three to six months to the war. He gathered that Eisenhower wanted to split the forces with the Americans heading towards Nancy and the British taking the northern coastal route. He decided he had to travel again and see Montgomery. Before he did so he attended a service in the crypt of St Paul's Cathedral to celebrate the liberation of Paris, and on hearing the thrilling French national anthem, *La Marseillaise*, it struck him that 'France seemed to wake again after being knocked out for five years.'

He prepared to visit Montgomery pondering Eisenhower's plans, as the American general was assuming the dual role of supreme commander as well as commander of land forces, which had been Montgomery's role. It was not an easy trip because of the weather, and he saw first-hand the scenes of battle before he reached Montgomery. This was the first phase of the controversy between what has been called the 'broad front' versus the 'narrow thrust' with Montgomery in favour of the 'single-sword' thrust compared to the 'bludgeon blow' preferred by Eisenhower.[44] Basically Montgomery wanted one single thrust, and the Americans several along a broad front. This writer can still remember Montgomery's televised postwar broadcasts as he explained the brilliance of his ideas. There was considerable tension between Montgomery and the Americans, and with the benefit of hindsight most historians agree that Montgomery's personality and egotistical ways of expressing himself did little to help. The whole issue never came before the CCOS and was resolved by Eisenhower himself. Brooke was more ambivalent and happier for some form of compromise, which he thought Montgomery had achieved. On his return to London, Brooke found Churchill had returned but was suffering from a 104-degree temperature. He explained the Eisenhower and Montgomery situation, and Churchill's response was to make Montgomery a field marshal; he may have deserved this honour, but it would never resolve the problem.

## Octagon Conference

During September, the Octagon Conference took place in Quebec. It was focused on the Japanese war, and preoccupied Brooke's thinking more than anything else, mainly because it led to even more heated exchanges with Churchill. He noted that Brussels was liberated, and there was a move on Antwerp, but his main entries, this being a personal diary and not a history, stayed away from these major events. The first V2s hit England (8 September), the Red Army entered Bulgaria which almost instantly and naturally changed sides, Finland surrendered, Montgomery carried out Operation *Market Garden*, the Allies had a few feet on German soil, and by the end of the month Hitler had mobilised all men aged between 16 and 60 in the *Volkssturm*. This last action of expending the lives of children and old men was a clear indicator of impending German disaster, and Hitler's desperate fanaticism. It was not announced until the following month, but it clearly indicated the German war machine was in a desperate state.

As the British political and military leaders boarded the *Queen Mary* liner there were a series of meetings which were generally cantankerous, and they did not seem to achieve much. Churchill came up with the idea that the Greek problem could be resolved by dropping an airborne division near Athens, and Brooke had to point out that this would only consist of some 2–3,000 men, and the Germans still had an estimated 150,000 troops in Greece. This suicidal idea was the opening of what would be a difficult journey, not because of weather, but due to the internal conflict, with Churchill, according to Brooke, believing the COS were ganging up against him. Brooke claimed Churchill was in a bad mood, and for his part Brooke admitted he 'found it hard to keep his temper with him' as there appeared absolutely nothing upon which they could agree, and the prime minister kept changing his mind, challenging past agreements, and misreading the facts. In some ways it 'showed Brooke at his most intolerant'.[45] It transpired that the major factor which dominated Brooke's critical approach to the prime minister was Churchill's tendency to want to be involved in the detail of military plans. This characteristic clash between these two men permeates Brooke's war diaries, and it was brought about by two very gifted but different men. Brooke could be overly critical when his views were challenged and angry; Churchill could be irritable and equally bad-tempered, as he often admitted, when he suffered from what he called his 'black dog' moods. This was a Victorian expression often used by nannies, leading some people to idiotically claim that Churchill was bipolar. Churchill and Brooke were both under intense strain during these years, Churchill the most because he carried the ultimate responsibility. It was the British system that permitted Churchill to be both the prime minister and minister of defence which gave him the constitutional right to ask questions, and to argue over strategic matters with COS as a matter of due process. It could be argued that Churchill had a better global perspective than Brooke, he could be more astute and see the broader global and political picture. On the other hand, Brooke was equally perceptive on the military details needed, he had a more pragmatic attitude and insight, and both were deeply conscious of their sense of national responsibility. As Brooke later added to his diary at this juncture, his criticisms were sometimes too harsh, but they were written at a time of 'sheer exasperation' and in an original entry he wrote that 'never have I admired and despised a man simultaneously to the same extent'. He thought that Churchill talked 'absurdities', it 'makes my blood boil to listen to his nonsense' and he was a 'public menace'. The vitriol was palpable, somewhat over the top, but almost understandable. What strikes the modern reader of these diaries is that Brooke never changed them, knowing that his views if widely read would cause rancour. However, he was always honest with himself, and others, and by adhering to this policy had left himself open to the criticism that he was a 'moaner and groaner', but he was a man prepared to live and die for his nation, and he never lost his respect and love for Churchill, despite all the frustrations of top command. What should have brought their minds together was that on 7 September as the *Queen Mary* sped toward Canada, they passed over or near a U-boat, intercepting its signal that they had been spotted: a sharp reminder that the real enemy was not to be found among themselves.

According to Brooke the trip, after they arrived and were met by the presidential train, appeared to go well. After a COS meeting followed by a CCOS, which was dominated by the Far East, there was general agreement on the main points. Brooke lunched with Marshall, Leahy and Dill. As he had noted before, Dill had been ill, and Brooke was deeply disturbed to see his old friend 'wasting away'. At dinner, the great and the good met, and Brooke found himself seated at the right-hand side of the president, with whom he found conversation amazingly easy and pleasant. The next day Churchill gave a talk on the situation, stating that the next two objectives were to 'march on Vienna' and 'recapture Singapore'. Neither of these issues had been established by COS at any time during their meetings, and Brooke had already agreed at COS and with Alexander the inherent dangers in heading towards the Austrian capital. They were simply not in the British plans, and this alone demonstrated some of the causes of Brooke's reaction to the impetuous and individualistic Churchill. The Americans accepted the British plans about Burma, and that the British fleet could make an appearance in the central Pacific within Admiral Nimitz's domain. The only objection arose from Admiral King who almost exploded with rage at the latter agreement. The situation was inadvertently helped by King's outburst because even the American side opposed him. Portal and others often suspected that some Americans, especially King, were waging a secret war against the British Empire, which most Americans disliked because of their country's origins.

There was another internal British dispute when Mountbatten wired Churchill asking for six and not just two divisions for Burma. This somehow prompted Churchill to think Pug Ismay had been deliberately withholding information and he lost his temper. Unlike Brooke, Pug Ismay was a patient man, and he was so hurt he threatened to resign. Brooke did not dissuade him on the grounds that such a move might pull Churchill back to his senses. Brooke went to see Churchill and discovered he was in a good mood and the Ismay problem had been resolved. He never knew for certain whether Ismay gave his letter of resignation to Churchill, but he thought he may have done, but Churchill had ignored the request. In these confrontations, Brooke was beginning to find Eden a more useful support in trying to make Churchill understand the military points of view. Brooke also concluded that the Americans 'admired' Churchill, but they were always 'suspicious' of him; there would be some justification in this speculation. Brooke found the Americans highly co-operative and there were agreements on most issues.

The conference ended on 16 September, and Brooke, Portal and others prepared for a fishing holiday, which was nearly spoilt by Churchill demanding another meeting, but he relented. They flew to Oriskany Lake where they enjoyed a few days' fishing for trout, with Portal catching the largest recorded number of trout at that time. As they returned, they received an amusing wire from Churchill which read: '*Gunfire (305): Following for CIGS and CAS from Prime Minister. Please let me know how many captives were taken by land and air forces respectively in Battle of Snow Lake.*' Portal framed a reply, and this must have cheered the company up a great deal; having enjoyed a brief holiday may have set a better tone between politics and military. Had the Germans or Japanese intercepted this wire it would have caused considerable speculation.

The military fishermen then flew back to London arriving on 22 September, and Brooke immediately had a day's shooting and enjoyed Ferney Close home life. During his fishing and shooting holidays Brooke never mentioned Montgomery's Operation *Market Garden*, basically holding to his principle of not commenting in his diary on operations or expressing his opinions, though he held strong views about Montgomery's plans which he expressed later in October. The well-known battle of Arnhem had been a poorly planned attack, preceded by Dutch warnings about a strong German panzer presence which were ignored, and by sending in some of the best British fighting troops lightly armed, to a total disaster. Montgomery's plan was to shorten the war by crossing the Rhine and entering northern Germany almost by surprise. It has often been believed, by American historians especially, and probably correctly, that the Arnhem route was chosen by Montgomery because it was a 'British route' into Germany, and ahead of the Americans; certainly Brooke made 'no reference to the Remagen Bridge crossing in his diary'.[46] The fact that Eisenhower's policy was for a broad front to defeat Germany had brought sharp criticism from Montgomery, who believed the best way was a narrow 'punch line, or the sword thrust' mentioned above, through to Berlin. Experts have long argued about these strategic plans, but the Germans even in defeat were proving their professionalism at military arms, and this idea of a long deep thrust opened the nightmare of unprotected flanks. Even at the time many thought this was a misconceived project and believed, as Brooke noted the following month, that 'Montgomery's strategy was at fault...instead of making an advance on Arnhem he should have made certain of Antwerp first' as this port was essential for future success.[47] Montgomery naturally claimed Arnhem as a 90 per cent victory when it was an extremely serious defeat.

The first COS meeting on Brooke's arrival in London discussed how to capture Rangoon, not the ramifications of Arnhem. One of the implications or reminders of the Arnhem fiasco was the residual power of the German army to fight well even under extreme pressure. Brooke was pleased after this meeting to have lunch with his eldest daughter Rosemary before she travelled to India, followed by a quick Cabinet meeting because the prime minister was still travelling. They met him with the usual entourage at Euston Station the next day. There was little to do for the remaining days of September, except to answer the German request to send food to the Channel Islands, which was denied on the grounds that it was a German responsibility; given that these were British citizens this demonstrated the unpleasant nature of war. The next COS was cancelled because there appeared little to discuss; times were changing rapidly. It had been a month of serious conflict between Churchill and Brooke, but he had had a good fishing holiday, then came home to some shooting and his beloved Benita, which must have prepared him for the next round.

CHAPTER 9

# Final Months

## Anglo-American Tensions

Brooke had invited Montgomery for lunch and found him 'full of criticisms about the way Eisenhower was running the war'. Brooke had helped mould Montgomery who intimated this fact in his own memoirs, and they shared a common strategy, but Brooke was aware that Montgomery lacked any sense of tact and diplomatic wisdom, and at times his brusque comments and assertions were considered by many to be downright rude. Brooke always supported Montgomery, but too often he had been obliged to pick up the pieces after the constant confrontations, and this developing situation would soon become even more dire, if not ominous for Anglo-American relationships. The next day he met Cyril Falls, the military correspondent for *The Times*, who pointed out that Eisenhower by being supreme commander of the three military wings, as well as the controller of the land forces, was failing. Brooke pointed out that 'this was a political matter' and noted in his diary that he had obviously spoken to Montgomery. It can only be speculation, but it may have crossed Brooke's mind that Montgomery had probably set this journalist up to reinforce his arguments.

The Americans already suspected, according to General Omar Bradley's autobiography, that Montgomery was seeking total command of the land forces which he had once held in Normandy.[1] The Americans despised Montgomery, Patton hated him, and all were suspicious of his motives, possibly with some justification. Many of the leading generals were ambitious, often self-serving, but it was all too apparent in Montgomery's case. Brooke shared some of these feelings about Montgomery, but he kept them to his personal diary. He met Montgomery again the next day and wrote that he was 'still harping on' and 'he has got this on his brain as it affects his own personal position'.[2] As with *The Times*' journalist he explained to Montgomery that although he had some sympathy with him, there was not much he could do about the matter. This situation would not go away and before the end of the war would reach explosive proportions.

## Tolstoy Conference in Moscow

If most of Brooke's September had been consumed by the Octagon Conference in Quebec with its pleasurable fishing tour, October was the so-called Tolstoy Conference in Moscow, with some enjoyable tourism for Brooke. The war continued unabated and the Germans appeared to be losing against the Red Army in Hungary and evacuating Greece; the Scheldt estuary was being cleared; the Red Army with Yugoslavian partisans had entered Belgrade; the first German city fell to the Allies (Aachen); the Russians occupied Riga; and probably to Brooke's annoyance the USA and Britain recognised de Gaulle as the head of the French government. The month started for Brooke with discussions on the postwar situation, and he speculated this would become complicated. He later observed this potentially delicate issue developing in Moscow, and knew it was being constantly discussed at home. Normally, within British tradition the COS was not concerned with the aims or results of war; this belonged to the higher strategy of the elected government, quite properly. Brooke and his fellow leaders in the COS were at first concerned with the defence of the homeland which had been a major emergency in 1940 and 1941, and thereafter with trying to ensure campaigns and offensive operations were successful. The conduct of these campaigns was generally directed by the overall political aims, but now there was a Post Hostilities Planning Staff with the future very much under discussion and in the balance. The British were aware that the Americans, especially in the Far East, did not appreciate the British Empire; the Americans were now the dominant partner, and many of the more astute realised the end of the empire was in sight which would also be the end of Britain as a world power. The Americans and British were only now beginning to think of the future, but Stalin was ahead of them, looking to assume power in central and southern Europe, and possibly with some expansion in the East following the projected defeat of Japan. There was a growing awareness of this potential Stalin threat, and the dismemberment of Germany was the continuous focus in these often-secret discussions. Brooke thought that the Foreign Office could not foresee that the Soviet Union could soon become unfriendly and even hostile, with Eden supporting the military at this juncture. The more the situation was discussed, the more the division of Germany into zones came to be regarded as of considerable global strategic importance for the immediate future. Later in Moscow, Brooke summarised his thinking in a homespun parable about some hunters planning to shoot a bear, but they were so lost in the sale of the skin and arguing over the proceeds they forgot to shoot the bear. Brooke was a military minded man and probably understood the political future had to be secure, but he also realised that the Germans and Japanese were still fighting, and they had to be totally beaten and reduced to surrender first.

On the broader front there were problems in the Far East, and he was conscious that once again the Italian campaign was 'lagging'. He spoke to General Urquhart who had commanded the airborne division at Arnhem which he described as 'very interesting', but it had not escaped his observations that the Germans had fought back and won an important victory. Later, on 16 February 1945, he eventually caught up with John Hackett who had spent the interim time behind enemy lines, and who had led a parachute brigade. Brooke thought Montgomery's strategy had been wrong, but he never commented on the disaster of the planning.[*] On 4 October he flew to Versailles to visit Eisenhower and witnessed one of the dreaded V2 rockets fall on Paris. It was not going to be easy to bring the Germans down to unconditional surrender.

He talked with Eisenhower about the march on Antwerp which the Germans had carefully resisted by flooding the Scheldt estuary, and questioned himself whether Montgomery would have been better in placing his forces there and not in Arnhem. He admired the fact that Eisenhower shouldered the blame for Arnhem by stating that he had given Montgomery permission.[†] He was also impressed in the way Eisenhower ran his conference. He could not stay long because he had to fly back to London ready for his departure to Moscow, which Churchill had suddenly sprung on him; it was fundamentally a political conference and Brooke would rather not have attended. The fact that Churchill wanted Brooke's presence in what was essentially a political meeting spoke volumes for their interdependence, despite the often-heated rows; Brooke flew with Eden while Churchill went with his party in another plane. They landed in Naples to be met by Alexander, Jumbo Wilson, and Macmillan where plans were discussed, especially with Alexander whose forces were somewhat stuck in the Apennines. They then flew to Cairo with Eden joining Churchill's aircraft, but somewhat disconcertingly this plane damaged itself on landing. They then travelled in the same plane and because of the weather and terrain had to fly at a high altitude, which was difficult for Churchill who needed an oxygen supply. When they landed in Moscow, they developed yet more mechanical problems with their aircraft, when they had difficulty lowering the undercarriage. Brooke was pleased with his rooms in the National Hotel, Churchill had his own small house, and Eden was given space in the British Embassy. By this stage, although not mentioned by Brooke, they would all have been aware that their rooms were unquestionably bugged.

The meeting started well with a lunch given by Stalin, and as Brooke noted the best uniforms were out and everyone 'seemed in good form'. There was now an air of confidence because they knew the Germans were losing. The only speculation was how long and what would happen to Germany and the rest of Europe once peace was restored; this was the fundamental reason for the meeting. Stalin was in

---

[*] Not least, as noted, ignoring Dutch intelligence that a panzer division from the East was recuperating in the area, but also the risk of the ground troops covering the long distance to reach the lightly armed paratroopers,

[†] Omar Bradley wrote that 'in permitting Montgomery to launch Operation *Market Garden*, Ike committed his gravest tactical error of the war.' See Omar Bradley, *A General's Life*, (London: Sidgwick & Jackson,1983) p.333.

an 'affable mood' and congratulated Brooke on his promotion. In a brief speech both Churchill and Harriman, who was representing Roosevelt and the American party, spoke about the fact that both their respective countries had been unprepared for the war. Stalin responded by stating it was the same for the USSR, and the reason was that their three nations were 'peace-loving' countries. It would have brought an ironical thought to Brooke's mind that in September 1939 Stalin's Russia had joined with Germany in the attack on Poland.

Regarding the lunch, Brooke mentioned that this meal took three hours, and although he enjoyed alcohol he was always measured in his amounts and despised drunkenness, which prevailed at Russian banquets. Stalin loved to drink, and it has often been noted that Churchill also enjoyed his consumption and could keep pace with the Russian leader. It brought Brooke's criticism to the surface, as he noted in his diary that 'listening to half-inebriated politicians and diplomats informing each other of their devotion and affections, and expressing sentiments very detached from veracity' was difficult for him, begging the question whether 'international friendships are based on such products of drunken orgies'.[3] He was relieved that he managed to survive this ordeal with just one vodka and a glass of wine.

As the politicians and diplomats took themselves off in what Brooke described as a 'small huddle' to some room he was free to make a tour of Moscow, looked after by a contingent of Russian policemen. He was obviously relaxed, there was no longer any great need for him to be involved in military debate, and he intended to make this a holiday break whenever he could. He was fascinated if not enthralled by an exhibition in which the Russians showed all the German equipment they had captured, ranging from planes to guns and other military equipment.

Afterwards he had a brief meeting with Churchill who was seemingly desperate to do something for Mountbatten, and Brooke had to fight his political master to stop him removing troops from Italy merely for the sake of Churchill's friendship with 'the royal'. This was a brief interlude and Brooke was soon back relishing his tourism. He especially enjoyed the opera, ballet and various shows. He started with the opera *Prince Igor* which he found impressive, noting that London could not reach that standard of production. Over the next few days, he watched another opera, *Eugene Onegin*, a Gala Ballet performance, the ballet *Swan Lake*, Russian folk dances and songs, and the Red Army choir and music. He was bemused when he tried to find access for some of his party that sergeants were not allowed to attend because they were too far down the ranks, which he thought somewhat unusual for a society which based itself on equality. He was close to what George Orwell would one day predict in his dystopian novel *Animal Farm*, that the Russian version of communism merely supplanted the old system with its own political class structure. The new Russian elite had all moved into the homes and dachas of the tsarist privileged classes, and ordinary people experienced little substantial change in their poverty status.

Another discussion with Churchill arose over Montgomery receiving his field marshal's baton and as to whether he had received it yet. Brooke was taken by surprise and puzzled, explaining he was not aware as such, and maybe he had not yet been given the honour because, he explained, these batons were individually made. Churchill then exclaimed that when it happened 'he did not want the Mall' [Pall Mall] packed with people. When Brooke asked why that should happen Churchill replied, 'He will want to fill the Mall because he is Monty, and I will not have him filling the Mall.'[4] Brooke was somewhat taken aback by this attitude, reflecting that Churchill liked the 'limelight' and was jealous of anyone else blocking the view. Churchill, however, had perceived Montgomery's love of adulation and his huge ego, which would cause more problems in the months ahead, and Brooke was also quietly aware of Montgomery's propensity for wanting to be popular. Later Brooke warned Montgomery to keep his visit to Buckingham Palace as quiet as possible; he was, as always, in support of his commanders, and especially Montgomery.

Brooke met the Russian General Antonov who discussed Hungary and the general situation in that country. Brooke learnt from this Russian that handling the Hungarian army was never going to be easy if they attacked Germany through Hungary, because many of the Hungarian officers were German or Germanic in origin. That same evening (14 October) there was another major banquet with the Russian custom of toasts. Curiously, Brooke noted that one toast was not translated, and induced peals of laughter at the expense of his neighbour Ivan Maisky.[*] He asked Maisky what was happening, and he replied that Stalin had referred to him as the 'poet diplomat' because he had written some verses. He then told Brooke, who had obviously asked him why he looked so grim, that the last 'poet diplomat had been liquidated'. Eden's observation that Maisky could 'not be subdued by the sternest rebuffs' (see footnote) did not apply to Stalin's toasts. Brooke undoubtedly gathered another insight into Stalin's Russia. His mind was distracted from this conversation when Molotov proposed a toast, where he demanded that every person first had to drain a tumbler of champagne, as he toasted the Red Army. Brooke obeyed and wondered what effect it would have on him later that evening when he was expected to present a military report. As it transpired the evening military session was open and frank, and for Brooke 'revealing', though sadly he did not take this wide-reaching comment further.

The next day he was back to his tourism, leaving Moscow to visit the Zagorsk Monastery which he described as 'the Canterbury of Russia'. On his return there was another meeting in the Kremlin, where, with some concern, he thought Churchill was suffering from another fever. It was at this meeting he was convinced of Stalin's

---

[*] Ivan Maisky was once described by Eden as 'the most active and ingenious Ambassador' in London, who 'never missed a trick that could by any argument be his and was unsubdued by even the sternest of rebuffs.' See Eden, A., *The Eden Memoirs, Facing the Dictators* (London: Cassell, 1962) p.125 and p.407. Maisky under Stalin's orders kept demanding the Second Front which made him popular with many in the general public who often cheered him in the London streets and asked for his autograph.

military strategy, and he was deeply impressed by his immediate understanding of logistics, even to Stalin's awareness of the limitations of rail transports. There was also the happy belief that the Russians would assist in the war against the Japanese once the German threat had been resolved. This priority given to the war against Nazi Germany would have been music to Brooke's ears, but like others he knew that Stalin's offer to fight Japan would come at a price.

The next day when he returned to his tourism, he was shown around the tsarist grandeur of the Kremlin, noticing in the gardens three great tits, as if they were brave birds to be there. Now the military matters had been decided he wanted to return home, but delay followed delay (probably taken up by postwar Polish and Greek issues) and he went looking for a rare black woodpecker which sadly for him remained elusive. He went shopping, noting the price and worth of the goods on offer. Brooke obviously enjoyed his tours and apparently even the most 'junior members of the delegation found him the most relaxed of companions, and always asking whether there was some party to attend'.[5] This interesting insight was gleaned from a Joan Bright Astley, a shorthand typist who rose in the secretarial world, and who was privy to major papers and many of the key players.[6]

Brooke had previously noted that it was difficult to meet the ordinary everyday people and his Russian watchers were always in attendance, and when a Russian crowd surrounded them they were warned to move away from the westerners, which they did instantly and obediently.* Later, on his long flight back, Brooke ruminated on this Russian experience, comparing the Russian and German fascist styles of government, believing that 'it seems essential for humanity to subject itself to untold ordeals in order to achieve even slow progress towards perfection. The path of mankind in learning to "love its neighbours as itself" is a thorny and risky one.'[7] Brooke thought that one day mankind would achieve this goal, but it remains a long-drawn-out hope.

Before he left he visited more places, attended more banquets, with Molotov raising a toast to Brooke, and he was surprised that Stalin turned up at the airport to wish them farewell. They stopped off at Yalta and had a tour of the Crimea, which struck Brooke as more prosperous than anywhere else in Russia. They flew on to Cairo where he met and discussed plans with Mountbatten, and then via Benghazi to Naples to be met by the Italian overseers consisting of Jumbo Wilson, Alexander and Macmillan. They then flew back over southern France landing at Northolt where Churchill's wife Clemmie was waiting for him. A route over France would have been inconceivable a few months earlier. They had a good telegram from Marshall who believed the war would finish by the end of the year, and Brooke was interviewed in depth by the king.

---

* When this writer was in the Soviet Union during the early period of Leonid Brezhnev's leadership, he had the same experience of being steered clear of meeting everyday Russians.

## More Anglo-American Friction

During November 1944 President Roosevelt won his fourth presidential election with Harry Truman as his vice-president, an Allied convoy was able to use Antwerp, the Red Army crossed the Danube and Strasbourg was liberated, but this was the lull before the storm of success. This 'storm' was a result of a politically dangerous and delicate version of Anglo-American disagreement, which emerged regarding the unfortunate tensions between the two Allied camps, in which Brooke was caught up. Brooke was sometimes blamed, with claims he had over-indulged Montgomery and defended him too often, and it was often believed that Brooke 'campaigned to turn the ground war over to Montgomery', possibly on nationalistic grounds.[8] The latter criticism was somewhat unfair, but Brooke knew about Montgomery's egotistical faults and rudeness, and although it was Montgomery who was often the disturbing cog in the machinery of Anglo-American relationships, Brooke's constant support of him never helped. Brooke's criticisms of Eisenhower, when published later in Bryant's book *Triumph in the West*, caused a considerable deal of rancour and bad will in America.[9] The month started with some concern for Brooke over Canadian troops being badly led again, but he heard that his old friend McNaughton,

Bradley with General George Marshall (US Army)

of whom he had been highly critical, had replaced Ralston as defence minister and decided he had better keep a low profile. He later noted that during this month the political situation in Canada had 'not been rosy' but on 22 November the Canadians managed to send 16,000 conscripts for overseas duties.

Brooke gathered early in the month yet more rumblings that Eisenhower's strategy of a broad front, rather than the British proposal of selecting a single strategic target, was not appearing too successful, and he wondered whether this meant there would be a general halt along the length of the Rhine.

At a personal level he was knocked back when he heard of the death of his old friend Dill in America, writing that a 'prominent landmark of my life was gone... his loss is quite irreparable.' He later added to his entry that in his opinion Dill, more than any other general, was responsible for the final victory. Brooke was always furious that Churchill never saw Dill in the same light, and 'never forgave him' for not awarding a peerage to Dill, despite the pressure he and Grigg had applied on the prime minister. Dill, who was pleasant and diplomatic, was much loved by the Americans, and after the war Anthony Eden wrote in his diaries that he went to America 'to attend the unveiling by President Truman of the memorial to my friend Field Marshal Sir John Dill in Arlington Cemetery, an honour never before or since accorded to a British soldier.'[10] As a point of curiosity there are other British soldiers and airmen in that cemetery, but Dill had a special memorial. Had Dill not fallen ill the encroaching friction between the military and politicians might possibly have been somewhat alleviated.

The next problem was replacing Dill and changing the command structure, which caused further heated debate between COS and Churchill, who, Brooke claimed, never ever understood the intricacies of the command system. Later in the month (17 November) it was eventually agreed that Jumbo Wilson would replace Dill in America, Alexander would replace Wilson as commander, Mark Clark would take over from Alexander, and General Truscott from Clark. The president agreed, though Brooke had his usual doubts, noting that 'Alexander has just not got the brains for it', and he may have had doubts about Clark, but not about Truscott. Brooke knew that everything would depend on how Wilson related to Marshall. Brooke was not the only one with concerns, and the First Sea Lord Admiral Andrew Cunningham had serious doubts about Alexander becoming supreme commander, as he had always held him in incredibly low esteem. Later in the month Churchill suggested that both Alexander and Wilson should be field marshals. Brooke was aware that Wilson had never worked well with Alexander, and he hoped that it might be better if Alexander's chief of staff Harding were replaced. There had been considerable discussion at COS level over Dill's replacement, and eventually Churchill was happy that Wilson should be the right choice. In his history Churchill reprinted his formal minute that 'I can see no other officer of sufficient status to fill this gap except General Maitland Wilson,' giving the impression that no discussions had occurred.[11]

At the time of Dill's death Brooke heard that he was to go with Churchill to the Armistice ceremony in Paris which delighted him. He was concerned that the French had already made this too public, and that there might still be some Germans or German sympathisers there making it a risk for the prime minister's security. Later he remained unconvinced about French security measures. Before they went to France there were COS and political discussions on dividing Palestine for the benefit of the Jews, and it was decided that there should be no announcement until the war had concluded. This fraught issue was to be the future nightmare in the Middle East and remains so to this day with ongoing friction. There was a Cabinet meeting to discuss the food crisis in Norway, the Netherlands and the Channel Islands but with no decisive results. It was during this week of discussion that Brooke noted that Churchill was not always having his own way with the politicians and wondered whether he was losing his grip on the Cabinet.

On 10 November he joined Churchill's party consisting of his wife and daughter, Eden, Ismay and Cadogan at Northolt ready to fly to Paris, where they had a pleasant reception. There is a distinct impression in his diary entries and other writings that Brooke was now enjoying his trips abroad. He was placed in an excellent hotel where the French had lined his shelves with some priceless bird books. He was delighted; his love of ornithology was widely known, and it was apparent by this courteous action that Brooke was appreciated. That evening he joined Churchill at his residence in the Quai d'Orsay for dinner, Churchill recalling that the last time he was there, in 1940, was the occasion when the French were hurriedly burning their archives. The next day he was at the Arc de Triomphe waiting for Churchill and de Gaulle to arrive, but he found the security appalling; it could be said that Brooke was being over-sensitive, but he may have had some justification, because although the crowds shouted in adulation at Churchill, Brooke knew there were some who would have preferred him dead. They watched a military parade for an hour, and he met Giraud recovering from a wound, and who was concerned that his wife and children were still in German captivity and he had heard nothing about their safety.*

Brooke found it 'a dream' to be back in a 'restored France' and enjoyed a dinner given by General Alphonse Juin, although he could not enjoy the food so much because of an upset stomach. The next day he had a meeting with Juin and found him an easy person to talk with and very likeable. It appears from Ismay's memoirs that the French General Koenig was also present. According to Ismay, Juin begged Brooke and Ismay to encourage the Americans to help equip eight new French divisions, which as Ismay noted had some sound military reasoning but also carried political and psychological implications.[12] Ismay had been warned by a close French

---

* As noted earlier, Giraud had escaped the German POW camp which made him something of a hero. Some historians claimed his freedom was activated by Pétain's government, but they only tried to placate the Germans after the escape.

military friend that it would take years for the French to forgive the British for fighting on when they had caved in. The British had much to be grateful for in the existence of the English Channel.

This sense of French honour and dignity was always de Gaulle's understandable motivation, and on this occasion, Brooke even found de Gaulle affable, which given their previous mutual history was a momentous sea-change. However, he also met some French Resistance leaders who were not impressed by de Gaulle, asking 'what did he do' and then treating it as a rhetorical question with the answer that he merely 'evacuated his family and himself to London' and thereafter stated that '*Je suis la France.*' Brooke later wondered whether de Gaulle would be the person to unite France; he did, but it took time. He was to become one of France's best-known leaders, but he always remained suspicious of the Anglo-Saxons of England and America.

On 13 November, the British party were driven to Maîche where General Jean de Lattre de Tassigny had his forward headquarters, and where they anticipated being able to view a planned battle about to start. The viewing was not to happen because snow obscured the scene, so they had to make do with a description of the events while they were happening. Brooke, who had constantly been critical of Eisenhower's plans of attacking along the whole front line, was pleased to discover that the French agreed with him. On the way back they visited a French training camp with young Maquis recruits whom Brooke found to be excellent in their potential. Churchill arrived back at his residence frozen, and he had to have hot-water bottles and a warm brandy 'poured down his throat', which according to Brooke 'thawed him out'.

The next day was not good for Brooke as his feelings for Eisenhower deteriorated yet further when they met at Rheims. Eisenhower took them over his plans and dispositions which Brooke found too vague as to what precisely 'was going on'. He later added to his diary that he was highly disturbed to see Kay Summersby, Eisenhower's one-time chauffeur, now promoted to hostess and sitting at the head of the table next to Churchill. Brooke wrote this 'produced a lot of undesirable gossip that did him no good'.* That evening they all flew back to Northolt.

At the first COS meeting the nature of the atom bomb was discussed, upon which Brooke made no comment at this stage, but they also discussed Mountbatten's plans which Brooke regarded as 'half-baked as usual'. Earlier in the month he had heard from Philip Joubert de la Ferté (Air Chief Marshal in India) that within Mountbatten's headquarters the Anglo-American relationships were poor. Brooke also saw 'Boy' Browning, still recovering from the loss of his troops in Arnhem, and

---

* Kay Summersby went from being chauffeur to secretary to hostess. Some writers have claimed they were lovers, some simply good friends. Those who knew both people have rejected the claim they were lovers, as do most of Eisenhower's biographers; not that this was important, apart from Brooke's realistic observation that gossip of this nature can cause considerable damage.

told him that he was to go as chief of staff to Mountbatten; Brooke could detect his heart was not in this assignment, but 'he took it well'.

It was not Mountbatten who concerned Brooke most, but his view that Eisenhower was failing as a commander, that Bedell Smith was in Paris and out of touch, and the 'war was rudderless'. He attended Westminster Abbey for the American Thanksgiving Service which he found disappointing, and with Benita in company on the same evening they went to the Albert Hall in honour of Remembrance Day for the Americans, which he also found disheartening with its dull music. It was not that Brooke was anti-American, but Eisenhower and his various strategies were never far from his anxious mind. The next day he cleared the COS meeting of all the minors and asked Pug Ismay to stay with the purpose of speaking about what was happening in France. Whatever the later criticisms it was apparent that Brooke was genuinely anxious about the then current conduct of the war. He was critical not only of Eisenhower's strategy, but of how he spent his time, and it was the question of 'Eisenhower on the golf links at Rheims' which was the singular line which caused the most offence in America, when it appeared in Bryant's book *The Triumph in the West*.

For Brooke and the COS, it appeared to be necessary to change the command structure, putting Bradley in command of the land forces, Tedder with the air control responsibility, and having two armies, one in the north under Montgomery and the other in the south under Patton. There were three army groups: in the north the 21st British and Canadian under Montgomery, then the 12th (USA) under Omar Bradley, and the 6th (USA and French) under General Jacob (Jake) Devers. Most of the forces were now American, and it was most unusual for Brooke to interfere in the field command.

Montgomery flew from France and went for lunch at Ferney Close where he and Brooke decided on three fundamental strands. The first was to counter the 'pernicious American strategy' of attacking along the whole line; secondly there should be two army groups, not three; and finally they must appoint a commander for the land forces. The question was how to achieve this concept of having Bradley as commander of the land forces with Montgomery in the north and Patton in the south. This was perhaps a politically dangerous meeting by Brooke, as Montgomery did not need much igniting, and this gave Montgomery a sense that he had the backing of his superiors. They agreed that Montgomery would speak with Eisenhower and Brooke would consult Churchill about Marshall coming to Britain to discuss the issues. Brooke was aware that Churchill, typically of his character, was also concerned about the lack of pace in France. There was a general feeling that the war was being won, but there had been a slowing down of the tempo because 'euphoria bred delay'.[13]

A few days later Montgomery telegrammed Brooke to the effect that he had spoken to Eisenhower, who had agreed that the strategy was wrong but would not agree to a separate land commander. Montgomery gave the impression that the

General George Patton with Third Army Staff (Intelligence Knowledge Network)

meeting had gone well, but this was far from the truth according to the many other accounts. Montgomery's proposal that there should be a single thrust into the Ruhr to capture German industry did not go down well with Eisenhower, who, apart from disagreeing with the strategy, thought that Montgomery's overbearing manners and criticisms were directed at Eisenhower's ability – and Eisenhower was correct in his thinking. The meeting may have sounded good to Montgomery, but Eisenhower was incensed, causing a possible rift between the Allies. The British public may have applauded Montgomery and those who knew Brooke admired him, but in America both Marshall and Eisenhower were well known and highly popular.

In Britain there was the common assumption that they had fought the longest and survived for victory to be in sight. Whereas in in America their public knew they were supplying more forces and material, and they were convinced that because of Eisenhower and Marshall the victory would be secured. Both viewpoints had a degree of veracity. The British by surviving had provided a reasonably safe base for the vast resources of America, and the thousands of military personnel who came to fight. Without this America would have been isolated. On the other hand, the British were unlikely to be able to launch an attack against Germany without American muscle, and the result may possibly have meant a Soviet-dominated Europe. It was critical for Britain to maintain a harmonious relationship with the Americans, and Montgomery's meddling did not help.

In his December diary Brooke made no mention that in the first few days of the month, de Gaulle was in Paris signing a Franco-Soviet Pact with Stalin, or the Red Army had started the siege of Budapest, because he was preoccupied by meetings and his anxiety about Eisenhower's control of the war in France. However, from mid-December he was to be more deeply concerned about Rundstedt's counterattack through the Ardennes, often known as the Battle of the Bulge. This crisis was not just military, but it would create immense problems on the diplomatic front between the British and Americans. Also passed over by Brooke, at the end of the month Stalin had made the Lublin Committee the Provisional Government of the Polish Republic. This clearly indicated his postwar intentions, which had been foreseen by the more astute when Stalin refused to help in the Warsaw uprising, and Churchill could not budge him at the Tolstoy Conference in October.*

The month started with Brooke talking to Churchill in his birthday bed surrounded by presents, informing him of Montgomery's talk with Eisenhower. Unfortunately, they only had Montgomery's version, which perhaps they should have thought about, and Churchill was prompted with his usual impetuosity to contact the president, but Brooke managed to persuade him to give it more time. Churchill was equally preoccupied with the situation in Greece, desperately trying to ensure that this country was not taken over by the communists, and a sense of pre-war normality was restored. Brooke was less interested in this area but was obliged to co-operate. He had little time for Ambassador Leeper in Greece, or the way the situation was being managed. He recalled that Eden had originally asked for 5,000 troops and now 40,000 were engaged, and Leeper was claiming the military were underestimating the problem. Brooke wanted the paratroopers who had been sent to Greece returned to the front because, he argued, they were a 'specialist brigade'. What he was saying was that they were elite troops needed at the German battlefront, and not wasted in Greece. He stuck to this demand but had no choice, under political dictate, and had to allow two more brigades into Greece. The Americans were less keen on this venture; as Brooke wrote, 'they turned sour' and demanded their landing craft should not be used for ferrying troops into Greece. Even at the end of the month Churchill dashed off to Greece to 'sort out the mess'. This had all started with Operation *Manna* and British troops remained in Greece until 1949. Ambassador

---

* This was a sham government headed by Bierut and was later recognised by the USA and Britain in July 1945. The Poles had fought bravely against the Germans, but they were to be occupied by the Soviets and lost their independence until the collapse of the Soviet Union nearly 50 years later. The treatment of the Poles by the West begs a few questions.

Leeper and Macmillan had suggested the Greek Archbishop Damaskinos should be a regent, but the Greek king had disagreed, and this problem took time to resolve.*

As noted above the main issue for Brooke was Eisenhower's conduct of the war, based on his disposition of troops along the complete front and lacking concentration at strategic points, which suddenly appeared to exhibit its weakness by the German thrust through the Ardennes. This naturally raised the issue of the command structure mentioned above. Brooke liked Eisenhower as a person, had often recognised his ability to resolve and ameliorate tensions between the Allied commanders, but he never had much time for Eisenhower's understanding of strategy, and this issue was now coming to a head. Churchill also liked Eisenhower, and he probably had a better understanding than Brooke of Eisenhower's position as a valuable intermediary between the Anglo-American allies. He told Brooke that he found Eisenhower amenable to which Brooke replied: 'I could see little use in having an amenable Supreme Commander if he was totally unfit to win the war for him.'[14] He held these same opinions about Alexander. Bradley once described Brooke as 'hard-nosed' but as any soldier in the ranks would reflect, they would prefer to have an efficient officer in charge of them rather than just a pleasant chap.

It was not just Eisenhower who gave Brooke cause for concern in military abilities, and when Alexander attended a COS to discuss Italy (6 December) Brooke noted that it was only now Alexander could see some of the difficulties he was up against, and 'he is a mere child at it and does not begin to grasp what his task is'. It is essential at this juncture to note that although Brooke could often come across as angry and critical, most of his colleagues found him amenable, and this critical and harsh side of him found more expression in his personal diaries, which were a necessary vent for his pent-up feelings. He was certain that Alexander's chief of staff, Harding, was the cause of the problem, and he had tried for a long time to 'get rid' of him. He knew that Alexander was almost too loyal towards his staff, so he tried a manipulative move by suggesting that Alexander was holding Harding back from promotion which, because of Alexander's benevolent nature, caused him to think; Brooke could be cunning, but not often.

On 12 December there was a critical meeting with Eisenhower, but first Brooke had to try and gain Churchill's attention because he was preoccupied with Greece. Churchill was concerned about the postwar future, having gained Stalin's agreement that Greece, the recognised home of democracy, could stay within Western influence, and Churchill was determined to ensure this happened. That evening Eisenhower explained his plan of a double advance into Germany north of the Rhine and via Frankfurt, and he suggested that this would probably not happen until 1 May 1945.

---

* Archbishop Damaskinos was the regent of Greece between the German occupation force leaving in 1944 and the return of King George II to Greece in 1946. He held this position during the Civil War, recalling the king when the internal strife ceased.

For the first time Brooke was totally forthright, if not angry according to Eisenhower's confidante Bradley, not just about the projected timing, but Eisenhower's 'violating the principle of concentration of forces'. Brooke felt Tedder was speaking 'nonsense' and that Churchill could not understand the military principles involved. Brooke was annoyed that Churchill seemingly leapt to the defence of Eisenhower, and that night he even considered resigning, probably suffering from a moment's petulance. The next day he discovered that Churchill agreed with him, and he had only defended Eisenhower because he was the only American present and Brooke 'was a bit rough on him'. There was probably a high amount of truth in Churchill's insight.

On 18 December Brooke heard that the Germans under Rundstedt had started a strong counter-offensive through the Ardennes against the Americans who had no immediate reserves. Brooke believed they could hold the line, but he thought this offensive had happened because of Eisenhower's disposition of thinly spread troops. He even wondered if Rundstedt as a 'good German' wanted to bring the war to a rapid conclusion by recklessly rushing forward. It was Rundstedt in charge, but the plan had originated from Hitler, living on the hope the Anglo-Americans would face another Dunkirk. Brooke speculated that Rundstedt had gathered how widely dispersed the American troops were, and he wrote that it was only 'Montgomery's prompt action' which saved the day. Montgomery was there, he was prompt in assuming control, but this would later pose many serious problems. Although Brooke trusted Montgomery in the field, he knew his self-conceit could be dangerous, and he 'was dreading how he [Montgomery] would behave on finally receiving the command he wanted, and Montgomery confirmed his worst fears.'[15]

This Battle of the Bulge had been planned by Hitler for several months, undoubtedly because 'a decisive German victory on the battlefield might well implant fatal discord between the British and the Americans.'[16] It transpired that his plans created havoc and panic amongst the Allies; it failed as a German victory, but Hitler's hope that it would divide the Allies came close to working, mainly because of Montgomery's egotistical behaviour. The havoc and panic were created simply because the Allied commanders had become complacent; they ignored intelligence warnings, and simply refused to believe the enemy would initiate such an audacious attack. Eisenhower had to succumb to the suggestion that Montgomery took over the northern sector, whilst Patton turned north towards the gathering debacle. Patton had moved with amazing speed, but it has been suggested that he had gleaned forward intelligence and had cunningly prepared for the emergency; the veracity of this information remains enigmatic.[17]

It was a time of tension. Bradley was understandably almost paranoid about Montgomery, and he decided that Brooke and Churchill were looking to the political advantages and saw Montgomery's bid to take control as a 'political triumph'.[18] Eisenhower, to Bradley's deepest chagrin, accepted Montgomery's help, and he gave the British field marshal control of Bradley's First and Ninth Army, causing Bradley to note that 'this was the darkest of times for me'.[19] When Bradley met Montgomery he recalled that 'Monty was more arrogant and egotistical than I had ever seen him, he began lecturing and scolding me like a schoolboy.'[20]

There seems little doubt that Montgomery saw the Ardennes offensive as an opportunity to take total control, and he wrote to Eisenhower in this vein in his characteristically blunt and rude fashion. Bradley described the letter as 'arrogant' which was a natural response because Montgomery was arrogant, and he was suggesting that Bradley and his armies be put under his control to save the situation. This all happened as the British newspapers were selling Montgomery as the saviour of the Americans. Montgomery, whose public reputation had somewhat diminished after Caen and Arnhem, needed this success for his own vanity: he wanted to be regarded as the all-conquering victor.

There is little doubt that Brooke believed that Montgomery could save the day, but he was concerned that Montgomery would make too much out of this for his personal aggrandisement, and on 21 December, Brooke wrote to him 'that events and enemy action have forced on Eisenhower the setting up of a more satisfactory system of command. I feel it is most important that you should not even in the slightest degree appear to rub this undoubted fact in.'[21] Montgomery had followed his usual 'slow methodical approach to a counter-stroke, which came far too late to prevent the Germans from withdrawing the bulk of their forces', a criticism which for many years would not have sat well with his adoring British public.[22] For Brooke it had exposed his criticisms about Eisenhower's faulty disposition of forces, and the system of command Eisenhower had deployed. From the historical point of view, although Montgomery was enabled to have oversight, the battle was fought and won by American soldiers and the fast-moving Patton. However, Brooke's letter of warning to Montgomery was a clear indication he was sensitive, unlike Montgomery, to the Anglo-American relationships. As the German offensive started to grind to a halt and having warned Montgomery to be circumspect in what he said, Brooke took a week's leave due to him to celebrate Christmas with his family. This was not, however, the end of Montgomery's debacle in projecting himself as the saviour, and damaging relationships with the Americans.

## The Final Year of War, 1945

The Russians had promised a winter offensive and it started well during the first month of 1945. Churchill had been anxious about this and had asked Stalin when it would happen, assuring him, 'I shall not pass this most secret information to anyone except Field Marshal Brooke and General Eisenhower…only under the conditions of utmost secrecy.'[23] Churchill did not have to wait for a reply because the Red Army was already attacking East Prussia, taking Warsaw and crossing the Pomerania and Brandenburg Rivers. In Western Europe there were fears that a German counterattack in the Alsace-Lorraine area might jeopardise Strasbourg, the Ardennes attack was being mopped up, and the debate over Eisenhower's strategy continued.

In a speech at Harvard University when Churchill was given an honorary degree (6 September 1943) Churchill had said 'I would not say there are never divergences of views among these high professional authorities. It would be unnatural if there were not. When they meet, they thrash things out with great candour and plain, blunt speech, but after a few days the President and me find ourselves furnished with sincere and united advice.'[24] Churchill was fairly accurate in stating this, and as noted, there had been several CCOS meetings when the minor attendees had been asked to vacate the room in order that essential issues could be ironed out, and most times there was a sense of some agreement. The clash at the lower level, created by Montgomery in his attack on Eisenhower and with his boasting, was not so easily resolved as even the worst clashes at the CCOS level. Late on 8 December the prime minister called for Brooke to discuss 'all the evils of Montgomery's press conference'; the bitterness was escalating and worrying Churchill and Brooke.

When Montgomery had been asked to restore order as the Germans had counterattacked through the Ardennes, he had responded with a defensive system, and he used the British XXX Corps as a strategic reserve. However, it was Patton's army which was 90 miles to the south which switched direction to the north to rescue the situation, and despite the appalling weather, broke through to take Bastogne, as the Germans ran out of fuel. This had been a battle of major proportions and significance, but it was fought by American soldiers, and it was not helped when Montgomery persisted in proclaiming, 'he had won the day'. In a notorious press release Montgomery claimed the victory 'as his own' which understandably infuriated the Americans who had done the fighting and become the eventual victors. These were comments which had ignited a jubilant British press and made the issue so publicly widespread. This sense of continuous self-glorification almost exploded in Montgomery's face because the Americans complained bitterly; it reached the highest military and political positions, and Montgomery had to be reprimanded and put in his place. Montgomery had made it abundantly and extravagantly evident that in his opinion it was he who had defeated the Germans and not the Americans. It was put most succinctly by one of Marshall's biographers who wrote that Montgomery had implied at the press conference that 'a canny Montgomery had saved the situation and the British Army had rescued the hapless Americans.'[25]

Eisenhower preferred Alexander, put up with Brooke, but several times the military alliance was in danger because of Montgomery's lack of tact. After the war Montgomery would continue in his upward promotion, but he did little to help his reputation as a self-seeking glory hunter, with his postwar radio and television broadcasts, as well as his memoirs published in 1958. In his memoirs his criticisms struck at Eisenhower, but also Field Marshal Auchinleck who threatened legal action, which obliged Montgomery to give a radio broadcast in 1958, declaring his gratitude to Auchinleck for stabilising the front at the first Battle of Alamein.

He had created his own personality cult and tried to enhance his reputation as a great military commander, and although many maintain he was a great general, others held contrary opinions. The trouble was that because of Brooke's unstinting support of him, his own reputation was somewhat tarnished by Montgomery's behaviour. In some ways Brooke let himself down because he had known this problem of Montgomery for a long time, had issued him warnings, but perhaps not strongly enough.

Brooke and Churchill phoned Eisenhower and sent Brendan Bracken to try and heal the situation. On the American side there was sheer understandable fury; Montgomery was already disliked because of his blunt rudeness, and he came dangerously close to creating a serious rift between the Allies. In short, 'Montgomery had made a fool of himself by making it appear as if he personally retrieved – with British forces – of which practically none were engaged – a disaster created by the Americans.'[26] Montgomery had created a major rift and Brooke's over-indulgence of his erstwhile colleague had not helped.

Brooke hoped as the New Year started that it would be the last year of the war, but, as usual, there were the normal everyday frustrations. On New Year's Day back in his office Brooke received unnecessary minutes from Churchill which took time to answer; the next day he described them as 'poisonous'. This was promptly followed by an argument with Churchill over why Alexander should go to Moscow when he had a war to fight, then listening to Churchill demanding that British troops should have more of the limelight even at the expense of the Americans. Given the embarrassment of Montgomery claiming an American victory as his own, which was still widely public, it now seems curious that Churchill was pressing this nationalistically inclined viewpoint. Moreover, Brooke was sad to hear of the death of Admiral Ramsay. He had died as his plane took off in France and crashed, and for Brooke it was a 'desperate loss' because he respected Ramsay and always regarded him as a good friend. Ramsay had been the key figure behind Dunkirk, and incredibly important in the D-Day planning. It is only recently that a good modern biography has been published about him.[*]

On 3 January Brooke and Churchill took a plane from Northolt to Paris, where they were met by Eisenhower and taken to his residence at Versailles. While there they discovered that de Gaulle had taken exception to Eisenhower's disposition of troops because it had left Alsace and Lorraine somewhat vulnerable, and it placed in danger the recently liberated city of Strasbourg. During their conversations Churchill eventually agreed that it was pointless that Alexander should attempt to break through to Vienna, and that Tedder was needed back home; Churchill suggested Alexander should take his place alongside Eisenhower. Brooke tended to agree with this

---

[*] Izzard, Brian, *Mastermind of Dunkirk and D-Day* (Oxford: Casemate, 2020).

despite his reservations about Alexander, Eisenhower also agreed, and Alexander was delighted. Brooke always partially backtracked on his condemnations of Alexander because he liked his company and he was a gentleman; these would have been the very characteristics which Eisenhower would have appreciated. Because of heavy snow they had to take the train to Montgomery who met them the next morning. It was the usual meeting with Montgomery who was complaining that some of the American divisions were understrength, and it must have been a relief for Brooke to escape him and to travel by car to Brussels. During which journey he reflected on the situation in 1940, when he had to flee France, with the current situation of invading a few years later. They flew home, and Brooke returned to the comfort of Ferney Close. After the weekend they all attended a service at Westminster Abbey in memory of Admiral Ramsay the naval genius behind Dunkirk.

The following week was concerned with the Montgomery debacle of a news conference mentioned above, and Alexander's view that there were too many troops in Greece. At the first COS meeting it was agreed that a priority had to be given to concluding the Greek problem, to bring the troops back to Italy where Kesselring was to be contained at Adige (the second longest river in Italy), and thereby be able to provide troops for France. Brooke, in one of his usual forays into Alexander's perceived lack of ability, felt he was 'completely lost in this damned Greek business' and depended too much on Macmillan. He always felt that his old friend was too reliant on advisers, especially Harding, Montgomery, Oliver Leese, and even politicians like Macmillan. Brooke asked himself the question as to who oversaw the Mediterranean operation, whether it was Alexander or Macmillan? This caused him to sit back and reflect, writing in his diary: 'My God how difficult war is to run owing to the personalities one has to handle, and how terribly dull it would be if they were all soulless cog wheels without any personal idiosyncrasies! But to handle them you must be young and full of vigour and enthusiasm, whereas every day I feel older, more tired, less inclined to face difficulties, less capable to face problems.' These priceless personal thoughts, which Brooke often placed in his diary, clearly indicated the strain he felt and the commitment he gave to his work. Brooke saw the same effects on Churchill who was often tired and prone to illness. He knew that Churchill was constantly worried about Greece, and by sending troops to Greece for political reasons had run counter to Brooke's military advice, but at least Brooke understood Churchill's wish to put Greece back on its democratic feet, and supported him. Throughout his diary Brooke constantly threw abuse at Churchill for a variety of reasons, but during this month he reflected on his attitudes. He admitted that 'I retained the same boundless admiration' and 'one could not help also being filled with the deepest admiration for such a genius super man.' He admitted his sentiments were 'mixed' but 'always feelings of real affection for the better side of him'. It is known that when Churchill later read extracts from Brooke's diary, he was angry, but it must have been alleviated by these occasional reflections when Brooke was not simply reacting to a momentary clash, a madcap idea or an incident.

In a curious note Brooke had seen Jumbo Wilson before he was setting off for Washington, and he failed to dissuade him from taking his wife with him, adding that 'I am certain she will crash him in Washington.' It seemed a curious note and it can only be assumed from Brooke's observation that he knew something about Wilson's wife which disturbed him. Brooke was happier with the news from the Russian front where there was considerable progress. The hatred and brutality of the Eastern Front, and the fear the Germans felt about Soviet retribution, meant that the major bulk of their forces were contained in the East, and not opposing the Western Allies. There were also signs of progress in Burma where Brooke felt the Japanese were showing signs of 'crumpling' and he met Browning who had been sent by Mountbatten 'pleading for more aircraft'. Again, he met the Polish General Anders who wanted the Polish forces to fight in France under his command. Brooke recognised that there would be political ramifications to this request. He understood the Poles regarded Russia as an enemy not only because of their mutual history, but the Soviets had joined Hitler in the 1939 invasion, and the Poles had long realised that Stalin was responsible for the Katyń massacre and not the Germans. On the other hand, the Western Allies recognised that Soviet Russia was bearing the brunt of the conflict, and they needed Stalin on side even though it was known that he had ambitions in central Europe, especially Poland. The Poles had fought bravely in Italy, provided some fearless fighter pilots during the Battle of Britain, and after the war were treated very badly by the West. Brooke went no further with his comment because he regarded it as a 'political problem' but he was aware of the ramifications. The other issues Brooke heard were the same as before: Montgomery depressed over American strategy and Herbert Morrison continuing to complain about rocket attacks on London.

At the end of the month, on 29 January, Brooke flew to Malta for the Argonaut Conference and a meeting with the Americans. The good news was that Churchill agreed that some divisions could be withdrawn from Greece for Italy; the bad news was that Brooke and the COS remained uncertain about Eisenhower's plans. Eisenhower projected that his plans were threefold. First, to reach the Rhine and ensure its entire length was closed on the western banks; second, to cross it; and finally to invade Germany. He was still proposing two bridgeheads, one in Montgomery's sector and the other south in Bradley's area of command. It struck Brooke that the British and Americans were not that far apart, but there 'was much American indignation at what they regarded as gratuitous mistrust of Eisenhower's ability'.[27] On reflection this was perhaps understandable, and it had not been helped by Montgomery's constant carping and criticisms which he always made far too public.

## Yalta

The Argonaut conference in Malta started with the British concerned with shipping shortages and stocks of oil at home, but the issue regarding Eisenhower's conduct of the war still dominated the session, and on 1 February, Marshall asked for a closed session because he was concerned about the 'cramping of Eisenhower's style' by the issuing of directions to Eisenhower while busy in the field of command. Brooke's response was that he 'would take note' of what Marshall asked, but he could not promise what Marshall had demanded. Generally, it has been suggested that it appeared that Marshall tended to blame Montgomery more than Brooke, which was a fair assessment.[28] Brooke's reply seemed to indicate by his slightly ambiguous statement that force of circumstances, namely the sheer size of the American contribution, left Brooke little choice in the matter. Brooke had observed many times that he admired Eisenhower's ability to attract loyalty from most nationalities and heal rifts, but he had often disapproved of Eisenhower on a professional basis. 'He proceeded from that disagreement to underrate him as a soldier and a man. Eisenhower was trusted by those who served him. In war that is a very great deal. And he won.'[29] Brooke privately observed that Bedell Smith was closer to the British point of view, though that may have been conversational politeness, and Brooke had, in this writer's opinion, allowed himself to be overly influenced by Montgomery. However, Brooke was probably closer to the truth when Eisenhower first started, but the Ardennes fiasco helped focus Eisenhower's attention. Brooke conceded that after Rundstedt's failure in the Ardennes the state of the morale of German forces had probably deteriorated, or was at a lower ebb, and a wider front might have held some advantage. Brooke had taken note of the fighting in Arnhem, the Colman pocket and the Ardennes, and knew the Germans would continue fighting fiercely. Later he observed to the Joint Intelligence Committee (20 February) that although German forces were crumbling, they had not cracked, and he was correct because they fought to the last moment, right up to Hitler's corpse in the bunker.

It was just after this confrontation with Marshall that Brooke heard the personally devastating news that his close friend Barney) had died in a plane crash near Pantellaria. It was what he described as a 'frightful blow' which according to his diary and letters left him feeling deeply bereft, and 'was one of the worst blows I had during the war'. He had been emotionally close to Barney, sharing his flat with him; they had been together during Dunkirk, and he had been a man who Brooke had found totally trustworthy, while enjoying his cheerful company. The human side of Brooke very much emerged on hearing this devastating news, and during the momentous days of Malta and Yalta his mind kept turning from world events to the loss of his close friend.

After a plenary session on the president's battleship they flew to the Crimea and the beautiful city of Yalta. There Brooke stayed in the ex-German commander's house which had remained in excellent condition compared to the ruins elsewhere, because, he gathered, a German officer had been promised this house as a personal residence after the war. The suggestion that Alexander should replace Tedder as Eisenhower's man had been discussed and largely welcomed, but there was some concern that the American public would be suspicious that this move might be taking place because of Eisenhower's perceived failure in the Ardennes, and it was eventually decided to give it at least six weeks, before the transfer happened. This was a foretaste of Yalta and the ensuing months when political issues started to dominate more than military matters. The Yalta meeting was focused on the political issues of the potential postwar situation and the immediate future, in which Brooke was not involved, picking up bits and pieces of the discussions from Churchill. In this conference Brooke was very much on the side-lines.

There was a meeting at the American headquarters situated in the tsar's palace, making Brooke somewhat amused by Marshall having the tsarina's bedroom and Admiral King her boudoir. There was then a conference with Stalin who had Maisky as his interpreter. It was apparent that Brooke was held in some esteem because at a joint meeting of the three Allies he was asked each time to chair the meeting. The focus of their discussions was to explore the question of the various theatres of operations and necessary co-operation, including the co-ordination of the strategic bombing, which was then left to the 'air experts'. The Russians assured their Western Allies they would be keeping the Eastern offensive going if possible, and the meetings on military matters gave the impression of co-operation without too many issues.

General Antonov, obviously prompted by Stalin, privately asked Brooke whether Allied forces would break through the Ljubljana Gap (sometimes called Ljubljana Gate – a transition area between the Alps and Dinaric Alps leading to Trieste and Ljubljana). Brooke responded by pointing out the difficulties involved, but on later reflection wondered whether the Soviets were testing Western intentions regarding Yugoslavia. According to 'Rear Admiral Morison the Ljubljana Gap was a narrow tortuous route, dominated by mountain peaks, and would have been a tactical cul-de-sac.'[30] It was by now well understood that the difficulties experienced during the Italian campaign had largely arisen by the nature of this sort of terrain. This type of countryside, as noted, was easier to defend than attack. However, it was, as Brooke knew, primarily a political meeting. Later Brooke seemed to change his mind about breaking through to Vienna which was curious as it was not his normal habit to alter his opinions, but he may have become influenced by either Churchill for political reasons or by Alexander. This was a sudden surprise turn of opinion by Brooke 'to support Churchill's Vienna strategy, although he was later embarrassed by this lack of judgement'.[31] That evening Brooke found his relaxation viewing the birdlife outside his allotted residence, which probably caused some concern then bemusement from his undoubted Russian watchers.

That evening he caught up with Churchill who informed him of some of the decisions which had been made. The decision which immediately caught Brooke's attention was that the Americans had stated they would stay in Germany after the defeat for only two years, and that the French could assist in the army of occupation, but they would not be represented on the Inter-Allied Committee in Berlin. It was noticeable that Brooke had placed one of his many exclamation marks after he noted this agreement in his diary. He often withheld personal comments but implied them by this punctuation device. He also gathered that Stalin had been reluctant to offer a toast to the king because he was a republican, but toasted Churchill for the time he stood against Hitler alone. The politics were rapidly creeping into the toasts. Brooke also discussed with Churchill Macmillan's demand for more troops in Greece, cynically observing that Macmillan was regarding himself as the supreme commander, and then forgetting there was still the war against Germany to be concluded. The next day there was another joint military meeting at Antonov's headquarters which Brooke chaired again, concerned with bombing strategies, but this time there was no sign of Churchill.

The next day, 7 February, Brooke was back into his enjoyment of tourism and with a small party and some maps he had brought with him, looked at the 19th-century Crimean battlefields. While he was studying one of these maps one of their tourist group discovered nearby a full human skeleton from the more recent conflict. This was a stark reminder of the bitter fighting which typified that part of the world, and Brooke saw for himself the debris and detritus of the war in that area, writing about his admiration for those who had risen to the defence against overwhelming odds and with few resources. As he continued his tour, he still felt the presence of Barney like a 'black cloud' and was dreading returning to his flat alone.

The conference ended with the traditional Russian banquet of alcohol and toasts with a sense of friendship and good humour, and with Brooke's usual cynical observation that the standard of speeches was 'remarkably low and most consisted of insincere slimy sort of slush'. The penultimate day was a plenary meeting with the prime minister and president, and a dull dinner party, according to Brooke, with Churchill, Marshall and Alexander. After this social meeting Brooke held Alexander back and warned him that he was supreme commander and not Macmillan, once again observing, that true to form, Alexander 'took it well'. On the last day as they were departing the Russians gave each person a parcel to carry with them which was to have ramifications later in the month. When they returned to Malta Brooke went immediately to Barney's grave to lay a wreath, reflecting that his last words to his close friend had been 'we shall meet next in Malta'. It would take a long time for him to acclimatise to his friend's absence. Barney's death had unsettled Brooke more than anything else, and clearly indicated that behind the formidable field marshal's uniform was a warm if not loving personality.

The Yalta Conference, as observed, had been mainly a political meeting which many have regarded as a betrayal of prime responsibilities. Britain and France had technically gone to war in defence of Poland, but now Poland and much of central Europe, the Baltic States and the south-east of Europe were being assigned to Stalin; only Greece, thanks to Churchill, was staying within Western traditions. Many Poles understandably regarded this as an act of sheer treachery on the part of the Allies. Their main underground newspaper in Warsaw declared it 'A disgraceful and immoral betrayal.'[32] It could be argued that the overwhelming strength of the Soviet forces was a key factor, or that a need for a sense of peace was critical, or that Stalin was genuinely believed when he spoke of elections. However, Yalta prepared the basis for much of Europe to move from one form of oppression to another, and it set the scene for the Cold War by assigning much of Europe to the USSR. Brooke's biographer David Fraser commented that 'Yalta has come to stand for Western naivety or indifference, and Soviet brutality and cunning,' and this statement is not wide of the mark.[33] The Soviet objective was to dominate Europe and Brooke must have suspected this policy. When on 20 February he had been visited by Kopanski, the Polish chief of staff, Brooke was told the Poles wanted to fight on but not to return to Poland as a vassal state of Russia, again. A few days later he met Anders who explained he did not trust Stalin and wondered why Churchill and Roosevelt appeared to do so. Anders explained he had experienced being a prisoner of the communists and knew them better than the democratic leaders; his wife and family were still in Poland, and his fighting men expected him to find a solution. Brooke felt sorry for Anders, but the political world was not part of his domain.

Within a few years Anders was proved correct in his predictions about the Soviet takeover of Poland: Poles and Germans suffered in this country after the war, and unnecessarily. Stalin had promised Poland some German territory, and 'six million Poles and eleven million Germans were duly forced from their homes—a scale of ethnic cleansing that went beyond anything yet seen in the war' – this alongside a brutal secret police who had a paranoid suspicion of every Pole alive.[34] The subsequent Russian behaviour would have appalled most people in the West, but during the war it was often seen that Uncle Joe and his people were suffering the most, and it would take time for such sentiments to be changed. The Western world held Stalin in affectionate high regard, and later, on VE day, Soviet flags were prominent in London. There was a genuine sympathy for the Russians created by the bloodletting of the Red Army, but it would take years before Stalin's barbarity would come into the public consciousness.

It was at Yalta that the shooting of German leaders was discussed, during which Churchill famously walked out of the meeting. It was further agreed that all deserters or traitors should be returned to their country of origin. This would have heart-rending repercussions, especially when the British returned many of the Cossacks to the USSR where they knew execution or starvation awaited them. As noted, Brooke was not politically involved and felt sorry for Anders, but still had a war to run.

## Post Yalta

Back in London he took Barney's wife Diana to lunch and could feel her palpable grief which he also shared, but he was a pragmatist, and he desperately missed Barney's discretion and efficiency. He eventually arranged for Rollie Charrington, another old and trusted acquaintance, to take his place. His ADC had to be someone whom he could be comfortable with and totally trust. During his absence the war had continued unabated: the Germans had surrendered Budapest, the Soviets crossed the Oder, in the West the Colman pocket had been cleared to the relief of de Gaulle, and Dresden was bombed.* Elsewhere the Americans had landed in Iwo Jima and Turkey had declared war on Germany, as had many South American countries, now it was safe.

Back at his desk there were further discussions on the rocket attacks, and given the impossibility of defending against them, the COS realised the only certain method was for ground troops to overrun the launch sites. It was the old land-air debate, experienced by Göring versus Kesselring: the latter persistently claimed that to win foot soldiers had to be on the ground. Bomber Harris, as Göring had once claimed with Britain, had also argued that Germany could be brought down only by bombing; it helped but was not the reason for capitulation. Brooke also heard that the SS General Wolff was discussing surrender in Italy, and although there was some truth in this Wolff did not carry enough authority.

There was an ironic twist at the end of the month when the British were invited to an evening at the Russian Embassy to celebrate Red Army Day, and it was only then discovered that they were expected to bring the packages given to them at the Yalta airfield. When the packages had been opened, they had contained vodka and caviar, most of which was soon gratefully consumed. The Foreign Office came to the rescue and sent the Russian Embassy crates of champagne. No one in the Crimea had told their visitors that the packages were not personal gifts, but they were carrying the parcels as postmen. This was undoubtedly a mere oversight, but in a poetic way reflected Yalta in so far that the Russian intentions were often misleading.

During March it became clear the Germans were crumpling rapidly with the Russian offensive in the East and the Anglo-American incursions in the West. The Americans found a way across the Rhine at the now famous Remagen Bridge, and just over two weeks later Montgomery's men crossed the Rhine between Rees and Wesel with Brooke and Churchill watching events. A few days earlier the Americans had taken Koblenz, Worms, Saarbrücken and Ludwigshafen. The Red Army had entered Austria during this month, also taking Danzig on the Baltic Sea. It was clear that the German military was in a state of total collapse. On 19 March Yugoslavian

---

* The Colman pocket was a German bridgehead west of the Rhine and south of Strasbourg. The Allied casualties were more than 18,000 and yet more for the Germans. It had endangered Eisenhower's plan for closing the Rhine.

partisans had launched an offensive towards Trieste; this must have caused Brooke to reflect on Antonov or Stalin's seemingly harmless question as to whether the West would go through the Ljubljana Gap, which Brooke had thought even at that time might be testing the waters. Tito was declared the president of the Federal People's Republic of Yugoslavia, while elsewhere the British had taken Mandalay, Iwo Jima fell to the Americans, and most of the Philippines were liberated. Apart from a few fanatical Nazis it was clear the German war was lost, and in Japan most would have detected the turn of the tide. With the end of war in sight for many ordinary soldiers, their understandable hope was of simply surviving; for Brooke it was a matter of realising his greatest wish, the end of Nazism.

The first COS meeting, not surprisingly, discussed the limited shipping with the need to return POWs, serving soldiers and others back to their countries at the end of the war: a numerically massive task. It would take time, but COS was already pondering the issue. Postwar Europe would be fermenting with displaced persons for more than a decade. Following years of critical defence measures, working with Allies and planning offensives and campaigns, life for Brooke had suddenly become much easier. It was almost holiday time, and he was, because of Churchill's similar attitude, able to spend a good deal of the month in Europe, seeing for themselves what was happening and studying the final projected plans. On 2 February he and Rollie took off with Churchill and others in Churchill's new C54 plane, which Brooke described as comfortable.* First they flew to Brussels then on to Eindhoven where they met Montgomery and stayed overnight in Eisenhower's train which he had sent for them. They had dinner with Montgomery and Brooke attended Montgomery's usual daily briefing which he found 'impressive'.

Next day they motored to Maastricht and met Simpson and the Ninth American Army then under Montgomery's command. They then pressed on towards Aachen, pausing at the Siegfried Line, where Churchill decided to stop and deliberately relieved his bladder over the tank traps, as Brooke hurriedly stopped excited photographers capturing the shot of a lifetime. Later in the month Brooke watched Churchill do the same in the Rhine with self-evident pleasure and to Brooke's bemusement. They visited Aachen and saw the extensive damage, and Brooke wrote that at least the buildings were German, not British, Belgian or French. He was curious on inspecting a citadel brick fort which had been attacked using flame throwers after the doors had been blasted open with artillery. He was always interested in military innovations. They moved on rapidly towards Nijmegen and met Crerar with his Canadian forces, then encountered the 51st Highland Division which Brooke could recall so vividly from his time in 1940 France. Throughout this journey so close to the front line, Brooke's mind kept reflecting on how far they had travelled over the

---

* The C54 was derived from the commercial DC-4 airliner, and the C54 Skymaster, as it was known, was used by the American land and sea forces.

last four to five years, from retreat and defeat at Dunkirk to standing on the borders of Germany as an invasion force. This was a significant time in history in which Brooke revelled. Churchill was equally enthralled and wanted to be close to the action and watch the crossing of the Rhine. It is easy to gain the impression from the more restrained diary entries that Brooke felt the same excitement as Churchill without expressing it directly.

They had time with Eisenhower, and Brooke spoke privately to him about Alexander, telling him to be honest over whether he needed Alexander or not; Brooke had become aware that Eisenhower was conscious that he did not want to unsettle his current team. Despite the moment of growing success by the American commander, Brooke could not restrain his personal sense of criticism, noting that 'there is no doubt that he is a most attractive personality and at the same time a very very small brain from a strategic point of view'.[35] He pondered on the problem that Eisenhower's relationship with Montgomery was insoluble, mainly because Eisenhower was only capable of seeing Montgomery's worse side, which to be fair to Eisenhower, was not easy to avoid. When Eisenhower's later personal records are read, as well as those of others, it was equally surprising that Brooke failed to see how obnoxious and infuriating Montgomery could be. Brooke may have thought little of Alexander's military ability, but at least he behaved in a gentlemanly way and made friends and not enemies out of his own allies. Montgomery unquestionably behaved better when he was in the company of Brooke and Churchill, but both men could see behind the outward convivial appearance.

On 7 December Churchill and Brooke were back home with a COS meeting once again discussing the issue of the German rockets, and Herbert Morrison remained persistent with his pleas to do something about the problem. The Germans were on the verge of collapse and Morrison's demands may have irritated Brooke, but they were understandable given the renewed destruction at the end of the war, and the induced fear amongst the public. For many in the British public it seemed unpleasantly strange that the Allies were knocking on Germany's front door, yet the V2 rockets persisted in their destructive attacks. The shipping problems had yet to be resolved and the Dutch prime minister was pleading for food supplies to the still-occupied part of the Netherlands, where starvation had become a critical issue if not a grim emergency. In times of extreme war some basic humanitarian cries for help were often neglected. There was starvation in the Channel Islands, and the news of the extermination camps (where Jews and others were being systematically liquidated) was arriving and met with surprisingly little response, mainly because everything was dominated by the singular goal of finally crushing the Nazi regime. There was still a pocket of German occupation in the Netherlands, which was best described as a gnawing problem, but in response to the Dutch plea Brooke decided that Montgomery's plans for crossing the Rhine could not be changed. For Brooke it was much more important to push into Germany than 'clean up the mess in

Holland' which was mainly created by the debacle at Arnhem, and the political and military wish which had been to beat the Americans across the Rhine; this was the political heat of war.

Montgomery was planning to cross the Rhine on the 24th, two weeks after Brooke had met the Dutch prime minister, and he had warned Montgomery not to send dismissive letters to the prime minister. Montgomery responded by sending Churchill and Brooke an invitation to come and watch the battle taking place. Brooke knew he would not be able to stop Churchill – 'nothing on earth will stop him' – but he was concerned he might be in danger and make a nuisance of himself.

During these days Brooke heard more about the possibility of the peace terms in Italy being organised around the figure of SS General Wolff, but he was uncertain about this move and regarded it as somewhat 'fishy'. Brooke was right to regard the development as 'fishy'; what he did not know at the time was that as he returned to London and was discussing 'shopping issues' on 8 March, Karl Wolff and Kesselring had been discussing the future of the Italian campaign, but Kesselring was ordered to Berlin to be given new orders and 'told to hurry'.[36] 'Nothing since the 20 July plot had agitated Hitler so much as the capture of the bridge at Remagen' which gave him the excuse to sack Rundstedt, who according to Hitler 'seemed only to want to retreat', though of course Rundstedt had little option.[37] Kesselring suggested to Hitler's office that he was needed in Italy and was suffering from an injury, but was told by Keitel this 'would hold no water with the Führer'.[38] Hitler had prided himself on the defences of the Western Wall but after Remagen was lost, 'the barrel flowed over.'[39] Hitler trusted Kesselring, stating at a Führer conference on 9 Jan 1945 that 'as you saw with Kesselring, if someone does it right, it does work.'[40] Kesselring had a reputation as a 'tough commander-in-chief...a leader of high professional competence who took care to keep out of politics. He was an arch-loyalist...however grim the military situation', in some ways Brooke's German counterpart, but Brooke was not a war criminal.[41]

In Switzerland SS General Wolff had held secret meetings with Allen Dulles to finish the war in Italy for fear of a communist take-over.[*] Harold Macmillan claimed that 'the first indications that some of Kesselring's officers wished to treat for terms had reached us on 8 March' and that Wolff, together with an OKW representative, was presumably from Kesselring's staff.[42] At this stage it was pure speculation on the part of Macmillan. The British assumed that Kesselring was cognisant, and Eugen Dollmann, postwar, claimed he was.[43] Wolff visited Kesselring on 23 March to persuade him to allow Vietinghoff to surrender. Kesselring was obviously aware

---

[*] It is has been suggested that Wolff was not seeking peace, but working for Himmler to create problems with Stalin's paranoia that the West was making peace. When Wolff sent an optimistic message to Dulles that Kesselring was ready for further discussion it has been suggested it 'was intended for Stalin's agents.' See Padfield, Peter, *Himmler Reichs Führer-SS* (London: Cassell & Co, 2001) pp. 574/6.

of this operation which the Allies had named Operation *Sunrise*.* Following a row with Wolff, Kesselring had 'backed the steps that were being taken and agreed to be associated with them, but then added 'that an end only came into question for him if the Führer was no longer alive.'[44]

Brooke was right without knowing all the complex circumstances on the German side, and later in the month Churchill received an angry letter from Molotov wanting to know whether the British were holding separate peace talks, which had unsettled the prime minister. As the rumblings of what might or might not be happening in Italy crossed his desk, Brooke found time to lunch again with Diana Charlesworth (his deceased ADC's wife), and his close friend Adam (General Sir Ronald Adam), and he later arranged for Diana to go to Rheims to start a hotel for inter-allied soldiers. Brooke was no longer under the same pressure, and before he returned to France with Churchill, he enjoyed an evening with the British Ornithological Union followed by an 'excellent film on birds'. From bird meetings to the front line, and on the 23rd Brooke set off with Churchill in a Dakota and headed towards Venlo, the place where in November 1939 two SIS operatives had been snatched across the border by the Germans, not that this embarrassment was mentioned by Brooke.[†]

The next day they were driven to the front to observe the action; it was a hazy day, but they could still see the operation taking place. Brooke found it a 'wonderful sight' watching transport planes with paratroopers followed by the gliders. Later Brooke took a plane flight with Montgomery to observe the target areas. The plan was working well, but the 51st Highland Division lost their commander in some bitter fighting, because in their sector they met an experienced and battle-hardened German parachute regiment. It was so successful that Brooke wondered whether the Germans would now consider surrendering. 'It seems unlikely,' he wrote, 'that the German soldier in the East will be induced to go on fighting when he hears the German soldier in the West had packed up.' He was wrong in this perception. What he would learn later was that the war on the Eastern Front was far from a 'clean-war' but it was bitter with recrimination and retribution, rape and massacre, and for many Germans it was better to die in the heat of battle than become a Soviet prisoner. The Germans and Russians treated and viewed one another as mere scum to be eliminated, and they fought one another to the doors of Hitler's bunker.

Brooke and Churchill celebrated Palm Sunday in Venlo, and then they visited Wesel (North Rhine-Westphalia and Wesel which was the capital of this district)

---

* The Americans appeared to trust Wolff and when later 'Nuremberg prosecutors gathered three folders of evidence relevant to Wolf's administrative involvement in war crimes, including the extermination of European Jewry' he still found protection from Dulles; see Salter, Michael, *Nazi War Crimes, US Intelligence & Selective Prosecution at Nuremberg* (Oxford: Routledge-Cavendish, 2007) p.25.

† Best and Stevens were the two agents working for the 'Z' organisation; see Payne Best, Captain S., *The Venlo Incident* (Barnsley: Frontline Books, 2009).

only to discover it was not German free, but snipers were still present with shelling just ahead of them, and also behind their position. Brooke could see that Churchill was thrilled to be in this situation, but the commander, Simpson, told them he was responsible for their safety and they had to leave quickly. Brooke was amused that 'the look on Winston's face was just like that of a small boy being called away from his sandcastles by his nurse'.[45] He was pleased that Churchill was 'obedient' and they managed to extricate him from the battle. They also picked up the news that Patton's forces were moving successfully in the south.

Brooke's hopes that the Germans would surrender soon, as noted, were not to be fulfilled, but the end was now in sight, and the German civilians were as unhappy as the French had been with the carnage in Normandy. Kesselring also reported that the population 'was playing a negative role in the struggle against the advancing American forces' in so far that town and village deputations were begging German officers to go around them, and many of them were yielding to these desperate pleas.[46] Hitler was not impressed, claiming 'that can't be any concern any longer, get them out', and it was not until 'the Americans were advancing on all fronts, both Kesselring and Model decided against any more destruction.'[47] Westphal claimed that Kesselring ignored Keitel's and Bormann's instruction that every town and village should be defended, by commanding that positions be taken up outside the boundaries.[48] War was bloody and destructive, but the population in the West was happier to admit defeat than those more terrified in the Eastern zones of Soviet operations.

Churchill and Brooke arrived back in London on 27 March and their boisterous equilibrium was immediately disturbed by news that Eisenhower had been directly in touch with Stalin, which in Bradley's views unsettled the British. He was right in this observation because both Brooke and Churchill belonged to the traditional school of thought that a general's job was military and not political (this pattern of perceived political interference would be replicated by MacArthur in later years), and Brooke's vitriol was further raised on reading the telegram which, in his opinion, was so 'badly worded' he could hardly understand what it was asking. The basic message of the telegram was Eisenhower's effort to try and co-ordinate operational plans with Stalin, which Brooke regarded as above Eisenhower's pay grade. There were of course some serious political and military ramifications to this episode. In terms of a general oversight, Eisenhower was proposing to drive on a main axis via Erfurt to Leipzig towards Dresden, taking the Allies to the upper Elbe. There was no mention of the north or Berlin. Eisenhower also planned to direct Simpson's Ninth Army away from Montgomery's command and back to that of Bradley. Brooke was inclined to see this as symptomatic of issues in national prestige, which was surfacing all too rapidly, but he warned Montgomery not to make personal representations to Eisenhower. Stalin had replied to Eisenhower claiming that he was happy, and that Berlin was no longer politically or militarily important, which was self-evidently deceptive. Whether Eisenhower was right or wrong will long be debated, with

American and British nationalism too often involved. It would be during April that the tensions would rise, but in the meantime Brooke took himself off salmon fishing in the River Test on the Broadlands estate (Mountbatten's home), only to be called back by Churchill for a meeting at 11.30 a.m. on Easter Sunday morning.

The first day of April was consumed by the Chequers meeting with Churchill, who was concerned about Eisenhower and especially his intercourse with Stalin, and he wanted to send a telegram to the president. Brooke appeared somewhat more circumspect, noting that Eisenhower had not changed his plans that much, but was heading for Leipzig instead of Berlin – although at no time did it appear that Eisenhower had been directed to head for Berlin, only to win the war. Most Americans, including their president and their COS, felt that there was nothing wrong in the supreme commander adjusting his plans or communicating with Stalin. It had become yet another issue in the Anglo-American camp, and Brooke recalled Churchill's quip that 'there is only one thing worse than fighting with Allies, and that is fighting without them.'[49] Two days later Tedder attended the COS meeting to explain why Eisenhower had taken this decision, stating that Eisenhower had taken exception to a directive issued by Montgomery. Brooke was astonished that Eisenhower should 'call on Stalin in order to control Montgomery'. Brooke had once said it was a shame that Eisenhower only saw the one side of Montgomery, but it was also conversely true that Brooke only saw the better side. Perhaps he should not have been surprised that Montgomery was somewhere mixed up within this recent problem. A week later there was a difficult COS meeting as they tried to understand one of Churchill's Minutes, which was so obscure Brooke thought he must have dictated it when he was 'tight'. This memo was an abusive wire to Tedder about failing in his post for not letting the British know what Eisenhower was thinking. Brooke thought this unfair because often Churchill would communicate with Eisenhower directly, keeping Tedder out of the loop.

The British were not the only ones to question why the Allied thrust should head to Leipzig and not Berlin, and why stop at the Elbe. Patton had wanted to take Berlin, and do so quickly, but more wisely Bradley had forecast that it could cost about 100,000 casualties, which was close to the mark when Russian casualty figures became known. When Simpson reached the Elbe, he suggested that he should be given permission to head towards the German capital, but he had received a firm negative response to the suggestion. Some jeeps drove to the outskirts of Berlin without resistance, but the Germans were fighting in the East. Eisenhower gave three reasons to reporters why they had stopped: their armies were already beyond the agreed zones with the Soviets, he wanted to keep casualties down, and Berlin was only a political objective and not a military one, which should have been music to Brooke's ears. Most commentators regarded Eisenhower's wish to keep Allied casualties down as the real reason, and many believed this was the correct decision given the massive Russian death toll in taking Berlin. However, although this decision was probably right, there is the argument that perhaps the Germans would have surrendered more quickly in Berlin against the Western Allies, who were regarded as less brutal.

The Russian viewpoint was somewhat different, Stalin was fixated on taking Berlin, and in a telegram to Molotov (19 April 1945) he mentioned that 'we are 35 kilometres from Berlin. Zhukov moves at 4–5 km a day, Konev is faster at 10–12 km. As for allies, they are as far as can be seen, stuck at the Elbe.' In his reply to Eisenhower, Stalin had been his usual cunning self and told Eisenhower that Berlin was no longer of military or political interest, when in fact he was desperate to be the one who entered the Nazi centre at any cost.

The resisting Germans were clearly no match for General Zhukov's army advancing on Berlin who poured troops in to ensure he was there before others: 'He was probably to lose more men in this one operation than the US army lost in the whole of the war.'[50] If this assertion is correct, which it probably is, it demonstrated the lack of Soviet care for its soldiers, the fanaticism of the German defenders, and the fear of Stalin who had demanded this success at any cost from his military commanders. The benefit of hindsight provides the possibility that the Germans may have surrendered more quickly to the Western Allies, but Brooke, Eisenhower, Churchill and few others could risk this speculation, and Omar Bradley was close to the mark with his projected casualty forecasts.

As the European war was heading towards this bloody conclusion, Brooke must have felt as if he were almost on holiday, looking for a specialist book on ducks, only to be called back by Churchill. The prime minister was concerned about a Soviet accusatory telegram that the British were 'faking a surrender of Kesselring's forces on the Western front'. The Americans had experienced the same biting communication, and as Brooke noted, it at least had the effect of drawing the Anglo-Americans together again. There was a quick COS meeting and Brooke was back in the shops to find his book on ducks. It was also decided that Montgomery would be the 'Gauleiter' for the British zone, a German word used with an ironic twist, and a task which Brooke did not envy him. It was at this stage (10 April) that Brooke felt the war was stagnating once more, unless Stalin 'kicked-off again', which he was doing by ordering his commanders to race towards Berlin as mentioned above.

Brooke was pleased that Grigg asked if he would stay on as CIGS after the election, telling Brooke with Benita present that he was 'one of the few he had seen Winston would listen to'. Brooke said he would, but he intended to resign after the war had finished. On 17 April Brooke attended a memorial service for Roosevelt at St Paul's Cathedral, which for a reader of his diary is a sharp reminder that it is not a history book or chronicle, because Roosevelt had died on the 12th of the month, unmentioned by Brooke. On the same day as this service Brooke heard more sad news from Alexander that his grand-nephew Henry (whose parents were Basil and Cynthia) had been killed. Following the death of Roosevelt, Marshall became more robust, but Britain was suffering serious financial problems, the Americans had more troops and resources in Europe than the British and Commonwealth together, which both Churchill and Brooke recognised; Brooke was reduced to expressing his opinions only in his diary. Neither Churchill, Brooke nor anyone else could change the tide of events that meant Britain was losing its status as a world power. The empire, most realised, was on the verge of seeking independence, the financial deficit would not be resolved until the next century, and American and Russian military power and resources were self-evident; this was not to do with individuals, but the march of history.

The next day discussions were back to postwar decision-making, and the formation and designation of the French zone. The general feeling was that the French should not be next door to the Russians, not split the Anglo-Americans, and not stop American communications with Bremerhaven, and no satisfactory decision could be arrived at on such a delicate and nebulous policy. Generally, apart from the Anglo-American friction over the British attitude towards Eisenhower's telegram, this month was more holiday time for Brooke, and he intended to go fishing in the last week of April. Before he did so, on 20 April, he wrote in his diary that if Hitler committed suicide it would bring the European war to a conclusion; while he was fishing in Scotland Hitler obliged and shot himself on the 30th, leaving the hapless Dönitz to take charge as the Nazi regime folded in on itself.

Brooke did not hear about the death of Hitler until he heard the news broadcast and found himself strangely unmoved by this event which he had hoped to hear. On reflection he decided that 'I think that I could have become so war weary with the continual strain of the war that my brain is numbed, and incapable of feeling intensely.'[51] Even a week later, just before the official VE Day, he was reflecting that 'I can't feel thrilled, my main sensation is one of infinite mental weariness.' When he was summoned next morning to see Churchill, the prime minister was explaining the situation on the phone to the king, and Brooke could see that Churchill 'was evidently seriously affected by the fact that the war was to all intents and purposes over as far as Germany was concerned.' However, Brooke continued to worry and wonder as to whether the surrender processes by Keitel would control the 50-odd German divisions still in Czechoslovakia.

The month of May 1945 was a momentous time; the Red Army took Berlin on 2 May, and two days later on Lüneburg Heath Montgomery took the surrender of the Germans in north Germany, Denmark and the Netherlands, and later found himself with the problem of caring for one million German POWs and 400,000 Russians. The Germans surrendered in Italy and Norway, Jodl signed the unconditional surrender at Rheims, and Keitel confirmed this in Berlin. Stalin had protested it all had to be done in the German capital, despite his previous claim it held no political value, and it was eventually agreed that 8 May would thereafter become known as VE Day (Victory in Europe). As this was happening in Europe the British had taken Rangoon, and Burma was cleared of the Japanese army. This was a timely reminder that German surrender in Europe was accomplished, but Japan was still fighting, and at the first COS meeting in May, even before they had realised that Hitler had killed himself, there were discussions about long-range bombers near Formosa, the British taking over the south-west Pacific area, and managing British manpower for the Far East.

In Europe, the war had all but ceased apart from some few forgotten units, but Europe was in an unbelievable mess: impoverished, destroyed in places beyond recognition, demoralised and with millions of displaced persons. Prisoner of War camps had to be emptied and men returned to their homes; the horror of the extermination camps was being seen first-hand; German soldiers were imprisoned and checked for war criminals, and the SS was looked at with meticulous scrutiny. There had been seismic population changes, and this was not going to stop. The military situation in Europe was closing in combat terms, but the political problems were soon accruing.

When Churchill raised the question of a General Election the military leaders, including Brooke, were wary that this might lead to a dispersal of effort; not that the COS could pontificate their strategy on democratic elections. Amidst all this turbulence of joyful cheering and emerging concerns Brooke still managed, because it was May and bird nesting time, to take more days off than he ever had before to photograph bullfinches, black caps, hawfinches and nightingales whose names punctuate notes of a more global nature. He even found time to mend his broken rabbit hutch.

As noted earlier many Germans had been more inclined to surrender to the West rather than to Soviet troops of whom they were terrified, but the issue was resolved by sheer force and having no choice. The first problems were emerging as Alexander reported that there were glitches in Trieste where Tito was making claims. But first came the joyful 8 May VE Day celebrations, of which Brooke amusingly noted it was a day 'disorganised by victory' that 'I can put up with.' He made his way through the crowds to a meeting at Buckingham Palace then back to a balcony in Whitehall. Lady Grigg later told him that she had watched the crowds looking at him and realised they did not know who he was, the 'man who had won the war'. Brooke's obscurity was often commented on by friends and colleagues, but he never sought the limelight, and most people had never heard of the COS. Churchill rarely mentioned this main War Committee in his speeches. It was more spectacular to be a field commander such as Montgomery, Alexander, Eisenhower, Patton or Bradley, but few realised that these men depended on directions from the COS and men like Brooke. Victory in Europe Day caused Brooke to reflect on his faith, writing that 'I am not really a highly religious individual according to many people's outlook. I am however convinced that there is a God all powerful looking after the destiny of the world,' and his conviction had been made deeper by the war in which he had perceived 'God's guiding hand'. Ecclesiastical historians had noted that church attendance had dropped after the devastation of the Great War, but Brooke was one of those people who knew that humanity had free will and had brought the devastation upon itself. VE Day Two, 9 May, was declared a national holiday, and Brooke, a man who enjoyed the solitary life in the countryside, amusingly noted that 'Englishmen apparently enjoy spending such a holiday by crowding together into the smallest possible space.'

After the two days celebrating the end of the German war Brooke was back in his office with meetings concerning the Far Eastern war and the signs of emerging problems in Europe. Of growing concern was de Gaulle who was seeking to restore the glory of France by re-gathering the remnants of the French Empire. The Americans, who would soon seek worldwide influence, were against the old European empires, and were not happy about France looking to reassert itself in Indochina (Vietnam, Cambodia and Laos) and in Syria and the Lebanon (the Levant). Brooke could see 'trouble brewing up' as de Gaulle wanted 'his clutches on his share of the world'. The COS meetings were looking at this issue and the question of Tito in Trieste, as well as the problems arising from the Soviet Russian presence. Churchill was pleased that the new President Truman was inclined to be 'tough' on the Tito situation. Tito was refusing to withdraw from Istria (the largest peninsula in the Adriatic Sea between the Gulf of Trieste and the Kvarner Gulf) and de Gaulle was sending forces to the Levant, but he would not remove his troops from north-west Italy over which the Italians protested; as Brooke noted, the 'vultures of Europe were gathering'. The European war had stopped, but already new tensions were emerging from the detritus of the conflict, and this may well have occupied Brooke's mind as he attended the service of Thanksgiving in St Paul's Cathedral.

There were discussions with Churchill about and with Eisenhower, and over Montgomery's deputy (Weeks) in his role of ruling the British zone in Germany. None of this hindered Brooke from his enjoyment with fishing alongside Andrew Cunningham at Broadland and his photographing of birds. COS meetings were consumed by the Foreign Office proposals for starting the Allied Commission in Germany, closing Eisenhower's headquarters. There was some concern over Churchill's proposal to hold back on certain areas, which had been agreed would come under Soviet dominance, but Churchill now wanted to use them as bargaining chips. Churchill never lost his suspicions about communism or Stalin, and he knew that hard-nosed bargaining was all the Russian dictator understood. Nevertheless, Brooke thought this was wrong, but decided 'this is a political matter and politics are as crooked as rams' horns'. The COS meetings were not as frenetic or as busy as they had once been. They studied with the planners the operations in the Far East, and the growing concern over Soviet Russia's intentions. The possibility of a military confrontation with Russia was raised, which Brooke rightly considered as 'fantastic and the chances of success quite impossible,' writing that there was no doubt that from this time onwards 'Russia is all powerful in Europe.' Brooke considered a war with Russia as simply 'unthinkable'. This situation should have been obvious with the Russian ascendency in military strength, and the concessions and agreements made at Yalta. Concerns continued to grow over de Gaulle's actions in the Levant and how they could deal with this new situation, but Churchill was content to let 'the French and Syrians cut their own throats'. When George Bernard Shaw had once warned that 'we learn from history that we learn nothing from history', this quip may well have crossed Brooke's thinking, and the minds of many others at this juncture, because within days of the end of the German war nationalistic demands and fears were re-emerging. Brooke concluded the month of May with more fishing and watching kingfishers, the only real peace available.

## The Final War Months

During the last months of the European war the main issue was ongoing conflict with Japan, which for most people was finished surprisingly quickly with the invention of the atom bomb; this was good news at the time for Japan's enemies. However, this invidious new weapon, along with the emerging Soviet threat, started to cast shadows over the future, as the Cold War with its inherent dangers started to develop in a world full of habitual mistrust. In June, the concerns of the aftermath of the European war dominated Brooke and others, as they attempted to work their way through other problems of risk areas and the strategy of the Far East. There was, as far as Brooke was concerned, still concern about de Gaulle's 'mad antics' in Syria, and Tito's aspirations in the Trieste area. The Foreign Office was suggesting that British troops should be moved out of Persia to encourage the Russians to do the same, indicating a degree of unbelievable naivety about Stalin.

Brooke had lunch with General Anders in early June who was still understandably concerned about his own troops and wishing to restore Polish independence. Brooke observed the Polish general's anger, noting that 'he is capable of doing the most dangerous things and will require watching carefully.' A month later the Americans and British recognised the Polish Provisional Government set up by Stalin as his puppets. Later historians have questioned the way the Poles who fought for the Western Allies had been treated. Over two hundred thousand Poles had fought for the Allies, and at the later Victory parade they were not represented because of political sensitivities. Churchill was concerned that the Soviet presence reached too far into Western Europe, but short of an unthinkable war this could not be changed overnight; but neglecting the Polish contribution appeared as a serious moral error by the West. Brooke was British through and through, and the fact that Poland had once again become a victim of its more powerful neighbours was not high on his priority list of observations. Britain was safe, the Nazis crushed, and for Brooke this had been his sole priority and ambition. In July there was a degree of concern about how the

Polish forces would react, especially when the communist government in their country was formally recognised; it was an act of betrayal as far as the Poles were concerned.

Brooke was more concerned in these early weeks of June with British troop movements being unsettled by his close friend Grigg (secretary of state) announcing a shorter time of service for soldiers serving overseas. After the German surrender it had been agreed that overseas service be limited to three years and eight months, and now the War Office was reducing this by four months. This was for soldiers who had been fighting away from home the very news they had wanted to hear, especially after the main threat of Germany had gone. This powerful feeling of wanting to come home was entirely understandable, but the SEAC (South East Asia Command) still needed men to be deployed for their military operations. This cutting back of overseas service brought protests from Mountbatten, supported by Portal and Cunningham, and Brooke had a high degree of sympathy for the viewpoint of his colleagues. Brooke put it down to mere 'electioneering' but he never challenged the decision because of his rule of keeping out of politics, and Grigg had become a close friend. Brooke may well have been right with his views on this sudden change in policy being an electioneering device: it was widely known that thousands and thousands of potential voters were overseas. Brooke was also concerned about the shipping logistics, that the new order was 'releasing more men than we had shipping to bring them home'.

On 12 June he listened to a series of speeches given by Eisenhower when he was presented with the Freedom of the City, and Brooke was impressed by his presentation. He had, as frequently noted in his diary, little time for Eisenhower's strategy during the war, but on hearing him speak he started to realise the depth and command of this American general. He wrote that 'I had never realised that Eisenhower was a big man until I heard his performance today.' He was also worried, as was Churchill, that the Americans appeared to be holding to their intention of staying in Europe for only two more years.

Brooke was able to spend more time with his family, enjoying the company of his wife and children Pooks and Ti, and he was pleased to see more of his eldest son Tom, home on leave. As the month ended, plans were discussed for the moment when Singapore fell. There was also the arising question of the last conference between the three powers, called Terminal but better known as Potsdam, and preparations had to be considered. The king had signalled his wish to be included, and although President Truman was happy, Stalin was not, and Montgomery was concerned for his safety so the matter was quietly dropped. Brooke was also contemplating retiring as soon as he could, but Churchill informed him that if he won the forthcoming election, which Brooke had warned him against holding (on the military grounds of dispersing effort) he would not hear of this proposal. Churchill informed Brooke he would be essential to help reorganise the army, and if necessary, Alexander could be brought back to assist him. Neither of these thoughts much appealed to Brooke.

On 28 June Brooke travelled down to Bletchley Park where he addressed some four hundred of their staff, 'thanking and congratulating them for their extraordinary contribution to the Allied war effort.'[52] He may occasionally have been at odds with the JIC, but he had appreciated the clever people who had made such a massive contribution in decoding, deciphering and ensuring the necessary information was transmitted to the vital operational areas.

In early July he noted that Churchill looked exhausted from his electioneering campaign, with polling day due on 5 July. The results would not be rapidly known because of the massive number of military personnel who were entitled to vote, spread widely around the globe. Brooke also heard that there was a rumour he might be offered the role of governor general in Canada, which he initially thought would go to Harry Crerar. This was a post he later admitted he would have enjoyed.

Two days after he picked up this rumour, and following polling day, there were serious riots by Canadian forces in Aldershot which lasted for two nights. Churchill demanded to know what the military police were doing, but Brooke warned him that the British forces should not deal with a Canadian problem. The Canadian military police had tried, but the riots, based on the false rumour that three Canadians were in a police cell, continued with much local damage done in the town of Aldershot. It was followed by court martials and prison sentences, and the Canadian government paid compensation to the local shopkeepers and others who suffered from the damage. The local council graciously responded by giving the Canadians the freedom of the town; an appropriate recognition that they had fought and died in the war, which was more important than a local riot based on misinformation.

Before Brooke went to Potsdam, he went to see a Mr Wyatt at Lloyds bank to borrow money for purchasing a house. Brooke may have dined at the Ritz and Claridge's, but he was poor when compared to most people in his position. His finances were to be an ongoing problem, later having to sell some of his treasured bird books to pay his way. His final gratuity was an appalling £311, whereas following the Great War Haig had been given £100,000 by a grateful nation. Brooke never financially benefited from his critical wartime duties. He was cheered up by his home life and having Tom with them for a time, and he was thrilled to meet Eric Hosking the famous ornithologist well known for his bird photographs. Hosking had arrived on Brooke's doorstep unexpectedly, hoping for his help in photographing a rare bird, the hobby (a small bird of prey), which delighted Brooke. In his autobiography Hosking wrote that it was 'with some trepidation I knocked on his door' and it was 'answered by a man wearing an old open-necked shirt, vivid red braces, and old khaki trousers'.[53] This homely looking figure was Brooke, who explained to this new friend that he was just off to Berlin, but offered the initial help in building the hide, obtaining the necessary permit, and promising to catch up once his business in Germany was finished. He even phoned Hosking from Potsdam to ask how it was going. It is not difficult to imagine Eric Hosking's reaction that the top British military commander, due in Berlin of all places, was so easily prepared to give his time and even phone him from the major world conference in Potsdam, to see how the enterprise was doing.

## Potsdam

Brooke flew to Potsdam on 15 July, was met with a guard of honour, and was placed in 'a dwelling called Babelsberg!' His exclamation mark pointed out the affiliation name of the tower of Babel, an aetiological story to explain why people spoke different languages and often referring to verbal nonsense. The irony of this name was not lost on Brooke. That evening he was relaxed enough to try fishing for a pike in the lake outside his house. The next day there was the usual COS meeting with Jumbo Wilson in attendance, but it was not until after the meeting that Churchill took him aside with the news that the king had asked for Alexander to be governor general of Canada, the very post Brooke had hoped for. This was one of a series of disappointments that Brooke had to contend with, which he always managed with ease on the surface, only allowing his sorrow to be exposed in his diaries. He had turned down the field command in North Africa because he believed he was needed elsewhere, had been promised the post of supreme commander for *Overlord* only to be told the Americans demanded control of this position because of their contribution, and now Canada, a job, he wrote, that 'I would have given a great deal for.' He was, as always, gracious enough to understand that Alexander was suited for the post, and congratulated his thrilled colleague, but admitted that 'I remain with a few heartburns.'

The meeting with the Americans and Marshall went surprisingly well, and as soon as it was over, they came together and made a tour of Berlin. Brooke walked around the sheer chaos of the German capital, and he wrote that 'I was very impressed by the degree of destruction' and on seeing members of the public thought they did not look 'too thin but on the whole pathetic and surly.' To the modern ear this may sound somewhat harsh, but it was the conclusion of a bitter war permeated by hatred and the popular demand for retribution, causing Brooke to note that they had suffered what they dealt out but with '100% interest'. They looked around Hitler's old office with his marble-topped desk tipped upside down and surrounded by Iron Crosses; a Russian soldier gave him one still in its presentation box. It must have been a strange experience for Brooke and others, strolling around the devastated German capital as tourists of destruction, only six years after the war started, and when Germany had once appeared invincible.

The next day the British COS received the American responses which were better than Brooke had anticipated, including an agreement that British forces could join in the final attack on Japan. The British had been operating in south-east Asia with good results, they had fought a protracted and bitter campaign in Burma, and mainly forgotten was the fact they had inflicted on the Japanese Army its largest single defeat. The British now asked for a quarter share in the Pacific operations, but the Americans appeared somewhat reluctant. The other issue was reaching some accord on 'basic agreements,' but there was no sense of hostility. The Far Eastern war was American controlled, they had the vast superiority in men and materials, and as mentioned earlier they were often suspicious of the European empire-holders demanding their so-called territories back. Brooke was taken on a visit to meet the American 2nd Armoured Division, and he was impressed by the tanks and their equipment, but less so with the men. He did not elucidate further on this observation, but the factors at play in his evaluation might have been the difference between the background of the British army, which was much more rigid in its traditions than its American allies, and that like many British troops they wanted to go home and not be inspected by the 'high-ups.'

The next day he went with Churchill to inspect Montgomery's Seventh Army Division (the Desert Rats) in Berlin's Charlottestrasse, and he found himself pondering how these men had started their war in Egypt, fought their way through North Africa, into Italy and then France and now they were in Berlin. They were now parading where Nazi soldiers had 'goose-stepped' in the same place, which left him feeling 'cold'.

Relationships with the Americans were good, certainly much better than the previous fraught years, and the next day they had another tour of the 1936 Olympic stadium and walked through Hitler's bunker which, according to Brooke, was one 'heaving mess'.* After another COS meeting he and Portal took a plane and travelled south to Schongau, where they were taken by Bedell Smith's men to Oberammergau. Here he found beautiful scenery seemingly untouched by the war; there were no conference demands, just an opportunity to fish. He noticed that there were Americans nearby fishing with worms (which he obviously found distasteful as a fishing expert, or snob) and he heard the fish were not in fine fettle because some German SS had used hand-grenades to catch them. Fish for these men had been food, not sport. Worms and hand-grenades could be effective, but it was not Brooke's classical sporting style. They were obliged to fly back early to Berlin because of the weather, and the German capital had been hit by a serious storm which Brooke described as a typhoon. This would have added yet more misery for the capital's residents mainly living in cellars or open rooms, not that the occupying troops or visitors would have cared at this stage.

---

* The Führerbunker, which was an underground complex, remained undisturbed until 1989–90 despite some attempts at demolition. Most of it was destroyed in the rebuilding of Berlin, and until 2006 the site remained unmarked, but a small plaque was placed there with a diagram. Some corridors remain, but they are sealed off from the public. For many modern Germans it is an unpleasant reminder of what many look upon as an aberration in their history.

On their return Churchill took Brooke aside and told him of the successful test of the atom bomb (16 July). Churchill was excited and said there was no longer any reason to involve the Soviets in the Japanese war: the Soviets may have had larger forces, but the new bomb ruled out this need. Brooke thought the prime minister was far too optimistic and tried to calm him down. Later he admitted that Churchill had been more correct in his assessment than he had managed in his own thinking. The emergence of nuclear weapons changed the world overnight with its dreadful inherent threat of global annihilation. The Russians already had spies working on this new weapon with Beria's agents infiltrating scientists in America, and soon caught up with the same type of device. Brooke also heard from Churchill about the discussion of the big three, Truman, Churchill and Stalin, and concluded that one thing stood out, namely it was 'more clear than any other that nothing is ever settled'.[54] That evening Churchill gave a dinner for all three allies backed by the RAF band, only spoilt, according to Brooke, by 'the continuous speeches'. In a reply to a toast Brooke offered his 'to those men who were wanted in war and forgotten in peace', following which he found Stalin pleasant towards him and shaking his hand. Brooke had looked at the Russian General Antonov as he gave the toast, feeling he probably felt the same way.

The following day there was a tripartite meeting in a building called Cecilienhoft which had been the German Crown Prince's home in Potsdam. The Japanese war was discussed, and it was abundantly clear that the Americans held the upper hand, but it was the easiest of meetings, and the next day they flew home. There Brooke was astounded to hear the election results had voted Attlee and the Labour party in, and Churchill was finished as prime minister. Brooke was shocked by the results, and Stalin, when the conference resumed, was amazed to see Attlee in Churchill's place, a situation beyond his comprehension.

Brooke could not help recalling that he had warned against the election, but it was not because he thought Churchill would fail, just that there were more important matters afoot than political elections. Churchill was and remains a great favourite with the British public even long after his death, but he was admired as a war leader, not as a man who could necessarily be trusted to restore the economy and ensure life improved for the working man, many of whom who were still returning from fighting overseas. The unemployment and poverty after the Great War remained a potent memory, and it was hoped a socialist Labour government would be better placed to organise a healthier social future than the Conservatives would ever achieve, given their track record in peace. The Tory party in the interbellum years did not have a good reputation of success in such matters as far as the working classes were concerned. Brooke was sad to see his friend Grigg leave office, and when it came to saying farewell to Churchill, Brooke confessed he could not say much for fear of 'breaking down'. For Brooke to admit that he could 'break down' said much for his deep feelings towards a man he had often poured his private scorn on. He noted that Churchill 'was standing the blow wonderfully well' but it is known that Churchill was shaken by the public's response. He had not conducted the campaign well, comparing the Labour party with the Nazi elements which was language too extreme, because Attlee was well known for not being a dictator.

Churchill's departure caused Brooke in his nightly entries to reflect on his acrimonious relationship with the prime minister. It had started when Brooke had returned to Brittany in 1940, when he had told Churchill over the phone that it was a waste of time and life to fight on in France at that stage, and the personal battles between the two had risen, waned, and soared again in a ceaseless tide of confrontations. It was a long entry that night in which he spilt into writing his emotions which generally only found exposure in his private diary. He marvelled 'even now that as a result of some of our differences he did not replace me' but that it was 'impossible for us to go on striving together unless a deep bond of friendship had existed' and on looking back at his diaries he later wrote that 'I have repeatedly felt ashamed of the abuse I have poured upon him.'[55] He concluded with the thought 'for that I thank God that I was given an opportunity of working alongside such a man.'[56] He was genuinely sad to see Churchill go, and also Grigg who had become such a close friend.

## Post-Churchill Days

July ended with a short COS meeting where 'clouds were gathering on the north Greek frontier'. It had been calculated that there were at least seven Yugoslavian divisions at the border which was concerning. The Foreign Office had originally asked for 10,000 troops and Brooke had told them it would need 80,000. They had informed him that he knew nothing about the mere political situation, but eventually there were 90,000 on duty in Greece to restore law and order, and now they might be needed to defend the borders.

He ended July with Eric Hosking watching the hobby on its nest, and he started August high up in the hide filming this rare bird. This hide which Brooke had helped build was, according to Hosking's autobiography, some 64 feet high and precarious.[57] His time out was short, and he had a COS meeting with Mountbatten in company with an Australian called General Lloyd. He found the Australian 'excellent and clear headed' but as always, he was critical of Mountbatten, writing that he 'was as usual quite impossible and wasted a lot of our time'. That evening he attended his first Labour Cabinet meeting where he was asked to outline his broad strategy. He was impressed with the way Attlee ran the meeting and his way of keeping the Cabinet to the agenda. The next day he had another cantankerous meeting with Mountbatten who wanted Brooke 'to pull his chestnuts out of the fire'. Mountbatten was trying to secure an aircraft carrier from the Pacific and asked Brooke to ask the First Sea Lord for him. Brooke's answer was short and to the point: 'I told him to do his own dirty work.' This time Churchill was not around to support Mountbatten as he often had in the past. Brooke found Mountbatten intolerable, perhaps in his own mind going back to the raid on Dieppe where Mountbatten's planning and decision making had produced a downright disaster. He noted in his diary on 10 August that 'I find it very hard to remain pleasant when he turns up. He is the most crashing bore I have on a committee, is always fiddling about with unimportant matters and wasting other people's time.'[58] The day was made more memorable, despite Mountbatten's presence, because the war in Japan was drawing to a rapid close with Hiroshima struck by an atomic bomb (6 August), then Nagasaki (9 August) and the knowledge that one way or another the Japanese had little choice but to surrender. It was somewhat ironic that Portal at the Casablanca conference had suggested bombing Japan into submission rather than risk invasion, and now with these new weapons of mass destruction it had been achieved.

The next day he picked up Nancy Dill, his friend's widow, and with his family spent a few relaxing days by the seashore at Sandgate. When he returned he found the three chiefs in COS had been created barons, though he was appalled that it would incur him the cost of about £200 which he could not avoid. He also, as the king's ADC, had to attend the opening of Parliament which he found 'interesting but not inspiring' and this was followed by the new secretary of state, Jack Lawson, asking him to do another year as CIGS. The three Chiefs had already talked about their successors, and Montgomery had the support of Portal and Cunningham even though he was unpopular with a large portion of the army.

## CHAPTER 10

# After the War

## Postwar Duties

Brooke was uncertain about his personal future, and he longed for some public and private peace. However, Attlee told him and everyone else that he had the greatest confidence in Brooke, and the new secretary of state Lawson repeated this to him, telling him the new government needed a 'good CIGS'. It was not until January 1946 that Brooke managed to persuade Attlee that he should hand over his tasks to Montgomery. The new work was to become involved in army reorganisation and new deployments, with the massive task of the demobilisation that would demand careful consideration. It was not until June 1946 that this could happen. During these months Brooke was busy on a world tour, following discussions with the government in which he was searching for a global defence system based on zones of interest. Germany was no longer a threat, but the growth of communism, the main fear during the interbellum years, had returned with a vengeance, enhanced by the figure of Stalin and the power of the Soviet Union, as well as some emerging fears of China's possible direction down a similar route.

Brooke had always thought in imperial terms which was part of his title, his military education, the basic premise of his post, and he hoped that British territories and interests could form a basic and formal command structure for global defence and strategy. The days of empire were rapidly closing, and the war had signalled a new future for many of the so-called colonies. Nevertheless, there was a hope at the time for a unified front based on the configurations of the past. In October 1945 he set off on a massive world tour in which he travelled an estimated 40,000 plus miles. It was a colossal task during which he met every conceivable leader from leading generals to prime ministers and even had an audience with the Pope. It might have seemed to some of his critics that it was a government holiday, and undoubtedly Brooke enjoyed the experience, but it was a government mission trying to seek a way to maintain a sense of peace, in a world still reeling from a major conflict. The Attlee government obviously trusted him with a lengthy fact-finding exercise. It was also a sure sign that Prime Minister Attlee had perceived that Brooke was a non-political soldier, who would serve his country under Conservatives, Liberals or Labour.

In Greece he immediately realised that a clearer policy was needed against the constant communist bid for power, and to overcome the ghastly violence which had dominated that country. In October he wrote 'What is Greece going to cost us in treasure and men? Can we afford to meet this liability? Will America take a share?'[1] Because it was a fight against the renewed threat of communism this was a reasonable hope, and Greece was never part of the old British Empire, although often seen as a place of British interests. The Americans were opposed to the old empire states, British, French, Dutch and many others. Greece, however, was an ancient country in a critical geographical situation in the Balkans, and if Greece remained stable and Turkey neutral, it gave a sense of more safety in this area with a long history of geopolitical unrest. Churchill had long realised the importance of this balancing act of power in that region, and Brooke, now the Germans were defeated, paid it similar attention, but remained concerned at the resources Greece needed in support.

He travelled through parts of the Middle East, and in Iraq, Saudi Arabia and Transjordan picked up the same messages concerning the fear about communist influence and infiltration; it was widespread. This threat of communist expansion was real enough, and it would soon dominate American thinking and strategy for a long time, becoming at times almost a state of paranoia. He was pleased that Saudi Arabia was especially keen on a defence co-operation scheme, which in the years ahead would lead to lucrative and often questionable trade deals in military hardware. In Palestine he met Gort who was the high commissioner and thought he looked seriously ill. He was correct in his observations, and it was during this visit that Gort physically collapsed in Brooke's presence and was flown back to London where he died five months later. In this ancient country Brooke was concerned about the growing Jewish terrorist movements, and correctly foresaw the long-term problems which would emerge following the end of the Mandate.*

In Egypt he met a less enthusiastic response to his global plans over a defence federation, though he found King Farouk more in favour. This was a testing of the waters which would soon culminate in the well-known Suez Crisis in 1956 during which Britain, France and Israel conspired against the emerging Nasser, which led to a political conflict with the Americans under Eisenhower, resulting in the downfall of Eden as prime minister. The Americans, who were later deeply concerned about the situation in 1956 Hungary with the Soviet Russian occupation, could hardly have protested at the Russians moving their military forces into Hungary, if the British and French had done the same in Egypt. In Iran Brooke looked at the oil installations, and then he flew onto Delhi in India, which was a place he had enjoyed as a young subaltern and which brought back a flood of memories. His letters and diary indicate that as in World War II he detested any long absence from Benita and his family,

---

* The Mandate was created in 1918 and assigned to the British at the San Remo Conference, with Transjordan being added in1921. It was repealed in May 1948 which saw the emergence of the State of Israel and the Arab–Jewish conflict which continues to this day.

Chiefs of Staff in Delhi (Interservices Public Relations Directorate)

but this was a task he regarded as critical for the long-term safety of the Western world and for British interests. He spoke to Wavell, the viceroy, and Auchinleck, the commander-in-chief, and he astutely gathered a sense of the imminent storm arising on the subcontinent. When a few months later the Attlee government accepted that independence had to be granted with some form of partition, Brooke believed this to be the right decision even though he regarded India as a key point in his global defence strategy. The partition in India would be a disaster leading to innumerable deaths, and was organised by Mountbatten, Brooke's *bête noire*, which later drew down heavy criticism in the way Mountbatten handled the situation. Brooke had always loved India since his days as a young hunting officer, but while he recognised its strategic importance, he seemed to have some understanding for its right of independence.

In Burma Brooke detected a 'degree of apathy' among the 'natives' about restoring their country. This was hardly surprising given the amount of violence they had experienced by the incursions of overseas powers. His son Tom was stationed in Mandalay, and he enjoyed his company as they took time out to tour some of the battle sites.[*] Being with his son Tom, who had nearly died from his illness in France

---

[*]  Mandalay was a port on the Irrawaddy River in central Burma (Myanmar).

1940, was a great joy for Brooke, and made this part of his tour memorable. Having experienced the death of many close friends in a war which claimed millions of lives, he would have been grateful for Tom's survival and company. Tom became in time the 2nd Viscount Alanbrooke, a writer and water colour artist. He never married, and when he died in 1972 the title passed to his half-brother Victor who died in 2018, and the title then became extinct.

In November, on this massive global whistle-stop tour he visited Hong Kong, and then Japan where he was welcomed at the airport by MacArthur, whom he had often admired but had never met before. He had always valued MacArthur's strategy, appreciated his sense of firm approach towards the 'Russian menace,' but this time he detected a 'theatrical streak' in him. MacArthur was to crash from power during the Korean War as he suffered political aspirations and a form of egotism which Brooke normally detested. Brooke had always been suspicious of politicians, sometimes detested them, and although he had his own political views as a professional soldier he steered clear of involvement in politics, whereas some leading generals used their military status as a form of political advancement, Eisenhower successfully, but MacArthur disastrously.

Part of Brooke's far-reaching strategy was that each zone needed a 'lead country' and he had hoped that Australia would fulfil this role, but he was disappointed that after just a few days there he thought the country would be inadequate for such a task. He found that the politicians lived in their own world and the military in another. He detected what he thought to be a lack of realism in so far that Australian leaders could not foresee any more dangers, did not recognise communist Russia as a threat, and were overly dependent on the newly created United Nations. In many ways he was probably experiencing that sense of robust independence that Australia demanded, often questioning whether it should be a republic, and it was and remains only the nature of the current royal family with its constant visits which keeps this question at bay.

He did, however, enjoy his visit to New Zealand, a country which he loved, not least because of its birds, wildlife, and a rural scene like that in Britain. As noted in the interbellum years he had once considered moving there for a new life. The people of New Zealand felt closer to Britain than most others, and this aspect along with their countryside made New Zealand an attractive place for Brooke. Both New Zealand and Australia had contributed in a vast way to the defeat of Germany and Japan, and although some have claimed New Zealanders are civilised Australians, Brooke knew both countries were pivotal for the future; but they were, especially Australia, more in the geopolitical influence of America and Asia than Europe.

He then travelled to Mountbatten's headquarters situated in Singapore, and within this new context found it much easier to relate to Mountbatten. He recognised that there were intractable problems in south-east Asia, not helped by the Dutch who expected the portion of their perceived ownership of the East Indies simply to be 'handed back'. The Japanese during the war had made wide-ranging promises of local independence in many territories, which they had little intention of keeping, but these had engendered a view of a different future for many people. Brooke was optimistic about the French in Indochina, but wrong in this hope, as the French were virtually driven out, and this eventually led to the Vietnam war in which America was also defeated. His next stop was Kenya which he had projected as a base for the Middle East, but Brooke decided it was simply in the wrong geographical place.

He flew to the Sudan, South Arabia (now centred on the Republic of Yemen) and then Italy. It was there he fell into an open drain, damaging his Achilles tendon and causing him considerable pain, but he refused a recommended visit to an x-ray unit because he had an audience with the Pope. To overcome the pain his batman gave him a huge glass of brandy and he hobbled into the holy presence on two sticks, wondering whether the Pope would regard him as another drunken Ulster Protestant. He later observed 'the Pope was charming and never disclosed his feelings.'[2] He arrived home on 23 December having visited some 22 countries or territories. It must have been exhausting at one level, enjoyable at another; he missed his family, but he had met a variety of people. His anticipated strategy never found any realistic future in a world rapidly changing, because of the unsettling ramifications of the war, the growth of the so-called superpowers, and the loss of world status by the British.

He had another six months in office, and he often disagreed with the government, but he enjoyed and respected Attlee and others like Bevan, whom he especially admired. He could also see and understand that his world trip to explore a defensive strategy was already unravelling with India in ferment and the military leaving Egypt. This brought a robust Churchillian letter to Brooke expressing surprise at Brooke apparently acquiescing, not that he had much choice, and Churchill especially raising concerns about the safety of the Suez Canal. He accused Brooke of being misled, to which Brooke replied firmly but pleasantly.

This was a time when Brooke had honour after honour conferred upon him. First, in September 1945, the peerage with which he had been elevated and made a baron, adopting the title of Alanbrooke of Brookeborough in Fermanagh. Many high-ranking people thought this insufficient, and he was raised with the other two Chiefs of Staff to the status of viscount, invested as a Knight of the Garter and awarded the Grand Cross of the Victorian Order. He received similar awards from France, Denmark, the Netherlands, Sweden and Portugal, and the United States awarded him the Distinguished Service medal. It has been estimated that he was awarded some 13 foreign honours, more than any other military commander, which spoke volumes about his international reputation and the high regard in which he was held, but he remained remote in the general public's ambit of interest.

He received several honorary doctorates and degrees from various universities, all of which, given his personality, would have pleased and bemused him at the same time. He was a man who never sought the limelight and had little time for public applause. It was, however, an acknowledgement of his work and the way he had carried out his duties during some of the most fraught years of the 20th century. As he left the service he had two major concerns which he always held, the first was the threat of communism coloured by the Russian variation, and the second was the need for the Commonwealth countries to draw closer together in a sense of friendship and unity. He always remained concerned that there would be an eventual conflict with the Soviet Union unless it broke down, which it did nearly a quarter of a century after he died. He always believed that Europe had to make a rapid economic recovery and there had to be a spiritual revival; the former happened by the 1960s, but the spiritual recovery is still awaited.[3]

One of his last public duties as CIGS was to travel with the other two Service Chiefs in the same car during the Great Victory Parade in London on 8 June 1946; there were no Poles in the procession and most people would have looked at Brooke in the car and wondered who he was – the unknown field marshal who had been Churchill's right-hand man and critic.

## Retirement

In June 1946 Brooke handed the position of CIGS to his pupil Montgomery, the guardian passing on the baton to the one he had robustly nurtured for many years, often to the detriment of his own reputation. Brooke eventually settled at Ferney Close in a permanent way as a private man for the first time in over four decades. He would enjoy most of the rest of his life, despite the fact he was impoverished compared to many other senior and top military men of his status. He was obligated by his poor finances to sell his home in Ferney Close and moved into a refurbished cottage in the grounds, and he even had to sell his treasured Gould bird books, although he was pleased they made a profit. Both these decisions must have been heart-rending. Nevertheless, he still travelled widely, enjoyed his pursuit of nature, and was held in high regard and liked by those who knew or met him.

Having once been the CIGS he was given many honorary positions which, as far as is known, he never declined, and they were, given his character, all positions which he took seriously. It was an endless list of commitments and posts which kept him busy. He was president of the Forces Help Society, the Royal United Kingdom Benevolent Association, the Star and Garter Home for Disabled Servicemen, the London Union of Youth Clubs and many others, many of which are still functioning today with slight name changes and variations. Brooke was never a name at the top of headed paper, but he took an active interest in their affairs and progress, visiting, speaking, advising and sometimes in his old style 'inspecting'. He was an outstanding speaker and on one occasion it was reported that the audience were 'spellbound'.[3] Given that he had considerable experience of talking to large gatherings, world leaders, top military commanders in an international crisis, and had been asked to be chairman at Russian, American and British meetings, this ability was not surprising. He had a sense of timing, was able to imitate others, had an outstanding linguistic ability (orally), a sense of humour and a warm personality which made him a popular choice. For the first time he felt able to mix the skills he had learnt in his professional life with the social skills of the officer's mess. Few people realised, for example, that he could excel and be entertaining with his mimicry, and that he had a broad sense of humour. He also had huge confidence based on his experience of addressing major international conferences. During the war years some people had viewed him as 'aloof, stern and an isolate' but the era of peace released the inner man which had only, hitherto, been cherished by close friends and family. Many still stood in awe of him because of what he had once been, but all were surprised at the 'peace-variation' of Brooke. In the critical war years, he had felt obliged to give considerable thought and planning to his speeches, lectures and addresses, knowing he would be surrounded by critical listeners, and in peace he gave the same commitment. Like many, including Churchill, he would write out his speech in full, pondering phrases and expressions, then reduce it to bullet headings so he spoke naturally, not reading a written lecture. His natural intelligence, experience, and innate ability also meant he was able to give impromptu speeches which made his presence highly desirable at any function.

It was probably at this point of retirement that Brooke started to consolidate his diaries and started to form them into a possible sequence which Bryant rapidly utilised – which caused him so many problems, as mentioned in the Introduction, because of his downright honesty. This literary effort was to have a major impact both from the public point of view and for him.

Because of his financial limitations mentioned above, he had to seek some form of remuneration for his family funds. Many knew or guessed he was in a parlous state financially, and the field marshal soon became a businessman. He was appointed as the government-nominated director of the Anglo-Iranian Oil Company not long after he left the corridors of Whitehall.* There followed, almost rapidly, other appointments as director to the Midland Bank, and to many companies such as the National Discount, Triplex Glass, Belfast Banking and the London Tanker business. It would be easy to speculate that these commercial concerns were only interested in having 'big names' on their list, and since time immemorial firms would do anything to have 'By Royal Appointment' above their premises and on their letter headings. There may have been an element of this commercial self-seeking, but Brooke soon became admired for what he had to offer as an individual. In the war years he had been selected because of the toughness of his character, his incisive mind, his ability

---

\* In brief, this company was founded in 1908 and Britain bought 51 per cent of the shares in 1914; it was renamed in 1954 by the well-known name British Petroleum, BP.

to grasp the essential features of a problem, his immediate assessment of people, and the critical issues which had to be addressed. These life-long habits were the very features demanded by those who worked in business, and his contribution was soon valued because of what he brought with him rather than who he had once been, above all his tendency to say what he thought and always tell the truth as he perceived it to be.

There were other benefits for Brooke beside remuneration, and when in 1948 he was made a director of the Hudson Bay Company, a post which he held for 11 years, he found immense pleasure in travelling to Canada for business reasons. It was an extensive visit with every detail recorded for Benita, even down to his inevitable fishing exploits and birdwatching. He was invited across the border and had dinner with Marshall and others, and he visited Dill's memorial in Arlington cemetery where the Americans had demonstrated their appreciation of Brooke's friend with a magnificent equestrian statue. The fact that he and Marshall could enjoy one another's company was a sure sign that their critical dialogues and heated arguments had not interfered at the personal level. 'Big men', as Brooke would have said, were beyond that sense of ongoing pettiness caused in times of stress.

It was a time of salmon fishing in British Columbia, sledge rides with Inuit people and huskies, and he adored Canada's rural landscape. He visited the company's various posts just as he had done in military days, inspecting the sites and the books, and talking to the personnel. As had been his habit in the war years he gave support to those in the field and his observations were mainly about progress and the way forward. As mentioned above Alexander was Canada's governor general; he often joined Brooke on some of his exhausting long treks, and under the new circumstances sealed a life-long friendship. As with Marshall the debates and criticisms of the past were left behind, and the real friendships could blossom again without the heat of conflict. His letters to Benita were extensive, but his business reports often proved commercially invaluable. He was there for corporate business reasons and personal pleasure, but he was technically a guest of the Canadian government, and his presence was often requested in the military world, not least for the occasional parade.

At home in the UK this association with the military side of his life continued to function and grow. Since 1939 he had been the colonel commandant of the Royal Artillery, and of the Royal Horse Artillery since 1940. In 1946 he was appointed the master gunner of St James's Park (where he had spent hours watching for the scaup duck), a post which apparently dated back to the 13th century, but which then meant he was the colonel and the presiding authority over the whole of the Royal Regiment. From 1946 to 1954 he was the president and colonel commandant of the Honourable Artillery Company; in 1950 he was made lord lieutenant of London, and Constable of the Tower. In 1953 he was given, historically, the highest military office as lord high constable of England, in which position he rode in the procession of Queen Elizabeth's coronation as a major officer of the State. He rarely 'kept on' about the war and never wrote an autobiography or memoirs, warning young officers in occasional lectures that 'they should learn from the past but not live in it'.[4] He used to speak annually at the Camberley Staff College on the role of the CIGS, the COS, and what was expected of officers in the army. He had been a serving soldier all his life, and it was natural that his experience was demanded and deeply valued.

He served in many charities, worked as a businessman, held to postwar military duties when requested, but now had the time to pursue matters at the top of his agenda, his family and his love of nature, especially birds where he was not a professional, but regarded as a highly respected and gifted amateur, especially for his photography and cine-camera captures. He continued his fishing in Scotland, Ireland and even Norway, sending Benita detailed summaries of his catches of the day. He became the president of the London Zoological Society and the Severn Wildfowl Trust, and the Vice-President of the RSPB.[*]

Ornithology was his main pleasure and hobby, and unquestionably this had helped him retain his sanity during the war years. As noted above, when Churchill took his afternoon nap Brooke would disappear for up to three hours pursuing bird books in the local shops. Kennedy recalled dinners at Ferney Close when they watched bird films and the 'war was forgotten'.[5] His friend also recalled the time Brooke had excitedly explained how he had photographed a marsh tit by putting a small branch over the nest to slow the bird down, to enable his camera shot, and all this during a formal dinner.

His love of birds never ceased but increased in retirement. He led bird expeditions to places such as the Bass Rock and the Farne Islands, where he would have recalled the time in 1942 when he had once slipped from the naval boat and disappeared in the water, and to the Hebrides. These expeditions could be exhausting for those who lacked Brooke's physique and self-evident robust fitness. He could spend hours up to his waist in water (as he once did in the French Camargue looking for flamingos), not least because his favourite birds were waders, which is not an implied pun. He was fascinated by rare birds, as exemplified by his time in war-torn Russia looking for the black woodpecker, often following their speculated movements to track them down – such birds as the golden oriole and the little bittern. On one occasion, he helped in an expedition to Spain to the Coto Dañana (a reserve in Andalusia in southern Spain) with the two professionals Eric Hosking and Guy Mountfort, with Brooke writing a foreword for the latter's new book.

In his autobiography the bird specialist Eric Hosking provided a very human picture of Brooke, because in the company of other bird lovers Brooke's more basic and intimate personality emerged. Hosking described how in 1951 Portal had discovered a pair of goshawks nesting near Midhurst and had invited Brooke

---

[*] The Severn Wildfowl Trust was established in 1946 by the artist and ornithologist Sir Peter Scott.

to see them, who immediately took his friend Hosking with him.* Hosking with a few friends had set off on an expedition in the late 1940s to Hilbre (Dee Estuary area) and speculated as to whether Brooke would like to join them. They wondered whether he could put up with the conditions they were living under, guessing that as a soldier he could, and he was more than happy to accept their invitation. Hosking met him at Waterloo Railway Station, and drove him up north, noting that 'the Field Marshal was a remarkably interesting and amusing conversationalist' and he was a 'most modest man and rarely spoke about himself'.[6] The weather at Hilbre was appalling and their hide in danger of flooding as Brooke joined in as one of the group, after which Brooke wrote a letter of thanks, which Hosking described as 'typical of Lord Alanbrooke. Nothing that was done for him, however trivial, went unaccepted.'[7] To give this view further credence Hosking mentioned the time they had shared a lift in the Savoy, and before they stepped from the elevator Brooke stopped, turned and thanked the lift operator. His birder friends never found him 'haughty and forbidding' and on the occasion he had been made Constable of the Tower he arrived late at the bird-site, where the group had made a little cake with a union jack on it with a toy gun. He joined in the humour, took a bayonet used for poking the fire, made Hosking kneel and dubbed him with the words, 'Rise Lord Hilbre.' In this picture is painted the inner man, a companionable 'one of us chaps' with a good sense of humour.

When they had been preparing for the expedition to Coto Dañana mentioned above, Hosking explained they were having difficulty arranging for the poles needed to build a hide be transported to Spain. He was astonished when Brooke organised it through Mountbatten (then the First Sea Lord) and the material arrived in a Royal Naval vessel. This would later provoke questions being raised in Parliament, but they were brushed aside.[8] In Spain, Hosking noted that Brooke and his wife Benita were the only two members of the party who made it to Palacio in five hours because both of them 'were more accustomed to horseback riding than the rest of us'.[9] Brooke was self-evidently very fit for a man in his seventies, and 'he agilely climbed the thirty foot pylon with its three feet steps, and made light of the gruelling heat in the hide' and was less tired than the rest of them.[10] These few insights by the ornithologist are invaluable in portraying the man known for his stern looks, nicknamed Shrapnel, feared by many and who had recently been in the company of the world leaders.

Brooke loved Ireland, he was a freeman of Belfast (and London) and the president (yet again) of the London Ulster Association and chancellor of Queen's University, Belfast. In 1960 he was awarded the famous Boyne Medal, but he elected to live in England, despite his distinctive Irish heritage, and as mentioned in the early chapters had been born in France and received his basic education there. He and

---

* Portal was a keen falconer, and believed the goshawks had escaped captivity, met and mated.

Benita made a trip together back to his French origins, first to Pau where he had started his hunting, and then Bagnères-de-Bigorre where he had been born.

This visit occurred because there had been a rumour in some French circles after the war that an English general had been heard speaking their dialect and this raised a huge amount of curiosity and led to an invitation. While at Pau he met an old hunting friend, and visited his old school and the Villa Jourence which his family had once purchased. He was made a freeman of Pau (and later Bagnères-de-Bigorre) and outside the villa was a statue of French soldiers and a plaque to commemorate Brooke. He gave an impromptu speech in French stating he was half-French and half-English, which understandably was met with delight, but the crowd, to use modern parlance, went 'ballistic' when he paused for a moment, and suddenly spoke to them in their own local dialect known as Béarnais, associated with the Pyrenees area. They had discovered that a British field marshal was one of them, and he knew their sons. At Bagnères-de-Bigorre he was met with the same adulation when he used their dialect and opened another plaque, and for Brooke, he was almost overwhelmed. He reflected that his mother had once said she had hoped for his public recognition one day, even when he had been a subaltern, and he visited the house and the room where he had been born. They even presented Brooke with a copy of his birth certificate, as a reminder that he was 'one of us'. Of all the memories he had accumulated, this reception by French village and townspeople meant much to him.

These postwar years were for Brooke the happiest he had known, and he was thrilled that for once Benita was with him. He was able for the first time, despite his commitments, to stay in control of what he did and when, and he spent many hours at home with his family. He no longer had to respond to the calls from the prime minister, to drop everything and attend a meeting, sit waiting for the next emergency and prepare for another confrontation. In these final years of his life he was seen by many as 'essentially gentle, as humble, as charming, and as exceptionally good with the young'.[11] There are indications that these characteristics were not a late development, but had always been part of his personality, which had to be suppressed because of the nature of his profession; Brooke served with the dedication of a calling or a vocation. When considering the nature and conduct of war the normal human propensities must often be put aside out of sheer necessity, and the strains and demands of war would hide the normal person. Even in his seventies he remained robust and in good health but slowing down because of the natural decline of old age. He enjoyed pottering around in the house and tending the garden, though he had several serious mishaps while gardening, once nearly electrocuting himself with a hedge trimmer, and another time breaking some eight of his ribs on a rotary scythe.

His youngest daughter Kathleen, known as Pooks, married in 1953 (his eldest daughter Rosemary had married in 1945), and there is no question that during the war years, although he loved all his four children, the gift of the two younger ones gave him a 'spring in his step'. When Kathleen died as a result of a riding accident in November 1961 both Brooke and Benita were understandably devastated. This was news which would cause deep emotional pain for anyone. He withdrew from public life, but he had been looking forward to two special occasions. The first was that some friends had put a subscription list together to re-purchase his set of treasured Gould bird books. The second was on 17 June 1963 when he had anticipated attending the Garter Service at Windsor's St George's, but while having a cup of tea in bed with Benita in the room he unexpectedly died, quickly and quietly from a sudden heart attack. His funeral was held at Windsor, and his body interred at St Mary's churchyard near his home at Hartley Wintney.

## CHAPTER 11

# Contemporaries

## Military Contemporaries

In trying to understand the character of Brooke, a man often regarded as isolated and aloof, not easy to 'chum with', and a man of authority who many feared because of his right as the top military man to demote, sack, or promote, it is interesting to hear the views of some of his military contemporaries.

In his memoirs **Montgomery,** in referring to his corps commander Brooke in 1939 France, wrote he had a 'great liking and an enormous respect for him', adding that 'I consider he is the best soldier that *any* nation has produced for many years.'[1] He admitted that Brooke had given him 'backhanders many times' which he deserved, and on several occasions admitted that Brooke had saved him from trouble and always supported him. He referred to the time he was criticised for his venereal disease letter and the way Brooke told him off, but finally backed him. Montgomery was egotistical, undiplomatic to the point of being tactless, always believed he made the right decisions, and even in the case of the venereal disease matter, he later claimed that 'the venereal disease ceased' which was a downright stupid claim to make. He was a difficult man to support, but Brooke managed to do so, perceiving in him a combat commander who trained men well. Later, with Montgomery holding the critical post of helping to plan Operation *Overlord*, Brooke had to bail him out from his habitual problems caused by his impetuous behaviour, which brought him to the point of a serious clash with Secretary of State for War Grigg. Brooke skilfully organised a meal for them, Grigg accepted Montgomery's apology and they became friends for life. Brooke often had to placate others on Montgomery's behalf, not least an angry Churchill. At the end of his memoirs Montgomery was addressing Brooke as 'Brookie' which many called him behind his back, and only his closest friends to him directly. Montgomery looked back and concluded there had been four men who had influenced him the most: his father, Brooke, Churchill, and in later years Eisenhower. In 1946, when Montgomery took over from Brooke as CIGS, he was very much aware of Brooke's help behind the scenes. He wrote that 'I was well tuned to my short-comings,' recalling from previous years that when he had been 'hell-bent on some particular course' the last path of resort his senior staff officers could play was 'Have you consulted the CIGS, sir?'[2]

Montgomery wrote that Brooke was 'not an easy person to get to know, but once you have penetrated his quiet reserve, you see there the splendid qualities that one is so conscious of lacking oneself'.[3] Montgomery concluded his remarks on Brooke by stating he and Churchill together did more to win the war than anyone else, and they were a great pair. Brooke may have winced at this on two grounds, the first his natural modesty and secondly the years of effort he had made to restrain Churchill's more impetuous ideas, ranging from Trondheim to Kos to Sumatra and listening to Mountbatten's project of ice-made aircraft carriers. Montgomery hit the nail on the head when he wrote that Brooke 'is the most retiring and modest man I have ever met'.[4] Montgomery was quite the opposite: never modest, tactless, putting himself forward, and at times egotistical beyond belief, but at least on reflection, he had the good sense and humility to pinpoint Brooke's main characteristics. Moran noted that Churchill admired Montgomery as a 'professional soldier, but he is put off by his boastfulness' and Brooke felt the same, but always stood by this commander despite these personal traits which he found repulsive, and Montgomery always recognised this steadfastness of loyalty.[5] This informs us more about Brooke than Montgomery, and it is possible to speculate that Brooke's constant support for Montgomery may have saved his colleague. This loyalty towards Montgomery often made life difficult for Brooke, caused the Americans to be suspicious of him, and for some critics cast a small degree of doubt on his judgement in his total support of a difficult man.

The criticism has been made that Brooke selected only those men he had trained, or who had served under him, and had an 'aversion to the Indian army'.[6] This sweeping statement seems untenable, and while it is clear that Brooke appreciated certain aspects of Montgomery's military talents, it was only in some aspects, and Brooke's diary and writings abound with criticisms of Montgomery's character and some of his military decisions. Montgomery would have been aware of Brooke's views, yet still held him in the highest esteem, which was unusual for a man like Montgomery.

There is little doubt that Brooke was held in high esteem if not a degree of respected fear and some trepidation. In his official biography of **Mountbatten**, the author Philip Ziegler, who described Brooke as the 'acerbic and intolerant Alan Brooke', wrote that Mountbatten stood in awe of him.[7] Mountbatten was an extremely self-confident man as a member of the royal family, and he therefore had the support of Churchill most of the time, but Ziegler wrote that a member of staff had noticed how Mountbatten, 'who ordinarily stood in awe of no man but the King, approached Brooke with considerable caution and was ready to abandon a project at once if he knew the CIGS was likely to oppose it'.[8] Mountbatten's official biographer also wrote that Mountbatten 'would if necessary fight the Admiralty and the First Sea Lord to the last ditch but not the CIGS'.[9] In this biography it is clear that Mountbatten knew he was regarded as an interloper in the COS, and Brooke's evident attitude 'disturbed him deeply'.[10] Mountbatten must have been fully aware of Brooke's criticism of his ideas, policy and military knowledge, for example telling General Pownall when he became Mountbatten's chief of staff in the Far East, to be a benevolent uncle curbing Mountbatten's headstrong excesses, and Brooke even later criticised his Christmas broadcast.[11] Without doing an arithmetical count and weighing up the language of abuse, there remains the general impression that after Churchill, Mountbatten received the most criticisms and waspish words, even more than de Gaulle and Admiral Pound. As Mountbatten's biographer made clear, Mountbatten knew Brooke regarded him as a mere amateur, even if he were a cousin of the king. In fact, Brooke gives the distinct impression he despised Mountbatten's approach in all military matters. As noted above Brooke thought Dieppe was a disaster, which nearly led to a serious confrontation.

The important element is that Mountbatten obviously respected Brooke, not because of his position, otherwise he would not have clashed with the First Sea Lord, but as a professional person who knew his military matters at a higher level. Brooke could be cynical, harsh, and perhaps unpleasant in the various discussions, but they seldom left the room (except to go in his diary where they were often magnified), and he admitted that he enjoyed Mountbatten's company at a social level, with Mountbatten giving him freedom on his estates for fishing with Portal. After the war when they met in Singapore it was a more pleasant atmosphere for their relationship, and they formed a much better personal friendship. It had been the heat of war with its inevitable tensions which had led to their problems, which were soon put aside once the Nazi regime was crushed.

A close associate working alongside Brooke as Churchill's military assistant and staff officer, connecting the prime minister to the COS, was Pug **Ismay**. His real name was Hastings Lionel Ismay and he had been known most of his life as Pug because of his bull-dog jaw; it was a useful nickname because it sometimes concealed his identity. He probably saw more of Brooke than most people, mainly because he worked alongside him, travelling with him extensively over a long period of time. He wrote that Brooke 'was by general consent the best all-rounder' in the army, that he had been 'an unqualified success in all staff appointments he had held in peace and war' with a 'reputation as a fighting commander in France'.[12] He noted in a positive way, unlike many, that 'in council he was so quick on the uptake that he was sometimes impatient with those who were slower witted' but 'his habit of expressing his opinions in positive terms led those who did not know him well to regard him as unnecessarily abrupt.'[13] This had been the initial reaction of Portal and Pound when he first joined the COS, but it was a matter of understanding the nature of the man. When people became used to him and became 'accustomed to his mannerisms, they formed a respect for his competence as a soldier, and a liking for his character as a man'.[14] Ismay made the highly relevant observation that Brooke's diaries were intended for his wife, adding that 'there is however, a danger that posterity, not knowing the circumstance, will take the assertions and criticisms in the diaries at their face value' and readers might think him self-satisfied, self-pitying, ungenerous and disloyal when in reality 'he was none of these things'.[15] Ismay pointed out that Brooke wrote these diaries last thing at night when he was exhausted, but for many, as the American historian John Toland wrote, although Brooke was 'outwardly charming, he reserved his acid wit for the diary he faithfully kept'.[16] It was more frustration and exhaustion than wit. In reading and studying Brooke's life, Ismay's views are important, because they help expose the fact that the diary entries do not reflect the man who appeared during the day. They revealed the deep feelings of frustration and sometimes the gloom he felt late at night after an exhausting day. The question some people raised at the time and to this day was why he later allowed the diaries to be published without expunging some of the more bitter personal comments, over which Ismay expressed some concern. It was possibly an element of forthright honesty, or a demand of integrity, of revealing what he was thinking at the time of writing, and somewhat reminiscent of Wellington's well-known statement, 'publish and be dammed'. It may even have been the impoverished financial state Brooke found himself in after the war, hoping book sales would increase his income, a possibility in past days.

Watching Brooke in COS meetings, Ismay wrote, 'I would unhesitatingly say that Brooke was the best of them all.' Pug Ismay's account of Brooke came from a man who knew him well as a professional colleague, and the clue in understanding Brooke is to dig beneath the diaries, the stern countenance of the photographs, and look for his emotions, passions, and the man himself; a dedicated soldier who cared.

**Alexander** was a quite different character from Montgomery, coming from that level of English society which meant he was regarded by many as more of a gentleman, which endeared him to Churchill and the Americans. Brooke also liked him as a person, probably more so than Montgomery (whom he preferred on military grounds), admired his courage and his selfless adherence to duty and commands, but as his diary unfolded it became clear that Brooke thought less and less of Alexander's military capability in command and strategy. Alexander must have known Brooke's feelings towards him. Early on in the war, during the *Bumper* exercise (see Chapter Five) Alexander thought he had played his part well, only to be criticised in the post-exercise conference by Brooke for a seeming failure in one manoeuvre, and he considered protesting. The soldier and gentleman in him resisted the temptation on the grounds that it would 'be an attack on military discipline'.[17] During the Battle of France and retreat to Dunkirk Alexander recalled that Brooke had been the corps commander who was 'the most concerned in stemming the German attacks, and handled the situation in a most able manner'.[18] When Brooke was promoted to the position of CIGS, Alexander considered that the prime minister could not have found a 'wiser, firmer, or more understanding military chief to guide and look after our interests'. He then added that 'Brookie, as we always called him, is a fine soldier in every sense, trusted and admired by the whole army…furthermore, he had a broader military background than other competitors for the post of CIGS…and was and is a man of strong character.'[19] Alexander's observation that Brooke was a 'strong character' was an insight that few would disagree with, from Churchill to all the COS members on both sides of the Atlantic, and this was even acknowledged by Stalin. Brooke needed this strength of character to do his duties often against the odds and the overwhelming opposition at times from his colleagues and American allies. At the end of the war it was intimated that Alexander would take over as CIGS from Brooke, which given Brooke's constant doubts about his ability seemed strange. Alexander in his memoirs explained how Churchill took him aside and explained that although he was expected to be the CIGS, Canada had requested him to be their governor general, which he became. This was a post which Brooke had hoped for, but it was clear the Canadians preferred Alexander's style and personality.[20] However, there is just the suspicious, possibly unjustifiable thought, that offering Alexander Canada avoided the dilemma of Alexander becoming CIGS. As an individual Alexander was astute, pleasant, honest and courageous and his insights into Brooke underlined what people thought but rarely expressed.

Major-General John **Kennedy** had been deputy director of military operations in the War Office in 1938; he served as Commander of the 52 Royal Artillery Division in France, and on his return became director of military operations. From October 1943 to February 1945 he was the assistant chief of the Imperial General Staff. He was high in the military rankings, privy to what was happening, and an astute observer. He had seen active service with Brooke, knew him well and shared his love of birds; none of this stopped him being critical, but when Brooke arrived in the War Office as the CIGS, he wrote 'it was delightful to work with him. He was quick and decided; his freshness made a new impact; he infected the War Office and COS with his own vitality; the change of temp was immediate and immense.'[21] He noted the times when Brooke looked exhausted from his arguments with Churchill, but amusingly also observed that Brooke quickly spotted Churchill liked an afternoon nap, and Brooke would disappear for up to three hours, usually browsing bookshops for bird books.

It was through Kennedy's memoirs that it is possible to hear how Smuts had regarded Brooke, telling his listener that 'I have the greatest respect for him. I believe him to be a really great man.'[22] It had been Smuts who suggested that it should be Brooke who took over to prepare for the battle of El Alamein, and he admired the way Brooke slept on it for one night but decided his place was alongside the prime minister. The relationship between Brooke and Kennedy was interesting; it was helped by their love of birds, but Kennedy fell into that small category of people whom Brooke treated as a good friend during the war years, when a close friendship was not always easy.

Brooke could and did have furious arguments with **Portal**; he did not always agree with the other COS member **Cunningham**; but these were powerful figures with personal depth, and like Brooke they could put aside their differences and dash off fishing together, and once again Portal's love of birds (of prey) clearly indicates a deep friendship which lasted. It needs some careful reading in the war diaries to uncover these friendships under the strained atmosphere of those days. It took a man like Portal to listen to Brooke and thereby avoid a planned bombing exercise on a remote island to avoid destroying a rare tern colony, and after the war to connect with Brooke over nesting goshawks.

This brief selection of Brooke's British military colleagues indicated that although sometimes suffering from his criticisms, they had a deep confidence in him as the top military man, and they all admired his military knowledge and wisdom. They all recognised his strength of personality, and generally they liked him as a person, and despite the tensions of the war saw him as a friend.

His American colleagues had their own perspective on Brooke, although it was frequently coupled with their views on his boss Churchill, and often overly influenced by Brooke's pupil Montgomery. The insights provided by Omar **Bradley** in his autobiography are often coloured by his self-evident and understandable distaste of Montgomery. Bradley's aide recorded that Brooke was a 'severe man who says little but looks querulously out from behind his horn-rimmed glasses'.[23] Naturally Bradley himself saw Brooke more often and closely, and wrote that 'in company, he was soft-spoken, retiring, self-effacing, a British version of George Marshall. Excluding Churchill, Alan Brooke was the principal architect of the British war strategy.'[24] Bradley was American through and through and there were disagreements with Brooke over strategy, but Bradley admired Brooke and liked his company, whereas he detested Montgomery. He wrote that 'despite our differences in strategic outlook, I developed a deep admiration for Alan Brooke. He had a truly brilliant global mind… with an equal facility and a hard-nosed grasp of realities and political realities.'[25] In his memoirs at least Bradley was able to separate Brooke from his pupil Montgomery.

Like many others he could see that he and Churchill bounced off one another like two granite rocks, but noted of Brooke that 'his common sense, patience and tact kept the impulsive Churchill in rein, a nearly full-time job it itself.'[26] This was an astute observation too often missed by others and many historians. Brooke would have agreed with this because time and time again when he felt as if he were at the end of his tether, it was usually because of a recent unpleasant verbal clash with Churchill. Bradley was aware that Brooke and Churchill had opposed the timing of the American plans for *Overlord*, preferring the 'British strategy in the Mediterranean campaign, the indirect approach to the heart of Germany through the soft underbelly.'[27] Later however, he had the grace to realise that Brooke had been absolutely right: 'I came to the conclusion that it was fortunate that the British view prevailed, that the US Army first met the enemy on the periphery, in Africa rather than on the beaches of France. In Africa we learnt to crawl, to walk and then run. Had that learning process been launched in France it would surely have, as Alan

Brooke argued, resulted in an unthinkable disaster.'[28] Unlike most of the American team Brooke had fought the Germans and knew that they were in the senior class when it came to military proficiency, and that training and experience were essential to defeat them. Bradley wrote that he knew and admired Brooke, but admitted that in America he was unknown, as Churchill and Montgomery dominated the headlines. Montgomery was somewhat like the American Mark Clark and the royal Mountbatten, good at ensuring they always had the best news coverage, whereas Brooke would not have cared one way or the other. He may have been unknown in America, but this was equally true in Britain where few of the public had any idea who he was, or his major contribution during the war years.

The problem for Brooke was his close association with Montgomery whom the Americans disliked. Bradley said of Montgomery that 'what he most liked, it seemed to me, was a stage'.[29] When Bradley thought that Brooke was trying to boost Montgomery's appointment to command the land forces in November–December 1944, he thought he discerned the motive: 'the prestige that would accrue to Britain was entirely obvious.'[30] This may have been in Churchill's mind, possibly, but it was less prominent in the thinking of Brooke who had the one aim, which was to crush Nazi Germany, and he genuinely believed Montgomery was able to achieve this goal. The Americans at this juncture thought the British were intent on challenging American command, and the idea that Montgomery should have his way was anathema to the American generals and politicians. After the so-called Battle of the Bulge when the Germans struck through the Ardennes, the Montgomery crisis emerged again with greater ferocity and vitriol, and Bradley informed Eisenhower he would never serve under Montgomery. Marshall complained there 'was an overdose of Montgomery' and the friction between the British and Americans became dangerously brittle.[31] On the relief side Marshall believed Brooke had been unduly influenced by Montgomery.[32] There is no question that Bradley a top American general, liked and admired Brooke, but Montgomery with his lack of tact and downright rudeness overshadowed much of the American appreciation of Montgomery's boss.

Brooke's opposite American number was George **Marshall** who was much more a politician than Brooke. They clashed time and time again over various issues, especially over the question of *Anvil*, the plans and dates for *Overlord*, the necessity of the Mediterranean campaigns, proposals over the Istria Peninsula, but apart from one stand-off regarding Stilwell, most of the arguments were not overheated. They shared much in common, not least when 'both George Marshall and Alan Brooke fretted about Churchill's influence upon Roosevelt'.[33]

From the American point of view the British could be stubborn and men like Montgomery did little to calm a growing element of Anglophobia. Clark, Patton and Stilwell were typical field commanders who had no time for the British, and in his diary, Stilwell wrote of a typical clash between King and Brooke when 'King almost climbed over the table at Brooke. God he was mad. I wish he had socked him.'[34] The tensions between the Allies were at times almost palpable, and although Brooke in his diaries typically exploded with his frustrations and with some unpleasant personal observations, he refrained from doing so in public. Both Marshall and Brooke had many problems in common, not least Churchill, with Marshall noting that 'no battle with the prime minister stayed won but had to be fought and refought against dogged resistance.'[35]

Brooke did not always go down well with the American generals, one describing him as 'spindly-legged and slope-shouldered; that appearance and his delight in birdwatching belied his combat experience'.[36] General Wedemeyer, Marshall's chief consultant in the early years, distrusted and disliked Brooke. Hopkins spoke to the president about Brooke, saying that 'while he may be a good fighting man he hasn't got Dill's brains'.[37] Dill, often described as the 'honest broker', had the charms and diplomacy which Brooke often lacked, but no one else would challenge Brooke's intelligence – even Churchill's observant secretary once described Brooke as 'a man of exceptional intelligence' – this reflected the heat of disagreement between Allies rather than the so-called brain power.[38] If one person disagrees with another it is sometimes too easy to denigrate their intelligence as an explanation.

The Americans, aware that their public wanted the Japanese war won first, having been attacked by Japan, probably felt the British were always pushing them too much in Europe. They thought that Brooke 'who understood less than he realised, treated the United States' China policy with a lofty disdain'.[39] There was a high degree of validity in this claim, because Brooke's main goal had always been the defeat of Hitler, who, perhaps quite rightly, he regarded as the main threat to world order. However, Marshall was a rational person looking to the victory as much as Brooke, and if he considered Brooke correct would accept the facts if well presented. As such 'Marshall reluctantly bowed to the logistical reality and acknowledged that a simultaneous *Overlord/Anvil* was impossible.'[40]

The Anglo-American debate became more vitriolic over the constant British mistrust of Eisenhower, and Brooke was as guilty of this as Montgomery whom he over-indulged with trust. When at one discussion Bedell Smith demanded to put the facts of this debate on the table, Brooke explained that in his opinion Eisenhower was too influenced by his field commanders such as Patton and Bradley. When Marshall heard this, he responded that the Americans were equally worried about the pressure Eisenhower was under by the directions and influence of Churchill, which was a valid point. As victory came into sight these tensions were not helped by the geopolitical situation with the Americans moving into Austria, Churchill unhappy about suddenly being the junior partner, and Montgomery's press conference when he suggested the British army had saved the 'hapless Americans'.

Several observers noted that Marshall and Brooke had much in common in their approach and humanity. Moran wrote that Marshall was not one of 'these Americans who sneered at birdwatching…and Marshall felt at home with a soldier who liked birds, gardening, and fine horses'.[41] One time at Marshall's home they shared breakfast together and both were fascinated by a robin feeding its young.

As two men Marshall and Brooke appreciated one another, and even in the heated controversies of 1942 Marshall sent Brooke a large Smithfield ham along with cooking instructions from his wife. In June 1958, the year before Marshall died, Brooke went to the London office of the American broadcasting network NBC for an interview about Marshall. He spoke openly about the past, saying 'we were bound to have our differences, and we had many differences during the war, but we were always able, even after the heated discussion in conference, to walk arm in arm, and go to lunch together still exactly the same friends.'[42] This was a reflection on the past by Brooke and he may well have felt like that at the time of the events he described, despite his diary entries, and he offered some telling insights: 'Marshall always shone, but he was perfectly ready to discuss, he put his cards on the table and we shuffled them around until we found some pattern out of it.'[43] It was intriguing and gave an interesting insight that on the occasion when Voroshilov attacked Brooke over his lack of enthusiasm for *Overlord*, it was Marshall who rose to his defence, informing Voroshilov that crossing the Channel was not the same as crossing a river, almost quoting Brooke's previous arguments.

Despite all their arduous arguments and conflicts Brooke and Marshall retained a warmth and respect for one another, and when Brooke later visited Canada as a Hudson Bay Company director, nothing gave him more pleasure than being invited over the border to dine with Marshall. Marshall must have felt the same way in offering the invitation. In a similar picturesque vein, when Marshall was an American representative at Queen Elizabeth's coronation, he was pleased when Brooke, Churchill and Montgomery in 'their robes as Lords of the Realm pointedly turned out of the procession to shake Marshall's hand.'[44] Marshall had always believed his strategy was correct but admired the way Brooke presented his views, and his courage to do so in the face of major opposition. Brooke always acknowledged that he had warmed towards Marshall, and the feeling was mutual: 'Marshall and Brooke furthermore respected each other as gentlemen, even when profoundly disagreeing over grand strategy.'[45]

Of all the American contemporaries **Eisenhower** had the most reason not to appreciate or even like Brooke because of his constant criticisms. Person to person their social interaction was pleasant enough, but there is no doubt that Eisenhower was totally aware of Brooke's views of his abilities. He wrote in his immediate postwar memoirs that Brooke was 'impulsive by nature, as became his Irish ancestry [Dill whom he liked was also an Ulsterman], he was highly intelligent and earnestly devoted to winning the war. When I first met him in November 1941, he seemed to me adroit rather than deep, and shrewd rather than wise.'[46] Given the way Brooke had heaped criticism on Eisenhower this was rather pleasant, but Eisenhower was himself an 'adroit' politician. He added that 'gradually I came to realise that his mannerisms, which seemed strange to me, were merely accidental, that he was sincere and, though he lacked that ability so characteristic of Marshall to weigh calmly the conflicting factors in a problem and so reach a rock-like decision, I soon found it easy to work with him. He did not hesitate to differ sharply and vehemently, but he did forthrightly and honestly…it never affected the friendliness of his personal contacts or the unqualified character of his support, he must be classed as a brilliant soldier.'[47] This was praise indeed from a man who had been the butt of much sharp criticism by Brooke. Later Brooke ameliorated the strain of criticism by congratulating Eisenhower on his success, but never to the degree that Eisenhower suggested.* Brooke did, however, acknowledge in his diary after hearing Eisenhower speak in postwar London that he had missed 'the big man' in Eisenhower, which for Brooke was almost accepting a personally reformed view. The strains of major conflict marred their relationship based on opposing strategies, and it is a thoughtful reminder that these two prominent figures in history could retain a respect for one another.

The American-British relationship as allies had its difficulties, but in the initial phases the Americans were dependent on British experience and later needed the British Isles as a launching pad to destroy Nazi Germany. The British desperately needed American resources and later their manpower if ever the German Wehrmacht were to be defeated in occupied Europe. They needed one another, but the British were often critical about American military strategy and inexperience, and there developed on the American side of the friendly divide a degree of Anglophobia often epitomised by the Colonel Blimp image. Nevertheless, Bradley accepted that Brooke had been right in suggesting the Americans needed real battle expertise before crossing the Channel, and that his experience of German military professionalism had been correct. He also acknowledged that Brooke was the powerhouse behind the British strategy. Marshall and Brooke had much in common, not just because of their shared apprehensions about their political masters, but they were in many ways similar characters. They developed their own personal relationship which survived the war years and flourished. Eisenhower once described Brooke as sincere, but many of his observations were understandably coloured by their clashes, though he described him as a 'brilliant soldier'. There seems little doubt on reading the postwar accounts that Brooke was respected by the Americans, was generally regarded as the one man who could restrain Churchill, and that he had the necessary experience.

## Civilian Observers

Outside of the military contract, Brooke was not often commented on. General Bradley in his autobiography had said that in America Churchill and Montgomery

---

* According to Eisenhower, Brooke said 'Thank God you stuck to your plans,' when all Brooke did was simply congratulate him. See Toland, *The Last 100 Days*, p.282.

were well known, whereas Brooke was virtually unknown. Certainly in Britain Brooke was not as famous as Montgomery and even some other field commanders. In his diaries **Colville**, Churchill's secretary who was frequently at Chequers, often with the unwilling Brooke, makes few observations about him, although he is prolific about many of the guests.[48] As a matter of curiosity in his otherwise very full diary he only mentions Brooke seven times, and that is only to list the fact he was one of the company on a particular day; he did however give him more time in his postwar publication of *The Churchillians*.[49]

However, he was frequently observed by Churchill's doctor Lord **Moran** who was astute in his observations about the people he met. In 1942 when Brooke had been left in London while the other COS members were in America with Churchill, Moran observed they 'missed Brooke, the peace-loving Dill is no substitute. What he lacks is the he-man stuff.'[50] Brooke always regarded Dill as a good friend, and above all he admired his in-depth reasoning powers and sense of diplomacy. What Brooke had in addition to Dill's reasoning powers was what Moran called 'the he-man stuff' because Brooke could be strong and tough across the debating tables, never prepared to compromise, but making the point as he deemed it should be understood. It is little wonder that many of his own colleagues, British and American, and even Stalin had a deep respect for him. Stalin had even organised for Brooke to be awarded the Order of Suvorov (First Class) by the Soviet government, indicating that his 'he-man stuff' in answering Stalin's toast at Teheran had been observed by the Soviet dictator. Churchill also regarded Brooke in a similar light, with Moran observing that Churchill was 'too knowledgeable in military matters' (which Brooke would have disagreed with) to take Pug Ismay seriously, but 'if Brooke says something the Prime Minister listens to it attentively because it is the CIGS speaking.'[51] Their meetings may have been frequently stormy and bad-tempered, but Churchill often came back the next day and agreed with Brooke's views. Sir Edward Bridges, the cabinet secretary, claimed that Brooke had 'shown great judgement in his dealings with the Prime Minister, giving his opinion firmly and independently, but without making it too assertive'.[52] Many accounts of Brooke tend to indicate he was assertive, but Bridges' observation was closer to the truth. Brooke could be angry, and in his own words 'peevish', but he was rarely rude and was carefully polite in his stubbornness for establishing the truth of the issues under discussion when he presented his arguments.

There were times when he may have appeared remote if not stand-offish, and at a formal lunch it was noted that the CIGS sat between Herbert Morrison and a lady called Dorothy, with 'the capacity for looking straight ahead of him and can do so for a long time on end without any feeling of embarrassment.'[53] In difficult times Brooke could be bored with idle chatter which he considered a waste of valuable time, but the chances were that he was lost in his own reflections looking to the time when, as he said later, he wanted 'to get out of uniform, to turn his back on London streets and return to a country life', which Moran noted was 'the sum of his ambitions.'[54] When Brooke offered personal friendship, as many discovered, it was invaluable, because as Montgomery wrote he was a difficult man to know, and Moran wrote that 'his friendliness gave me pleasure, for as the years have passed I have come to respect his character, his complete integrity, his contempt for flattery, his indifference alike to praise and blame, and his great longing for peace. He said to me tonight "I have felt that every day of this war was taking off a month of my life."'[55] Moran was an outsider to the military discussions and political machinations, but he was able to observe the results and the people involved. Moran saw beyond the Sam Browne-belted formal uniform and the badges of rank, and he wrote that Brooke lived 'for the day when he can forget Europe and resume his country pursuits, especially photographing birds. He hates the war and all its ways, a little unusual in the senior soldier of his country in a world war.'[56]

Brooke was by many military standards of behaviour a quite different sort of officer. Like all good commanders he was deeply committed to his task of organising a successful war, which he hated because he preferred peace. Moran wrote that 'he gave all he had to his work: a simple, gentle, selfless soul, a warning to us all not to give up hope about mankind.'[57] This statement, for many observers of the man Brooke, was perceptive.

The king's private secretary, Alan **Lascelles** knew Brooke reasonably well, often meeting him at formal dinner parties, and they shared a love of birds. Lascelles recorded a dinner party (14 June 1944) when Churchill and Brooke argued over the stores being transported on D-Day, and that Brooke 'stubbornly' argued with Churchill, pointing out that 'no army could fight, let alone progress unless it had adequate supplies of ammunition'.[58] Lascelles recognised in Brooke that 'stubborn' and tough form of character which would not acquiesce to a point of view, even when surrounded by the king and the prime minister; it was not a matter of conceit, but of principle. Lascelles also knew he could trust Brooke and relied on him to tell him the best time to send Alexander a congratulatory telegram from the king.[59] Later, when the king wanted to travel to Eindhoven, and Montgomery had objected, it was from Brooke that Lascelles sought the necessary help. This happened again after the war when Montgomery wanted to visit Canada just when Alexander had been made governor general. Lascelles turned to Brooke for help in this embarrassing situation, concerned with the hovering suspicion that Montgomery would try and steal the limelight. Lascelles understood that Brooke was totally trustworthy and held a firm grip even over people like Montgomery. Brooke was not Lascelles' boss, and Lascelles despite winning an MC in the Great War was a civilian like Moran – and like Moran could see Brooke's inner strength.

When people write their memoirs, they frequently carry the hidden agenda of self-importance, or apologia or explanation. For politicians it is generally a matter of self-importance. When Harold **Macmillan** published his war diaries the text did not portray that sense, but the photographs showed him at the important meetings and with the important people; he barely mentioned Brooke except to say he disagreed with him. He did, however, like many others have a deep respect for the man, as his 8 December 1943 entry noted: 'After a search all day I tracked down General Brooke and had an hour's talk with him. He is clearly an able man, and he has a lucid and flexible mind. But I do not agree with him.'[60] The disagreement was over the appointment of Jumbo Wilson and not Alexander. In his own account, as mentioned in the text, Brooke concluded that Macmillan had no idea what the task of a commander was all about, and he was interfering. Macmillan thought 'Wilson too old and too set', which ironically had once been Brooke's view, but he had changed his views and recognised that Wilson was able and tough enough to stand up to the politicians, and Brooke was proved right. Macmillan was a typical politician, adding that 'of course, I have to tread very carefully in all this, for if the Wilson appointment is made—as I believe it will be—I do not want to start on the wrong foot with him.'[61] Undoubtedly Macmillan was also mindful that Brooke, who had argued in his presence with Churchill at a very heated level, would probably succeed with Wilson's appointment. In August 1944 when Macmillan met Brooke and Portal in Rome, he was almost grateful that 'they were both very friendly and had approved altogether of the plan which we have prepared on Saturday'.[62] This was a meeting with Churchill, and Macmillan was simply in attendance on his political master, but it is easy to gain the impression in this entry that Macmillan was grateful he did not clash with Brooke and his fellow heavyweight, Portal.

# CHAPTER 12

# Historians

Historical truth tends to defy easy explanations, original documents when available can be suspect, some memoirs and autobiographies can too easily become self-serving or self-justifying and therefore misleading. Even the more objective biographies too often veer in favour of the subject, especially when they are official, that is authorised by the subject or the family. There is the additional problem of nationalistic historians or those holding a political viewpoint, and their perception may vary from a view of a person under study to the more important issues of the historical background. If nationalistically inclined historians write about World War II their accounts will frequently differ in emphasis. The British often claim they won the war when in fact they survived, and they can only gloat that they did so when standing alone in their famous 'finest hour'. The French suffered a catastrophic defeat, and their histories stress the Resistance movement; de Gaulle helped transform French self-perception from the defeated to the victors. The Germans and Italians sometimes focus on the issue that Hitler and Mussolini were historical aberrations, and regard themselves as victims of history and war. The Americans frequently reflect they came to the rescue which in many ways they did, after Japan attacked them and Hitler obliged Britain by declaring war on them. The Russians simply claim they 'won the war' against the Nazis with whom they had once been allied, but given the staggering losses they endured, and their defence and final attack, their claim has its own degree of justification. Most historians try and elevate their work above such nationalistic trends, many succeed, but like an obnoxious virus nationalism can occasionally creep into the best works.

Brooke was a British Ulsterman, typifying British traditions and viewpoints. He rarely regarded himself as misguided, but an objective history may indicate that the Mediterranean strategy he so strongly supported was flawed. The British historian Richard Overy 'convincingly argued that because Britain had no large settlements in the Mediterranean, nor vital economic interests, and took much of her oil from the new world by 1942' they were only fighting a corner of the world they could win.[1] This would not have been music to Brooke's ears, though for many its veracity is undeniable. On the other hand, the American General Omar Bradley, watching

American troops fight Germans for the first time in North Africa, admitted he was glad that Brooke had warned them about crossing the Channel too soon. History is never straightforward, it struggles to be objective, and it is against this confusing background that the reactions and insights into Brooke – or the omissions – of some 12 popular historians will be briefly explored.

**Stephen Ambrose**, the well-known American historian, wrote in his biography of Eisenhower that Brooke was a 'fiery Irishman with impressive credentials, who carried throughout the war the handicap of a deep-seated prejudice against the Americans'.[2] However, it was not because they were Americans – the 'fiery Irishman' constantly attacked anyone who opposed his own strategy, including Churchill, British politicians and his own national military comrades, as well as the French, Canadians, Australians and onwards. The Russians escaped to a smaller degree because Brooke noted that they were successfully turning the tide in their bloody conflict to reduce German power, and he knew nothing could influence Russia beyond Stalin himself. Brooke never trusted Stalin, but he liked Roosevelt as a person. Even if his vitriolic comments were at times sharp, he was never that nationalistic; there was only one objective, the defeat of Hitler. In his biography of Eisenhower, Ambrose at least admits that Eisenhower had American critics as well, including Patton and Bradley, as well as the British Montgomery, with their 'diaries and letters and conversations full of denunciations of Eisenhower'.[3]

**Thomas Zeiler**, a professor of history and serious American academic, in his book on *Global Military History* selected Brooke as 'one of the few officials who stood up to Churchill and managed through his intellect, clear communications skills, and professional demeanour to shape decisions.'[4] Zeiler, who is well known for his objective approach, in this singular sentence summarised one of Brooke's important contributions during the war years. Whatever opinion many people may hold of Churchill, for better or worse, he was a highly powerful presence on the world stage, persuasive, gifted, some would claim a genius, but prone to impulsive and sometimes mad ideas, and it needed a Brooke to contain or tone him down and channel him in the right direction. Since the time of that first argument over the phone from the proposed Brittany redoubt, Churchill knew he had to be surrounded by strong men and not fawners. It was reminiscent of the line from Shakespeare's *Julius Caesar*: 'Let me have men about me that are fat; sleek-headed men, and such a sleep o' nights. Yond Cassius has a lean and hungry look; he thinks too much: such men are dangerous' (Act 1 Scene ii). Churchill knew he needed strong gifted men around him, not like the adoration groups trooping after Hitler and Stalin, and the 'yes men' in their weak varieties so prevalent in democratic societies as well, which is probably why he selected Brooke and kept him in post.

A German-born American who is noted for his military and diplomatic history, **Gerhard Ludwig Weinberg**, made some 35 references to Brooke in his major historical work *A World at Arms*.[5] The work is well balanced in its view of Brooke, critical about some of his comments, even his strategy, but always reasoned and sensible. He noted that the disputes between Marshall and Brooke over *Anvil* 'left behind an endless trail of nasty comments about Marshall in Brooke's diary', which since the personal diaries were published seems a reasonable viewpoint.[6] On the other hand, contrary to many popular American views, Weinberg wrote that 'it is not, in my judgement, correct to assert that the British opposed a landing in Northwest Europe, but they were not yet willing it the kind of priority…' which once again was a fair appraisal of a complex scenario.[7] Near the end of his massive study he gave a brief overview of the various commanders, writing that 'some inspired respect by the obvious force of their personalities and intellect: Field Marshal Brooke and General Slim, to mention two examples.'[8] Weinberg tends in this work to support the American strategy, but argued in such a way that it precludes any sense of nationalism, just objective history.

**B. H. Liddell Hart** who had once worked alongside Brooke, in what appears to have been a somewhat uneasy relationship, was a well-known military expert who published his history in 1970. It was an immense study with major and minor details, but there is not a single reference to the part played by Brooke, not even in the battles and withdrawal from France in 1940.[9] There had once been debates between them on the use of tanks, as noted in Chapter Two exploring the interbellum years, and Liddell Hart had worked closely with Hore-Belisha whom Brooke had once found distasteful. In 1937 Liddell Hart had argued that Hobart and not Brooke should be given charge of a newly formed mobile division. There may have been a touch of personal animosity between Liddell Hart and Brooke. In Liddell Hart's history the question of the possible redoubt in France is passed by, and, typically of Liddell Hart there is considerable insight and time given to the German machinations, what he often referred to as the 'other side of the hill'. It was known that Liddell Hart and Brooke had clashed at times; this may not have been the reason for not mentioning Brooke or his role, but this important early academic study certainly did not help the unknown field marshal to be better known.

In his popular history of World War II, which amounts to some 750 pages, **Martin Gilbert** only mentioned Brooke twice, and both times *en passant*: the first that Brooke was in France, and much later that he told Churchill he was concerned about the Germans breaking into the Persian oilfields.[10] On the other hand Alexander is mentioned 11 times and Montgomery 16, which tends to demonstrate that despite the immense value of the work, it is more highly descriptive of explicit battle action, rather than what was happening behind the scenes, which was important because it dictated the events on the stage. Prior to the battle of El Alamein there were major command changes and instructions given to the commanders in the field. Many historians focus on Churchill's role, when in reality he was highly dependent on Brooke, who in this instance had gathered his own doubts about Auchinleck and fought various corners by refusing to take over himself, demonstrating the importance of the high command. This factor can be gleaned by the authenticity of war diaries usually written on the same day, even if late at night.

Naturally history books take a different slant or angle when portraying a designated piece of history, some of the older ones being nationalistic in their approach, some paying more attention to military history, others the political ramifications, and others challenging old concepts and views. Into this latter category falls **Norman Davies'** history which makes for interesting and informed reading, but he never mentioned Brooke, although he refers to Marshall seven times, and Montgomery 16.[11]

By contrast **Andrew Roberts**, who described Brooke as a 'flinty Ulsterman' mentions his role 28 times, and exposes Brooke's significance with his position in the High Command: Hitler never learnt from his mistakes, but 'Brooke and Marshall felt under no obligation to refrain from pointing out earlier errors made by Churchill and Roosevelt, and *vice versa*.'[12]

**Anthony Beevor's** study refers to Brooke's role some 45 times, and tends, understandably, to use Brooke as a reference point based on his reliable diary entries.[13] It is an uncluttered in-depth exploration of the war and not a biography, and he underlined Brooke's 'staccato style' of presentation of argument, and his work having to restrain Churchill 'from charging off on another pet project, [such as Sumatra].'[14] Brooke's contribution and relevance is noted by the number of times he crops up in a text. **Max Hastings'** study of World War II mentions Brooke some eight times, and, although Hastings is often critical of the British army, except for the artillery which would have pleased Brooke, he gave a valuable summary of Brooke's role. 'Brooke handled Churchill superbly well, and he made a notable contribution to Allied strategy between 1941 and 1943. Thereafter, however, he somewhat diminished in stature by condescension towards the Americans and stubborn enthusiasm for the Mediterranean operations.'[15] Many historians would agree with this brief summation, but how far he diminished in stature begs a few questions; Brooke received many awards and positions in Britain and 13 foreign decorations. Despite the valid point made by Hastings, this clearly indicated his status remained high, and his counsel sought to the very end.

Most histories which include Brooke's role nearly always focus on the way he related to Churchill and the prime minister's thinking. In his book *Moral Combat*, **Michael Burleigh** noted that 'the indefatigable British prime minister found his wilder strategic flights brought down to earth by the strong men with whom he surrounded himself, knowing he needed their discipline, notably the stubborn military bureaucrat Alan Brooke.'[16] Burleigh also clearly understood the relevance of Brooke's diaries, not dwelling on the barbs and blemishes, but pointing that they 'go to the heart of command at the highest level, revealing emotions that he otherwise repressed'.[17] Burleigh in these lines from his text makes a most relevant observation about Brooke's role.

The French historian **Henri Michel** referred to Brooke's role several times, quoting from Marshall who had said that 'one of the main tasks of his [Churchill's]

General Staff was to stop him making strategic blunders', which was a reasonable insight, given that inventive as he was, Churchill's over-zealousness came up with many madcap ideas.[18] Michel noted that Brooke's 'pessimistic view that by trying to do everything at once ran the risk of losing all over the board'.[19] Michel gives the distinct impression that he had a grasp of Brooke's role during the war and saw it as reflective of the British who 'over their long history, had learnt to appreciate the cost of failure and the virtue of patience'. He also mentioned Brooke's critical role in France in convincing Churchill not to try to continue the war in Brittany, which Liddell Hart virtually ignored.

All historians are different, have or take different approaches, look to different goals or explanations, but when dealing with World War II in general terms it is difficult to avoid the military background, the leaders and their advisers, the problems of the Anglo-American alliance, the understated role of Russia, and many other ramifications. Nevertheless, it remains somewhat mystifying as to why so many history books on World War II concentrate on the battles and the field commanders, and barely mention the serious background strategy which led to these battles. Many are too content to concentrate on Churchill, even putting the emphasis on Churchill as the controlling genius, and while not doubting Churchill's leadership qualities in war, he was advised, toned down and more often than not redirected by Brooke. The attempt to hold the redoubt in Brittany would have been a life-giving fiasco, and the project against Trondheim, invading Sumatra or islands in the eastern Mediterranean could have been as disastrous in human life as Gallipoli in World War I, and the failure in Norway in 1940. It was Brooke who had the courage to oppose Churchill in some ideas and support him in others. He was the one man to whom Churchill would pay serious attention. The many popular histories which avoid mentioning Brooke may have their reasons, but they have helped make him the unknown field marshal despite his self-evident contributions and overall value as Churchill's critic.

## CHAPTER 13

# Brookie

Brooke was first and foremost a soldier; with his family background it was virtually in his DNA. He is of interest and importance to historians because he rose to high command during the critical period of World War II, but he had also experienced conflict first-hand during the Great War, and he was a field commander in war-torn France 1939–40 where he experienced once again the bitter struggle against the very professional German military. Even when he held the 'top post' he was living in central London, experiencing the bombing, even having to retreat under his bed and having to avoid collapsing buildings and flying shrapnel. He lost close friends – in the Wellington Barracks bombing, and especially his closest friend, his ADC Barney, in a plane crash – and members of his wider family, and he travelled extensively seeing the battlefields of Europe and later globally.

In a single statement his first biographer summarised Brooke's major contribution to the war effort when he wrote that he 'infused realism' into the direction that the British and their Allies would pursue in their war against Germany.[1] He had his own views on the Far Eastern conflict with Japan, but he knew this was essentially an American theatre of operations, and that the military power of the Nazi regime had to be crushed first and foremost. His invaluable diaries, which focus more on Europe than the Japanese conflict, reflect his views, they are not a history; their only chronology reflects his personal life and immediate professional interests.

As noted, he was the best man Churchill could have chosen for the role of CIGS because of his realism. Before the Great War he was imbued with military life, having experienced combat between 1914 and 1918, then during the interbellum years academically and intellectually pursued the nature of international conflict. By 1939 he was already prepared for a field if not higher command. From 1940 Brooke's life became one of confrontation and argument both nationally and internationally. Decision making was no easy matter in a world torn apart by a major global conflict, and Brooke's critical war diaries clearly indicated his life was consumed by personal battles to assert what he deemed, from a lifetime in the army, to be the best military policies and strategy, based on personal experience, listening to others, and academic study. Even during the war, he always found time to listen and question those men returning from the frontline action, not just the leading officers but all ranks.

It was this confidence in his own experience and judgement that led to Brooke's many confrontations and heated debates, frequently with Churchill, but also with many of his own colleagues, including the other Chiefs of Staff, especially with Pound, and even his good fishing and birding friend Portal. He found himself in more serious conflicts with his American friends and colleagues, at variance with and suspicious of the Soviets, critical of the French and anyone else who objected to what he regarded as 'sound strategy': the key phrase which constantly motivated his thinking.

The conflict with Churchill, which has always received the greatest public criticism, was a major item in Brooke's diaries, and it was often bitter, although he would later retract his fury and explain how he 'loved and admired' the prime minister. For his part Churchill may have viewed Brooke as a difficult subordinate; however, he later wrote that Brooke 'was, by general verdict, fearless, formidable, articulate, and in the end convincing'.[2] Churchill probably held a wider and more balanced political global strategy than Brooke, but he was a romantic warrior in many ways, in contrast to Brooke's realism and pragmatism. Brooke believed that Churchill lacked the strategic ability of others such as Stalin; when Stalin appeared aware of the logistical railway problems of carrying enough troop numbers through Siberia, for example, this caught Brooke's admiration.

Such different approaches inevitably led to collisions in matters of individual operations, as when Churchill wanted Trondheim or Sumatra occupied, while Brooke and others argued it would have no real effect on the pursuit of a successful war. Churchill would too frequently raise some impulsive idea for a possible military operation, but Brooke would immediately note the practical requirements and often tell Churchill it was 'unachievable or pointless' in his usual blunt fashion, which was probably the only way to hold Churchill's attention. It was noted by many that at least Churchill tended to listen to what Brooke said, which he rarely did with others. Churchill's romantic love for martial exploits needed Brooke's tempering to hold the prime minister in line. Brooke was not the sort of person who could be bullied, not even by Churchill. In the later years of the war Brooke wondered whether Churchill, who was frequently ill from overwork, was losing the 'balance of his mind' and whether his dislike of American power taking precedence over his hitherto leading world position had blurred his reasoning powers. By this stage of the war both Churchill and Brooke were probably both exhausted, and their mutual behaviour reflected this aspect. Even later, when Churchill had lost the election, he still criticised Brooke with a letter through the post over the Egyptian situation and the safety of the Suez Canal. At a personal level Churchill grumbled, understandably, on the publication of Brooke's early diaries through Bryant, with their personal comments retained in the text. Churchill was somewhat unhappy, but there is no denying that there was a genuine friendship between these two men during the war years. Churchill's doctor Moran observed this friendly yet hostile relationship as did many others, and Brooke's use of the name Winston and Churchill's 'Brookie' underlines this aspect, though this was in writing; Brooke always addressed the prime minister as 'Sir' in any meetings, formal or social. Had Churchill not liked or trusted Brooke there is no question that he would have replaced him. There were times when Brooke admitted that it transpired that Churchill held the better perspective as, for example, in his comprehension of the political ramifications of the atom bomb revealed at Potsdam. It was because Churchill at times could be impulsive and unpredictable, that Brooke became more rigid and less flexible in his immediate responses. Despite Churchill's early military career, he was fundamentally an outstanding politician, whereas Brooke was military through and through, and while Churchill argued politically, Brooke always argued as a military man; it was a bizarre combination. It was often as a result of such conflicts with Churchill that Brooke in his angry late-night diary entries attacked the system of democracy, a system he adhered to all his life, accepting the role of the elected politician, and later rescinded his own outburst. This element serves to demonstrate the depth of his feelings following his conflicts with Churchill.

Brooke's 'fearless, formidable, articulate' qualities came to the fore in his relationships with the Americans, who tended to hold him in high regard, while always remaining suspicious of him. Their attitude was coloured somewhat because they were sceptical about Churchill, but also Brooke's bearing and delivery of his arguments. They soon discovered from their first meetings that Brooke was a master of detail, lucid in the way he presented his arguments, highly articulate and always blunt and to the point. Even his old adversary, the 'pro-Pacific first' campaigner Admiral King, admitted that Brooke always presented his plans in an impressive way and was a master of detail. There was nothing more damming when the Americans presented their side of a policy than to hear Brooke snap back that 'I disagree', with his well-known habit of snapping his pencil at the same time. His depth of feeling and passion was demonstrated by this habit. Despite their profound respect for him they were conscious that he was like Churchill, with British Empire ambitions somewhere lurking within his arguments. This initially arose with Brooke's insistence on the Mediterranean campaign. Curiously, when he had been commanding the defence of the British Isles, Brooke had queried Churchill over the same issue, although it was, for Brooke, not a matter of empire but in those early years the realistic strategy of home defence for the sake of the country's survival.

Later, with the threat of *Sea Lion* somewhat diminished, he once again stuck to his guns in the face of American disagreement over the next priorities. Brooke wanted to fight the Germans in North Africa where the British could realistically perform, distract their attention, reduce their resources, tackle their military strength, and take Italy out of the war, imposing an obligation on the Germans to come to their rescue. This made imminent sense in the early stages of the war, but whether Brooke and the British were right in pursuing this policy to the bitter end remains for many a serious question mark. For Brooke, standing firm in Egypt and North Africa was intended to keep a holding base, clearing the Mediterranean for shipping, and it gave a protection not just for India but the Middle East with its oil reserves. For Brooke this was not an empire issue; he had the one aim, namely, to crush Nazi Germany. However, always the realist, Brooke understood that Germany could lose in the Mediterranean and North Africa, but they would remain undefeated and a serious threat in mainland central Europe. This explained his attitude that crossing the Channel for a head-on attack would need precise timing, more resources, a sound preparation period for the best plans, and a weakened Germany. Many people, historians, military experts, politicians, have criticised the need to take the whole of North Africa, and they have regarded the persuasive arguments for Operation *Torch* as a means of stopping a too-early cross-Channel attack; these questions have always formed a nucleus of debate, especially in America. From their earliest meetings the Americans, from Marshall to Admiral King and most of their COS, simply could not believe in Brooke's overall strategy. However, his strength of character and forceful presentation of sound, reasoned arguments eventually persuaded the Americans to do things his way, despite their misgivings. In the end some even conceded he had been right, as when Omar Bradley admitted that 'it was fortunate that the British view prevailed' and that the American army had gained initial combat experience in North Africa. 'Had that learning process been launched in France it would surely have, as Alan Brooke argued, resulted in an unthinkable disaster.'[3] At least this one American general later understood some of Brooke's arguments, though it was the experience of his troops fighting the Germans which changed his mind.

The Americans tended to see the British as obstinate, especially Brooke, but they always paid serious attention to his arguments and papers. Whether Brooke was right to carry on the battle in Italy was another dispute with the Americans, who were enthusiastic about their plans to land in southern France. Kesselring had decided that this explained why the Allies were in Italy, but like Alexander, thought that while German soldiers were committed to that country so were many more Allied troops, because, as noted many times, Italy's terrain was easier to defend than attack. However, at this juncture, Brooke also knew that the German army and Luftwaffe were still strong, and the Russians, though turning the tide, were not yet on the offensive. Brooke was sometimes criticised for overestimating the strength of the German military, which comes only with the benefit of hindsight, or that he held the adversary in too high a respect. He was correct during the time of the Mediterranean days because it was not until the Russian offensive made substantial progress that most German troops became preoccupied in the East. Had the Russians sat back, lost ground or made peace, a cross-Channel invasion of Britain could have been a renewed and a frightening possibility for the British. He was always correct to hold the German opponents with appropriate respect because they were highly trained, backed by a national Prussian tradition of soldiering, and they were battle experienced. The accruing American resources hugely out-proportioned Germany, but too early a cross-Channel attack with the inevitable loss of life would have caused problems in a democratic political system. At one stage the arguments over Eisenhower became almost too acrimonious, and Brooke may have been at fault here for listening too carefully to Montgomery, his pupil, knowing his strengths, but also aware of his personal egotistical weakness and ambitions.

Brooke developed a military respect for the Russians, and as noted, especially Stalin's strategic down-to-earth attitude. As mentioned in the text he once clashed with Stalin over a toast, but Brooke's strength of steely character appealed to Stalin, who later ensured the military award of the Order of Suvorov was presented to Brooke. After the 'toasting affair' Churchill later recalled that 'it seemed to me that all the clouds had passed away, and in fact Stalin's confidence in my friend [Brooke] was established on a foundation of respect and goodwill which was never shaken while we all worked together.'[4] In some ways Brooke's robust response was better received by the Russians than the Americans, but Brooke also held a realistic appraisal of Stalin's long-term aims for the postwar period, which, it has been suggested by many historians, was why the Russians respected him for his incisive mind.

On the domestic front, frequent clashes occurred between Brooke and the other two COS Chiefs where the gloves of politeness were off as they discussed major plans and policies. However, he never regarded himself as the supremo, but one of the three Chiefs who happened to be the chairman, and their debates had to be open and frank to be able to present the way forward to Churchill and the War Cabinet. He was often at variance with the Royal Navy, especially during the time of Pound, who Brooke was constantly attacking for being asleep like a 'parrot on the perch'. This changed once Brooke knew Pound was seriously ill and he lamented his comments when Pound died. He still had issues with the navy even under the leadership of Pound's successor Cunningham, but they became good friends and the clashes were only over strategy, they never became personal. The same situation persisted with Portal who backed Harris in his total support of the bombing war, whereas Brooke wanted the RAF in support of the army. It has been suggested that Portal was right and Brooke wrong. There is no doubt that the horrendous bombing of Germany weakened that country; it did not break their will power, but it destroyed industry, broke communications and created mayhem. Nevertheless, as many generals have remarked, defeat demanded troops on the ground, and the initial German Blitzkrieg had demonstrated the power of air and land forces working together. Despite the differences of military opinion Portal and Brooke remained good friends, sharing the same hobbies of fishing and birds. In 1945 Portal, who admired Brooke, wrote to him that 'I take away with me what I know will be an enduring memory of your friendship, and from what I have learnt from you.'[5]

Brooke always held to the policy that the field commander on the spot knew better than those safely behind Whitehall desks – to the point where, in the field in

1940 France, he reflected that he wished he could be like Wellington with no phone system. Some of the more bitter quarrels with Churchill were over his derogatory attacks on commanders, on one occasion exploding in a War Cabinet when Churchill did this in front of other politicians. It is notable that he was able to remain friends with officers he castigated in his diary as he let off steam at their misdirections or weaknesses – and indeed he maintained friendships with people he had demoted or retired. Brooke watched, examined, and thought about the field commanders, expressing his feelings strongly in his diary and waiting for the moment to change commands. It was never a matter of favourites, as many have claimed, but a simple policy of having the best available man in the right place. He frequently accused Alexander of being 'out of his depth' and expressed his concern that Churchill might also spot this weakness. He felt the same about Auchinleck and he was probably right in these assessments, but he never allowed personal attachments to be harmed in these delicate and personally difficult changes. Later in life they would all retain their friendships.

Some have claimed that he only pointed out the weaknesses and not a person's strengths, which of course was true, but it was the weaknesses which concerned Brooke during a terrible war. His praise when it did come was never as ebullient as his criticisms were fierce. He had few intimates, looking to Adam, Dill, Kennedy and Wavell; he liked Smuts and Sikorski, but when he lashed out it could be scathing. He had a constant loathing of de Gaulle, and many would have agreed with him, looking at the aloof and arrogant man and not what he was trying to do in restoring France. Mountbatten's presence irritated him beyond even his more vitriolic vocabulary. He found Mountbatten easier to be with during the immediate postwar years on his trip around the world, but during the war he found it difficult to cope with him. For this Brooke has been criticised, but in the light of various studies on Mountbatten, from his fiasco in Dieppe through to the partition of India, he has had his share of contemporary and historical critics. Eisenhower received the whiplash of his diary, but he also acknowledged that Eisenhower could unite people of different nationalities, and when he heard him speak in postwar London he admitted he had underestimated the 'big man' in Eisenhower. Had Brooke been made supreme commander in *Overlord* few people doubt that he would have been superior to Eisenhower in strategic matters, but whether he would have been successful in conducting the necessary international human relationships may have been another matter, and he would probably have run into political difficulties somewhat sooner than later.

Brooke has often been accused of being a moaner and groaner, and of making assessments of other people that were too hasty, overstated, and at times vicious. The only justification for this was allowing the diaries to be published, because they exposed his personal thinking and his style of forthright expression at times of stress, a point once made by Churchill as he read them. He did not always make the correct analysis of another person, but he was as fallible as any other human being; sometimes he was all too accurate. He was perhaps over-indulgent with Montgomery, and too severe on Gort, and he later mentally criticised himself and admitted errors, the classic example being Jumbo Wilson whom at first he thought was too old and tired only to find he was totally wrong. His implied criticism of Wilson's wife when he was taking Dill's place in America was one of those entries which perhaps should have been scratched out before publication, but it helps to underline the diary's integrity as thoroughly original.

On concluding the intricate task of indexing and taking the necessary notes, it dawned on the author that Brooke's cantankerous references are equally balanced by his kinder words, and under the heading of *Life with Churchill* it becomes clear that they enjoyed as much time together as they spent quarrelling with one another. The trouble has been that readers of the diary tend to focus on the nasty jibes and vented criticisms rather than the friendlier and fun aspects. It also became crystal clear that under *Hobbies*, which originally was only going to number a few entries, there were on completion 24, which underlined the importance of birdwatching and fishing to help Brooke stay balanced in an unstable world, and these insights also brought out the personality behind the uniform.

It must not be forgotten that Brooke's diaries were written for Benita as his means of communication during long periods of absence, for letting off steam at times of stress and fatigue, and they revealed that at times he could be impulsive and felt deeply, but above all they were personal and reveal the man in depth, warts and all. Brooke was a well-read man, deep into history, always prudent and fundamentally conservative; he had a high intelligence, a sharp mind and was articulate, and although not perfect he had the right attributes for a first-class soldier. Whatever the subject, from tanks to birds, from military operations planning to fishing, he always made sure that he could be as expert as possible. His life from 1939 and throughout World War II was a series of confrontations, especially with Churchill and the American policies. In keeping the balance of this study it should be noted that it 'was part of the self-confident bigness of Winston Churchill that he appointed [Brooke] such a foil for his own genius, the best possible person to "keep his imagination in check" when many another, lesser politician would have opted for a yes-man in that post.'[6] From the time of the telephone call to Brittany in 1940 Churchill knew that Brooke could not be bullied, and he would be strong enough to resist him when necessary.

During the postwar years his trip around the world looking for a global defence strategy may well have been prompted by him to Attlee, and it indicated Brooke's long-term thinking processes. It held no real value in the end because the world was changing rapidly. The growth of various forms of communism was regarded as a serious threat to global stability. The Americans had become militarily powerful because of the war, and their influence was as powerful as an empire. They had huge resources which rapidly increased when they emerged from their long period of isolationism, and along with the Soviet Union were described with the new terminology as one of the new 'superpowers', with Britain a nation losing its empire and in serious debt to the Americans, which was not repaid until the next century. The British were no longer a world power, the Channel was no longer a defence, and the world was changing as Brooke travelled the globe, but at least it provided him with a well-earned holiday.

Brooke never financially benefitted from his service at this highest national level. He had worried about his coupons during the war, and afterwards he was obliged to sell his home and move into the gardener's cottage. His paltry income was almost a disgrace given the service he had given to the country. His aptitude was used by business appointments which helped alleviate his poverty, and his accumulation of awards and honorary positions all underlined an international gratitude which was not reflected in his bank accounts. He never let this concern him apart from domestic needs, and he kept to his principles and stood apart from politics. The Duke of Wellington later served as a prime minister, de Gaulle became the French president and Eisenhower the American president, but Brooke was happy enough to become the president of the London Zoological Society and the Severn Wildfowl Trust and the Vice-President of the RSPB.

This was all he ever wanted, and he was emotionally dependent on Benita with his family and his love of fishing and bird photography. Brooke's true personality emerged during these later years. His friendship with Hosking and other ornithologists was revealing in his love of the simple uncluttered life, his sense of friendship, humour and gentleness of character were the major aspects which were all revealed to those lucky enough to know him. Perhaps the most revealing moment was Hosking's revelation that when in his company at the Savoy, Brooke bothered to stop, turn back and thank the bellboy in the lift for pressing the button.

Brooke may not have been as well known as Rommel, Patton and Montgomery, but in the words of his first biographer 'he was the best Chief of the Imperial General Staff ever produced by the Army, and he was produced at the vital hours, Britain was fortunate indeed.'[7]

Moreover he was a decent forthright human being, admired and loved by those who knew him, a man who served his country and the wider world without ever seeking fame or fortune.

Brooke's statue in Whitehall (David Holt)

# Abbreviations

| | |
|---|---|
| AA | Anti-aircraft [guns] |
| ABDA | American, British, Dutch and Australian interests |
| ADC | Aide de camp |
| AQMG | Assistant Quartermaster-General |
| BEF | British Expeditionary Force |
| CAS | Chief of Air Staff |
| CCOS | Combined Chief(s) of Staff |
| CGS | Chief of General Staff |
| CIGS | Chief of the Imperial General Staff |
| CO | Commanding Officer or Combined Operations |
| COS | Chief(s) of Staff |
| COSSAC | Chief of Staff Supreme Allied Command |
| DMO | Director of Military Operations |
| GCB | Knight Grand Cross of the Order of the Bath |
| GHQ | General Headquarters |
| JIC | Joint Intelligence Committee |
| KCB | Knights Commander award |
| LDV | Local Defence Volunteers, later the Home Guard |
| MC | Military Cross |
| MG | Machine gun |
| MI5 | Home security |
| NAAFI | Navy Army Air Force Institutes |
| OKW | *Oberkommando der Wehrmacht* (German High Command) |
| OSS | Office of Strategic Services |
| QMS | Quartermaster-Sergeant |
| RA | Royal Artillery |
| RE | Royal Engineers |
| SEAC | South East Asia Command |
| SIS | Secret Intelligence Service, sometimes called MI6 |
| SOE | Special Operations Executive |
| TA | Territorial Army |
| VCIGS | Vice-Chief of Imperial General Staff |
| VE | Victory in Europe [Day] |

# List of Operations and Plans

As mentioned in text

| | |
|---|---|
| ANAKIM | Plans for recapture of Burma |
| ANVIL | Invasion of southern France, later *Dragoon* |
| ASCHE | German plan to disarm Italian soldiers |
| AVALANCHE | Landing at Salerno near Naples |
| BARBAROSSA | German attack on Soviet Union |
| BLAU | German operation in Russia |
| BOLERO | Plan to build up American forces in Britain |
| BUCCANEER | Proposed invasion of Andaman Islands |
| | Operation to cut off German army in Italy |
| BUMPER | Major defensive exercise in Britain |
| CHARIOT | The St Nazaire raid |
| DIADEM | Attack on Gustav Line in Italy |
| DRAGOON | New name for *Anvil* |
| DYLE PLAN | French plan to halt Germans at River Dyle |
| DYNAMO | Operation for Dunkirk |
| FELL GELB | German plan for invading the West |
| GIANT II | Projected plan for parachute drop on Rome |
| GYMNAST | First name for Operation *Torch* |
| HABBAKUK | Projected plan for ice-made aircraft carriers |
| HUSKY | Invasion of Sicily |
| IMPERATOR | Unrealised plan to take French port |
| IRONCLAD | Occupation of Madagascar |
| JUBILEE | Dieppe Raid, previously *Rutter* |
| MANNA | Embarking troops for Greece from Italy |
| MARKET GARDEN | Plans to take Arnhem |
| MICHAEL | German WWI offensive |
| NEPTUNE | Naval plans for D-Day Normandy |
| OVERLORD | Invasion of France, previously *Roundup* |
| PEDESTAL | Convoy plan for Malta |
| POINT BLANK | Proposed plan to invade Sardinia |
| RICHARD | Kesselring's plans for troop movements |
| ROUNDUP | Previous name for *Overlord* |

| | |
|---|---|
| RUTTER | Earlier name for *Jubilee* |
| SCHIEFFLEN | 1905 German plan for attacking the West |
| SEA LION | German plan to invade Britain |
| SHINGLE | Anzio landing |
| SICHELSCHNITT | German 1940 plan to encircle Allies in 1940 |
| SLEDGEHAMMER | Proposed plan to occupy Cotentin peninsula |
| SPARTAN | 1943 War Games exercise |
| SUNRISE | Plans for German surrender in 1945 Italy |
| TORCH | Invasion of North Africa, once called *Gymnast* |
| VICTOR | British defence exercise |

# Bibliography

## Primary Sources

Alanbrooke Papers, Section 4, King's College London

Alanbrooke, *Notes on my Life* (Section 3), King's College London

Alanbrooke, Field Marshal Lord, *War Diaries 1939–45* (London: Weidenfeld & Nicolson, 2001)

Bundesarchiv-Militärarchiv, Freiburg: N574–19, '*Kriegsende in Italien*'

Colville, John, *The Fringes of Power* (London: Hodder and Stoughton, 1985)

COS Meeting Papers and War Cabinet Papers, National Archives

Führer Conferences on Naval Affairs 1939–1945 (London: Chatham Publishers, 2005)

The *Guardian*, 12 June 1950

Hansard, 30 April 1958

Kew National Archives, HW1/1331

Lascelles, Sir Alan, *King's Counsellor* (London: Weidenfeld & Nicolson, 2006)

Macmillan, Harold, *War Diaries* (London: Macmillan, 1984)

NA-AMP, *The Rise and Fall of the German Air Force 1933–45* (The National Archives, Air Ministry Pamphlet, issued by Air Ministry 1948, 2008)

Orwell, George (ed. Peter Davison), *The Orwell Diaries* (London: Penguin Books, 2010)

Premier Papers, National Archives

Prime Minister's Personal Minutes 'Most Secret', National Archives

Taylor, Fred (trans.), *The Göbbels Diaries* (London: Hamish Hamilton, 1982)

*The Times,* 20 April 1944

*The Times*, 18 June 1963, *Obituary*

US Army Historical Division, *Mediterranean War Part V, campaign in Italy Part II*, MS C-064, Generalfeldmarschall Albert Kesselring, 1 May 1949

## Memoirs and Autobiographies

Alexander, Field Marshal Earl of Tunis, *The Alexander Memoirs, 1940–1945* (London: Frontline Books, 2010)

Bradley, Omar, *A General's Life* (London: Sidgwick & Jackson, 1983)

Churchill, Winston, *My Early Life* (London: Odhams, 1949)

Clark, Mark, *Calculated Risk* (New York: Harper and Brothers, 1950)

Dollmann, Eugen, *The Interpreter, Memoirs of Doktor Eugen Dollmann* (London: Hutchinson, 1967)

Eden, Anthony, *The Eden Memoirs, Facing the Dictators* (London: Cassell, 1962)

Eden, Anthony, *The Reckoning* (London: Cassell, 1965)

Eisenhower, Dwight, *Crusade in Europe* (London: Heinemann, 1948)

Hosking, Eric, *An Eye for a Bird* (London: Hutchinson, 1970)

Humbert, Agnes, *Résistance* (London: Bloomsbury, 2009)

Ismay, General Lord, *The Memoirs of Lord Ismay* (London: Heinemann, 1960)

Kennedy, Sir John, Major-General, *The Business of War* (London: Hutchinson, 1957)

Kesselring, Albert, *The Memoirs of a Field-Marshal* (London: William Kimber, 1953)

Liddell Hart, B. H. (ed.), *The Rommel Papers* (New York: De Capo Press, 1953)

Manstein, Erich von, *Lost Victories* (Minneapolis: Zenith, 1982)

Montgomery, B. L., *The Memoirs of Field Marshal the Viscount Montgomery of Alamein, K. G.* (New York: The World Publishing Company, 1958)

Moran, Lord, *Churchill at War 1940–46* (London: Robinson, 1966)

Nel, Elizabeth, *Winston Churchill by his Personal Secretary* (New York: iUniverse, 2007)

Schraepler, Hans-Joachim, *At Rommel's Side, The Lost letters of Hans-Joachim Schraepler* (London: Frontline Books, 2009)

Von Senger und Etterlin, General Frido, *Neither Fear nor Hope* (London: Macdonald, 1963)

Vassiltchikov, Maries, *The Berlin Diaries 1939-45* (London: Pimlico, 1999)

Wedemeyer, General Albert C., *Wedemeyer Reports!* (New York: 1958)

Westphal, Siegfried, *The German Army in the West* (London: Cassell, 1951)

# Biographies

Ambrose, Stephen, *Eisenhower, Soldier and President* (London: Pocket Books, 2003)

Cray, Ed, *General to the Army, George C Marshall, Soldier and Statesman* (New York: Cooper Square Press, 2000)

Fenby, Jonathan, *The General Charles de Gaulle and The France He Saved* (London: Simon and Schuster, 2010)

Fraser, David, *Alanbrooke* (London: Collins, 1982)

Gilbert, Martin, *Finest Hour, Winston S Churchill 1939–41* (London: Heinemann, 1983)

Izzard, Brian, *Mastermind of Dunkirk and D-Day* (Oxford: Casemate, 2020)

Khlevniuk, V. Oleg, *Stalin, New Biography of a Dictator* (London: Yale UP, 2015)

Mosley, Leonard, *Marshall: Organizer of Victory* (New York: Hearst Books, 1982)

Padfield, Peter, *Himmler Reichs Führer-SS* (London: Cassell & Co, 2001)

Roberts, Andrew, *Eminent Churchillians* (London: Weidenfeld & Nicolson, 1994)

Sebag-Montefiore, Hugh, *Stalin, The Court of the Red Tsar* (London: Weidenfeld & Nicolson, 2003)

Service, Robert, *Stalin* (London: Pan Books, 2010)

Stephen, Leslie (ed.), *Sir Victor Brooke, Sportsman and Naturalist* (London: Forgotten Books, 2018)

Young, Desmond, *Rommel* (London: Book Club Associates, 1973)

Zeigler, Philip, *Mountbatten, The Official Biography* (London: Collins, 1985)

# Other Cited Published Works

Andrew, Christopher and Gordievsky, Oleg, *KGB The Inside Story of its Foreign Operations from Lenin to Gorbachev* (London: Hodder & Stoughton, 1990)

Applebaum, Anne, *Iron Curtain: The Crushing of Eastern Europe, 1944–1956* (London: Penguin, 2017)

Astley, Joan Bright, *The Inner Circle* (London: Hutchinson, 1971)

Atkinson, Rick, *The Day of Battle, The War in Sicily and Italy 1943–44* (London: Abacus, 2013)

Beevor, Anthony, *The Second World War* (London: Weidenfeld & Nicolson, 2012)

Blatt, Joel (ed.) *The French Defeat of 1940: Reassessments* (Oxford: Berghahn, 1998)

Bryant Arthur, *Triumph in the West* and *Turn of the Tide* (London: Collins, 1965)

Bryant A, *Triumph in the West* (London: The Reprint Society, 1960)

Burleigh, Michael, *Moral Combat* (London: Harper Press, 2010)

Churchill, Winston, *The Second World War, Vol II* (London: Cassell and Company, 1949)

Churchill, Winston, *The Second World War, Vol III* (London: Cassell and Company, 1950)

Churchill, Winston, *The Second World War, Vol IV* (London: Cassell and Company, 1951)

Churchill, Winston, *The Second World War, Vol V* (London: Cassell and Company, 1952)

Churchill, Winston, *The Second World War, Vol VI* (London: Cassell and Company, 1954)

Colville, John, *The Churchillians* (London: Weidenfeld & Nicolson, 1981)

Corrigan, Gordon, *The Second World War, A Military History* (London: Atlantic Books, 2012)

Davies, Norman, *A History of Europe* (London: Pimlico, 1997)

Davies, Norman, *No Simple Victory* (London: Viking, 2006)

Deighton, Len, *Blitzkrieg* (London: Pimlico, 1996)

D'Este, Carlo, *Fatal Decision* (London: Fontana, 1991)

D'Este, Carlo, *Decision in Normandy: The Unwritten Story of Montgomery and the Allied Campaign* (London: Pan Books, 1984)

Dimbleby, Jonathan, *Destiny in the Desert* (London: Profile Books, 2013)

Eade, Charles (compiler), *Onwards to Victory, War Speeches by Churchill* (London: Cassell and Company, 1944)

Fairweather, Jack, *The Volunteer* (London: Penguin, 2019)

Ferris, John and Ewan Maudsley, *The Cambridge History of The Second World War Vol 1* (Cambridge: CUP, 2015)

French, David and Holden Reid, Brian, *The British General Staff, Reform and Innovation, c.1890–1939* (London: Frank Cass Publishers, 2002)

Fuller, J. F. C., *Tanks in the Great War* (New York: E. Dutton and Company, 1920)

Fuller, J. F. C., *A Military History of the Western World. From the American Civil War to the End of World War II*. Volume III (London: Minerva Press, 1956)

Gardiner, Juliet, *Wartime Britain 1939–1945* (London: Headline Books, 2005)

Gellately, Robert, *Stalin's Curse, Battling for Communism in War and Cold War* (Oxford: OUP, 2013)

Gilbert, Martin, *Second World War* (London: Phoenix, 1997)

Graham, Dominic and Bidwell, Shelford, *Tug of War: The Battle for Italy 1943–45* (Yorkshire: Pen and Sword, 2004)

Hastings, Max, *All Hell Let Loose* (London: Harper, 2011)

Hastings, Max, *The Secret War* (London: William Collins, 2015)

Heiber, Helmut and Glantz, David (eds.), *Hitler and his Generals* (London: Greenhill Books, 2002)

Hodges, Richard, 'Tempting providence: The Bombing of Monte Cassino', *History Today* (Volume 44, Issue 2, 1994)

Holmes, Richard, *The World at War, The Landmark Oral History* (London: Ebury Press, 2007)

Horne, Alistair, *To Lose a Battle, France 1940* (London: Macmillan, 1969)

Howard, Michael, *The Continental Commitment: The Dilemma of British Defence Policy in the Era of the Two World Wars* (London: Ashfield Press, 1989)

Hoyt, Edwin, *Back Water War, The Allied Campaign in Italy* (Mechanicsburg: Stackpole, 2007)

Infield-Glen, *Disaster at Bari* (New York: Bantam, 1988)

Jackson, Julian, *The Fall of France* (Oxford: OUP, 2003)

Jackson, Julian, *France: The Dark Years 1940–44* (Oxford: OUP, 2003)

Jeffrey, Keith, *MI6: The History of the Secret Service 1909–1949* (London: Bloomsbury, 2010)

Kershaw, Ian, *The End: Hitler's Germany* (London: Allen Lane, 2011)

Lewin, Ronald (ed.), *The War on Land 1939–1915* (London: Vintage Books, 2007)

Lewis, Jon (ed.), *World War II The Autobiography* (London: Constable/Robinson, 2009)

Liddell Hart, B. H., *History of the Second World War* (London: Book Club Associates, 1973)

Liebling, A. J., *Liebling: World War II Writings* (New York, 2008, Penguin Putnam)

Lingen, Kerstin von, *Kesselring's Last Battle: Crimes Trials and Cold War Politics* (Kansas: Kansas Press, 2009)

Macksey, Kenneth, *Military Errors of World War Two II* (London: Arms and Armour Press, 1987)

Macmillan, Harold, *The Blast of War* (London: Macmillan, 1967)

Michel, Henri (translated by D. Parmée), *The Second World War* (London: Andre Deutsch, 1975)

Neizel, Sönke, *Tapping Hitler's Generals* (Barnsley: Frontline Books, 2007)

*Oxford Dictionary of National Biography* (Oxford: OUP, 2008)

Payne Best, Captain S., *The Venlo Incident* (Barnsley: Frontline Books, 2009)

Picknett, Lynn, Prince, Clive and Prior, Stephen, *War of the Windsors* (London: Mainstream, 2002)

Powell, Anthony, *The Military Philosophers* (London: Arrow Books, 2019)

Redford, Duncan, *A History of the Royal Navy* (London: IB Tauris, 2014)

Roberts, Andrew, *Masters and Commanders* (London: Penguin Books, 2009)

Roberts, Andrew, *The Storm of War* (London: Allen Lane, 2009)

Salter, Michael, *Nazi War Crimes, US Intelligence & Selective Prosecution at Nuremberg* (Oxford: Routledge-Cavendish, 2007)

Sangster, Andrew & Battistelli, Pier Paolo, *Myths, Amnesia and Reality in Military Conflicts 1935–1945* (Newcastle: Cambridge Scholars, 2016)

Sangster, Andrew, *The Agony of France* (Newcastle: Cambridge Scholars, 2016)

Sangster, Andrew, *The Times, Life and Moral Dilemma of Beria* (Newcastle: Cambridge Scholars, 2019)

Schuker, Stephen Finney Patrick, (ed.), *The Origins of the Second World War* (London: Arnold, 1997)

Sebag-Montefiore, Hugh, *Dunkirk* (London: Penguin Books, 2007)

Sereny, Gitta, *Albert Speer: His Battle with Truth* (London: Macmillan, 1995)

Smart, Nick, *Biographical Dictionary of British Generals of the Second World War* (Barnsley: Pen and Sword, 2005)

Smith, Brigadier-General Greg, 'British Strategic Culture and General Sir Alan Brooke During the Second World War', *Canadian Military Journal*, Volume 18, Number 1.

Speer, Albert, *Inside the Third Reich* (London: Weidenfeld & Nicolson, 1970)

Stafford, David, *Churchill and Secret Service* (London: Abacus, 2001)

The *Telegraph*, 6 May 2001

Titmuss, Richard M., *Problems of Social Policy* (London: HMSO, Longmans Green: 1950)

*The Concise Dictionary of National Biography*, Volume I (Oxford: OUP, 1995)

*The Concise Dictionary of National Biography*, Volume II (Oxford: OUP, 1995)

Thomas, R. T., *Britain and Vichy, The Dilemma of Anglo-French Relations 1940–1942* (London: Macmillan, 1979)

Toland, John, *The Last Hundred Days* (New York: Modern Library, 2003)

Trevelyan, Raleigh, *Rome '44 The Battle for the Eternal City* (London: Pimlico, 2004)

Villa, L. Brian, *Unauthorised Action* (Oxford: OUP, 1989)

Weinberg, Gerhard L., *A World at Arms, A Global History of World War II* (Cambridge: CUP, 1994)

Whicker, Alan, *Whicker's War* (London: Harpers, 2005)

Whiting, Charles, *The Field Marshal's Revenge* (Staplehurst: Spellmount, 2004)

Wilt, Alan F., *The Journal of Military History* (Vol. 65, No. 4, October 2001)

Zeiler, Thomas W., *Annihilation: A Global Military History of World War II* (Oxford: OUP, 2011)

# Endnotes

## Preface

1  Jonathan Dimbleby, *Destiny in the Desert* (London: Profile Books, 2013).
2  Nick Smart, *Biographical Dictionary of British Generals of the Second World War* (Barnsley: Pen and Sword, 2005) p.43.

## Introduction

1  Anthony Powell, *The Military Philosophers* (London: Arrow Books, 2019) pp.60–1.
2  Ibid., p.61.
3  *The Times*, 18 June 1963, *Obituary.*
4  John Ferris and Ewan Maudsley, *The Cambridge History of The Second World War Vol 1* (Cambridge UP, 2015) p.548.
5  See introduction by Frank Lan in Eric Hosking, *An Eye for a Bird* (London: Hutchinson, 1970) p.xvii.
6  Smart, *Biographical Dictionary*, pp.45ff.
7  John Colville, *The Fringes of Power* (London: Hodder and Stoughton, 1985) p.256.
8  John Toland, *The Last 100 Days* (New York: Modern Library, 2003) p.41.
9  *The Times*, 18 June 1963, *Obituary.*
10  Field Marshal Lord Alanbrooke, *War Diaries 1939–45* (London: Weidenfeld & Nicolson, 2001) p.xxii.
11  The *Telegraph*, 6 May 2001.
12  See Epilogue of David Fraser, *Alanbrooke* (London: Collins,1982), written by Bryant.
13  Winston Churchill, *The Second World War, Vol VI* (London: Cassell and Company, 1954) p.131.
14  Churchill, *The Second World War, Vol VI*, pp.670–1.
15  Elizabeth Nel, *Winston Churchill by his Personal Secretary* (New York: iUniverse, 2007) p.44.
16  See the *Telegraph*, 6 May 2001.
17  Ibid.
18  Ibid.
19  Alan F. Wilt, *The Journal of Military History* (Vol. 65, No. 4, October 2001) pp.1152–4.
20  Ibid., pp.1152–4.
21  Ibid.
22  Quoted in Andrew Roberts, *Masters and Commanders* (London: Penguin Books, 2009) p.91.
23  Wilt, *The Journal of Military History*, pp.1152–4.
24  Major-General Sir John Kennedy, *The Business of War* (London: Hutchinson, 1957) p.xv.
25  See Nel, *Winston Churchill*, p.44.
26  Roberts, *Masters and Commanders*, p.277.
27  Michael Burleigh, *Moral Combat* (London: Harper Press, 2010) p.340.

28  Gordon Corrigan, *The Second World War, A Military History* (London: Atlantic Books, 2012) p.528.
29  Kennedy, *The Business of War*, p.275.
30  Ibid., p.268.
31  Smart, *Biographical Dictionary*, p.43.
32  See Roberts, *Masters and Commanders*, p.42.
33  John Colville, *The Churchillians* (London: Weidenfeld & Nicolson, 1981) p.143.
34  *The Times*, 18 June 1963, *Obituary*.
35  Philip Zeigler, *Mountbatten, The Official Biography* (London: Collins, 1985) p.179.
36  Kennedy, *The Business of War*, p.xvii.
37  Henri Michel (translated by D. Parmée) *The Second World War* (London: Andre Deutsch, 1975) p.610.
38  See Burleigh, *Moral Combat*, p.311.
39  Ibid., p.320.

## Chapter One

1   Statistics gleaned from Burleigh, *Moral Combat*, p.339.
2   David Fraser, *Alanbrooke* (London: Collins, 1982) p.41.
3   From introduction in V. A. Brooke and Stephen L. Brooke, *Sir Victor Brooke, Sportsman and Naturalist* (London: Forgotten Books, 2018) p.6.
4   Fraser, *Alanbrooke*, p.45.
5   See Winston Churchill, *My Early Life* (London: Odhams, 1949).
6   David, *Alanbrooke*, p.53.
7   Ibid., p.65.
8   Kerstin von Lingen, *Kesselring's Last Battle: Crimes Trials and Cold War Politics* (Kansas: Kansas Press, 2009) p.19.
9   See David, *Alanbrooke*, p.72.
10  Ibid.
11  From his early letters and quoted in Fraser, *Alanbrooke*, p.79.

## Chapter Two

1   Andrew Sangster and Pier Paolo Battistelli, *Myths, Amnesia and Reality in Military Conflicts 1935–1945* (Newcastle: Cambridge Scholars, 2016) pp. 68f.
2   *The Times*, 18 June 1963, *Obituary.*
3   Fraser, *Alanbrooke*, p.83.
4   J. F. C. Fuller, *Tanks in the Great War* (New York; E Dutton and Company, 1920) p.308.
5   Fuller, *Tanks,* p.321.
6   Quoted in Fraser, *Alanbrooke*, p.92.
7   Norman Davies, *A History of Europe* (London: Pimlico, 1997) p.938.
8   Fraser, *Alanbrooke*, p.93.
9   Alanbrooke Papers, Section 4.
10  Alanbrooke, *Notes on my Life*, (Section 3).
11  See David French, in David French & Brian Holden Reid, *The British General Staff, Reform and Innovation, c.1890–1939* (London: Frank Cass Publishers, 2002).
12  Fraser, *Alanbrooke*, p.110.

13  See J. F. C. Fuller, *A Military History of the Western World. From the American Civil War to the End of World War II.* Volume III (London: Minerva Press, 1956) p.380.
14  French, *The British General Staff*, p.145.


## Chapter Three

1   Ronald Lewin (ed.), *The War on Land 1939–1915* (London: Vintage Books, 2007) p.19.
2   Julian Jackson, *The Fall of France* (Oxford: OUP, 2003) p.79.
3   C. John Cairns in J. Blatt (ed.), *The French Defeat of 1940: Reassessments* (Oxford: Berghahn, 1998) p.283.
4   Jackson, *The Fall*, p.85.
5   William Philpott in David French and Brian Holden Reid, *The British General Staff, Reform and Innovation, c.1890–1939* (London: Frank Cass Publishers, 2002) p.86.
6   Jackson, *The Fall*, p.78 and Alistair Horne, *To Lose a Battle, France 1940* (London: Macmillan, 1969) p.434.
7   Jackson, *The Fall*, p.159.
8   Ibid., p.199.
9   S. Martin Alexander in J. Blatt (ed.), *The French Defeat of 1940: Reassessments,* (Oxford: Berghahn, 1998) p.297.
10  Andrew Sangster, *The Agony of France* (Newcastle: Cambridge Scholars, 2016) p.59.
11  Fred Taylor (trans.), *The Göbbels Diaries* (London: Hamish Hamilton, 1982) p.87.
12  Ibid., p.89.
13  Richard Holmes, *The World at War, The Landmark Oral History* (London: Ebury Press, 2007) p.97.
14  Jackson, *The Fall*, p.164.
15  See A. J. Liebling, *Liebling, World War II Writings* (New York, 2008, Penguin Putnam).
16  Alanbrooke, *War Diaries,* p.50.
17  Ibid., p.3.
18  See Fraser, *Alanbrooke*, p.131.
19  Ibid., p.139.
20  Ibid., p.131.
21  Len Deighton, *Blitzkrieg* (London: Pimlico, 1996) p.69.
22  Fraser, *Alanbrooke*, p.134 (footnote).
23  Jon Lewis (ed.), *World War II: The Autobiography* (London: Constable/Robinson, 2009) p.21.
24  Horne, *To Lose a Battle*, p.36.
25  Stephen Schuker and Patrick Finney (eds.), *The Origins of the Second World War* (London: Arnold, 1997) p.255.
26  Alanbrooke, *War Diaries,* p.8.
27  Thomas W. Zeiler, *Annihilation* (Oxford: OUP, 2011) p.207.
28  Alanbrooke, *War Diaries,* p.8.
29  Ibid., p.15.
30  Ibid., p.19.
31  Field Marshal Alexander, Earl of Tunis, *The Alexander Memoirs, 1940–1945* (London: Frontline Books, 2010) p.16.
32  Alanbrooke, *War Diaries,* p.18.
33  Jackson, *The Fall*, p.78 and Horne, *To Lose a Battle*, p.434.
34  Kennedy, *The Business of War*, p.35.

35  Alanbrooke, *War Diaries*, p.26.
36  Kenneth Macksey, *Military Errors of World War Two II* (London: Arms and Armour Press, 1987) p.18.
37  Alanbrooke, *War Diaries*, p.37.
38  Ibid., p.27.

## Chapter Four

1   Richard M. Titmuss, *Problems of Social Policy* (London: HMSO, Longmans Green: 1950) p.111.
2   Juliet Gardiner, *Wartime Britain 1939–1945* (London: Headline Books, 2005) p.180.
3   Alanbrooke, *War Diaries*, p.34.
4   Ibid., pp.30–1.
5   Alanbrooke, *War Diaries*, p.32.
6   Ibid., p.36.
7   Ibid., p.38.
8   II Samuel Chapter 11, verse 1 of the English Standard Version.
9   Alanbrooke, *War Diaries*, p.41.
10  Ibid., p.45.
11  Ibid., p.55.
12  Jackson, *The Fall*, p.32.
13  Fraser, *Alanbrooke*, p.143.
14  Smart, *Biographical Dictionary*, p.42.
15  Fraser, *Alanbrooke*, p.145.
16  Alanbrooke, *War Diaries*, p.67.
17  Churchill, *The Second World War, Vol II*, p.84.
18  Hugh Sebag-Montefiore, *Dunkirk* (London: Penguin Books, 2007) p.175.
19  See Michel, *The Second World War*, p.83.
20  Anthony Beevor, *The Second World War* (London: Weidenfeld & Nicolson, 2012) p.97.
21  Zeiler, *Annihilation*, p.87
22  Ferris and Maudsley, *The Cambridge History of the Second World War Vol 1*.
23  See Duncan Redford, *A History of the Royal Navy* (London: IB Tauris, 2014) p.30.
24  Alanbrooke, *War Diaries*, p.71
25  Agnes Humbert, *Résistance* (London: Bloomsbury, 2009).
26  Quoted in Carole Fink in J. Blatt (ed.), *The French Defeat of 1940: Reassessments,* (Oxford: Berghahn, 1998) p.53.
27  See Churchill, *The Second World War, Vol II*, p.169.
28  Alanbrooke, *War Diaries*, p.73.
29  B. L. Montgomery, *The Memoirs of Field Marshal the Viscount Montgomery of Alamein, K. G.* (New York: The World Publishing Company, 1958) p.58
30  *The Times*, 18 June 1963, *Obituary.*
31  Alanbrooke, *War Diaries*, p.79.
32  Michel, *The Second World War*, pp.130–1.
33  Churchill, *The Second World War, Vol II*, p.171.
34  General the Lord Ismay, *The Memoirs of Lord Ismay* (London: Heinemann, 1960) p.142.
35  Alanbrooke, *War Diaries*, p.83.
36  Julian Jackson, *France: The Dark Years 1940–44* (Oxford: OUP, 2003) p.126.
37  Alanbrooke, *War Diaries*, p.87.
38  *The Times*, 18 June 1963, *Obituary.*

39   Alanbrooke, *War Diaries*, p.89.
40   Erich von Manstein, *Lost Victories* (Minneapolis: Zenith, 1982) p.155.
41   Smart, *Biographical Dictionary*, p.43.
42   Alanbrooke, *War Diaries*, p.93.
43   Churchill, *The Second World War, Vol II*, p.233.
44   See Roberts, *Masters and Commanders*, p.46.
45   Prime Minister's Personal Minutes 'Most Secret.' M.1052/1 17 November.
46   *The Times*, 18 June 1963, *Obituary.*
47   Premier Papers 3/4696/2 Folios 2–16.
48   Alanbrooke, *War Diaries*, p.94.
49   Kennedy, *The Business of War*, p.91.
50   Alanbrooke, *War Diaries*, p.98.
51   Ibid., p.100.
52   Colville, *The Fringes of Power*, p.186.
53   Churchill, *The Second World War, Vol II*, p.263.
54   Alanbrooke, *War Diaries*, p,108.
55   Ibid., p.112.
56   Fraser, *Alanbrooke*, p.188.
57   Jonathan Fenby, *The General Charles de Gaulle and The France He Saved* (London: Simon and Schuster, 2010) p.35.
58   Alanbrooke, *War Diaries*, p.113.
59   Ibid., p.114.
60   COS Meeting Papers and War Cabinet Papers, COS N0 260 of 1940 12 August 1940 10.15 am and Cabinet Papers 79/6.
61   Alanbrooke, *War Diaries*, p.117.
62   Ibid., p.121.
63   Colville, *The Fringes of Power*, p.316.
64   Alanbrooke, *War Diaries*, p.121.
65   Martin Gilbert, *Finest Hour, Winston S Churchill 1939–41* (London: Heinemann, 1983) p.861.

## Chapter Five

1    Alanbrooke, *War Diaries*, p.148.
2    Ibid., p.138.
3    Ibid., p.143.
4    Ibid., p.145.
5    Ibid., p.161.
6    Fraser, *Alanbrooke*, p.198.
7    Alanbrooke, *War Diaries*, p.165.
8    Quoted in Gerhard L. Weinberg, *A World at Arms, A Global History of World War II* (Cambridge: CUP, 1994) p.283.
9    Alanbrooke, *War Diaries*, p.185.
10   Ibid., p.170.
11   Winston Churchill, *The Second World War, Vol III* (London: Cassell and Company, 1950) p.716.
12   Ibid., pp.693–4
13   Alanbrooke, *War Diaries*, p.183
14   George Orwell (ed. Peter Davison), *The Orwell Diaries* (London: Penguin Books, 2010) p.257.
15   Weinberg, *A World at Arms*, p.358.

16  Alanbrooke, *War Diaries*, p.190.

17  Colville, *The Fringes of Power*, p.443.

18  Alanbrooke, *War Diaries*, p.197.

19  Ibid., p.198.

20  Kennedy, *The Business of War*, p.162.

21  Ibid., p.179.

22  Alanbrooke, *War Diaries*, p.199.

23  Roberts, *Masters and Commanders*, p.58.

24  Churchill, *The Second World War, Vol II*, p.19.

25  Colville, *The Churchillians*, p.142.

26  Ibid., p.142.

27  See Fraser, *Alanbrooke*, p.204.

28  Churchill, *The Second World War, Vol II*, p.234.

29  See Kennedy, *The Business of War*, p.204.

30  Brigadier-General Greg Smith, 'British Strategic Thinking and General SIR Alan Booke in the Second World War'. *Canadian Military Journal*, Volume 18, Number 1, p.32.

31  Michael Howard, *The Continental Commitment: The Dilemma of British Defence Policy in the Era of the Two World Wars* (London: Ashfield Press, 1989) p.52.

32  Quoted in Carlo D'Este, *Decision in Normandy: The Unwritten Story of Montgomery and the Allied Campaign* (London: Pan Books, 1984) p.25.

33  As claimed in A. Bryant, *Triumph in the West* (London: The Reprint Society, 1960) p.28.

34  Philpott, *The British General Staff*, p.80.

35  Ibid., p.80.

36  Zeigler, *Mountbatten*, p.168.

37  Roberts, *Masters and Commanders*, p.107.

38  *The Times*, 18 June 1963, *Obituary.*

39  Fraser, *Alanbrooke*, p.215.

40  Alanbrooke, *War Diaries*, p.207.

## Chapter Six

1  NA-AMP, *The Rise and Fall of the German Air Force 1933–45* (The National Archives, Air Ministry Pamphlet, Issued by Air Ministry 1948, 2008.) p.53.

2  Andrew Roberts, *The Storm of War* (London: Allen Lane, 2009) p.437.

3  See ibid., p.440.

4  Quoted in Max Hastings, *All Hell Let Loose* (London: Harper, 2011) p.666.

5  Alanbrooke, *War Diaries*, p.226.

6  See Smart, *Biographical Dictionary*, p.45.

7  Fraser, *Alanbrooke*, p.236.

8  Simon Ball, *The Mediterranean and North Africa, 1940–1944* in *The Cambridge History of The Second World War Vol 1* (Cambridge UP, 2015), p.364.

9  Führer Conferences on Naval Affairs 1939–1945 (London: Chatham Publishers, 2005) p.329.

10  Ball, *The Mediterranean*, p.364.

11  Alanbrooke, *War Diaries*, p.237.

12  Ibid., p.236.

13  Ibid., p.243.

14  Kennedy, *The Business of War*, p.257.

15  Alanbrooke, *War Diaries*, p.246.

16  Ibid., p.248.
17  Leonard Mosley, *Marshall: Organizer of Victory* (New York: Hearst Books, 1982) p.202.
18  General Albert C. Wedemeyer, *Wedemeyer Reports!* (New York: 1958) pp.105–6.
19  Alanbrooke, *War Diaries,* p.253.
20  David Stafford, *Churchill and Secret Service* (London: Abacus, 2001) p.285.
21  Keith Jeffrey, *MI6: The History of the Secret Service 1909–1949* (London: Bloomsbury, 2010) p.742.
22  Max Hastings, *The Secret War* (London: William Collins, 2015) p.201.
23  Ibid., p.554.
24  Alanbrooke, *War Diaries,* p.268.
25  Fraser, *Alanbrooke,* p.261.
26  Quoted in Roberts, *Masters and Commanders,* p.204.
27  Wedemeyer, *Wedemeyer Reports,* p.141.
28  Winston Churchill, *The Second World War, Vol IV* (London: Cassell and Company, 1951) p.339.
29  Ismay, *The Memoirs,* p.255.
30  Ed Cray, *General to the Army, George C Marshall, Soldier and Statesman* (New York: Cooper Square Press, 2000), p.325.
31  Alanbrooke, *War Diaries,* p.275.
32  Stephen Ambrose, *Eisenhower, Soldier and President* (London: Pocket Books, 2003) p.204.
33  Fraser, *Alanbrooke,* p.263.
34  Churchill, *The Second World War, Vol IV,* p.410.
35  Desmond Young, *Rommel* (London: Book Club Associates, 1973) p.99.
36  Hans-Joachim Schraepler, *At Rommel's Side, The Lost letters of Hans-Joachim Schraepler* (London: Frontline Books, 2009) p.93.
37  US Army Historical Division, *Mediterranean War Part V, campaign in Italy Part II,* MS C-064, Generalfeldmarschall Albert Kesselring 1 May 1949 -007732 ref: 007718.
38  B. H. Liddell Hart (ed.), *The Rommel Papers* (New York: De Capo Press, 1953) p.120.
39  Colville, *The Fringes of Power,* p.271.
40  Roberts, *Masters and Commanders,* p.265.
41  Ibid., p.267.
42  Churchill, *The Second World War, Vol IV,* p.413.
43  Alanbrooke Papers, Section 12.
44  Roberts, *The Storm,* p.603.
45  Alanbrooke Papers, Section 10.
46  Fraser, *Alanbrooke,* p.292.
47  Alanbrooke, *War Diaries,* p.299.
48  Ibid., p.301.
49  Norman Davies, *No Simple Victory* (London: Viking, 2006) p.102.
50  Roberts, *Masters and Commanders,* p.273.
51  Zeigler, *Mountbatten,* p.195.
52  Alanbrooke, *War Diaries,* p.324.
53  Fraser, *Alanbrooke,* p.296.
54  Alanbrooke, *War Diaries,* p.318.
55  Ibid., p.332.
56  Ibid., p.332.
57  R. T. Thomas, *Britain and Vichy, The Dilemma of Anglo-French Relations 1940–1942* (London: Macmillan, 1979) p.5.
58  Jackson, *France,* p.179.
59  Alanbrooke, *War Diaries,* p.343.

60  Christopher Andrew and Oleg Gordievsky, *KGB The Inside Story of its Foreign Operations from Lenin to Gorbachev* (London: Hodder & Stoughton, 1990) p.220.
61  See Hugh Sebag-Montefiore, *Stalin, The Court of the Red Tsar* (London: Weidenfeld & Nicolson, 2003) p.336.
62  V. Oleg Khlevniuk, *Stalin, New Biography of a Dictator* (London: Yale UP, 2015) p.203.

## Chapter Seven

1   Alanbrooke, *War Diaries*, p.355.
2   Ibid., p.357.
3   Wedemeyer, *Wedemeyer Reports*, p.181.
4   Alanbrooke, *War Diaries*, p.361.
5   Mosley, *Marshall: Organizer of Victory*, p.227.
6   Wedemeyer, *Wedemeyer Reports*, p.179.
7   Alanbrooke, *War Diaries*, p.363.
8   Ibid., p.383.
9   Ibid., p.383.
10  Ibid., p.396.
11  Dwight Eisenhower, *Crusade in Europe* (London: Heinemann, 1948) p.157.
12  Roberts, *The Storm*, p.312.
13  Eisenhower, *Crusade*, p.163.
14  Beevor, *The Second World War*, p.411.
15  Kew National Archives, document, HW1/1331.
16  Alexander, *The Alexander Memoirs*, p.159.
17  *Guardian*, 12 June 1950, p.6.
18  See Zeiler, *Annihilation*, p.220.
19  Alanbrooke, *War Diaries*, p.398.
20  See Sir Alan Lascelles, *King's Counsellor* (London: Weidenfeld & Nicolson, 2006) pp.128–9.
21  Roberts, *Masters and Commanders*, p.366.
22  Alanbrooke, *War Diaries*, p.405.
23  Fraser, *Alanbrooke*, p.349.
24  Carlo D'Este, *Fatal Decision* (London: Fontana, 1991) p.26.
25  Eisenhower, *Crusade*, p.195.
26  Hastings, *All Hell*, p.449.
27  Ibid., p.450.
28  Roberts, *Masters and Commanders*, p.91.
29  Astley, Joan Bright, *The Inner Circle* (London: Hutchinson, 1971) pp.103–4.
30  Winston Churchill, *The Second World War, Vol V* (London: Cassell and Company, 1952) p.76.
31  Roberts, *Masters and Commanders*, p.382.
32  Omar Bradley, *A General's Life* (London: Sidgwick & Jackson, 1983), p.203.
33  See Michel, *The Second World War*, p.614.
34  Colville, *The Churchillians*, p.143.
35  Eisenhower, *Crusade*, p.215.
36  Beevor, *The Second World War*, p.500.
37  Ismay, *The Memoirs*, p.311.
38  Alanbrooke, *War Diaries*, p.443.
39  Ibid., p.444.
40  Ibid., p.447.

41 See Churchill, *The Second World War, Vol V*, p.105.
42 See Roberts, *Masters and Commanders*, p.22.
43 See Alanbrooke, *War Diaries*, p.451.
44 Alan Whicker, *Whicker's War* (London: Harpers, 2005) p.85–6.
45 Weinberg, *A World at Arms*, p.3600.
46 Alanbrooke, *War Diaries*, p.457.
47 Ferris and Maudsley, *The Cambridge History of The Second World War Vol 1*, p.577.
48 Alanbrooke, *War Diaries*, pp.458–9.
49 Alanbrooke Personal Files and quoted in Fraser, *Alanbrooke*, p.367.
50 Churchill, *The Second World War, Vol V*, p.271.
51 Churchill, *The Second World War, Vol V*, p.375.
52 Lord Moran, *Churchill at War 1940–46* (London: Robinson, 1966) p.152.
53 Harold Macmillan, *War Diaries* (London: Macmillan, 1984) p.304.
54 Macmillan, *War Diaries*, p.304.
55 Robert Gellately, *Stalin's Curse, Battling for Communism in War and Cold War* (Oxford: OUP, 2013) p.80.
56 Alanbrooke, *War Diaries*, p.484.
57 Ibid., p.485.
58 Ibid., p.486.
59 Moran, *Churchill*, p.164.
60 Initially from Churchill's *Second World War* and quoted in Robert Service, *Stalin* (London: Pan Books, 2010) p.467.
61 Fraser, *Alanbrooke*, p.385.
62 Macmillan, *War Diaries*, p.322.
63 Moran, *Churchill*, p.132.
64 See Infield-Glen, *Disaster at Bari* (New York: Bantam, 1988), which is a book based on this disaster.

## Chapter Eight

1 Alanbrooke, *War Diaries*, p.536.
2 Ibid., p.511.
3 D'Este, *Fatal Decision*, p.255.
4 Rick Atkinson, *The Day of Battle, The War in Sicily and Italy 1943–44* (London: Abacus, 2013) p.363.
5 D'Este, *Fatal Decision*, p.404.
6 Atkinson, *The Day of Battle*, p.354.
7 D'Este, *Fatal Decision*, p.184.
8 Raleigh Trevelyan, *Rome '44 The Battle for the Eternal City* (London: Pimlico, 2004) p.107.
9 See Fraser, *Alanbrooke*, p.421.
10 Alanbrooke, *War Diaries*, p.530.
11 Ibid., p.534.
12 Mark Clark, *Calculated Risk* (New York: Harper and Brothers, 1950) p.348.
13 Alanbrooke, *War Diaries*, p.535.
14 Frido Senger von und Etterlin, *Neither Fear nor Hope* (London: Macdonald, 1963) p.187.
15 Richard Hodges, 'Tempting providence: The Bombing of Monte Cassino', *History Today* (Volume 44, Issue 2, 1994).
16 Maries Vassiltchikov, *The Berlin Diaries 1939–45* (London: Pimlico, 1999) p.151.
17 *The Times* 20 April 1944, p.3.

18  Alexander, *The Alexander Memoirs*, p.139.
19  Alanbrooke, *War Diaries*, p.543.
20  See Beevor, *The Second World War*, p.581.
21  Alanbrooke, *War Diaries*, p.541.
22  Ibid., p.544.
23  Ibid., p.546.
24  Ibid., p.552.
25  Roberts, *Eminent Churchillians* (London: Weidenfeld & Nicolson,1994) p.133.
26  Brian L. Villa, *Unauthorised Action* (Oxford: OUP, 1989) p.4.
27  Roberts, *Eminent Churchillians*, p.55.
28  Lynn Picknett, Clive Prince and Stephen Prior, *War of the Windsors* (London: Mainstream, 2002) p.43.
29  Zeigler, *Mountbatten*, p.701.
30  Alanbrooke, *War Diaries*, p.546.
31  Lascelles, *King's Counsellor*, p.216 and p.308.
32  II Samuel Chapter 11 verse 1.
33  Alanbrooke, *War Diaries*, p.555.
34  Ibid., p.552.
35  Whicker, *Whicker's War*, p.182.
36  D'Este, *Fatal Decision*, p.365.
37  Dominic Graham and Shelford Bidwell, *Tug of War, The Battle for Italy 1943–45* (Yorkshire: Pen and Sword, 2004) p.315.
38  Winston Churchill, *The Second World War, Vol VI* (London: Cassell and Company, 1954) p.11.
39  Bradley, *A General's Life*, p.288.
40  Ambrose, *Eisenhower, p.143.*
41  See Anthony Eden, *The Reckoning* (London: Cassell, 1965) pp. 461–2.
42  Alanbrooke, *War Diaries*, p.570.
43  Jack Fairweather, *The Volunteer* (London: Penguin, 2019) p.339.
44  See Fraser, *Alanbrooke*, p.348.
45  Ibid., p.442.
46  Weinberg, *A World at Arms*, p.701.
47  Alanbrooke, *War Diaries*, p.600.

## Chapter Nine

1   Bradley, *A General's Life*.
2   Alanbrooke, *War Diaries*, p.620.
3   Alanbrooke, *War Diaries*, p.603.
4   Ibid., p.605.
5   Fraser, *Alanbrooke*, p.448.
6   See Astley, Joan Bright, *The Inner Circle* (London: Hutchinson, 1971).
7   Alanbrooke, *War Diaries*, p.614.
8   See Zeiler, *Annihilation*, p.344.
9   See a modern publication of A. Bryant, *Triumph in the West* and *Turn of the Tide* (London: Collins, 1965).
10  Anthony Eden, *The Eden Memoirs, Facing the Dictators* (London: Cassell, 1962) p.568.
11  Churchill, *The Second World War, Vol VI*, p.610.
12  Ismay, *The Memoirs*, p.381.

13  Fraser, *Alanbrooke*, p.453.
14  Alanbrooke, *War Diaries*, p.632.
15  Beevor, *The Second World War*, p.663.
16  Ferris and Maudsley, *The Cambridge History of The Second World War Vol 1*, p.409.
17  Charles Whiting, *The Field Marshal's Revenge* (Staplehurst: Spellmount, 2004) p.151.
18  Bradley, *A General's Life*, p.365.
19  Ibid., p.368.
20  Ibid., p.369.
21  Alanbrooke Papers, and quoted in Fraser, *Alanbrooke*, p.461.
22  Weinberg, *A World at Arms*, p.768.
23  Churchill, *The Second World War, Vol VI*, p.243.
24  Charles Eade (compiler), *Onwards to Victory, War Speeches by Churchill* (London: Cassell and Company, 1944) p.183.
25  Cray, *General to the Army*, p.495.
26  Weinberg, *A World at Arms*, p.768.
27  Fraser, *Alanbrooke*, p.466.
28  See Toland, *The Last 100 Days*, p.48.
29  Fraser, *Alanbrooke*, p.468.
30  See Roberts, *Masters and Commanders*, p.517.
31  Beevor, *The Second World War*, p.637.
32  Fairweather, *The Volunteer*, p.345.
33  Fraser, *Alanbrooke*, p.475.
34  Anne Applebaum, *Iron Curtain: The Crushing of Eastern Europe, 1944–1956* (London: Penguin, 2017) p.104.
35  Alanbrooke, *War Diaries*, p.669.
36  Toland, *The Last 100 Days*, p.213.
37  Ibid., p.213.
38  Ibid., p.221.
39  Siegfried Westphal, *The German Army in the West* (London: Cassell, 1951) p.191.
40  Helmut Heiber and David Glantz (eds.), *Hitler and his Generals* (London: Greenhill Books, 2002) p.585.
41  Ian Kershaw, *The End: Hitler's Germany* (London: Allen Lane, 2011) p.303.
42  Harold Macmillan, *The Blast of War* (London: Macmillan, 1967) p.707.
43  Eugen Dollmann, *The Interpreter, Memoirs of Doktor Eugen Dollman* (London: Hutchinson, 1967) p.333.
44  Bundesarchiv-Militärarchiv, Freiburg: N574–19, '*Kriegsende in Italien.*' pp.53–54; and Kershaw, *The End*, p.364.
45  Alanbrooke, *War Diaries*, p.677.
46  Albert Speer, *Inside the Third Reich* (London: Weidenfeld & Nicolson, 1970) p.438.
47  Gitta Sereny, *Albert Speer; His Battle with Truth* (London: Macmillan,1995) p.485; p.487.
48  Westphal, *The German Army*, p.196.
49  Alanbrooke, *War Diaries*, p.680.
50  Davies, *A History of Europe*, p.1045.
51  Alanbrooke, *War Diaries*, p.686.
52  Hastings, *The Secret War*, p.545.
53  Hosking, *An Eye for a Bird*, p.155.
54  Alanbrooke, *War Diaries*, p.710.
55  Ibid., p.712.

56  Ibid., p.713.
57  See Introduction by Frank Lane in Eric Hosking, *An Eye for a Bird*.
58  Alanbrooke, *War Diaries*, p.716.

## Chapter Ten

1   Alanbrooke, *War Diaries*, p.716.
2   Ibid.
3   See Fraser, *Alanbrooke*, p.514.
4   Ibid., p.513.
5   Ibid., p.517.
6   Kennedy, *The Business of War*, p.290.
7   Hosking, *An Eye for a Bird*, p.128.
8   Ibid., p.129.
9   See Hansard, 30 April 1958.
10  Hosking, *An Eye for a Bird*, p.181.
11  Ibid., p.185.
12  Fraser, *Alanbrooke*, p.523

## Chapter Eleven

1   Montgomery, *The Memoirs*, p.55.
2   Ibid., p.479.
3   Ibid., p.479.
4   Ibid., p.480.
5   Moran, *Churchill*, p.198.
6   Smart, *Biographical Dictionary*, see pp.44–5.
7   Zeigler, *Mountbatten*, p.157.
8   Ibid., pp.169–170.
9   Ibid., p.170.
10  Ibid., p.169.
11  Ibid., see p.231 and p.256.
12  Ismay, *The Memoirs*, p.317.
13  Ibid., p.317.
14  Ibid., p.317.
15  Ibid., p.318.
16  Toland, *The Last 100 Days*, p.28.
17  Alexander, *The Alexander Memoirs*, p.81.
18  Ibid., p.77.
19  Ibid., pp.79–80.
20  See Alanbrooke, *War Diaries*, p.xii.
21  Kennedy, *The Business of War*, p.181.
22  Ibid., p.317.
23  Bradley, *A General's Life*, p.402.
24  Ibid., p.230.
25  Ibid., p.230.
26  Ibid., p.230.

27  Ibid., p.230.
28  Ibid., p.159.
29  Ibid., p.232.
30  Ibid., p.365.
31  Ibid., p.412.
32  Ibid., p.391.
33  Cray, *General to the Army*, p.321.
34  Quoted in Cray, *General to the Army*, p.424.
35  Cray, *General to the Army*, p.308.
36  Ibid., p.308.
37  Ibid., p.309.
38  Nel, *Winston Churchill*, p.43.
39  Cray, *General to the Army*, p.424.
40  Ibid., p.457.
41  Quoted in Roberts, *Masters and Commanders*, p.142.
42  Roberts, *Masters and Commanders*, p.201.
43  Ibid., pp.368–9.
44  Cray, *General to the Army*, p.462.
45  Roberts, *The Storm*, p.302.
46  Eisenhower, *Crusade*, p.185.
47  Ibid., p.185.
48  See Colville, *The Fringes of Power*.
49  See Colville, *The Churchillians*.
50  Moran, *Churchill*, p.22.
51  Ibid., p.137.
52  Ibid., p.271.
53  Ibid., p.295.
54  Ibid., p.268.
55  Ibid., p.348.
56  Ibid., p.239.
57  Ibid., p.136.
58  Lascelles, *King's Counsellor*, p.233.
59  See Lascelles, *King's Counsellor*, p.221.
60  Macmillan, *War Diaries*, p.322.
61  Ibid., p.322.
62  Ibid., p.505.

## Chapter Twelve

1  Roberts, *Masters and Commanders*, p.220.
2  Ambrose, *Eisenhower*, p. 59.
3  Ibid., p.155.
4  Zeiler, *Annihilation*, p.206.
5  Weinberg, *A World at Arms*.
6  Ibid., p.593.
7  Ibid., p.612.
8  Ibid., p.918.
9  B. H. Liddell Hart, *History of the Second World War* (London: Book Club Associates, 1973).

10 Martin Gilbert, *Second World War* (London: Phoenix, 1997) p.93 and pp.347–8.
11 Norman Davies, *No Simple Victory* (London: Viking, 2006).
12 Roberts, *The Storm*, p.302 and p.594.
13 Beevor, *The Second World War*.
14 Ibid., p.487.
15 Hastings, *All Hell*, p.666.
16 Burleigh, *Moral Combat*, p.319.
17 Ibid., p.339.
18 Michel, *The Second World War*, p.149.
19 Ibid., p.545.

## Chapter Thirteen

1 Fraser, *Alanbrooke*, p.525.
2 Ibid., p.532.
3 Bradley, *A General's Life*, p.159.
4 Churchill, *The Second World War, Vol V*, p.342.
5 Fraser, *Alanbrooke*, p.529.
6 Roberts, *Masters and Commanders*, p.106.
7 Fraser, *Alanbrooke*, p.539.

# Index